KATIA

WIFE BEFORE GOD

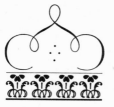

KATIA

WIFE BEFORE GOD

∴

BY Alexandre Tarsaïdzé

THE MACMILLAN COMPANY

The Macmillan Company
866 Third Avenue, New York, N.Y. 10022
Collier-Macmillan Canada Ltd., Toronto, Ontario
Library of Congress Catalog Card Number: 69-10467

FIRST PRINTING

Printed in the United States of America

Acknowledgments

It is surprising that about a century after the events described, one can find, if not actual witnesses of the tragic era, at least many persons, among them relatives and descendants of Katia, who knew her intimately or often spoke with her or with "actors and actresses" in her drama. During the past years, in which I have gathered material on Katia, I was more than lucky to have many conversations with these "witnesses" without whose assistance, advice, and reminiscences this book could not appear in its present form. Their help was particularly valuable to me in view of my inability and unwillingness for obvious reasons to examine personally the archives in Soviet Russia. Strangely, most of my "witnesses" have resided in the United States or in South America since the Russian Revolution.

It would be impossible for me to thank all the people to whom I am indebted for the guidance and useful information they gave me. However, I am mostly indebted to the late Count Boris G. Berg of New York, nephew of Katia (her sister Marie's son), whose most valuable unpublished family archives, memoirs, and innumerable documents were generously loaned to me during the preparation of this book. I more than appreciate the graciousness of his widow, Countess Sophia Berg, also of New York, for allowing me to keep her husband's literary legacies all these years.

My thanks must be also extended to Colonel Serge Obolensky of New York, former husband of Katia's daughter, whose personal reminiscences of his mother-in-law while residing in France before and after the Revolution of 1917 were invaluable to me.

To Count Vasilli Adlerberg of New York, whose granduncle, as a Minister of the Court and a childhood friend of Emperor

[5]

Alexander II, played such an important role in the *ménage à trois*, I owe my appreciation for remarkable and correct evaluation of the past events described to him by his family.

To the late Countess Marguerite Cassini, who knew Katia in France before the Revolution of 1917, I also owe a debt of gratitude for information on the personality of the Princess. I also should not forget the late Colonel N. D. Pleshko, director of the Russian Nobility Association in the United States, whose valuable archives were placed at my disposal.

To Count Basil Loris-Melikoff of New York, the grandson of the last Minister of the Interior and virtually the Premier during the last period of Emperor Alexander II's reign, and whose brother is Katia's granddaughter's husband, I owe appreciation for help and the family reminiscences he recounted to me.

To Mr. Andrey Sedykh of New York I extend my gratitude for allowing me to reprint his interesting article on Princess Yourievsky which appeared in the New York magazine *Novosselye* in August, 1942. For several unpublished photographs and other material loaned to me by Alexander Schaffer of A La Vieille Russie, an antique shop in New York City, I also extend my sincerest thanks.

I wish to thank Ray Roberts, James Daly, and Alison Newhouse for their efforts in editing my manuscript.

I would also like to thank Miss Marie-Hélène Martin, who, with a great deal of perseverance and talent, deciphered my handwritten hieroglyphics by retyping the whole of my manuscript.

Needless to say, the characterization of my "heroes," as well as the evaluation and judgment of the people in the narrative, is entirely my own responsibility.

All dates are given according to the new Gregorian calendar— that is, in the nineteenth century, twelve days after their actual occurrence, and in the twentieth century, thirteen days after— unless otherwise specified.

A. T.

Contents

Preface

THE LAST ACT FIRST

*". . . an episode which in the index of
history enjoyed a modest place . . ."*
STANLEY LOOMIS, *Du Barry*

On Sunday, July 18, 1880, an event that rocked the Empire took
place in "Holy Russia." It was the sudden morganatic marriage
of the aging Czar, a widower of forty days, to his young mistress
of more than fourteen years. When, seven months later, the Czar-
Liberator, as he was called, was assassinated, some people saw in
his murder the "hand of God."

On June 6, 1931, the Hotel Drouot in Paris, a traditional site
of auctions of rare collections, *bibelots, objets d'art*, and antiques,
is holding one of its many sessions. The salon is not crowded, but
one can discern among the usual types of bidder quite a few
solemn old men, shabbily but neatly dressed, with sad eyes—un-
mistakable attributes of many "White" Russian émigrés, now
making their enforced homes in Paris.

The monotonous voice of the *commissaire-priseur* conducts the
sale. "*Et voilà,*" he triumphantly exclaims, holding a sheaf of
yellowed pages in his hands, "here we have the authentic love
letters of the Czar Alexander II to his *maîtresse la belle* Princesse
Katia! Any bids?" "Only two foreigners," a "White" Russian
spectator noted much later, "bid fiercely for the possession of the
correspondence, with the sole aim to resell the collection to
American dealers. . . ."

The *billets-doux* are successfully sold, and the *commissaire-
priseur* holding an object high above his head, shouts: "We end

[9]

today's session with the *pièce-de-résistance*—the Czar's personal key to the secret apartment of the Princesse at the Winter Palace! Any bids, *Messieurs?*"

Ten years later, while France groaned under the German-Nazi occupation, an auction for the balance of the same Czar's intimate letters takes place, but this time in Nice, in the "free" zone of Vichy. Here is how, years later, a well-known Russian writer, now in the United States, described the event:[*1]

"The last two years [1941 and 1942] I spent in France living in Nice, the town which is connected with so many Russian memories. For a whole century Russian people were coming here to rest, to lose money playing roulette, to die. During the cold winter the titled and high ranking nobility of Moscow and St. Petersburg, rich business people and political emigrants came to the sunny Riviera. Nice held something particularly attractive for the Russian northerners which Tyutchev[†] expressed so well in his verse:

Oh this south, oh, this Nice!

"At one time Russians were welcomed here as dear and desired guests. It was in those prehistoric times, when in Europe we were not yet considered as impoverished and horribly boring relatives to everyone. In the aristocratic quarter of Cimiez, palaces stand, which were at one time built by enormously rich Russians. There are two Orthodox cathedrals. The chapel on the Boulevard Cesarevich, built in memory of the heir to the Russian throne, whose fate prevented his becoming the Emperor, and who died in Nice [in 1865] of tuberculosis. There are some Russian libraries, charitable institutions, in which old chamberlains and former ladies-in-waiting of Her Imperial Majesty are ending their lives until the present time. Old time residents will show you the house where Marie Bashkirtzeva[‡] lived and in the Massena Museum is a whole display devoted to this amazing and eccentric girl.

---

[*] Sedykh, author of many books, is now on the staff of the oldest New York Russian daily, *Novoye Russkoye Slovo*.

[†] Feodor I. Tutchev (1803–73) a lyric poet, whose three hundred poems were very popular in Russia in his later years.

[‡] A Russian painter and author of the famous autobiographical *Journal* which she kept from the age of twelve until eleven days before her death in France at the age of twenty-four in 1884.

"In the Russian cemetery in Nice there are many famous Russian graves. Here is buried Alexander Herzen and not far from him stands the mausoleum of Her Serene Highness Princess Ekaterina Mikhaylovna Yurievskaya, who spent long years in Nice and died there in 1922. The old Russian inhabitants of Nice still remember this little vivacious but aged lady, who on holidays arrived at the cathedral in her very old-fashioned carriage.

"During the summer of 1941, an ad appeared in the local papers stating a part of the archives of Princess Yurievskaya would be sold at public auction . . . the intimate letters of Alexander II and rare photographic pictures.

"I went to examine these things at the auction hall and the Paris expert Andrier obligingly opened a display case for me, in which were lying time-yellowed photographs and letters of Princess Yurievskaya. This consisted of two hundred and five large sized pages sewn together.

"E. M. Yurievskaya wrote on paper with a mourning border soon after the death of Alexander II in a large bold handwriting. As I was turning over the leaves and was reading page after page, the amazing story of this woman came to life in my memory. She was only ten years old at the time when she saw her future most august spouse. He came to the estate of her father, Prince Dolgorukov, directly from manoeuvres, covered with dust and tired. Little Katia made an awkward curtsy. The Czar glanced at her with a smile, immediately turned to the master of the house and started to discuss some important things with him. Later she was again presented to the Czar at a Ball at the Smolny Institute. She was already a dazzlingly beautiful slender girl and this time the Czar's eyes lingered on her attentively for a long while. Then started something incomprehensible and vertiginous—a frightening and secret love. Meetings in the Summer Garden, a long desperate resistance and finally the inevitable.

"She was already living in the Winter Palace, had children by the Czar and was suffering unbearably from her ambiguous position. He could see her only at his moments of leisure which were far from happening every day; wrote to her desperate notes and she spent her entire days at home waiting. Suddenly something happened which she never could have expected: The Empress Maria Alexandrovna died. Several weeks later without waiting for the ending of the official mourning, before God and people she became the morganatic wife of the Czar. The wedding took place in the Winter Palace on July 18, 1880, attended by a few close friends.

"Quite a good deal was written about the morganatic wife of Alexander II. Several years ago a novel was written on her life and a film called *Katya* made out of it. However, nowhere was the image of this interesting Russian woman presented as sharply and as clearly as in her own letters. The correspondence stops with the murder of Alexander II.

"Princess Yurievskaya does not tell us anything further of her fate; her role is ended and she leaves the stage. Alexander III who respected the memory of his father, felt towards Ekaterina Mikhaylovna as he would towards the dowager Empress. The palace of Prince Bezborodko was bought for her and a lifelong pension of forty thousand gold rubles was granted to her. Nevertheless, life in Russia reminded her of everything of her happy and dead past and was upsetting to her. She soon left for France and settled herself in Nice and lived there for almost forty years.

"Old inhabitants of Russian Nice said that she lived in luxury which was unusual even for those days. Foreign monarchs and the Russian Grand Duke when in Nice came to pay her an official visit at her mansion on the Boulevard de Bouchage. She lived in grand style, in a Russian manner; she did not know how to count money. Lots of money was spent during the war arranging a military hospital in her place, and when her pension was suddenly stopped in 1917 it turned out that she had nothing but debts. She lived five years longer and died a seventy-three-year-old lady. Her mansion and all of her possessions were sold at auction for debts. The mansion was later remodelled and turned into luxury apartments.

"Now some remaining part of the archives again fell into the hands of the auctioneers.

"Quite a few people came for the sale which took place several days later in the Hotel Savoy. Russian speech could be heard in the auction hall as many people wanted to know into whose hands would fall the letters and the 'Czar's relics.' The man in charge of the auction said several words about the letters

and did not forget to mention the film *Katya.** This it seemed
produced on the public the desired impression which was exactly
such as the expert counted on. Then in his customary voice,
speaking very quickly, he said: 'The letters of Her Serene Highness Princess Yurievskaya are for sale. We start with 500 francs,
who will give me more?' '550,' an unsure feminine voice said from
a corner of the room. '600,' a Russian bibliophile answered.
'1,000 . . .'

"The price was rising quickly. It was mounting by 100 francs.
Towards the end, the struggle was led by two men, a Russian
bibliophile and a Frenchman, Mr. V., owner of a luggage and
travel accessory store. The remaining public no longer partici-
pated in the sale and only watched with curiosity this unexpected
drama of the auction.

"When they had reached 3,500 francs, the Russian bibliophile
suppressed a sigh and negatively shook his head. The victor
turned out to be the man who was selling suitcases for 4,000
francs each in his store on the Cour Albert I. The 3,500 francs
represented a small amount of money to him and apparently at
one time he had enjoyed the film *Katya.* I am writing not without
bitterness because after the auction Mr. V. calmly informed me
that he did not intend to publish the correspondence—that it was
a simple investment for him during the difficult time when money
was losing value every day. It also was he who bought the greater
part of the letters and autographs of Alexander II and of Princess
Yurievskaya.

"A letter written by Alexander II to the Princess immediately
after the abortive attempt [in Paris] on his life by Berezovsky
sold for the highest amount. The letter was dated July 6, 1867 at
5:30 P.M. and 2,100 francs were paid for it. There was still another remarkable unpublished letter written in great hurry and
excitement, half in French and half in Russian, June 8 at eleven
o'clock in the morning [year is not mentioned]. His Majesty
wrote:

" 'My angel I am in despair that you waited for me in vain

---

* The film was produced in 1935 with Danielle Darrieux as Katya
and John Loder as Emperor Alexander II.

this morning. . . . I am in despair and I love you to the point of madness. . . .' This letter was sold for 1,300 francs. All the rest were sold for a trifle even considering the French devaluated francs*: 400 francs for the New Testament [actually a recent edition] which belonged to Alexander II, and only 200 francs for the whole pile of reports to Count Rumiantzev and to Baron Stroganov†, dated 1808–1812. Over sixty documents!

"The photograph of Princess Yurievskaya was sold for 520 francs. The photograph represented a young, slender woman in a white satin dress with a thin wasplike waist and magnificent shoulders. A photograph of the Czar with a touching inscription was sold for . . . 100 francs, which means three dollars by the official quote! The impoverished Russian emigres sitting in the auction room couldn't buy anything. All the documents and all the photographs fell into the commercial hands of Mr. V.

"The man in charge of the auction was yawning from time to time and was in a hurry:

" 'An interesting letter of Nicholas II to Princess Yurievskaya on the occasion of the betrothal of her daughter, fifty francs— who will bid more?'

"100 francs was offered and then 200 francs.

"The man in charge of the auction, with a crash, lowered his gavel which was made out of bone. . . . The last letters and photographs were going, the ghosts of a long ago lost and sunken world. The gavel was falling more and more quickly, and it seemed to me that someone was hurriedly hammering in the last nails in the coffin of Ekaterina Mikhaylovna Yurievskaya. . . ."

Eventually most of these letters happily reached America and became the property of a lover of Russian history, who very kindly gave permission to the author of this book to use them at his discretion.

---

* In 1940 the devalued French franc was quoted as about two U.S. cents. See the *World Almanac*, 1942, p. 515.

† Probably Count Nicholas Rumiantzev (1754–1826), statesman and a book and art lover, who donated a museum to the city of Moscow. Baron Alexander (later Count) Stroganov (1733–1811), a descendant of a famous northern merchant family, was a great patron of art and education.

Practically all the correspondence between the Czar and the Princess was written in French, with a few Russian words and phrases here and there. They all were translated into English by the late Prince Nicholas V. Orlov, a descendant of the famous Orlov family. Being an expert interpreter and translator in the employ of the United Nations, Prince Orlov was made the personal interpreter for Nikita Khrushchev when the Soviet Premier made his memorable tour of the United States prior to his downfall. Apparently, the Prince and the "Communist Boss" got along well: Khrushchev called Orlov "Prince" all during their travels.[2]

KATIA

WIFE BEFORE GOD

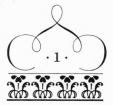

THE OVERTURE

It was the middle of June, 1815. The last chords of music had died out, and the tired and exhausted royalty of Europe—statesmen, diplomats, ladies of fashion, courtesans, and others of lesser fame—had left Vienna, the gay capital of Austria, and had gone home. The "dance" was over.[1]

Three days later, when the Congress of Vienna became history, an event took place in a little village by the name of Waterloo, a few miles from Brussels, then in the Netherlands—an incident that redrew the map of Europe, to remain virtually unchanged for a century. The victorious Allies had once more returned to occupy France, and the scene that had taken place in Paris in 1814 was repeated in July of 1815. The Parisians still remembered the "liberation" of their city in March of 1814, when Emperor* Alexander I of Russia, at the head of the Allied troops, made his triumphal entry into the capital of France. With him that day were his two younger brothers, the Grand Dukes Nicholas and Michael,

---

* In Old Russia only the lower strata called the Emperor "Czar" (peasants even addressed him as "Thou Czar-Batiushka" [Little Father]). For the sake of clarity, "Czar" will be used here more frequently than "Emperor." Upper classes and often upper-middle classes addressed their sovereign as "Your Imperial Majesty" or "Your Majesty"; in a conversation about the Czar one said "Gosudar" or "Gosudar-Imperator" (Sire-Emperor), rarely "Czar." The Empress was also "Czaritza" and the daughters "Czarevni." The heir to the throne was called Cesarevich (formally) or Czarevich (informally).

and Prince Leopold of Saxe-Coburg, then just a general in the Russian service and the brother-in-law of Alexander, Constantine, Nicholas, and Michael. This impoverished Coburg prince entered the Russian service (1797–1817) during the Napoleonic Wars with the rank of general,* which "favor he owed" to his sister Julia, then married to the heir apparent, the Grand Duke Constantine, the brother of Alexander I. Later, Leopold, as King of the Belgians, became indirectly the creator of four other dynasties—English, Portuguese, Roumanian, and Bulgarian, but excluding the Russian dynasty because the Grand Duke Constantine, to the "horror" of Leopold, "repudiated" and then divorced his sister in 1820.[2] Leopold, who, according to Hector Bolitho, "had the chameleon quality of the Coburgs" (he tried to serve Napoleon too), was able to induce Princess Charlotte of Great Britain to break her engagement to the Prince of Orange and become his wife in 1816. He was later naturalized in England under the title of Duke of Kendal. His German fellow princes nicknamed him Monsieur Peu-à-peu or Marquis Tout-doucement. He was, of course, Queen Victoria's "beloved Uncle Leopold."

From the spring of 1814, while Napoleon was "safely" in Elba, the popularity of Russia in Europe was at its height; yet the Russian troops as conquerors continued to occupy Paris, Berlin, and Warsaw. In Germany the Russians were particularly popular. Beethoven dedicated three sonatas to Alexander I, and three quartets, numbers 7, 8, and 9, all on "Russian themes," to Count Razumovsky, the Russian plenipotentiary at the Congress of Vienna. In Berlin the Alexander Platz, a square so named in 1813, always reminded the Germans of the "Liberators of Prussia."† At

---

* An oil painting of Leopold still graces the Winter Palace "Gallery of 1812" in Leningrad. He wears a Russian uniform of the Cuirassier Gardes Regiment, which he then commanded. His sister became the future Queen Victoria's mother, and his brother's son, Albert, the nephew, was to marry his niece, Queen Victoria! Through election in 1831, Leopold himself became the first King of the Belgians.

† Ironically, the same *Platz* played a historical role when on May 5, 1945, the Soviet troops, on capturing Berlin, hoisted their Red Banner at the "Tor" (Tower) near the Alexander Platz, still, even in the Communist parts of Berlin, bearing through all these years the name of the "Liberator of Prussia."[3]

Napoleonic France, as well, remembered its "Liberators," by renaming

the same time, many German regiments, including the crack "Russian Kaiser Alexander [I] Garde Grenadiers Regiment," were named after the Czars, retaining those honors through World War I of 1914–18.*

But it was in England that the admiration for the Russian Allies reached the proportion of mass hysteria. Forgotten were the *Drang nach* India in Czar Paul's days, the Tilsit Peace Treaty, and the costly and bloody war between Russia and England, which lasted until the very day Napoleon invaded Russian soil. The Russians were feted, lionized, and extolled virtually by all classes of England. Even women's and men's fashions were affected. "Suwarrow [Suvorov] boots," the Kutuzov mantle, and the Bagration hat were the rage with smart Londoners.†5

However, what all Britishers should have remembered was what happened in 1797 when England stood almost alone against the might of Revolutionary France.6 That year, with England nearly bankrupt, with widespread popular discontent, and with a crisis on hand, more than fifty thousand men in 113 warships in Portsmouth, Plymouth, Spithead, and Nore, refused orders, expelled their officers, hoisted *red* flags and set up a parody on Soviet ships of 1917. The British government had no alternative but to appeal to the Allied Russians Squadron, then in the British waters, to put down the rebellion. The Squadron was successful, and as a result Russian Admiral Makarov received from George III a golden saber with a dedication, dated June 12, 1797, camouflaged as if for the joint cooperation against Revolutionary France in the waters of the Netherlands.‡7

---

their bars "Les Bistros," from the Russian soldiers' impatient cry for quick or "bistro" service of drinks.4

* Russians, on the other hand, at the beginning of the World War, immediately changed their German chefs for Russian ones.

† The Kutuzov mantle was made of pale pink or scarlet cloth, trimmed with a Kutuzov hat with matching pink and scarlet feathers. A London contemporary observed that a "Russian wrapper, with long sleeves edged with swansdown begins to be a favorite" and a "cossack hat" of white satin in the shape of a helmet crowned with small white feathers "was very fashionable."

‡ Curiously enough this grave crisis is rarely mentioned in British history books. The 1967 Encyclopaedia Britannica devotes to this mutiny only a few lines. See French Rev. Wars p. 921 Vol. 9, p. 366 Vol. 20.

Even in faraway America, in Boston, the citizens were invited to celebrate "the downfall of France and to be united in a grateful and national festival of honoring Russia." Two thousand people attended a banquet at the Exchange Coffee House, appropriately decorated for the event with a transparent likeness of Alexander I in full uniform with the motto "Alexander—the Deliverer of Europe." Flanking the portrait of the Czar were pictures of generals Kutuzov and Bagration and the ataman Count Platov.[8] When Platov visited England in 1814 he was given a golden saber, a warship was named in his honor, and Oxford University bestowed on him an *honoris causa*—even though the hero was not fluent even in Russian.[9] The celebrated Lawrence painted his portrait (which now hangs in Windsor Palace), and Sir Walter Scott interviewed him and related some of the ataman exploits in his life of Napoleon.

But this was not all. Platov was received in the best homes, and smart women wore lockets bearing his portrait and begged him to be the godfather of their children. However, it was his horse Leonid, which the cossack general had brought to England, that suffered Platov's fame the most. It was fashionable then to wear medallions with a lock of hair, and the poor horse so fulfilled the trend that he lost his tail entirely. One nameless English lady—a widow—made a vow to devote her entire life to the ataman, and despite his having a perfectly good wife at home, she followed him first to St. Petersburg, then to the Don Province, where she remained until her death in 1818. Her vow thus had been fulfilled.

Countless engravings were issued in Platov's honor, several depicting his daughter, "Miss Platov," "a lady with a 50,000 crown dowry." One picture showed the ataman saying, "I, General Count Platov, solemnly promise to give away my daughter into marriage and 2000 roubles to a cossack, a Russian, Prussian, German, Swede, Turk, John Bull or any other Bull, who will bring me the head of the Little Boney"—all this while Napoleon was a prisoner in Elba.[10]

No less sensation was created by the simple cossack private Alexander Zemlenukhin, who in his uniform, with a martial spear in his hands, was received by the Lord Mayor. "With this instrument," cried his Lordship at the reception in honor of the Russian, "this cossack killed 39 Frenchmen." Countless newspaper articles were devoted to him, and several engravings were sold as soon as they were printed. Zemlenukhin was presented to the Prince Regent and received a silver saber, and a warship, the *Cossack*, was named in his honor. Several other men-of-war bearing such historical names as *Prince Kutuzov, Borodino, Moscow, Smolensk,* and *Vilno* were launched in honor of the Russians.*

Nor were commercial advantages overlooked. British manufacturers of ceramics flooded the markets with "Russian China" depicting the Czar, cossacks, peasants, and bucolic scenes *a la Russe*, with the result that "Russian China" milk jugs, teacups, dishes and goblets found their way into many English and continental homes.†[11]

Somewhat different from, and less impressive than, the presence of the Russian officers and troops was the long-awaited entry into the English capital of Czar Alexander I in June, 1814, the first Russian monarch to visit Britain since his ancestor Peter the Great touched the soil in 1698. Alexander was accompanied by the King of Prussia, Frederick Wilhelm III, and the same Prince Leopold of Saxe-Coburg. Alexander decided to travel incognito. Thousands of people in London lined the route in the hope of catching a glimpse of the two victorious allied sovereigns, but they were disappointed in their expectations and in fact took them for their aides-de-camp, which prompted the witty Countess

---

* This was the second *Cossack* in the British navy; the first was launched in 1806. But the fifth ship of that name was the one that made history in World War II. On February 16, 1940, H.M.S. destroyer *Cossack* entered neutral Norwegian waters and intercepted the German auxiliary tanker *Altmark*, a floating prison for the crews of Allied ships sunk by Germany. The *Altmark* was returning after a cruise in the South Atlantic with the *Graf Spee*. This incident gave a spur to the invasion of Norway by Hitler. However, the British Information Service in New York disclaimed any reason for naming British warships *Cossack*.[12] Captain of the *Cossack*, later Admiral, Philip Vian died on May 28, 1968, in London.[13]

† The best and most complete collection of British-made "Russian China" can be seen in the Brighton Museum.

Lieven, the wife of the Russian Ambassador to England, to remark: "The English people loves royalty to show itself in state, it loves also like every other to have its pleasure and its money's worth: it has been robbed of both."[14]

From that moment everything went wrong. To pave the way for his arrival in London, Alexander sent before him his favorite sister, the beautiful twenty-five-year-old Grand Duchess Catherine, the young widow of her first cousin, the Prince of Oldenburg (their mothers were sisters). Her public relations, to use a modern phrase, were far from successful. When the Regent's younger brother, the asthmatic and gouty Duke of Clarence (the future King William IV), already tired of his mistress's fading charms and in a race for a possible heir, twice offered the Russian Duchess his hand and heart, he was rudely rejected. "He is a mere, vain sailor," she confided in a letter to her brother, the Czar, "who says things to make you die of laughter. . . . Although at a decent distance he sniffed round the pot, I made believe not to understand. . . . This only I know for certain that I should not become Madame Clarence." Or, to quote Countess Lieven again: "He [Clarence] had no knowledge and [had] vulgar English habits and manners; his conversation is also vulgar . . . [he is] the least educated of all the English princes."

The Regent fared no better. Catherine considered him "ill bred" and had several unpleasant incidents of verbal fencing with him which prompted him in a "loud voice" to dub the situation intolerable. In view of such a "pleasant" relationship, it was not surprising that Alexander, whose brotherly love for his sister was known to be more than friendly, insisted on staying with her at the Pultney Hotel, instead of in St. James's Palace, where the Regent had placed a suite of apartments at the Czar's disposal. The Regent was expected to pay his respects by calling on the Russian Emperor. But at the appointed hour no one appeared, and finally after the Czar had waited for three hours a messenger came with a note from Count Lieven. It was not even a personal note; it was the Regent's secretary's missive. It read: "His Royal Highness has been treated with annoyance in the street if he shows himself. It is therefore impossible for him to come and see the Emperor." Indeed this was a plausible excuse for the unpopular Regent.

Meanwhile the crowds waiting outside the Pultney Hotel to glimpse the Czar had grown denser and all the surrounding roads were blocked. Impatient roars from the crowds prompted the Czar to step out on to the balcony to acknowledge the cheers. Later, whenever he appeared in the street, people struggled wildly to shake hands with him. He acceded, a gesture that delighted the mob and made him even more popular.

Thus the relations between the Regent and the Czar went from bad to worse. When at a state ball the Regent presented his mistress, Lady Hertford, Alexander bowed and said nothing. The Regent, who thought that Alexander did not hear the name (in fact the Czar was conveniently deaf), repeated in a loud voice, "This *is* Lady Hertford." Alexander was still silent, and as the Marchioness made a low curtsy she threw at the Russian sovereign one of her haughtiest glances. "The fate of this whole visit," mused Countess Lieven, "seemed to me written in this glance."

A few days later, at another ball, Countess Lieven herself made an attempt to reintroduce Lady Hertford, but all in vain. "There, Sire," she said, "is someone who awaits and hopes for a word from you." But the Czar was adamant. "She is mighty old," he said, and abruptly left the scene. But despite this petty bickering between two sovereigns (the Regent was considered a sovereign because of George III's madness), Alexander was a great success in society, with the population and with the younger ladies. He made a special effort to seek out the Regent's former mistress, Lady Jersey, naturally to the "intense annoyance" of the Regent. Alexander asked Lady Jersey to give him a ball on June 15, but the Regent purposely arranged for the Czar to visit Oxford to receive an honorary degree on the fourteenth, in the hope that Alexander would miss the ball. He did not, but managed after returning to London to change his clothes and appear on the early morning of the sixteenth at Lady Jersey's house and to dance the reel until 5 A.M.

Finally the visit to London was over, and the Czar, accompanied by his beloved sister, left England, never to return.[15]

An entirely different royal reception awaited Grand Duke Nicholas, Alexander's nineteen-year-old bachelor brother, in England. "Go to England," the Czar said to him. "England is the best school of constitutionalism in the world."[16] By November of 1815, Nicholas had arrived there. Peace now reigned in Europe, or at least, so it seemed. Napoleon, "this poisoner, an assassin and an incendiary," in the words of *The Times* of London, was[17] at last safely ensconced at St. Helena, and the Holy Alliance, set to make the world safe for the monarchies, was an accomplished fact.

The young Duke Nicholas, whose engagement to the lovely Princess Charlotte of Prussia had just been announced, was conveyed from Calais aboard the yacht *Royal Sovereign*, sent on behalf of George III.* For three months the young Duke Nicholas attended balls, routs, dinners, plays, and race meetings in the English countryside. He too was well received by the people. "He is devilishly handsome," exclaimed a Mrs. Campbell, "he will be the best looking man in Europe." "A tall and handsome man always pleases John Bull, such is their *faiblesse nationale*," the German Baroness of Bunsen wrote to her husband. And in Scotland, Sir Walter Scott, whom Nicholas met, addressed verses to him—a "sprig of grandeur from the Russian tree."

Nicholas inspected the inevitable arsenals, industrial centers, coal mines, prisons, and hospitals. In return the Grand Duke invited the Prince Regent and his brothers to a reception aboard a Russian frigate lying at anchor in the Thames. The Regent was more than enthusiastic this time. Jovially he praised the Russian sailors, whom he considered to be "as good as England's tars," and Nicholas in his turn gallantly remarked how insignificant the Russian fleet was in comparison with the English Armada. "Let us divide the Empire," exclaimed the Regent in jest, "we will keep the ocean and leave the North Sea to you." Soon, to the relief of

---

* Charlotte was the daughter of King Frederick Wilhelm III of Prussia and the "heroic" Louisa of Mecklenburg-Strelitz, remembered for her unsuccessful love affair with Napoleon. Charlotte was also the sister of the future Emperor of Germany, Wilhelm I, and a great-niece and god-daughter of Queen Charlotte of Great Britain, the wife of King George III, who had also been born a princess of Mecklenburg-Strelitz.

the Russians, the portly Regent and his brothers left the Russian frigate to the tune of "God Save the King." Nicholas's mission was thus brilliantly accomplished, and the happy Grand Duke returned early in 1816 to the Continent to inspect the Russian troops then in the occupation of France and to prepare for his forthcoming marriage, to take place in July, 1817, in St. Petersburg.

Meanwhile in England the House of Hanover slowly but inevitably was nearing its end, at least in the male line of succession. The ailing King George III had only three years to live. His only legitimate grandchild was the daughter of his son the Regent, twenty-year-old Princess Charlotte, heir presumptive, who was married to Leopold of Saxe-Coburg, the future "beloved Uncle Leopold." But Princess Charlotte died suddenly in 1817. "Charlotte is dead," the old Duchess of Saxe-Coburg wrote in her diary. "I cannot realize the gigantic tragedy. I cannot bear it. Poor Leopold [her son]. She is dead, the beautiful, charming, good woman, the hope of the large population of England over which she would have ruled."

To make the matter worse, none of the remaining six sons and six daughters of King George III was at that time a prospect as possible heir. The King had fifteen children in all, but the youngest at this time was thirty-eight. Apart from the Regent, deep in trouble with his attempted divorce, the Duke of York, though married, was childless; the Duke of Clarence, the future King William IV, had a large but illegitimate family by the actress Mrs. Jordan; the fifty-year-old Edward, Duke of Kent, unmarried, had been living for almost thirty years with a Frenchwoman with a name as long as their liaison lasted, Madame Alphonsine Thérèse Bernardine Julie de Montgenet de St. Lorenz, Baronne de Fortisson; the Duke of Cumberland had only one child, who died at birth; the Duke of Sussex had two children by Lady Augusta Murray, to whom he was married, but this marriage, inasmuch as it violated the Royal Marriage Act, had been declared void and the offspring barred from succession. The daughters of King George III were either unmarried or had no children, at least by legitimate husbands.[18]

"At the time of Charlotte's death [in 1817]," said one English historian, "as matters then stood, after the deaths of her uncles, aunts and two middle-aged cousins, the [Hanoverian] Duke of Brunswick, nephew of the Regent's hated wife Caroline and the first cousin once removed of the Regent himself, then a boy of thirteen, would have succeeded to the English throne."*

But an English heir to the throne had to be provided at all cost, and provided it was. The man to fulfill this destiny was the Duke of Kent, the "least profligate" of King George's sons but "the greatest rascal that ever went unhung," to quote the famous diarist Charles Greville. The Duke of Kent, as he himself confessed, sacrificed for it his "personal life and the woman he loved." The year was 1818.

Now the scene shifts to a large bedroom at Kensington Palace in London, where, at about 4 A.M. on May 24, 1819, the thirty-year-old Victoire, Duchess of Kent,† gave birth to a child, "plump as a partridge"—a girl. The Duke of Kent, who incidentally was twenty-one years older than his wife, had taken no chances and had seen to it that the Duke of Wellington, the Archbishop of Canterbury, the Bishop of London, and others of no less importance were present looking on at this historic event.

Exactly one month later the christening of the baby took place. The exasperated Regent, who, as one author says, "was furious at the Kents for their pre-arranged pomp and circumstances" for the arrival of the baby, "as if it were the unquestionable heir to the throne," nevertheless consented to be one of his niece's godparents. Among other godparents—there were alto-

---

* This boy, who was a theoretical successor to the throne of England, lived, after the revolution of 1830, in Hanover, and as an exile in Paris, where he died in 1873. With his brilliantly painted face, black wig, and shirt front and fingers blazing with diamonds, he was a familiar figure to many Parisians. It was he, says Creston, "that Providence saved the English from having to accept as their King." [19]

† Victoire, Duchess of Kent, was born Princess of Saxe-Coburg, the sister of "Uncle Leopold" and the widow of Prince Leiningen-Dachsburg-Hardenburg. It was her sister Julie who was married to Grand Duke Constantine, brother of Alexander I and Grand Duke Nicholas. Thus she was by marriage related to the Russian Royal Family.

gether five—was Czar Alexander I of Russia, represented by the Duke of York.

The atmosphere was tense as everyone eagerly awaited the Regent and speculated whether he would appear. The observant Countess Lieven wrote that "in spite of the caresses the [future] King [George IV] lavished on her, I could see that he did not like dandling on his sixty-four-year-old knees this little bit of future." Finally the portly and "disagreeable Regent," with his face "redder than usual," made his belated appearance. "My Lords," he said, "I suppose the ceremony may now begin?" Then an incredible scene took place. It is charmingly told by Creston: "There arrived the moment for naming the baby. The Archbishop, the foamy bundle lying in his arms, asked, 'By what name does it please Your Royal Highness to call this child?' No answer. There came a long pause. But something had to be done. Gazing at the Royal Godfather, the Archbishop gave rise to 'Georgiana.' Still silence! Shall she be called 'Georgiana'? repeated the Archbishop. 'On no account,' rapped out the Regent. 'Charlotte, after your Royal Mother and the child's Royal Aunt?' 'Certainly not.' The ambitious Duke of Kent, who had aspired earlier to name the baby 'Elizabeth,' (his brother, who detected the 'influence,' vetoed it), hoped at least to substitute it for the name of Alexandrina, in honor of the Russian Emperor Alexander I, the ally of England, and the 'Liberator of Europe,' whose personality unfortunately for years back eclipsed the Regent in London. The Archbishop became more definite. Still silence. 'What name is it Your Royal Highness's pleasure to command? What is her mother's name?' Victoria, answered the Duke of Kent. Finally, the Duke of York, who earlier advised his brother to leave the question of naming his child unsettled, and then 'suddenly bring it out at the christening,' now came out with a suggestion: 'Alexandrina-Victoria.' After all he was representing the child's godfather, Emperor Alexander."[20]

This was accepted, and from that moment and for many years thereafter the future Queen Victoria was known as Alexandrina, or "Drina" for short, not quite realizing herself—nor was it clear to her future subjects—that the name she bore was in honor of an emperor whose country, except for one short period, she was not only to remain on cold terms with all her life but was even to go to war against.*

---

* The earlier issues of the *Almanach de Gotha* always listed Queen Victoria as "Reine Alexandrine-Victoire I." (See for instance the edition of 1845.) Only at the end of the nineteenth century was it changed to "Victoire-Alexandrine, Reine du Royaume de Grande Bretagne." At her accession in 1837, the Privy Council, in its "Declaration to the Kingdom" referred to the young Queen as "Alexandrina-Victoria," and on that day all peers swore allegiance to her under these names. Only on the next day was her designation altered to Victoria, "necessitating no end of trouble in the issues of a new declaration and a re-signing of the peers' roll." [21] Yet the appellation "Victoria" was objected to by many in England, including Sir Walter Scott, and two influential members of Parliament, who urged that on her accession she assume the name of Queen Elizabeth II. "Victoria," they stated, "was not in accord with the feelings of the English people." They thought it was a "foreign name." At any rate, until she reached her ninth year, she was always called "Drina" by her family.

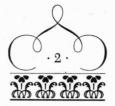

ALEXANDER

Shortly before the historic christening of the future Queen Victoria took place, in faraway Russia—victorious but exhausted from the ravages of the Napoleonic Wars—a boy was born and given the name of Alexander, Sasha for short.* Symbolically, the boy, first child in the family, destined to make history, was born on Russian Easter Sunday, on April 29, 1818.† The place of birth was the modest quarters of the Chudov Monastery in Moscow, which still bore the scars of the fires of 1812. The boy was the son of the young Grand Duke Nicholas, whom we already have met in England, and of the Grand Duchess Alexandra Feodorovna, as the former Princess Charlotte of Prussia was now known. Although the parents of Alexandrina-Victoria had at least some hopes for a future throne for their child, the parents of Sasha had none, inasmuch as the elder brother of Nicholas, Constantine,‡ was at that time the heir to the throne of Russia— the Cesarevich.

---

* Alexander's mother was the grandniece and goddaughter of Queen Charlotte of England, the wife of George III, and therefore was related to the future Queen Victoria. It is very possible that when Alexander was born, Charlotte of England congratulated her great-grandnephew and just as plausible that Nicholas congratulated the English royal family on the arrival of a new relative—his niece Alexandrina.

† Six days later in a small Rhenish Prussian town, a male baby was born to Jewish German parents and was named Karl Heinrich Marx.

‡ When he was seventeen Grand Duke Constantine, "by orders of"

For the Grand Duke and Duchess life was quiet and uneventful the first eight years of marriage. "Our Life," Charlotte confessed to her brother, the future Emperor of Germany, Wilhelm I, "is quite bourgeois." Their stay first in Moscow, then in St. Petersburg, followed a century-old routine. "We went out into society very little," wrote the Grand Duchess, "usually on Sundays we dined with Mama [the widow of Emperor Paul I] . . . and in the evening we returned to form a circle and to play macao [a fashionable card game]. At these gatherings the society was terribly old and rococo and consisted mainly of aged half-blind senators and great nobles of the days of the Empress Catherine." Charlotte, or "Mouffy" to her husband, was truly a beautiful woman. She was only twenty at the birth of her son. Her husband was two years older.

The young couple were very much in love (their marriage was an exception among royalty because it really was a love match; "our world is in our hearts," Charlotte wrote to her brother). They read a lot, particularly the novels of Walter Scott—in English since both knew the language well. *"Corinne,"* and *"Malek Adel,"* the rages of that time, were their favorites. At home the Grand Duchess knitted or embroidered and, like every *hausfrau,* devoted her spare time to interior décor. Charlotte adored hothouse flowers, singing birds and fountains, and her rooms became a fairyland of exotic blooms, Harz canaries, and other trilling birds. She even faithfully reproduced her Berlin sitting room and thus satisfied the nostalgia of her *Heimat.*

Nicholas, on the other hand, when not busy soldiering, and busy he was (he commanded a guard division), took a great deal of interest in regimental music and even composed some operatic arias and religious chants. Inasmuch as he was not in the line of succession, state affairs did not concern or interest him. He was not given even a small participation in them. "The Russians,"

---

his grandmother, Catherine the Great, married fifteen-year-old Princess Julia of Saxe-Coburg, the sister of Victoria's mother. The marriage was an unhappy one, and Constantine "repudiated" Julia in 1820. Alexander I consented to the divorce in April of the same year, on a specific condition that Constantine renounce his right to the throne, a condition which was not known to many, with disastrous results in 1825.[1]

wrote a contemporary, "know him very little." Nicholas continued to occupy an inconspicuous position in the army hierarchy and, despite custom, was not even made aide-de-camp to his eldest brother, Czar Alexander I. Yet he made no complaint but was content to lead the quiet, unobtrusive existence of a junior member of the dynasty, assuming as well the duties of a family man.

Children came with a clocklike precision. A year after the birth of Sasha, Marie arrived, then a stillborn child in 1820, Olga in 1822, and in June of 1825 another girl, Alexandra. "I had three children in two years; it is quite pleasant to have still another child in the family, but I would like to rest for a few years," Charlotte confided to her German brother-in-law in November, 1825. She was yet to produce three more sons—all this within six years.[2]

While Charlotte penned these lines, Alexander I was already in the south of Russia, in Taganrog, where, for reasons of health, he decided to spend a few months. On November 19 (December 1 new style), 1825, he was dead, and the tragic days of December, which changed the history of Russia and with it the destiny of Nicholas and his son and heir, Alexander, began.

Because Alexander had left no children (two daughters had died in infancy), his successor ordinarily would have been the elder of his brothers, Constantine. However, when, unknown to many, including his younger brother Nicholas, Constantine had renounced his right of succession, Alexander had then transferred the right to Nicholas, without informing the latter. Because of these circumstances, Nicholas, at the death of Alexander, took the oath of allegiance to Constantine, while Constantine swore allegiance to Nicholas at Warsaw. Russia found itself with two emperors!

On the fatal day of December 14 [26], 1825, in St. Petersburg —the day of swearing allegiance to the "new lawful Czar," that is, Nicholas I—members of the revolutionary group The Northern Union decided to utilize the confusion to further their own aims and proclaimed the constitution with Constantine as Czar. Shouts of hurrah for Constantine and his wife Constitutzia(!) misled simple people and soldiers, and they were induced to rebel.

Owing to the lack of any organization of the revolutionaries and the absence of real support from the garrison and population, however, the revolt was speedily suppressed, mainly through Nicholas's energy and resoluteness.

Nicholas revealed high personal courage that day when he rode his horse through the enormous, surging crowds assembled in the square near his palace. He faced the mutinous soldiers, their loaded muskets pointed at him, as he made repeated efforts to bring them to their senses. In midafternoon Nicholas sent for reinforcements, the Horse Guards, "the only two units" he could absolutely rely on.[3] The short winter day was fast drawing to a close, and the new Emperor knew that if the revolt was not broken before nightfall, he might lose his throne. Cannon were moved in, and an order to disperse the mob was given. But the soldiers refused to fire upon their own people. Finally, a young officer with the name of Bakunin (incidentally, the uncle of the future anarchist Michael Bakunin), whose soldiers had refused to take their stations around a cannon, manned it himself and fired three rounds.

As if by magic the crowd fled. In minutes the streets were empty.

The little Sasha—"le petit Sasha" as his parents called him— spent the morning on this fateful day with his anxious mother at their relatively small Anichkov Palace. As the revolt became more menacing, orders were given to transfer the young Empress and the children to the better-guarded Winter Palace. This was done, and they were secretly brought in by the back door. Since Alexander spent the rest of the day in the front drawing room, overlooking the Neva River and the Senate Square, where the main revolt took place, he must have heard cannon and rifle shots and the roars of the mob. Yet we know from witnesses that the seven-year-old boy was completely unaware of the tragedy and continued to color an engraving with an appropriate title: "The Crossing of Granicus by Alexander the Great in 334 B.C."

Then, suddenly, calm descended. At 6 P.M. Nicholas arrived at the Winter Palace, surrounded by enormous crowds of people, shouting, "Hurrah to the Emperor Nicholas I." "Our love to the Czar, our father!"

As he alighted from his horse, Nicholas greeted and thanked the loyal Sappers Guard Battalion, who had been the first to come to protect the royal family.* Then he entered the palace and in a moment returned to the people, holding in his arms the little Sasha, dressed for the occasion in the uniform of the Hussars of the Guards, whose Honorary Colonel he had been since his birth and whose uniform he would always love (he never forgot that it was given to him by his uncle Czar Alexander I).

"Love my son, as I love you," Nicholas cried out as the soldiers gathered around to kiss the young Grand Duke.

The night was growing colder and darker. In the palace backyard, the soldiers were lighting fires to keep themselves warm.

The revolution was over.

"Our beautiful bourgeois life is ended," the new Empress regretfully wrote to her father, the King of Prussia. "We cannot live again in our house [the Anichkov Palace]. We were so intimately linked together and so vividly shared all our sorrows and worries together. Now I can only occupy a small place in Nicholas' heart, the rest belongs to Russia. . . ." Even if we discount the German sentimentality, then so much in vogue, one must confess that the life of this "bourgeois family," now an imperial household, had changed completely.

Despite much of the drillmaster in him, Nicholas decided to give his son an education entirely different from his own. He would not repeat the mistakes of his father, Czar Paul I, and his grandmother, Catherine the Great, resulting in the shortcoming "a pêle-mêle of an education," as Nicholas wrote. "We were given to the care of Lambsdorff, our principal gouverneur. There were around us six more tutors . . . we loved some, detested others, but not a single one inspired in us confidence. Lambsdorff inspired only one sentiment—the fright . . . during the lessons quite often Lambsdorff inflicted on me very painful blows of a cane. . . ."[4]

---

* We will encounter this regiment later in more than tragic circumstances.

When Alexander was only five, Nicholas replaced the boy's English nurses with an army captain, Karl Moerder, as his first tutor.* Karl Karlovich Moerder, "an ugly . . . nonfashionable man," a grandson of a Saxon émigré in the Russian service, was a humane and an educated man. He was interested in men as men and not merely as soldiers or subjects of the Czar. Moerder was a Protestant, but he always talked of religion as Russian Orthodox, of course.

First of all, Alexander must live to please God. "Life itself," Moerder insisted, "was a school and God was the headmaster." But Alexander believed that religion was the doing of good and submitted humbly to the will of God. Appropriately, he had been born on an Easter Day, and he believed in resurrection in the new life.[5]

The results of Moerder's influence were soon forthcoming. "And how would you have punished the Decembrists, Sasha?" asked his father once. "I should have pardoned them," was the reply. (As a matter of fact, upon his succession to the throne in 1854, Alexander did pardon the Decembrists. The Decembrists and their direct descendants had been stripped of all their privileges; Alexander restored them.)

For the first time in the history of the upbringing of a Russian grand duke, the Czar selected as playmates for his son several boys of different social strata and nationalities. To begin with, there were three more Alexanders—the Russian Prince Alexander Bariatinsky, the future field marshal and liberal viceroy of Caucasus; Alexander Adlerberg (the descendant of a Swedo-Balt), the son of a childhood friend of Nicholas I, and the future minister of the Imperial Court and a lifelong friend of Alexander;† and Alexander Patkul, another Balt, of obscure background, who ended his days quietly as chief of police of St. Petersburg. The other playmates were a Pole, Count Josef Wieligorsky, a member

---

* "The choice of Moerder," wrote a contemporary, "surprised St. Petersburg society but proved the foresight of the Emperor." Moerder's granddaughter, a Russian émigrée, Countess Sophia Armfelt, died in 1963, in the United States, at the age of ninety-seven.

† Adlerberg's grandmother literally brought up Czar Nicholas.

of a famous family of Russian amateur musicians and Macaenes;* and finally, Count Alexis K. Tolstoy, a Russo-Ukrainian (whose grandfather was a Razumovsky, a relative of the famous shepherd who morganatically married the Empress Elizabeth) who was to become a celebrated dramatist and poet and a longtime friend of the future Czar.

The four Alexanders and the others, all the same age, were a happy, carefree lot. They roamed and played around the innumerable rooms of the Winter Palace, to which they were brought daily to study. Thus intimacy with the future Czar grew. Some of them even shared the same washbowl with him, at that time a great distinction.†

At an early age Alexander was initiated into the usual hardships of military life: he slept under canvas every summer during maneuvers at Krasnoye Selo, near St. Petersburg, his bed a mere wooden bench, and his tutor read history to him "until he went to sleep." His food was plain; his amusements—military games and gymnastic exercises—were taken in all weather. (It is very possible that this was the cause of Alexander's asthma, which he suffered for most of his life.) Even his bedroom wallpaper, his father's gift to him, depicted soldiers. In all, it was a typical military upbringing. Nevertheless, Alexander grew to be quite indifferent to military parades but open rather to romantic influences. The man who was to give this to him, when Alexander was eight years old, was Vasilli Zhukovsky, the famous Russian poet and formerly Sasha's mother's teacher of Russian. Zhukovsky, a contemporary of Pushkin, and whom Byron styled a Russian nightingale, was a rather curious choice as tutor for the son of a "reactionary" monarch. Considered by some a freethinker and a liberal, the new tutor was the "natural son" of a Russian landowner, Afanassy Bunin (of the same family as the White Russian exile, writer, and Nobel Prize winner of 1933, Ivan Bunin), and a sixteen-year-old Turkish slave girl, Fatima, a spoil of war.

---

* "This friendship" (of Patkul and Wieligorsky) wrote a contemporary known for her biting tongue, "was necessary" to the Czarevich "as spurs to a lazy horse." [6]

† Adlerberg's descendants possessed the historic washbowl in the family until the revolution of 1917. [7]

"Respect the law," Zhukovsky used to say to his royal pupil, "and by this example teach others to respect it. The law neglected by the Czar will never be honored by the people," he explained. "Love also education—this is the strongest help to an enlightened government—people without education is a nation without dignity. Respect public opinion, this is what enlightens the monarch and is his greatest support. Love your people, without which there will be no love for their Czar. Rule not by force but by order. The might of state is not in the number of soldiers but in the prosperity of its people." These were new words for young dukes of a royal family to hear.[8]

The education plan Zhukovsky drew up for the first twelve years was submitted to the Czar and heartily approved. It consisted of many subjects: religion, history, political economy, law, literature and military arts, mathematics, philosophy, applied arts and five languages—Russian, Latin, French, English, and Polish. The celebrated reformer Count Michael Speransky instructed Alexander in law. Diplomacy was taught by Baron Brunnow, later Russian Ambassador to England, and the Polish poet Adam Mickiewicz gave him lessons in Polish.

The advantages of free labor versus serf labor were especially stressed. Later, for advanced studies, Sasha was given two more teachers, Russians. (From this point on there would be no more foreign teachers, most unusual in the education of the Russian members of royalty.) They were Professor Constantine I. Arseniev and Professor Dimitri A. Kavelin, both expelled a few years earlier from St. Petersburg University for "teaching and instilling in students premeditated systems of unbelief, perniciousness, and destruction." Yet to these politically precocious teachers Nicholas, "the Gendarme of Europe, the despotic Emperor," confided his son and heir. To top it all, Kavelin was a Mason, then an unpardonable sin.

When, at sixteen, Alexander became of age and took the oath of fidelity to preserve the inviolability of the empire, Zhukovsky, in consultation with Arseniev, planned for him an extensive tour throughout European Russia and Siberia.* The trip began in the

---

* Male members of Russian royalty became of age at sixteen, other "mortals" at twenty-one. Nicholas did not bestow on Alexander the title

early spring of 1837, before the era of railways, by carriage and by boat. The royal cortège galloped from post station to post station in the fashion immortalized by Pushkin, and stopped and visited scores of Russian towns never seen by the Russian ruler with the exception perhaps of Alexander's ancestor the perpetual traveler Peter the Great. The historic cities of Central Russia, among them Tver, Yaroslavl', Kostroma, and finally Viatka were visited. At Viatka he met the young political exile Alexander Herzen (once more a reminder of Alexander I), and through the intercession of Alexander and Zhukovsky, the famous revolutionary-to-be and publicist obtained his freedom.

Herzen met the Czarevich Alexander at an exhibition in Viatka, where he acted as a guide to the royal guest. In the evening the exile was again presented at a ball given by the local society in honor of the Grand Duke (a situation absolutely impossible in Soviet Russia today). Eventually Herzen emigrated to England, where from a safe retreat in London he began his revolutionary activities by publishing the famous newspaper *Kolokol (The Bell)*, banned in Russia but said to be read even by the Czar himself. The three principal demands of *The Bell* were the emancipation of the serfs, abolition of corporal punishment, and the curtailment of censorship. Incidentally, all these reforms were enacted by Alexander in 1861.

A few days later the royal cortège crossed the Ural Mountains and approached the vastest expanse of Alexander's realm— Siberia. The Czarevich was more than well received by the population and the exiles who were not confined in the prisons in the towns of Tumen and Tobol'sk. As Alexander penetrated deeper and deeper into Siberia, he could not help notice that though the expanses were larger and the soil was richer and generally the whole life of the peasants was "fuller, freer and more prosperous" than in European Russia, the country here was not as thickly populated. "Did it not occur [it certainly did] to the educated youth [Alexander]," wrote a Russian author, "that

---

of Cesarevich or Heir Apparent to the Throne until 1831, the year of the death of Sasha's uncle the Grand Duke Constantine, the legitimate Czarevich, who, as we have seen, abdicated his rights earlier.

the reason why this country was way ahead of European Russia *was due to the fact* [emphasis by the author] that serfdom was always unknown here. Free labor of the free people."*

While in Siberia,† the Czarevich dispatched by special courier a plea to his father to ameliorate the conditions of the Decembrists. The favorable answer arrived by special courier while Alexander was still traveling in Siberia. As a result of this visit and plea, the living conditions of the Decembrists were much improved, though they and their families were at that time rather comfortable in their forced exile. Contrary to the general belief, some of the exiles, like the princes Troubetzkoy, Wolkonsky, and several others, each had twenty-five servants at his disposal and had salaried workers on a regular payroll. Many of them imported pianos, subscribed to magazines, and some bought out entire libraries in which, as one exile wrote, "one even found books forbidden in Russia."[9]

By Christmas of 1837, Alexander was back home in Czarskoye Selo, having visited such historical places as Moscow, Borodino, Simbirsk, Viazma, Sebastopol, Poltava, and Kiev. Owing to Zhukovsky and Arseniev's liberal guidance, the trip was a success and permitted Alexander, perhaps with limitations, to learn the true conditions of the country. There is no doubt that the Czarevich, because of the influence of his tutors and from his own impressions, came to the conclusion that sooner or later the serfs must be liberated. And the sooner the better, lest they take matters into their own hands and liberate themselves. As we will see later, this thought never left him.

Meanwhile, the Russian Siberian tour was soon to be followed by a European one. But the schedule of this trip was advanced. The reason—an age-old problem—a girl, but a "wrong" one:

---

* In the Civil War of 1917–22 many Siberians were staunch supporters of the anti-Bolshevik movement.

† In Siberia, the royal procession also stopped at Ekaterinburg, then a small Siberian mining town on the threshold of Europe and Asia. Could anyone in this group, from the Czarevich down, have imagined that eighty years later at that very spot his grandson with his entire family would be assassinated by the Communists, and the empire and its three-hundred-year-old dynasty would come to an end?

beautiful but a commoner, Polish and a Catholic at that!* Sasha
was twenty years old, handsome, and romantic. The girl was
Olga Kalinovskaya, of the same age as Sasha. An orphan, she was
the daughter of a Polish official, Ossip (Joseph) Kalinovski, who
remained loyal to Russia during the Polish insurrection of 1830
and was recompensed by the appointment of his daughter to the
most dazzling court in Europe, generally a remarkable favor but
particularly so for a subject of a rebellious nation. Olga, as a
lady-in-waiting to the Empress, occupied a very minor place in
the history of Russia except for the time she gave some worries
to the imperial parents.[10] This romance was not generally known
and was never made public in Russia until the Bolsheviks
ransacked the archives of the imperial palaces. In 1919 a metal
box was found containing "personal and secret" letters of
Alexander II in "His Majesty's Own Library" in the Winter
Palace of Petrograd (St. Petersburg). The Bolshevik historians
published the contents in 1926.

"We talked about Sasha," wrote the Czar to his wife, "he must
have more strength of character, otherwise he will be lost." The
Czar felt that his son was too amorous and weak and easily fell
under influences. "He must without fail," continued Nicholas,
"stay away from St. Petersburg. . . . Let us pray God that Olga
K. will get married."

Meanwhile the old remedy was applied: *Partir c'est mourir un
peu*, and by the spring of 1838, the unhappy Sasha was made
ready to leave home for his European visit. Now he was to be
under sterner tutelage, that of Count Christopher Lieven. Perhaps
better known as the husband of the celebrated but unfaithful
Princess Daria Lieven, General Aide-de-Camp Count (later

---

* When Alexander was about fifteen, "he flirted" with a young but
"very poor" lady-in-waiting, one "Natasha" Borozdina. But the young girl
was "sensible and laughed off [the Czarevich's] sighs," wrote Madame
Smirnova. Eventually Natasha married and ended her life as Mrs.
Kamenskaya in England, where she is buried in "Ganzee Green." [11]

Alexander's first love could have gone unnoticed if not for Pushkin's
immortal lines in *Eugene Onegin* (Chapter VII, stanza 26) in which he
mentioned Natasha and her sister as the two who received the Empress's
coveted "initials" or patent to be ladies-in-waiting to Nicholas I's wife,
the Empress.[12]

Prince) Christopher Andreievich Lieven (1777–1838) was the Russian Ambassador to St. James's from 1812 to 1834, when he was appointed head tutor to Czarevich Alexander. Sasha was again accompanied by his friend and teacher Zhukovsky and his usual playmates—Bariatinsky, Adlerberg, Patkul, Wieligorsky, and Tolstoy. In addition, a Colonel Simon A. Yourievich* took the place of the old Moerder, who had recently died.

The "forget-it-all" trip (Alexander knew only too well that the purpose of the advanced schedule was to separate him from his amorata; *however*, he did not suspect that the trip would be so lengthy) began by a state visit to Stockholm to the second Bernadotte ruler, Oscar I, then married to Josephine Beauharnais. (The Queen, the granddaughter of Empress Josephine, the wife of Napoleon I, was the sister of the Duke Maximilian Leuchtenberg de Beauharnais, who in 1839 was to marry the Grand Duchess Marie, Alexander's sister.)

Alexander's first visit was followed by a call on a distant relative, the King of Hanover. By July, the Czarevich and his suite stopped at the fashionable watering town of Ems to take "a cure and drink the waters." They arrived with twelve horse carriages and created a sensation. Here, for the first time, Alexander opened his heart to his father.

"You know how despondent I am," he wrote. "You probably noticed my relation with O.K. You and I had a conversation last winter *à coeur*. . . . Feelings which I have for her are feelings of a pure and real love, of attachment and respect. This increased every day and now continues. But the thought that this will lead to nowhere does not leave me. Just to the contrary, it tortures me more and more, and therefore I become dull and sad. I can't contain my tears." But the father comforted him: "I love Ossipovna [Olga Ossipovna, *i.e.*, Olga the daughter of Ossip] and love her as a charming girl. I will not blame her that she unwillingly roused in you feelings of love. From that point be quite at ease."[13]

Many witnesses have left us their impressions of the young

---

* He taught Polish to the Czarevich. Of Yourievich's two living descendants (girls), one is a British and the other an American citizen.

Alexander. One worth quoting came from the pen of the Marquis de Custine, the celebrated "78 days wonder" French "expert" on Russia, who saw Alexander in Ems.* "He is 20 and tall," wrote the Marquis, "but he seemed rather stout for his years. He looks rather like a German than a Russian, he is evidently suffering from some grief, as his eyelids are cast down with a sadness that shows the cares of a riper age. The Grand Duke of Russia is one of the finest models of a Prince I have ever met. If he ever comes to the throne he will obtain obedience through the constraint of a gracious character rather than by terror."[14]

But soon Ems and its "waters" were left behind, and the royal party stopped at Weimar, where the reigning Grand Duchess Marie was Sasha's paternal aunt. After a meeting with Nicholas (his father) at home, Alexander wrote, ". . . everything was cleared and explained," regarding Olga.

Then the entourage headed for the south—sunny Italy. Verona, Venice, Rome, and Genoa were all visited and studied, and soon

---

* "The expert" (1790–1857) was in a short time expelled from Russia on "moral grounds." Some authors feel that because of the above, his critical description of Russian life was a revengeful act, biased and unfair. Balzac, for instance, felt that the book was "essentially empty" nothing but epigrams about the weather.[15] The poet Vasilli Zhukovsky called him a "dog," and one recent European author, using a penname of Ghislain de Diesbach, a "scion of a [non-Russian] princely family," in his 1967 book *Secrets of the Gotha* discloses who was ". . . the object of [Custine's] passion [for which] de Custine had not hesitated to undertake a journey to St. Petersburg in order to ask the Czar to restore his young friend's property which had been confiscated. This rash step was by no means successful as Custine revenged himself writing his famous book 'Russia in 1839.'" Though the author does not give us the sources of his information, we know who Custine's *protégé* was. It was a young Pole, an adventurous émigré from Russia and a precursor of twentieth-century gigolos, one Count Ignatius Gurovsky, who eventually, in 1841, eloped with and married the twenty-year-old Infanta Isabella of Spain, a cousin of Queen Isabella and a descendant of King Charles IV of Spain.[16] The story of the elder Gurovsky brother, Count Adams, is no less interesting. Adams, taking part in the Polish Rebellion of 1830–31, emigrated to Paris, where he began his fierce anti-Russian propaganda campaign. In 1835 he suddenly changed his views and began to extol Russia, with the result that he was permitted by the Czar to return home. In 1848, restless as he was, Adams emigrated to the United States, where, in 1854, he published in English a book favorable to Russia under the title *Russia As It Is*. Apparently, he died in America in 1868 at the age of sixty-one.[17]

Prince Lieven, the diplomat and tutor, was able to report to his master, the Czar, that "Monseigneur is leading a very social and gay life and apparently is forgetting Mlle. K." But when the royal party reached Rome, the elderly Lieven fell ill. On January 10, 1839, His Serene Highness Prince Lieven breathed his last. A new *gouverneur en chef* was appointed and sped to his assignment. He was the General Count Alexis Orlov, the natural son of one Feodor Orlov, whose brother was the famous Gregory Orlov, Catherine the Great's "favorite."*

Count Orlov's instructions were explicit—to head north immediately and look for a suitable bride for the Czarevich. The future Cesarevna (*i.e.*, wife of the Cesarevich, Heir to the Throne) had to be not more than nineteen and Protestant and had to belong to one of the royal families of Europe. However, this was not all. The reputation of the future bride's family naturally had to be without blemish, a requirement, as we shall see later, not easy to meet. The prospective bride had to be reasonably good-looking, but what was more important, if beauty was lacking, she had to be *racée* (well bred) and absolutely no taller than her intended bridegroom (conveniently, Romanovs were all tall). Finally, she should not be too closely related, another requirement almost impossible to fulfill, inasmuch as Alexander was related to practically all the reigning non-Catholic Houses of Europe. At that time he was the nephew of the King of Prussia (his mother's brother), the nephew of the future Queen of the Netherlands (his father's sister), and nephew of the King and Queen of Württemberg. He was closely related to the grand dukes of Baden, Hesse-Darmstadt, Mecklenburg-Schwerin, and several others. We have already seen that he was also a cousin, and at the same time a nephew, of the young Queen Victoria. In the words of Bismarck, Prussia in the early nineteenth century was "an outpost of the Czar's Empire and a

---

* During the Decembrist revolt, Gregory Orlov was in command of the Horse Guards, which remained loyal to Nicholas. For this he was made a count. He fulfilled many diplomatic missions. For signing the Treaty of Paris, which ended the Crimean War in 1856, he was made a prince. In 1959, as we have seen, at the request of the United Nations, his direct descendant, the late Prince Nicholas V. Orlov, an American citizen and an expert on the Russian language, accompanied Premier Khrushchev as an interpreter on the latter's trip to the United States.

vassal of the House of Romanov." The Russian rulers and their male and female descendants from Peter the Great down traditionally and invariably married members of German royalties. Yet, although the Czarevich Alexander's blood was theoretically only 1/32 pure Russian, he was in every way a Russian, with the good and bad qualities that suggest a typical representative of the aristocratic breed of St. Petersburg. He could very well repeat the words of his *confrère* and grandnephew King George V of Great Britain, who in 1917, in the midst of World War I, in answer to H. G. Wells's public appeal to "get rid of the alien and uninspiring Court," remarked: "I may be uninspiring, but I'll be damned if I am alien."[18] If Alexander's sole 100 per cent Russian ancestor was Peter the Great (1689–1725), George V of Great Britain, the grandfather of the present Queen Elizabeth II, had no equivalent English ancestor unless one stretches the point and takes into consideration James I (1603–25), the son of Lord Darnley and Mary Queen of Scots and grandson of Mary of Lorraine (on his mother's side)!

The itinerary now included visiting *en passant et en touriste*, Vienna and Munich ("We were not looking there [in the Catholic countries] for brides," reported Orlov). Then there were stops at Stuttgart, the capital of Württemberg, at Karlsruhe, the capital of Baden; then to round out the trip, visits to The Hague, Copenhagen, and finally England, "just to pay a short courtesy call" on the youthful Queen Alexandrina-Victoria, who had then been crowned less than a year.

Meanwhile the quest for a bride continued, and the royal party descended on the friendly little kingdom of Württemberg, whose ruling family for many years was closely related to the Romanovs. There, in the charming atmosphere of a miniature court of a kingdom created by Napoleon only thirty-three years earlier, and so different from the brilliancy and the *éclat* of the Russian court, Alexander met for the first time the children of his uncle, King William I, his cousins, one of whom was soon to marry his sister Olga, the future Queen of Württemberg.°

° Alexander's grandmother, Empress Marie Feodorovna, the wife of Paul I and the mother of Czar Alexander I, was born Princess Sophia Dorothea of Württemberg (1759–1828) and the grandniece of Frederick the Great of Prussia. In 1816 her daughter, Grand Duchess Catherine,

Among his cousins, Alexander found only one young lady available as a marriage prospect. She was Princess Catherine, who was three years his junior but who, as Orlov sadly reported, was "decidedly not to His Imperial Highness's liking," even though Orlov himself felt that *"les cousines sont embellies, mais la Princesse Catherine est mieux."* (The King of Württemberg had two daughters by his first marriage to the Russian Grand Duchess Catherine, the sister of Czar Nicholas I, and two by his second one.)

Soon the royal entourage moved on. This time they visited Baden, whose rulers were also closely related. The princess in question here fared no better. "Here we are in Karlsruhe," wrote Orlov, "the 18 year-old Princess Alexandrine [again that shadow of the liberator], who was destined to the Grand Duke ["according to choice" suggested by his parents], has absolutely nothing which attracts anyone; she has an ordinary figure, is of unimportant height. Monseigneur arrived with the best of expectations and hopes [sic] but left absolutely disappointed." Three years later this would-be fiancée of Alexander married Prince Ernst of

---

married King Wilhelm I of Württemberg, her mother's nephew. To make the matter even more complicated, in 1846, Empress Marie's granddaughter Olga (the daughter of Czar Nicholas) married Charles I, the King of Württemberg, who was the son of the same Wilhelm I but by his second wife. Finally, in 1824, the Empress's son, the Grand Duke Michael, married her grandniece, Hélène, known in Russia as the Grand Duchess Elena Pavlovna (1806–73). She was an outstanding woman among any royalty. Of "encyclopaedic knowledge and wide interest," the Grand Duchess, though not Russian, was an enthusiastic worker for emancipation (she liberated her serfs at once). Her literary and artistic salon in St. Petersburg was famous throughout Europe. It is known that on the serf-emancipation question she wielded enormous and decisive influence on her nephew, Alexander II.

In general, one must admit that the members of the Württemberg family in Russia were an outstanding addition to Russian culture and progress. The Empress Marie herself was a woman of exceptionally good education and taste. Such gems of architecture as the palaces of Gatchina, Czarskoye, and the Winter Palace in St. Petersburg and the Hermitage were decorated and furnished under her personal guidance. Her most important heritage to Russia however was the establishment of the first Schools for Women as well as numerous charity organizations in the empire. These institutions existed until the Revolution of 1917. Her brother, Prince Alexander (1771–1833), was in the Russian Civil Service and built several waterways, bridges, etc. The Württemberg Waterway System is still in use and links the Volga with the North Dvina River.

Saxe-Coburg-Gotha, the brother of Albert, the future consort of Queen Victoria. Many years later, her niece, the Queen of Roumania, described Alexandrine as a "drooping, sad-looking old lady in shabby black, a large cameo brooch with the effigy of her ('a tyrant') husband whom she adored. A grisly beard covered her chin and two kindly beaded eyes protruded above a depressed-looking nose, hopelessly pear-shaped." Alexander had had a close shave.

However, Alexander's attention was attracted at last by the youngest princess of the smallest principality of Germany. She was Marie, Princess of Nassau, whom he met in Baden. "The Grand Duke," again Orlov dutifully reported, "told me that he likes very much the little Princess of Nassau, better than all presented to him before, but unfortunately she is too young." She was then fourteen. (In 1842 Marie married the German Prince of Wied. It was their grandson who, in 1914, was proclaimed the King of Albania, the comic-opera kingdom that came to an end with World War I.)

The "looking over" trip was so far a complete fiasco, particularly since all the major Protestant courts of Germany had been visited. At that time (1839) the territory of the future German Empire consisted of independent kingdoms of Prussia, Württemberg, Bavaria, Hanover, and Saxony and of several grand duchies, among them Mecklenburg-Strelitz, Oldenburg, Saxe-Weimar, Saxe-Coburg, Hesse-Darmstadt, and Baden, and of countless smaller duchies and principalities.*

Now the royal cortège was ready to head farther north to Holland, where more than a century earlier Alexander's ancestor Peter the Great left such unforgettable memories. They stopped in The Hague, where Alexander's aunt, Princess Anna of Orange, later Queen of the Netherlands, his father's sister, had only one,

---

* In 1793 there were three hundred separate and independent states in what is now Germany. However by 1815 these independent states, by amalgamation, were reduced to thirty. Even after 1870 some of them retained a certain independence, exchanging ambassadors and ministers within themselves and abroad, having their own governments, armed forces, royal courts, etc. Up to the 1870s one could not say abroad, "I am a German," could not pride himself that the German flag was flying from his vessel, could have no German consul in time of need, but had to explain: "I am a Hessian," "I am a Württemberger," "I am a Bavarian," etc.

much-too-young (eleven years old) daughter, and a first cousin of Alexander at that, and then, before going to England, in Copenhagen, where no marriageable princesses were available anyway. Finally Count Orlov, as a last resort and only half-heartedly, suggested a stop, simply for the sake of *"politesse,"* in the "unimportant" grand duchy of Hesse-Darmstadt, "where," as Orlov condescendingly wrote, "they praise very much a Princess of Hesse, whom I, however, did not see."

The Princess was not even on the list of prospective brides. Alexander at first refused to visit the duchy. "Let us outflank it," he said to Orlov. But at the insistence of the Count and his aide, A. A. Kavelin, the Czarevich gave in on condition that the stay· there be "just for a day." They stayed, it may seem strange, in a public hotel, the Traube (the Grape).

His mentors no doubt explained to Alexander that owing to the close relationship of the two courts, omitting a visit to Hesse-Darmstadt would be a *faux-pas*. As a matter of fact, the first wife of Czar Paul I, born Princess of Hesse-Darmstadt, was the aunt of Ludwig II, the reigning Duke. In addition, the wives of Ludwig II and Alexander I, both Baden princesses, were sisters. Inasmuch as the Hesse family was also related to Prussian royalty, Ludwig's children were "cousins three times over" of Czarevich Alexander.

"Where we looked for happiness, it was not there," Zhukovsky wrote on March 26, 1839, to Alexander's mother. "But where we did not expect it, it came by itself." The Grand Duke hated the prospect of a tedious and "full of etiquette" evening and wanted to leave at once for Mainz. But after a few minutes, the *Gross Herzog* (Grand Duke) himself arrived (Ludwig II of Hesse-Darmstadt) and invited the Czarevich to visit the royal theater to hear a rather dull but symbolic opera, *Vestale*, by Gasparo Spontini (1774–1851). A supper "with music" followed. The Czarevich, splendidly attired in his flaming red cossack uniform, but "extremely pale and *distrait*," was naturally the center of everyone's attention. The only daughter of the widowed Duke, the lovely-looking Princess Maximilienne-Wilhelmine-Auguste-Sophie-Marie, to give all her names, then not quite fifteen, was the hostess for the evening.

A surprise to everyone, including Orlov, ensued. "Today" (March 25, 1839), the Czarevich wrote late that night to his father, "perhaps will be the most decisive day of all my life. This morning I left Karlsruhe with a heavy heart, I confess, because I knew how much you wished what did not take place [betrothal of Alexander to Princess Alexandrine of Baden]. Tonight however I am going to bed with a hope of a future happiness. Here in Darmstadt I have met the daughter of the reigning *Gross Herzog*, Princess Marie. [In Darmstadt she was always called Wilhelmine.] She attracted me enormously from the first moment I saw her. Now Copenhagen, dear Papa, is not necessary, and if you will permit, after my visit to England, I once more will return to Darmstadt."

The worried Orlov at once dispatched a note to the Czar in which he described "the strong impression left on his Imperial Highness by Princess Marie," but at the same time, in extremely veiled and careful phrases, Orlov hinted about "prevailing gossips regarding the parenthood of the Princess." When the royal party was on its way to the Netherlands, through Rhine, Koeln, Düsseldorf, and Rotterdam, the Czar's answer arrived.

Nicholas was not even perturbed by the "touchy gossips." (This information was disclosed for the first time by Soviet historians in 1926.)[19] "The doubts about legitimacy of her birth," wrote the Czar to Orlov, "are more authentic than you think. It is a known fact that in her family they hardly tolerate her but she is recognized officially and bears the family name of her father, and therefore nobody can say anything against her." In March of that year, however, the Russian Ambassador to England, the venerable ex-Corsican, Count "Karl Ivanovitch" Pozzo di Borgo, requested the Russian Legation in Frankfurt to supply him with Princess Marie's vital statistics. Questions asked were: "How old is she now? Her height? Her figure? Who looks after her education and upbringing after the death of her mother? How strong are her moral achievements?" etc.[20]

By April the Grand Duke's party was in The Hague, and Orlov, who was rather surprised at the Czar's reaction, hastened to take the "right line": "Don't think, Sire," wrote Orlov, "that I kept a secret from the Grand Duke regarding the rumours of the

Princess' birth. He found out almost the same day he arrived to Darmstadt, but he reacted exactly like you did. He felt that it would have been better if it were otherwise [*i.e.*, if she were legitimate], however, she bears the name of her father and therefore legally nobody can make any objection." At the moment, correspondence regarding the touchy question ceased, and the royal party, headed by an "enormously pleased" Grand Duke, was approaching England for a state visit to the still unmarried Queen Alexandrina-Victoria.

Meanwhile the Czarevich, "with the name of Marie constantly on his lips," and his party—about forty in all, and once more in many dazzling carriages—were approaching The Hague, where they were to spend the Russian Easter holidays with Alexander's Russian aunt, the Princess Anna Pavlovna of Orange, the wife of the Heir Apparent. There, by the second of May, the royal party crossed the Channel on a steamer appropriately named *The Cerbes*, and landed in England.

While the Czarevich, surrounded by his usual companions and still "radiantly happy," speeds across England for a state visit to the youthful Queen, let us glance back to the small but ancient duchy of Hesse-Darmstadt and to the little girl officially known as Her Grand Ducal Highness Wilhelmina, "Princess Hesse-Darmstadt," the daughter of "the Reigning *Gross Herzog* Ludwig II and now "almost a fiancée" of a Prince Charming, someday to be ruler of one sixth of the globe.*

During and after the Napoleonic Wars, morals generally deteriorated and were more than lax among all the classes—a phenomenon not unlike the conditions that prevailed after World Wars I and II. Generally speaking, economic conditions and upheavals were the most important contributing factors, but the inevitable breakdown of the walls of class distinction in such difficult times played a part, particularly in the Napoleonic era, among the upper classes. As a result, there were many illegitimate children—or "natural" children and "wards," to use more polite

---

* At this time, the Hesse-Darmstadt duchy covered an area of about 154 square miles, with a population of more than 800,000 people, roughly twice the territory of the District of Columbia.

words—even among the royal families. The listing of *les bâtards royaux* and their descendants could fill a large volume.

Actually, it was known that the real father of Princess Marie was the "exceedingly good-looking" descendant of a Swiss émigré, one Baron August Ludwig de Senarclens-Grancy, the Master of Horses of Grand Duke Ludwig II.* Marie's mother, born Princess Wilhelmina of Baden, was not only good-looking but was "extremely well connected," one sister, as we have seen, having been married to Alexander I of Russia, the second to King Gustav IV (of the ancient Vasa line) of Sweden, the third to the Duke of Brunswick, and the fourth to King Maximilian I of Bavaria. She herself found no happiness. Life in the Grand Duke's castle of Darmstadt, in the fortress-like building, standing in a small town, was remarkably dull and stagnant. Married to the Duke at the age of sixteen, Wilhelmina went through all the hardships of the time, suffering poverty after the French occupation of 1806, even though her father and grandfather, the reigning Grand Duke of Baden, conveniently sided with Napoleon and fought with him at the battles of Jena and Moscow. Two boys were born to Wilhelmina and Ludwig. (One of them, Charles of Hesse, was the future grandfather of Princess Alix, the "Tragic Empress" and the wife of the last Czar of Russia, Nicholas II, who was assassinated with her and their children by the Communists in 1918.)

After a space of fourteen years, Wilhelmina "surprised" her husband† by giving birth to another boy‡ and, a year later, to a

---

* The man who unwittingly played such an important role in the destinies of Russia and Hesse-Darmstadt, a bachelor until November, 1836, nine months after the death of his *amorata*, the Princess, married a German countess. His three granddaughters died the same day in 1945 in Darmstadt in the Allied bombing of the city.

† Interviewed recently by an author regarding the above, Prince Ludwig of Hesse, the last member of this family branch (died in June, 1968) stated that "there was no foundation for it and that the gap of thirteen years [actually 14 & 15] between the births was nothing remarkable." The author seems to accept the version, based on "jealousy" but errs when she accepts that the story was "invented after 1839." We know that it was not so.[21] The latest work on the Hessen family by David Duff omits this question altogether![22]

‡ The boy, Prince Alexander of Hesse-Darmstadt, as he was always known, the first ancestor of the Battenberg-Mountbatten family made history too. We will hear more of him.

girl, Marie, our heroine in question. Princess Marie was only twelve when her mother died in 1836.* Eventually her "official" father, the Duke, entered a morganatic marriage and slid slowly from the pages of history.

---

* The Baden family, it seems, made another small contribution to history when in 1837 a girl was born to Sophia-Wilhelmina, the Princess of Sweden (of the old Vasa dynasty) and the wife of a reigning grand duke of Baden. The said baby was the daughter of a banker by the name of Haber. She eventually married Grand Duke Michael, the younger brother of Czar Alexander II. Czar Alexander III and his son Nicholas II, always jokingly referred to her as "our Auntie Haber." [23]

ALEXANDRINA

Czar Nicholas was more than anxious that his son and heir get the most from his visit to England. During his own first visit there in 1815, Nicholas had become a great admirer of England and everything English. He spoke and read fluent English: his first nurse, a Miss Lyon, was a Scot whom Nicholas admired and always called "my beautiful lioness." Only England did the stern Czar consider "equal to Russia."

"The English have lots of common sense," he wrote once. "They will understand me." Such was the attitude of a Russian Czar, the very one soon to war against the country he so much admired. Russians generally, and their monarchs particularly, were always a wonder to the English people. Aside from Peter the Great's short stay of two months in England in 1698 and the unsuccessful wooing "by mail" of the Virgin Queen by the many-times married Czar Ivan the Terrible,* no Russian ruler, with the exception of Alexander I and Nicholas, then a grand duke, had set foot in England since 1815. But now, in 1839, the impending state visit of a Russian grand duke—unmarried, handsome, and above all, heir to an empire immense, mysterious, so strange, and at the peak of its might—created a stir not only

---

*Queen Elizabeth I politely refused the hand and offered one of her court ladies for a substitute. The "royal" correspondence was never published in full, inasmuch as Ivan's letters contain quite a few unprintable words and phrases. In one, he called the Queen a "whore."

in the small circle of the young queen, now less than two years on the throne, but among all the classes of England.

"The young Tsarevitch is most charming," the widowed Princess Lieven hurriedly wrote from Russia to *the right people in London.* "You cannot imagine anyone more handsome. He is in every way interesting; he has a most interesting, sweet face, and all manners of speech and way they are all one can most desire."[1]

But the timing (that important factor in everything) was not propitious. "The year of 1839," wrote a recent biographer of the Queen, was to "turn England's 'baby of a Queen' from a figure of love into the target for censure, to convulse the whole country with arguments and partisanship, and to reverberate in all the capitals of Europe."[2] It was of course the famous Flora Hastings scandal case—the so-called "Bedchamber Plot"—which developed into a political racket of the day. The newspapers, particularly the *Morning Post*, continued to publish, in Victoria's own words, "the violent and libellous articles," and at Ascot, as the Queen stepped out on a balcony, a cry of "Mrs. Melbourne" came from the enclosure reserved for the "gentlemen in respect of rank."

Neither did Alexander escape attack, but it was an attack of a different kind. When the news about the forthcoming visit of the Czarevich to England reached the Polish émigrés who had fled to London after the unsuccessful revolt against the Russian rule in Poland in 1830, they decided, in the words of the Russian Ambassador Count Pozzo di Borgo, "to make an attempt on the life of His Imperial Highness." When this news was communicated to Alexander's father, he refused to cancel the trip.* "An inner voice tells me that Alexander will be safe," he wrote in return.[3]

In the midst of all the "excitement and fracasserie" surrounding the state visit of the Russian Czarevich, the goddaughter of Emperor Alexander I of Russia, Queen Alexandrina-Victoria, celebrated her birthday. "Friday, the 24th of May. This day I go out of my teens and become 20! It sounds so strange to me," the

---

* Neither did Nicholas escape Polish threats. During his visit to Victoria in 1844 a Polish emigrant tried to get into Windsor Palace by bribing a footman.[4] Victoria had her troubles too. Within six years after her ascension to the throne, she had been the victim of seven "alarming acts of hostility," including threats of killing her in 1839. The same year, two shots were fired at her. In all, more than a dozen attempts on her life were made during her reign.

Queen wrote in her journal that day. Indeed it probably did seem strange to Drina, who possessed everything in the world and yet lacked one thing, the dream of every girl—love. Not the love of her mother, or of innumerable uncles and aunts from almost equally innumerable principalities, or of her German governess, "Dear Lehzen," or of that "dear and excellent Lord Melbourne," her Prime Minister—no, she had enough of that. What she yearned for, wanted, and desired, but could not even mention, real, passionate love, was not there.

When quite young, Victoria had been "entranced" in turn by her singing teacher, "the Maestro Luigi Lablache"; the sexagenarian Prime Minister Lord Melbourne; and youthful Lord Alfred Paget ("my handsome Calmuck-looking gentleman," wrote Victoria). She of course had royal "suitors" in the past, but none of them (by 1839) had left any impression on her. When Alexandrina-Victoria was seventeen, her mother, in pursuit of an obvious plan worked out with her brother, the "beloved Uncle Leopold," invited their two young nephews, Ernst and Albert, to stay in Kensington Palace. But King William IV, who intensely disliked the "Coburg relatives" ("enough of Coburg blood," he used to say, having the Duchess of Kent and her relatives in view), tried for the same purpose to invite the young Prince Alexander of the Netherlands, the son of Princess Anna, the sister of Czar Nicholas I.

But he was late, and despite his protest that "no other [the Prince of Orange] marriage should take place" and that the Duke of Saxe-Coburg and his son (the elder Ernst was meant) must never put foot in this Court—"they should not be allowed to land and must go back whence they came"—the Coburg suitors safely arrived. The first meeting with her cousins Ernst and Albert, which took place in May, 1836, left Victoria decidedly lukewarm.

Three years later Victoria recorded in her diary a conversation she had on the subject with Lord Melbourne. When the question of marriage was brought up "I mustered up courage, and said that my uncle's [Leopold's] great wish was that I should marry my cousin Albert—He [Lord Melbourne] said: 'Cousins are not very good things,' and 'Those Coburgs are not popular abroad, the Russians hate them.' I then said, who was there else? We enumerated the various Princes, of whom no one, I said, would do. For myself, I said, at present my feeling was quite against ever marrying. I praised Albert very much; said he was younger than me. I said Uncle Ernest [father of Albert] pressed me much about."

She was equally uninterested in other visitors, including assorted cousins from Germany—the Württembergs, the Saxe-Weimars, and still other Coburgs. Now, early in May of 1839, the Queen received in state at Buckingham Palace an exalted and charming new guest, a year and a month older than herself, His Imperial Highness, the Grand Duke and Cesarevich Alexander. It is true he was another cousin and relative, but what a different figure this relative made. How different Alexander was from the habitual German "kissing cousins," with their heavily accented English and constant heel-clicking and stiff bows, and with parents always so poor and always begging for favors. But now, during these beautiful May days, the days that only England has, all had changed, as if by the wand of a magician.

Now at last came a man, a total stranger, a man of her age, immensely rich and to her good-looking and strong (this impressed her), dazzling, the first man in her life with whom she could talk with pleasure. She could confide in him, and with him she laughed and even dared to dance those weird dances so new and strange to her, the Polish mazurka and the *valse*, which the Russian guests introduced in the musty ballrooms of her palaces. The visit, scheduled to be short, almost upset the carefully planned "forget-it-all" journey. Alexandrina-Victoria was "fair, slim, elegant, active . . . with eyes blue and . . . half open mouth." Alexander fell in love with the Queen, and the Queen responded.*

The fateful day was Saturday, May 4, when the Russian Prince Charming was first presented to the Queen at Buckingham Palace. ". . . at half past one," she wrote rather reservedly in her diary, "I received the Grand Duke, who was introduced by Lord

---

* It is rather curious that this fact is not even alluded to in the well-known biographies of Queen Victoria. Russian official sources do not refer to this incident at all.

Savin, the Soviet historian, who specialized in research on the subject, states however that many pages and sentences of the Czar's correspondence of the period have been excised. An exception in this case is the latest work of Creston, who mentions it rather casually.[5]

Palmerston and accompanied by Count Orlov and Count Pozzo di Borgo.* I made the Grand Duke to sit down; he is tall with a fine figure, a pleasing, open countenance without being handsome, fine blue eyes, a short nose and a pretty mouth with a sweet smile. . . . I found the Grand Duke exceedingly agreeable, so good-natured, natural and merry. He is just a year older than I am."

The inventory taken by the young Queen is interesting since she had not been looking forward, as she herself confessed to Lord Melbourne, to meeting the Grand Duke.† She even found Count Orlov, rather a gruff soldier, "pleasing." When Melbourne, in a conversation with the Queen, described Orlov as looking exactly like Henry VIII, he was contradicted by Victoria. "I said I thought Henry VIII was not nearly so good-natured a man as Orlov." But she dismissed the brothers, the princes Alexander (once more named in honor of Alexander I) and Henry of Orange, the first cousins of Alexander who arrived with him from the Netherlands, "as timid young men." (Alexander of the Netherlands, as we have seen, was the unsuccessful candidate for the hand of Victoria, the choice of King William IV of Great Britain.)

Now her attention was centered only on the Russian and his suite. She took pains to give a few lines in her busy diary to each of his companions. "The Grand Duke and the gentlemen came after dinner," she wrote. "M. [Monsieur] Tolstoy (a young man and attaché here) [later the famous writer Count Alexis Tolstoy, a distant relative of Leo Tolstoy], Baron Lieven (cousin to Prince Lieven), M. Patkul (a young man of the Grand Duke's age and brought up with him), M. d'Adlerberg (also brought up with the Grand Duke, and his father brought up with the Emperor), Prince Bariatinsky (a young man, aide-de-camp to the Emperor, who distinguished himself very much in the war against the

---

* Victoria had met Count Orlov earlier, in 1837, the year of her accession, when the Count presented to her the "Order of St. Catherine all set in diamonds" (see her Diary, July 19, 1837) sent by the Emperor Nicholas I "to congratulate me."

† Metternich was particularly indignant at the Grand Duke's visit. "Nothing," he wrote to the Austrian Ambassador in St. Petersburg, "could be more compromising than the appearance of the Grand Duke in a country where everything should have forced him to keep out of it."[6]

Circassians and has a ball in his body), M. Yourievich* (an aide-
de-camp of the Emperor's and who has been with the Grand
Duke for fourteen years) and Prince Dolgoruki [sic] (an aide-
de-camp of the Emperor). They are all pleasing people and
rather easy to get on with. I like the Grand Duke extremely; he
is so natural and gay and so easy to get on with."

Next day the two young people met and went out riding
together in the park. The Queen was "exceedingly pleased" with
the Grand Duke, who was "so easily pleased with my horse he
was put on." Two days later the first ball in the honor of the
Czarevich took place. ". . . We kept it up (the ball)," wrote the
Queen the next morning to Lord Melbourne, "till a quarter past
three. . . . The Queen danced the first and last dance with the
Grand Duke, made him sit near her and tried to be very civil
to him. And I think [here she changed her style of writing] we
are all great friends already and get on very well; I like him
exceedingly," she ended this note.

In her diary she was more outspoken. ". . . at half past ten
we went in," she wrote, "it was rather formal, and everything
looked preoccupied. . . . When I had made the circle, dancing
began; I danced first with the Grand Duke. We went then into
the other room, when I danced with Prince Dolgoruky. We then
went again into the small ballroom, and saw the reels danced—
the Grand Duke sitting near me—and I concluded the Ball with
a quadrille with the Grand Duke. I left the ballroom at quarter
past three, much pleased, as my mind felt happy."

While the happy Queen began to like the Duke "exceedingly,"
Alexander did not escape her charms either. "Next day," after the
ball, jotted Colonel Yourievich (who also kept a diary),[7] "the
Czarevich talked only about the Queen. She impressed him with
her youthfulness, her charm and sense of humor. Alexander was
her constant partner at the ball, and I believe she also derives a

---

* Colonel Simon Yourievich, (1798–1865), teacher and tutor of
Alexander, later General. Baron Wilhelm Lieven, cousin of the former
Russian Ambassador, was attached to Count Orlov. Prince Vasilli Dolgorukov
(1804–68) was especially favored by Nicholas I for his loyalty during
the "December" days, Minister of War during the Crimean War.

Bariatinsky (1814–79) was wounded in the hip in Caucasus fighting
the mountaineers in 1835. He died at the age of sixty-five, then considered a "very" old age.

pleasure from his company. Indeed, together they are a perfect pair."

A few days later, one beautiful May evening, the two young cousins were alone at last. In the midst of the bedchamber scandal ("so much anxiety these days," wrote Victoria) both attended, but in separate boxes, a command performance at the theater. During the intermission, Alexander went to Victoria's box and stayed with her, as she noted with pleasure, "at least half an hour." There, in the royal box, the two human "love birds," shut from the outside world with the help of a heavy curtain, were alone that precious half-hour. Can one guess what they talked about? We know from her diary that Victoria had at last found someone, even though a foreigner, to whom she could confide her troubles. During that short and fleeting moment she opened her heart and poured out all that she had gone through—the abuses, the insults, and the slanders she suffered during the Bedchamber Affair. And the young Russian, brought up in an autocratic court, where such things were unheard of, with his fine blue eyes fixed on her half-open mouth, was properly and no doubt sincerely "shocked."

But the Czarevich began to worry his tutor Yourievich. In his diary on May 12 (eight days after meeting the Queen), the tutor wrote: "I am overwhelmed. Czarevich confessed to me that he loves the Queen and that he is convinced that the feeling is mutual. I begged him to give me a few days to consider the situation. Next day, the Grand Duke confronted me again. I pointed out to him that the marriage is an impossibility. He will have to renounce his future Crown and I added, that his conscience will not permit him to do that. He agreed with me, but it was apparent he was suffering. He was sad and pale." The worried tutor reported to Orlov, and both decided that Alexander should leave England as soon as possible.

The departure was set for May 30, but Alexander, wrote the tutor, "implored me to postpone it for a little longer." Yourievich explained that the "English visit is already a month too long—at no Court we stayed more than a few days." "For me," wrote Yourievich, the aide-de-camp, "there was not the slightest doubt that the Czarevich would have proposed to the Queen, she, without hesitation would have accepted him. . . ."

In desperation, Yourievich, who "feared" Nicholas ("His wrath is terrible"), approached the Fraulein Louisa Lehzen,* the German priest's daughter and the Queen's governess and later a confidante. "She told me that Her Majesty confessed her feelings for the Grand Duke, and told me that he is the first man she ever fell in love with. She is happy in his presence, is fascinated by his looks and charm. 'I am afraid,' said the Baroness, 'she would accept this proposal.' "

The two decided to act in concert to try at all cost to separate the couple in love. There was a good pretext—the usual spring departure of the Queen for Windsor. For Alexander, too, they found an occupation. The Grand Duke was kept away from the Queen by the inevitable military reviews and banquets. (At a London tavern banquet, arranged in his honor by the Russian Merchant Company, he responded in English to welcoming speeches.) He visited Parliament, was awarded a Doctor of Laws degree by Oxford University, made a sightseeing trip to London, and ended his adventures by attending the Epsom and Ascot races. And to the great surprise of its members, he bestowed three hundred pounds on the Jockey Club; he also founded a racing prize (the Cesarevich Newmarket Cup, which, along with the Irish Cesarevich Cup, is still very popular in England). He gave large sums to charity, particularly for the release of debtors he saw in prison, and while he "scattered diamonds, snuff boxes and rings in all directions," he made a favorable impression even on Lord Palmerston, who spoke of him as "humane and conscientious to a very remarkable degree."†[8]

Meanwhile the young Queen departed for Windsor; the Grand Duke and his entire suite were invited to join her later to stay for a few days. Now she was once more alone in her usual familiar surroundings—so dear to her in the past: "Spring in the country is always beautiful." But she missed the Grand Duke, and as she looked at her garden on that bright day, her "first impression," she wrote, "I know now why—beautiful as it looked

---

* Created Baroness in 1827.
† Diamond snuff boxes and rings, in addition to decorations (orders, medals, etc.) were usually "bestowed" by the Russian royalty. These gifts had several grades of importance, depending upon the deeds of the recipients. Usually they were given to foreigners of different religions.

and peaceful and bright—is always a triste one." Then one evening as she looked out of her window, Drina saw (she noted the exact time: "twenty minutes past seven") "an embellishment of the spring evening itself," to use the words of Creston, the Russian charmer arriving with his large suite.[9] As Alexander looked up, he saw the face now so dear to him, and bowed, as Victoria noted, "up to my window."

That night was the first of a series of enchanting evenings with the Russians. Victoria's journal speaks for itself. On June 2, 1839, she wrote in it: "Talked . . . [to Lord Melbourne] of the Grand Duke's having given 20,000 pounds to charities and of him having made a pretty speech about it before he went away. We agreed 20,000 pounds was immense.

"Windsor, Monday, 27th May, 1839. At quarter to eight we dined in St. George's Hall, which looked beautiful. [She noted the name of every Russian guest present.] "The Grand Duke, Count Orlov, Prince Dolgoruky, Prince Bariatinsky, Baron Lieven, General A. A. Kavelin, M. Joukovsky [Vasilli Zhukovsky*], M. Patkul, M. d'Adlerberg, M. Yourievich, Count and Countess Woronzov [Count, later Prince, Woronzov, the future viceroy of Caucasus (1781–1845)], whose daughter Elizabeth was married to Lord Pembroke, and the wealthy Polish heiress (the unmarried Countess Alexandrine Potoska† [Potocki]) and M. de Tolstoy." She also mentioned "Lord Albermarle, Lord Erroll, Lord and Lady Uxbridge, Duke of Argyll. . . . The Grand Duke led me in and I sat between him and Prince Henry [of the Netherlands]. I really am quite in love with the Grand Duke; he is a dear, delightful young man. At about a little after ten, we went into the red drawing-room . . . and the dancing began. I danced the first quadrille with the Grand Duke, then followed a valse, during

---

* Zhukovsky, who had a knowledge of English, translated into Russian Thomas Gray's "Elegy Written in a Country Church-Yard" and had it published in 1802—"my first printed poem." While in England with the Czarevich in 1839, Zhukovsky visited the celebrated churchyard of the Stoke Poges near Windsor and once more translated the poem, "closer to the original," and dedicated it to his old friend Alexander Turgenev. It was published in 1839 in the magazine *Sovremennik [Contemporary]*. Incidentally, Zhukovsky was also the author of the stirring words of the Russian national anthem, "God Save the Czar."

† Here is an amusing entry of the Queen: "I talked with Lord Melbourne. I pointed out Countess Potoska [sic] as having 30,000 pounds a

which I sat down. After the quadrille with M. de Tolstoy; this
was followed again by a valse (of course I and also the Grand
Duke sitting down during the valse). At a little after twelve, we
went into the dining room for supper; after supper, they [the
Russians] danced a mazurka for half an hour. . . . The Grand
Duke asked me to take a turn, which I did (never having done
it before) and which is very pleasant. The Grand Duke is so very
strong that in rushing around, you must follow quickly, and after
that you are whisked around like in a valse, which is very
pleasant. . . . Then danced a quadrille with Patkul, which was
followed by a valse. After we danced (what I had never ever
seen before) the Grossvater or Rerrant* and which is excessively
amusing, I danced with the Grand Duke and we had such fun
laughing; Patkul and the Countess Potoska led the way. This
concluded our little Ball at near 2 o'clock. I never enjoyed myself
more. We were all so merry; I got to bed by a quarter to 3, but
could not sleep till 5."

It was surprising that the "merry" young Queen could sleep
at all. There was no doubt that she was in love, in love for the
first time in her life! In the words of Victoria's recent biographer,
"those days for her were days of oscillation of life . . . of sweet
and fragrant air which impregnated the diurnal tune of the
Windsor Castle into a faster life. . . ."

Next day, May 28, a day before the forced departure of the
Duke, Victoria's journal became more and more outspoken. Now
one doesn't have to read between the lines of the usually reserved
journal. "The Grand Duke," she wrote, "talked of his very fine
reception here and said he would never forget it. 'Ce ne sont pas
seulement des paroles, je vous assure, Madame,' he said, but that

---

year, which he wouldn't believe. No girl ever marries if she wears a blue
gown." Countess Alexandrine Potocki was the daughter of Stanislav Potocki
and his wife, born Countess Catherine Branitzky. Shortly after the visit
to England, Alexandrine married a distant relative, Count August Potocki,
eventually a high officer at the court of Czar Alexander II.

* *Grossvatertanz*, an ancient German dance, usually accompanied by
songs, which got its name from a poem that started with the word "*grossvater.*" This is how Victoria described it herself: "It begins with a solemn
walk around the room . . . one figure, in which the lady and the gentleman
run down holding the pocket-handkerchief by each end and letting the
ladies on one side go under it and the gentlemen jump over; it is too
funny."

it is what he felt, and that he never would forget these days here, which I am sure I shall never also, for I really love this amiable and dear young man. . . ." The "great friend," "the dear, delightful young man," the "exceedingly agreeable" one, within a few days has become one she "loves."

The plot of the Baroness Lehzen and Colonel Yourievich to separate the young couple had been hatched, and the day of the departure, several times postponed (let us remember the "short courtesy visit"), at last was set for May 29. The sixty-year-old Lord Melbourne, the Prime Minister and Victoria's "mentor," was also taken in confidence and fully informed about the "love affair."

Victoria wrote, "I talked [about the Grand Duke and her feelings for him] to Lord Melbourne. . . . He said, 'I don't think the Grand Duke looks well; he looks rather livid.' " Later, Victoria once more had a "talk" with her Prime Minister. "I said," she wrote on May 29, the day of the departure, "all this excitement did me good. 'But you may suffer afterwards,' he said. 'You complain of that languor increasing and dislike for exertion; now it would be a dreadful thing for you if you were to take a dislike for business,' which I assured him I never should. 'You lead rather an unnatural life for a young person,' retorted the Minister, 'it's the life of a man.' " The Queen changed her conversation, centering it now on the Grand Duke and the Russian entourage.

"Talked [to Lord Melbourne] of Bariatinsky, dancing with that ball in his body, which Lord Melbourne said could kill him someday; of the Russians smoking [smoking was a complete taboo in Victoria's palaces; the Russians completely ignored it]. Talked of their wearing no whiskers, which Lord Melbourne said was because they thought it was French, and they hated French, that Orlov said we should one day see Louis Philippe deposed as easily as he had been put on the throne [a prediction that proved not too wrong: King Louis Philippe was deposed in 1848 and fled to England]. Lord Melbourne said that having the Grand Duke here [at Windsor], in this familiar way, was worth any fête in London."

The last dance finally took place, and Victoria regretfully noted that "after this [the last] valse, which was over at twenty to 3, I took leave of all the Grand Duke's gentlemen, with real regret, as I like them very much; Patkul and Adlerberg are 2 such merry young creatures. . . .[10]

"I then," wrote Victoria, "went to the little blue room next to my dressing room where Lord Palmerston brought in the Grand Duke to take leave. The Grand Duke took my hand and pressed it warmly; he looked pale and his voice faltered, as he said, 'Les paroles me manque pour exprime tout ce que je sens,' and he mentioned how deeply grateful he felt for all the kindness he met with, that he hoped to return again, and that he trusted that all this would only tend to strengthen the ties of friendship between England and Russia.* He then pressed and kissed my cheek in a very warm, affectionate manner, and we again warmly shook hands. I really felt more as if I was taking leave of a relative than of a stranger, I felt so sad to take leave of this dear amiable young man, whom I really think (talking jokingly) [sic] I was a little in love with, and certainly attached to; he is so frank, so really young and merry, has such a nice open countenance with a sweet smile, and such a manly, fine figure of appearance."†

The Czarevich's tutor's entry on May 30 is no less sad: "Last night," he wrote, "we said good-bye to the English Court. When Czarevich was alone with me, he threw himself into my arms and we both wept. He told me he will never forget Victoria. On parting, he kissed the Queen. It was his happiest and saddest moment of his life, he said."

---

* Actually Alexander returned to England only once, in 1874, to visit his daughter, Marie, married to Victoria's son, Alfred, Duke of Edinburgh. He never saw Victoria again.

† Very few British historians, either because of lack of material from the Russian sources or simply through prudishness, mention even briefly this love episode, and most treat the lines in Victoria's journal "this dear amiable young man whom I really think (talking jokingly) I was a little in love with" merely as a polite phrase. However, writing many years after (in 1965) Princess Alice, the Countess of Athlone, the only surviving granddaughter of Victoria, called Alexander "Grandmama Victoria's first beau."[11] We have even a more specific witness. In a letter of April 14, 1909, addressed to Queen Mary, then Princess of Wales, the granddaughter of George III and first cousin of Queen Victoria, Augusta Caroline, recounted "a scene I had with the Queen at a small Ball in the Gallery during the Tsarevich Alexander's stay in London when he was more attentive to me than to her." The Princess, eventually a Grand Duchess Mecklenburg-Strelitz, was three years younger than Victoria and outlived her by fifteen years.[12]

Sad as it was, Alexandrina-Victoria understood now, only too well, that a marriage between her, a queen and ruler of an enormous empire, to an heir of an even larger realm, was an impossibility. The usual dull routine and the usual dull people once more surrounded the Queen in love. A heavy, slightly dusty old velvet curtain descended on her existence. The departure of these "merry young creatures" brought a void; a sudden calm reigned in the gloomy and now deserted castle. "Someone played," she wrote on May 30, "the Grand Duke's and my favorite quadrille, called 'The Gay [sic] Loisir,' which made me quite melancholy, as it put me so in mind of all, and I felt sadly the change."

For her solace, she turned to her elderly friend and counselor, Lord Melbourne. "I talked to Lord M. of my feeling the change," she wrote, "and of its being so seldom that I had young people of my own rank with me, of my having so disliked the idea of the Grand Duke's coming, and that now I am so *very, very* sorry at his going. 'Very often the case,' said Lord M., 'as of the Grand Duke's being such a very good-natured young man.' Talked of this strange feeling when all the excitement was over, and that I feared that I would feel the difference now, being able to have these sort of dances. . . . I said a young person like me must sometimes have young people to laugh with. 'Nothing so natural,' replied the Lord M. with tears in his eyes, and I said I had that so seldom. . . ."

Next day, the sad Queen once more returned to her sweet memories. "We looked [Victoria and Lord Melbourne] at two of my large books of prints; in the first is a pretty picture of the Grand Duke when he was 11 years old, and which we agreed was still so like. . . ."

But life must go on, and so her duties. She must not forget what she had promised Lord Melbourne a few days before, never to take a "dislike" for business—royal, of course. Meanwhile, the Queen's alarmed "relatives" did everything in their power to make her forget the unintentional Russian "invasion."

Now that Prince Charming was gone—and gone forever, it was hoped—a "real" suitor arrived—another Grand Duke, this time the twenty-year-old Charles-Alexander (that name again)

Saxe-Weimar, a first cousin to the departed Grand Duke.* The comparison is striking. "The young Grand Duke," Victoria wrote, "is just the same age as *the* [emphasis by Victoria] Grand Duke; is not at all good-looking, but has a fine tall figure; but after the other Grand Duke, no one is seen to advantage. . . ." Victoria sulked and brooded; she was irritable and tense. "Talked to Lord Melbourne," she wrote two weeks after the departure of the Russian guests, "of my liking to live with young people, for that, then *I felt I was young* [emphasis by Victoria] which I really often forget, living so much, if not entirely, with people much older than myself. . . ."

Then one day a letter arrived from Alexander—a formal letter of thanks for Victoria's hospitality, and so on. But Victoria's answer had to be shown to her Prime Minister. "I showed Lord Melbourne the sketch of my letter to the Grand Duke, which touched him, and he said, 'That will do very well indeed; ought you however to say *bonne soeur?*' I said, 'He wrote, bon frère,' and Lord Melbourne agreed I could do no less. . . ."

About this time, at the end of June, a rumor spread at Windsor and naturally came to the attention of Victoria, of Alexander's forthcoming betrothal to the Princess of Hesse. "Talked of the report," she jotted nervously, "of the Grand Duke's intending to marry the Princess Mary [sic] of Darmstadt, who is only 15, which it seems he wished but Orlov stopped on account of her being in bad health. Lord M. says they'll marry him soon, though I doubted his liking to do so."

In a reaction typical of a woman in love, she rejected the possibility of Alexander's marrying anyone, and on hearing that the Lady Clanricarde (the wife of the British Ambassador to Russia) had just arrived in England, summoned her, eager to hear all the news about Russia. The Ambassadress—a gossiper *par excellence*—no doubt reported that Alexander had safely arrived in St. Petersburg, just in time to be present at his sister Marie's marriage to the Duke of Leuchtenberg, which was then the talk of the *beau monde*. But Melbourne was not pleased.

---

* Grand Duke Charles-Alexander Saxe-Weimar-Eisenach (1818–1901) was the son of the former Grand Duchess Marie, the sister of Nicholas I and the heir of the small duchy. Three years later he married the daughter of the King of the Netherlands.

"Lord M.," Victoria wrote, "said he hoped she [Lady Clanricarde] would not talk so much."

By the end of July, plans again of returning to Windsor Castle, which Victoria had always liked, particularly in summer, had begun to bore her. "Talked of my fearing of going to Windsor this year, of my getting tired of the place," she complained.

"Ah, Lady Lyttleton," exclaimed the Queen when at a ball in August, 1839, the musicians played her then favorite tune, "Le Gai Loisir," introduced by the Czarevich, "this room, this music— ain't it like old times?"[13] When at the end of summer that year, to dispel and counteract those nostalgic memories of the Russian, Victoria's mother and her brother "beloved Uncle Leopold" arranged an October visit of her Coburg cousins, Victoria, who of course understood the intent, began to grow more and more nervous and irritable.

"It must be understood," she wrote to her Uncle Leopold, "that there is no engagement between us" [*i.e.*, between her and her first cousin Albert]. She had a great repugnance to change her present position. She would not be guilty of any breach of promise, for she never gave any. She was even more explicit with Lord Melbourne. The Queen "had no great wish," she told him, "to see Albert and the whole subject was an odious one, to see him would be a disagreeable thing."* "I couldn't think of marrying for three or four years," she exclaimed, little realiz-

---

* A beautiful Russian wolfhound named Kazbek, presented by Alexander to Victoria, was—and would be for many years to come—part[14] of the Windsor household. He and his "descendants" were all that was left of the Russian "influence" at the court of the Queen. If this was the only good thing that was left in England of Russian "influence," Victoria's contribution to Russia was more than tragic. Now it is established almost with certainty that the Queen, through her mother, born Princess Saxe-Coburg, was a hemophilia transmitter, which spread this dreadful disease and killed and maimed many members of the royal houses, all decendants of Victoria, including, of course, her Russian great-grandson, the last Czarevich, the Grand Duke Alexis.

To the knowledge of this writer, the first to discover Victoria's "guilt" (formerly erroneously known as the Hessian or Spanish disease) was the British doctor-geneticist, J. B. S. Haldane, who published his conclusions on the subject with a chart to prove his thesis in the London magazine *Modern Quarterly* of March, 1938. (A translation of the article in Russian by Count Boris Berg appeared in the historical and genealogical magazine *Novik,* issued by the Russian Nobility Association in the United States in January, 1942.) An excellent and moving biography based on the above

ing that by October of that very year (Albert arrived on October 10, 1839; ten days later they were engaged, four months later they were married!)* the Russian mirage that still haunted her would fade away forever.†

---

disease and its influence on the fate of Russia's last rulers is, of course, Robert K. Massie's *Nicholas and Alexandra*, a best seller for two years.

* One wonders if Victoria, at that time, even heard the rumors of Albert's paternity. Hector Bolitho, in his *Queen Victoria*, relates that there were many books and printed documents which he examined in Coburg in 1931 which stated that the Duchess Luise, the wife of Duke Ernst of Saxe-Coburg-Gotha, "by her alleged infidelity brought Semitic blood into the Royal family." Bolitho also quoted from the book published in 1921 by Mac W. L. Voss, *England als Erzieher (England as Tutor)*, that "Prince Albert of Coburg, the Prince Consort, is to be described without contradiction as a half-Jew, so that since his time, Jewish blood has been circulating in the veins of the English royal family as well as in the veins of the Hohenzollern." Referring to the above even Lytton Strachey says in his *Queen Victoria*, that there were "scandals, one of the Court Chamberlains, a charming and cultivated man of Jewish extraction was talked of." When Albert was five, his father obtained a separation and never saw his wife again. She, after being divorced in 1826, married one Alexander von Haustein and died shortly after, in 1831.[15] Facts concerning the divorce of the Duchess Luise were taken by Bolitho from a German book, *Luise, Herzogin von Sachsen-Coburg-Saalfeld*, by Paul von Ebart, "a veteran of the Coburg who had access to the archives" and with whom the author had "conversation" in Coburg in 1931.

However, Frank Eyeck, a recent biographer of Prince Albert (*The Prince Consort*, N.Y., 1959, pp. 13ff.) stated that he was "unimpressed by the doubts which have been voiced as to Ernest I's paternity to Albert." The author goes further by explaining that "the Duke [Ernest I] . . . neglected his lively and somewhat frivolous wife. . . . The young mother sought distraction elsewhere [after the birth of Albert] and eventually found it in an officer of the court, Baron Von Haustein, later Count Pollzig."[16]

† In 1844, four years after Victoria's marriage, Nicholas once more visited England. He was "cordially" received and stayed at Buckingham Palace (the ground-floor apartments that he occupied were renamed the "1844 Room." In this very room in July, 1961, Major Yuri Gagarin, the Soviet space pioneer, was entertained at luncheon by Queen Elizabeth II, as was Premier Wilson in 1969). In a letter to his son Alexander, the Czar extolled the young Queen but described Windsor Palace as a "superb and rich prison." "What pleased me most," he wrote, "was the good impression you left after your visit. The Queen especially remembered you and praised you from all her heart." The twenty-five-year-old Victoria, on the other hand, was of a different opinion of the father of her "beloved Alexander," Czar Nicholas. "He is severe and gloomy," she wrote, "I don't think he is very intelligent; his mind is without any refinement; his education is very inadequate."[17]

INTERMEZZO

While Victoria sulked and fretted in Windsor, the lovesick Alexander ("I will never forget Victoria") hurriedly left the hospitable shores of England, spent one day in The Hague with his "Royal" aunt, stopped in Ems for a cure, where earlier Custine had sympathetically "observed" him, once more visited Darmstadt amid "close family surroundings" and finally, at Stettin, boarded a Russian war steamer. He landed in St. Petersburg just in time to be the best man at the wedding of his younger and impetuous sister Marie to the Duke Maximilian of Leuchtenberg.*

The summer festivities were soon over, and by October, 1839, Alexander learned about Victoria's betrothal. By now, however, all that had happened in England seemed to Alexander "ages ago." He had completely "forgotten" Victoria and was now "again drawn passionately" to Marie, "impatiently" awaiting permission to return to his "beloved" in Darmstadt. The greatest opposition to this new infatuation once more came from his mother. Though the official reason was, to use the Empress's

---

* The idea of this union at first shocked Nicholas, who considered the marriage a *"mésalliance"* and a "calamity." The groom, whom a Russian lady-in-waiting described as a "handsome rake and a gambler," was the grandson of Alexander de Beauharnais, the first husband of Empress Josephine and the son of the French Marshal Eugene de Beauharnais, who "captured" Moscow with Napoleon in 1812.[1]

own words, that "Wilhelmine [Marie] is too young" (it was true, she was then only fifteen), the undeniable but "painful" fact of course concerned the "circumstances" of her birth. To have an illegitimate—to use a milder word than *bâtarde*—for a daughter-in-law and a future Empress was to Alexander's mother, the proud Hohenzollern princess, "unthinkable." A little tin box that Soviet historians found in 1923 in the Winter Palace sheds some light on the "delicate" situation.[2] The box was sealed with a label reading: "Letters of Her Majesty, the Empress," and, in Sasha's own hand: "Matushki" (Mother's). In one of Sasha's letters to his father, written in the summer of 1840, he complained about "one word" that he found in "mother's letters." Sasha attributed this "offensive" word to the "Berlin influences," that is, his Prussian relatives, "because," as he wrote, "our good-natured mother with her heart of an angel could not suddenly change her kind opinion about Darmstadt" (read "Marie"). The letter containing the "word" was not in the box, but other letters, less offensive in character, were censored by the son. In one, dated June 12 [24], 1840, six lines are blacked out. This is the letter in which the Empress, at last "reconciled" with "fate," "opened her arms" to the future wife of her son. "Of course," she wrote, "Papa will permit you to return next year to visit your delightful Marie." We know now the reason for such a speedy surrender. As we have already seen, Nicholas was not at all disturbed by the "touchy gossips."*

So, in the same spring of 1840, and not "next year," as the Empress wished, Alexander, accompanied by the same Count Orlov, appeared once more in Darmstadt to "receive the consent of the reigning Duke." Yet the "ugly rumors" from Germany continued to flow into Russia. "Mean gossip from Berlin," wrote the Czar to Orlov, "spread by many, but primarily by my brother-in-law [Prince Charles of Prussia], do not stop of reviling poor Marie and are making noise regarding the forth-

---

* As early as spring, 1839, the Austrian Ambassador in St. Petersburg reported to Metternich the conversation he had with the Emperor regarding Marie. "Nicholas," he wrote, "knew all what was said, but as the Grand Duke [Alexander] took no notice of it, he [the Czar] found nothing to object."[3]

coming marriage of my son and of this 'mesalliance.' The gossips must be stopped at once," he remonstrated. And stopped they were.[4]

On September 8 [20], 1840, the fiancée of the Russian heir, "Her Grand-Ducal Highness Princess Maximilienne, Wilhelmine, Auguste, Sophie, Marie of Hesse-Darmstadt," as she was then styled, made a triumphal entry into the Russian capital of St. Petersburg.* The empress-to-be was accompanied to Russia by Sasha's childhood friend, the "dashing" Prince Alexander Bariatinsky, who, for the occasion, had made a special trip to Darmstadt. Marie brought with her also, for better or worse, her "dashing" brother, also named Alexander (the future progenitor of the Mountbatten "Dynasty"), and as her *dame de companie* or *gouvernante* Mademoiselle de Grancy, actually her aunt and the sister of her natural father. Amid the booming salutes of St. Peter and Paul fortress, the cortège slowly proceeded to its final destination, the Winter Palace. Multitudes of Marie's future subjects thronged the streets of St. Petersburg. The reception of the young Hessian bride by the population of the capital was "warm and spontaneous" and, as the official announcement stated: ". . . the long awaited bride chosen by the command of the heart of the Grand Duke" was received "with open arms and love by the Czar and by all the people."

For seven months prior to her marriage, Marie received instructions in the Russian Orthodox religion and finally, in December, "Wilhelmina" was rebaptized (she was of course a Lutheran). On December 6 [18], 1840, on the name's day of the Czar Nicholas, she was officially "betrothed" to Alexander. From that day on, "Wilhelmine, Sophie, Marie," and so on, ceased to exist. She was now known as "Her Imperial Highness Grand Duchess and Cesarevna Maria Alexandrovna."†

---

* Just about one hundred years earlier a fifteen-year-old obscure and poor German princess, known in the family circle as *"Fichen"* (diminutive of Sofia-Sofichen), also started for the Russian capital to make history. Later she was known as Catherine the Great.

† Almost immediately, Marie became an ardent Orthodox. This was a peculiar trait of almost all the German princesses marrying into the Russian royal family. It was noted by Bismarck and by many other German statesmen.

On the surface it seemed that at last everything was satis-factorily arranged. Yet we know for certain (again that little "box") that just prior to Marie's arrival in Russia, Alexander had once more tried to return to his old love, "O.K.," threatened to break relations with Darmstadt, and marry the Polish com-moner. This alarmed Sasha's parents no end. "What will happen to Russia," wrote his mother in her diary, "if a man who will one day rule her, cannot even control himself and permits passions to dominate him, not in the least resisting them?" Nicholas was even more perturbed. The romantic vacillations of his son exasperated him. Himself a puritan and, contrary to all the gossips, a virtuous man,[5] his son's "eternal" love for a commoner, then for a Queen, enraged Nicholas. "Sasha," he wrote to his wife, "is not serious enough, is open to all kinds of pleasures and is careless to my reprimands and instructions." Just three days before Marie reached St. Petersburg, Nicholas wrote to the Empress: "For me, my Empire is above all, and no matter how much I love my children, I love my Fatherland even more; the example of Peter the Great* is before me . . . waver I will not."[6]

Meanwhile, the parents took quick action to pour cold water on the flaming coals. The cooperation of "poor O.K.," of Olga Kalinovskaya, was obtained. "Don't let Olga," wrote the Empress, "be discharged from the Palace [Olga was still a lady-in-waiting to the Empress]. Olga fears that her dismissal will increase Sasha's passion, as he will consider it as a sacrifice. Don't you think that her promise to keep herself to her room [in the Winter Palace] is sufficient until Sasha is living here?" All this pending the arrival of Marie.[7]

For a while the "O.K." interlude died out, and Alexander and Marie were solemnly married on April 16 [28], 1841, on the eve of the bridegroom's twenty-third birthday. Now they were installed, as man and wife, in the same imposing Winter Palace, to "live happily ever after."

But what about the "little Marie?" Fortunately for us, the

---

* The allusion is to Peter the Great's son Alexis, who was arrested and tortured for alleged "treason." He died in prison.

diary of Anna Tutcheva, one of Marie's maids of honor, reveals a great deal:*[8] "Marie was hardly 17, when she was brought to Russia," wrote Anna. "Timid and bashful, the Grand Duchess told me how horrified she was by the brilliant future which suddenly faced her. Brought up practically in isolation, even in neglect [her mother died when Marie was twelve, her "father" married a "commoner" shortly after], in a small Hessian Schloss, Jugendheim," Marie was frightened rather than dazzled when she was transplanted to the "most sumptuous, brilliant and richest of all European Courts." Even though she had brought to Russia her brother (also illegitimate) and of course her *gouvernante*, Mademoiselle de Grancy,† she was lonely. "At night when Marie was alone," wrote Tutcheva, "she would give herself to tears. . . . To hide her eyes, red after a sleepless and tearful night, she would open the window to cool them off. This, no doubt, resulted in the illness—consumption—which eventually killed her. . . .

"The new Grand Duchess," continued Tutcheva, "did not give the impression of being a *belle femme*—she was too tall, lean and brittle [unpardonable and unfashionable traits in those days]. But she was exquisite in her elegance, an elegance which one finds in old German engravings. . . . Her features were not regular, yet her hair, her delicate skin, her large blue eyes . . . were beautiful. Her profile was not striking—her nose was not classic enough . . . her mouth was too thin with lips pressed too closely. . . . In general, she was extremely reserved without the slightest trait of animation or impetuousness. Her slightly ironic smile was in a strange contrast to her eyes. . . . I

---

* This interesting diary was published only after the Revolution in the Soviet Union in 1928. Anna was the daughter of the noted Russian poet Theodore Tutchev and was appointed to the court in 1853.

† Mademoiselle de Grancy (her first name is lost to posterity), according to Tutcheva, was "a friendly creature of bourgeois simplicity, who simply adored her Marie. She was not yet 40, yet she looked older—her hair was silver gray. She told me [Tutcheva] that her hair became gray as a result of worries during the almost fatal illness [consumption] of Marie when she was 12. . . ." Mademoiselle de Grancy stayed with Marie until 1853. "Now" [1853], wrote Tutcheva, "she is receiving a yearly pension of 3000 Rubles [equivalent to $1500 in gold] and visits Russia from time to time."

must insist on these details," wrote Tutcheva, "because I rarely saw a person whose face and appearance expressed such nuances and contrasts of an extremely complicated ego."[9]

Directly after the wedding, the young couple (their age totaled forty years!) settled, as we have seen, in the Winter Palace, occupying about ten rooms of the Palace's seventeen hundred chambers. Apparently there was no honeymoon trip. They could hardly call their quarters home, inasmuch as they were constantly subjected to parental inspection. Details of everyday life, their occupations and amusements, were strictly controlled. At the same time, Alexander was made member of the Council of the Empire—the highest institution in the State. It was a sign that the Czar felt that from then on his son had to take part in the government. In addition Alexander was appointed chancellor of Helsingfors University of Finland and began to preside over the "Secret Committee" in order to study the problem of serfdom with an ultimate aim of abolishing it.

Soon a pattern of "bourgeois happiness" followed; after all, wasn't it a love marriage? Yet, the couple's first child, a girl, imaginatively named Alexandra, died at the age of two. She was followed with traditional precision by six boys and a girl. But as often happens with many human beings, no less so with royal ones, Alexander began, as was his custom, to cast eyes around him. The year was 1853. By now he and Marie had been married for twelve years. To cast eyes in the "wrong" direction was not too difficult. The young, attractive, and numerous ladies of the court were the usual targets. The *mesdemoiselles d'honneur,* the unmarried ladies-in-waiting of the court, were known for their youth and financial insolvency. Most of them orphans of good families or daughters of poor state functionaries, they were not what was often claimed, *odalisques* of the imperial court. Their beauty was purely coincidental with their appointments. Though they lived in the Winter Palace "by kindness of the Empress," their quarters were even simpler than the lodgings of senior servants of the palace. "There were 12 of us," related the same Anna Tutcheva, "some picked by the Empress herself, others, due to her good disposition forced on her, so that the *Fräulein* quarters at the palace resembled a charitable institution for the needy, but genteel maidens. . . ."[10]

The first to fall for the "maidens" was Marie's dashing and handsome brother, Prince Alexander of Hesse. Promoted at the tender age of eighteen to a colonelcy, this poor relative of the Czar soon became a general with the highest orders of the empire bestowed on him. "Charming, elegant, mentally alert, full of animation," wrote Tutcheva, "Prince Alexander stood out amid the dull and banal members of the court."* Soon the usual story developed. Poor, plain, but "coquettish" orphan Julia Hauke, one of the ladies-in-waiting, "lost her heart" to the Prince Charming. ("There was no passion on either side," retorted Tutcheva.) The affair was an open secret before long, with the result that the Hessian prince was cashiered[11] and soon appeared in Breslau, where they were married. (Soon after, Julia was "created" Countess. Her descendants after 1917 became known as Mountbattens.)† The grief of the Prince's sister, Marie, was indescribable. Her closest relative had vanished from her sight. The same Tutcheva relates with a certain exaggeration that Marie cried her heart out and "from that day on lost her gaiety and animation."

Meanwhile, another interlude took place, which, if it didn't break Marie's heart, humiliated her and made her "resign to her fate." Olga Kalinovski, still unmarried and still a lady-in-waiting (ladies-in-waiting were appointed for life provided they didn't marry), was at that time (1845) twenty-seven years old and considered an old spinster. All the efforts of her parents as well as of the Czar to marry her off had been unsuccessful. "Let us pray," wrote the Czar earlier to his wife,

---

* E. H. Cookridge, author of *From Battenberg to Mountbatten*, who had access to the so-called Hartenau Archives (assembled by Prince Alexander of Battenberg) paints a different picture of the Prince. "A notorious Don Juan," Alexander after many flirtations, liaisons, and affairs, concentrated for a while on Olga, the younger sister of the Czarevich, but, as the author adds, the "family had had one misalliance already due to a Czarevich marriage and were unwilling to face another."

† "This Gallop" [music that the Hessian prince composed in honor of his "beloved,"] Nicholas I is said to have exclaimed, "will never be played" and sent Alexander to fight the "rebels" in Caucasus. It is more than amusing to speculate that had this "misalliance" taken place, there would be no Battenbergs, Mountbattens, or Edinburghs of today. Incidentally, in her memoirs Grand Duchess Olga does not devote even a line to this "flirtation."[12]

"that Olga Kalinovski gets married." But marry she didn't for a long time despite many brilliant offers. Finally, in the year of 1845, she married her brother-in-law, the wealthy Polish landowner and widower Prince Irénée Oginsky, previously the husband of Olga's elder sister Josephine. That the marriage was not a happy one can be judged from the fact that both sons born to her claimed later as their real fathers others than the one whose name they bore.* At any rate, it is indisputable that Sasha resumed his liaison with "O.K."[13]

By 1853, Olga was no longer an object of the Grand Duke's infatuation. That year there began a new chapter in Alexander's life, a chapter that was somewhat different from the others.

Princess Alexandra or Alexandrine (again that name) Dolgoruky I (of the second by that name we'll hear later) was another of Marie's ladies-in-waiting. Appointed to the court in 1853, Alexandrine was not yet seventeen. Eldest of five daughters of an impoverished branch of the famous Dolgoruky family, Alexandrine was precisely one of those "poor, but noble maidens" in the service of the imperial court.

"At first," recorded Anna Tutcheva, "this very young girl . . . tall, somewhat loosely patched up, . . . with pale and colorless face and stony eyes rather repelled you. But soon, as she became animated, the whole of her being was completely transformed. As if by magic, her face and figure became at once supple, her movements graceful, as if it was a young tigress at play. . . . She was permeated with something *je ne sais quoi*, which conquered not only men, but also women.[14]

Nicknamed *"La Grande Mademoiselle,"* Alexandrine, asserted Tutcheva, was "passionately attached to the Cesarevna. . . . There were no grounds to suspect her sincerity," added Tutcheva. She was also "ardently" attached to the Emperor and at the same time "never denied" herself a chance to flirt, particularly with the young Grand Duke, which naturally "created gossips at the court." There is no doubt that thirty-five-year-old

---

* Bogdan, born in 1848, "never made a secret" that he was the natural son of Sasha, while the other, Michael, born a year later, was, according to "family records," the son of a Russian guard officer, one Michael Vonlarlarsky.

Alexander, amorous, sensuous, and a great admirer of the weaker sex, was infatuated with this young "tigress," but as one English historian wrote,[15] she shared the Grand Duke's sympathy for political reform, his thoughts for the betterment of Russia, but probably not his bed. . . ." At any rate, perhaps the Dolgorukaya affair was over before it started.* Whether their "flirtation" developed into an affair later in the 1860s is open to question. Some authors, including the recent one Constantine de Grunwald, who had access to "unpublished documents preserved by her husband's descendants," feel that it is hard to believe in the platonic flirtation of Alexandrine. However, De Grunwald also believes that her devotion and loyalty to the Empress was even stronger. The same author quotes part of a letter of the Czar (August, 1865) to the already married Alexandrine in which the former talks about his "wounds which are difficult to heal and the heart which will forever suffer."[16]

That Alexander was particularly susceptible to feminine charms no one could deny. As one biographer wrote, Alexander

---

* Eventually Alexandrine married a guardsman, an illegitimate descendant of a Baltic Baron Albedil, one Peter Albedinsky, who later made a brilliant *carrière*. Albedinsky, "a handsome and brazen opportunist," a grandson of Princess Bagration of the former ruling House of Georgia and grandnephew of Piotr Bagration, the hero of 1812, did everything in his power to reach the top. "He," states Count Berg, "even began a liaison with the famous courtesan and the mistress of the aged Minister of the court, Count Alexander V. Adlerberg, one Mina Ivanovna, in order to receive her 'protection,' which he did." Made an aide-de-camp to the Emperor, he at one time was a military attaché at the Court of Napoleon III, where, after an alleged affair with the Empress Eugénie, he was recalled. His *carrière* was spectacular—commander of Hussar Guards, one of the most exclusive and expensive regiments in the Russian Army; general aide-de-camp to the Czar; governor general of Poland at the age of forty; and finally a member of the Highest Council of the State. He died in 1883 at the age of fifty-eight.[17]

It was said that Turgenev immortalized Alexandrine in his novel *Smoke* in the person of the "heartless" Princess Irene Ossinin. Published in 1867, the novel created a sensation. Alexandrine survived her husband by many years (he died in 1883). In 1913, at the age of seventy-seven, she was still listed as a "Senior Lady of the Court," but her name does not appear in the 1914 Court Calendar. Apparently she was dead by then. Her son, already an aged man, escaped from Russia after the Revolution of 1917. (This author saw him in Stockholm in a Russian Church in 1952.)[18]

"was not a flirt, nor could he be called immoral." He was simply not different from many of his contemporaries. He did all that a man of a certain circle, married or not, was expected to do. However, while *un homme comme il faut* could conduct himself rather openly and "never be found out," a member of the royal family and especially the heir to the throne, being under constant supervision, had little chance of escaping gossips, guilty or not. Leo Tolstoy's aunt, Madame Ergolsky, expressed the trend of the times when in a letter to her nephew she wrote that "nothing forms a young man better then an affair with a *comme il faut* woman," married of course.[19] This was denied to Alexander. To "cuckold" a friend, a subordinate, or simply a subject was simply not "done." Hence the unmarried women were the victims.

By 1853, two years before Alexander ascended the throne, at the age of thirty-seven, Marie, as we have seen before, bore him six children. This was not enough. By 1860 two more sons were added to the family. While Marie knew that she had "fulfilled" her duty, the complete marital break had not yet occurred. The domestic unhappiness of noble as well as bourgeois families was one thing. For royalty everything had to be "well" on the marital scene. Marie bore her humiliation proudly and sought compensation in religion, Orthodox, of course, and in the numerous charities she headed.* Intellectually, she was a remarkable woman—highly cultured ("super cultured," in the words of an American writer), possessing a great erudition, and unusually "subtle and refined." Yet there were insinuations at the court claiming that the "Empress Marie wished to germanize Russia" and hinting at[20] "circumstances" of her birth. Others gave her the appellation of a *bourgeoise Allemande*, reminiscent of one of Marie Antoinette's nicknames, *l'Autrichienne*. Some, very cautiously, tried to instill in Alexander's mind a

---

* She was the first Russian ruler to open high schools for women of "all the classes." By her personal initiative, parochial schools for women were inaugurated in 1860. Through her influence, women were allowed to attend courses at the universities, usually reserved for men only. This was a novelty then unpracticed even in Western Europe. Thousands of women benefited through Marie's innovations. One was the future wife of Lenin.

suspicion that Marie "with her intellectual superiority" would dominate him and in this way influence him in the conduct of political affairs. We know however that Marie, when an Empress, "many a night" read important papers and dispatches to Alexander. They "discussed" measures to take, and Alexander often listened to her advice.[21] Marie was a "staunch supporter" of liberal reforms and of complete liberation of the serfs. She mastered the Russian language and read all its classic literature.* Yet her life as a woman and a wife in those days (she was only thirty-six in 1860) was finished.† In 1865 a witness described Marie as "a skeleton with a white face covered with powder and rouge to hide her skin disease—she looked like a cadaver."[22]

It would be wrong to assume that Alexander devoted most of his adult years to girl chasing. We have already seen that Nicholas, the father, remembering his own shortcomings, began to train his son and heir to fulfill "the mission he was destined [for] by Providence."

The fulfillment of that "mission" came sooner than expected. The year was 1855.‡

---

* Turgenev was a frequent guest at her palace. One wonders if the novel *Smoke* was written in sympathy with her.

† Between 1843 and 1860, Marie gave birth to 8 children: 2 girls and 6 boys. All died by natural deaths, except the last two sons, Serge and Paul who were executed by the Revolutionaries in 1905 and 1919 respectively.

‡ Alexander succeeded to the throne of Russia amid the disastrous Crimean War. As a result, Nicholas, it was said, died of a broken heart (actually from pneumonia) in 1855.

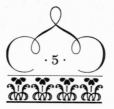

THE CZAR-LIBERATOR

Even though the first ten years of Czar Alexander's reign produced spectacular achievements in every sphere of Russian life—
millions of serfs were liberated, legal courts were reformed and
became known as "second to none in the world,"* local self-
governments were created, the educational system immensely
improved and liberalized, corporal punishment abolished, class
privileges of nobility drastically reduced—all these reforms
and more did not earn the "Czar-Liberator" the gratitude he
expected from his people. On the contrary, loose criticism,
open hostility, and discontent prevailed. "A [Russian] public
without political sense or experience," a British historian wrote
recently, "rigidly debarred for decades from all shares in
public affairs, took advantage . . . [of the liberal trend] to criticize
with complete irresponsibility every measure of the Emperor
and his government." Alexander,[1] the "father of his people,"
the "liberator," and the "reformer" to many of his people,
simply could not understand why he earned the wrath of his
subjects.† As a result of this attitude of his "beloved subjects,"

---

* "It must be emphasized," wrote Samuel Kucherov, "that between
1864 and 1917 Russia had courts second to none in the world as far as
civil and criminal cases without political character were concerned."[2]

† In all fairness one must stress that agitation came from a rather
small radical segment of society, mostly intellectuals, the *intelligentsia*
for whom these reforms were not "enough."

he became "bitter, irritable, melancholic and nervous." In vain his brother, the Grand Duke Constantine, advised him to attain "calmness." "Unhappily I know from my own experience," parried the Czar, "that this is difficult . . . but one must control oneself, and I find prayer the best means to this end."[3] Was the Russia of 1865 the same as it was in 1855? he asked. When in 1865 the Zemstos (self-governing body) of the St. Petersburg District demanded wider reforms, he exclaimed: "I suppose you consider that I refuse to give up any of my powers from motives of petty ambition. I give you my . . . word that this very minute . . . I would sign any constitution you like if I felt that this would be for the good of Russia. But I know, were I to do so today, tomorrow Russia would fall to pieces."[4] Much earlier, Vissarion Belinsky, the great Russian critic, "the literary revolutionary," and an outspoken foe of autocracy, surprisingly summed up the problem somewhat differently: "To give Russia in her present state [1837] Constitution means to ruin her. . . . The hope of Russia should be in education and not in upheavals, revolutions and constitutions." By 1865, to add to all of Alexander's troubles, his own health failed. An "old" man at forty-seven, Alexander suffered repeated attacks of asthma, the illness he had had since childhood. These attacks led some foreign diplomats to spread false rumors that he was afflicted with tuberculosis.

Then, like a bolt from the blue came the tragic and distressing news. President Abraham Lincoln was assassinated by a "fanatic" on April 14, 1865, the first of the many heads of state to fall that year as objects of political revenge.* Curiously the death of Lincoln, "the only friend" the Czar had in the 1854 and 1863 crises,† served him as a warning and, in a way, as a

---

* From 1865 to 1914, twenty-four monarchs, heads of state, and statesmen lost their lives through assassination.

† During the Crimean War of 1854–55, when the great powers (England, France, and Turkey) attacked Russia, the United States was "the only government to show a surprising amount of enthusiasm for the Czar's cause."[5] No less friendly an attitude was shown by the United States toward Russia during the 1863 upheaval in Poland, when the U.S. refused and "rejected" the invitation of the great powers "to exert influence on Russia."[6]

consolation that "emancipators" and "liberators" were not always appreciated by their own people.

To make matters worse for Alexander, his favorite, "most promising," and eldest son and heir, the twenty-two-year-old Grand Duke Nicholas, one on whom "so many hopes" were built, had died in faraway Nice. The Czar's mental attitude was clearly expressed in a note sent to Washington. "Scarcely has my August Master returned [from Nice to St. Petersburg] . . ." wrote the Russian chancellor Prince Gorchakov to President Andrew Johnson, "when he orders me to testify to you his grief at this painful event [the assassination of President Lincoln]. Tried himself by a woeful loss [of his son], which is also a cause of national mourning for Russia, the Emperor joins me in the unanimous regrets which encircle the memory of the eminent statesman, shattered away so suddenly and in so terrible a manner from his noble career."[7]

The Czar's life was usually an open book, not only to his entourage but to all his subjects. Almost his every move, every visit, every event—in short, almost every minute of his existence on earth—was made public, recorded, checked, double-checked, entered in several books especially kept for the purpose, viewed and reviewed by countless courtiers from high rank to low. Moreover, the "Imperial activities" were planned far in advance; specially bound booklets in red leather covers were printed for each occasion. Parades, church holidays (there were thirty-four yearly "non-working" days, aside from Sundays), visits to the Guard and Army regiments on various occasions—all these events were rigidly observed and personally attended by the Czar. Receptions for foreign sovereigns, diplomats, dignitaries, "family dinners" (there were thirty-two male and female Romanovs at that time), the "name's days" or "Saint's days" of relatives—events which were even more important in Russia than birthdays—funerals, baptisms, various marriages of relatives—all occupied the Czar. Finally, but not least of all, the "state affairs," the meetings with the cabinet ministers, took a great deal of the Czar's daytime hours. He was almost never alone.

The autocrat's "homework" occupied most of his time at night (provided there were no state dinners, theater performances, or balls). From the Czar's diaries we know that "state papers" meant reading "voluminous" reports from the four corners of the immense Russian Empire. Every report in those days (actually up to 1917), according to strict regulations, had to be handwritten. The home "reading," as it was universally done in Russia by all the officials, took place "after supper," that is, after 10 or 11 P.M. Time and time again the imperial diarist would note: "Worked on papers late after supper," or "I've read late—masses of papers to study," and so on. Every Russian sovereign, particularly Alexander II, wrote every resolution, decision, and answer, sometimes of several pages, in his own handwriting. The custom of employing "secretaries" had not been renewed since Catherine the Great's time.*

It was not surprising that the little time that was left Alexander for private life was more than precious, but even then it was open to minute scrutiny, under a guise of "security measures" (often unknown to the monarch).

One of Alexander's activities, less frequent, but more pleasant than dutiful, was visiting the Smolny Institute for the "noble maidens"—the special pet of his wife. It was an old and established tradition for the senior members of the imperial family, including the Czar, to pay calls on the school and on its inmates, the *desmoiselles*, as the girls were called. Officially named "The Imperial Educational Society of Noble Maidens," the Smolny Institute, founded by the Great Catherine in 1764, was the first school opened to women. (By 1917 there were thirteen such institutes in St. Petersburg alone, some opened to "all classes" of the empire's girls.) The institute educated girls from nine to eighteen years of age, with its curriculum somewhat like that of American high schools of that time but with an emphasis on foreign languages.† Even though all the

---

* History is indebted to Alexander V. Khrapovitzky (1749–1801), Catherine the Great's famous secretary, for his diaries—a major contribution to the study of the times.

† Smolny was built on the site of a tar storehouse—hence the name "Smolny" ("smola" = "tar"). The institute received world notoriety in

inmates of the institutes (or *institutki*, as they were called in Russian) were of "noble families" (this was the requirement for entry into Smolny), most of them were neither rich nor of aristocratic families nor beautiful. On the contrary, the great majority of Smolny's *institutki* or Smolianki, unlike their rich and more prominent counterparts, who were usually educated at home with the aid of foreign governesses, were from impoverished families of nobles, daughters of civil or military officials,* who could not afford to give private education to their daughters. Many of the girls were orphans, and their tuition was paid by the state. Quite a few royal princesses of states annexed or acquired by Russia, and foreign princesses as well, were also educated in Smolny. Impoverished royal princesses of the Kingdom of Georgia, exiles from the Persian royal house, even princesses from Montenegro and Abyssinia, were graduates of Smolny. All their tuition fees were assumed by the Russian state.

The institute was a "closed" school, which meant that the girls could leave the building only on "great holidays" to stay with their parents. The inmates were dressed according to seniority, in somber brown for the youngest, in blue, gray, or white "camelot" (a coarse woolen cloth generally worn at night) dresses for the seniors. On Sundays those who had no parents nearby were allowed to have "close relatives" as visitors. The visits were limited to an hour. At the institute no Russian language was allowed to be heard except in Russian "classes": French was the spoken word. Occasionally, a visit to the famous

---

1917 when Lenin and Trotsky forcibly seized it for use as "Bolshevik" headquarters. Smolny was built by the famous Italian craftsman Giacomo Quarengi (1744–1817), who was also the creator of such gems as the English Palace in Peterhof, the Hermitage theater in St. Petersburg and Alexandrinsky Palace in Czarskoye Selo. Today Smolny is a "Museum of the October–November Revolution."

* Since Peter the Great, it was not an insurmountable task to become a "noble." "Hereditary nobility" was open to anyone who attained a certain rank in any of the government services. Later, nobility "patents" were given to anyone achieving "higher education." Nobility "patents" were also bestowed for "valor" or lengthy services to the state. This procedure, rather a democratic one, did not exclude "non-Russian" elements, including Jews.[8]

Maryinsky Opera Theater (usually a matinee) was allowed, always in groups, however, and under the strict supervision of an institute *chaperon*. From time to time (mostly during the Easter holidays) the girls were allowed a short ride through the capital but always in enormous black coaches, usually drawn by six horses. Through the carriage windows the young and curious faces eagerly peeked out. Thus, for a short and fleeting moment, they became an integral part of St. Petersburg's enchanted scenery.

Sometimes a ball would be given on the institute premises, often attended by members of the imperial family, if not by the Emperor himself with his Empress, a great event in the girls' sheltered lives. Some young and "respectable" male relatives, chosen usually among the court pages or Army and Navy cadets, would be their partners in rigid *valses*, mazurkas, or polonaises—all this under the stern and watchful eyes of their *mesdames*, or *institutrices*. These rare occasions were, of course, "unforgettable" and brought animation and excitement into the dreary routine of the school. In their turn, the members of the royal family knew by heart the names of almost all the two hundred *desmoiselles*. After all, weren't these girls representatives of families who made Russia great? And coincidentally, many were not hard to look at.

After graduation (the whole stay in Smolny lasted six years), several of the more "deserving" *desmoiselles* were appointed to the imperial court as ladies-in-waiting, which helped some to find "glamorous" husbands and the unlucky ones their living. Often the Czar and Czarina would "befriend" or bestow "bounties" on the girls, daughters or orphans of "worthy" officials, and promised to look after them "forever." Others—and most of them—went out into the cold world to face life. Most of them found husbands, homes, and oblivion. Of the last group, the two young Dolgorukov princesses, Catherine (or Katia for short) and Marie (or Mouche), eighteen and sixteen years of age in 1865, certainly seemed destined to a relative obscurity.[9]

The Dolgoruky family claimed direct descendancy from the semilegendary founder of the dynasty of Rurikids, or Rurik, (the Ryurikovichis) in A.D. 879. More realistically, the family

is traced from Prince Michael of Tchernigov (eleventh generation from Rurik), who perished in 1246 as a result of tortures
inflicted on him by the Tatar invaders. For his resistance to
the Tatars he was canonized by the Church. His seventh direct
descendant (seventeenth from Rurik), Prince Ivan, inherited
the town of Obolensk (today a village near the town of
Kaluga, southwest of Moscow). He was actually long-armed,
and when he changed his name from Obolensky, which he
had assumed in accordance with the custom of the day, he
began to call himself Prince Ivan Dolgorukoy or Dolgoruky,
(Dolgorukov or Dolgoruky means long-armed ["ruka" = "arm"]
in Russian) thus becoming in the fourteenth century the ancestor
of the Dolgorukys or Dolgorukovs. His son, however, was
known as Dolgorukov, *i.e.*, the son of Dolgoruky. This nuance
(different spelling for father and son) divided the future
descendants, with the Dolgorukys considering themselves more
"noble" than the Dolgorukovs—probably more than anything
else because of wealth and influence acquired through their
"brilliant marriages."*

Though the Dolgorukov girls were descended from an old
and illustrious family of Great Russia, their branch, "Teplovka
line," as it was known because of the name of its estate in
the Poltava district, had not distinguished itself in the past
and became impoverished and therefore less prominent and
affluent. Moreover, this Dolgorukov branch was considered "provincial" and, lacking the correct contacts in the "high spheres,"
did not count much in the glittering capital.

But there were other reasons for this attitude. Katia's grandfather, the old Prince Michael Dolgorukov, was the only son
of a "non-political" exile to Siberia, whom the famous Russian
revolutionary Herzen, the co-exile of the Prince, characterized
as one of "those aristocratic idlers in the bad sense of the
word, who were but seldom found nowadays" (written in
1860). Katia's grandfather, continued Herzen, "had committed

---

* One should not confuse this Dolgorukov branch with its distant
relatives, the Dolgorukys, more prominent, more social, and more affluent
up to 1917. To that family belonged Princess Alexandrine Dolgoruky—*"the
Grande Mademoiselle."*

all sorts of tricks in Petersburg, Moscow and Paris. . . . He was a spoiled, impertinent and disgusting charlatan. . . . At last when his 'exploits' passed all bounds, he was ordered to live in Perm [near the Ural Mountains]." Finally, once more exiled for unsavory "tricks," the "penniless" prince died after a "brawl" in 1841.*[10]

Nor did Michael, his son, distinguish himself in any way. Born in a small town near the Ural Mountains, Michael, after a routine military upbringing, reached the rank of captain in one of the "less fashionable" cavalry regiments, married a rich Ukrainian heiress, one Vera Wishnevsky, soon retired, and settled on the estate of Teplovka, which his wife bought him as a dowry. The estate, about one hundred miles from the historical town of Poltava, received its name from the original owner, one Gregory Teplov,† a statesman of Catherine the Great. According to a contemporary, "Teplovka mansion was a three floor stone house without columns. . . . Grandiose, built in a style of foreign castles, the house was surrounded by an enormous park, reminiscent of an English estate, particularly due to a lake in which a flock of swans broke the silence with their cackle." Yet Teplovka, after all, was a typical Russian manor estate surrounded in every direction by "limitless steppes."[11]

---

* This "bad" Dolgorukov was married to a rich heiress, Sophia de Ribas, the daughter of a Neapolitan-Spaniard in the Russian service at the time of Catherine the Great. He was a boon companion of Admiral John Paul Jones, with whom he served in the Russian Black Sea Navy in the war against the Turks in 1788. The Deribassovskaya Street in Odessa, named in the honor of de Ribas, still bears his name.

Another "bad" Dolgorukov, Peter, was "rumored" to be the author of the insulting letter that led to the death of the celebrated poet Pushkin. "Dolgorukov," as wrote a recent author, "was of Heeckeren homosexual set."[12] Baron de Heeckeren was the Netherlands minister to the Court of St. Petersburg.

Their common ancestor Prince Alexis Dolgorukov received prominence in 1727 when his daughter Catherine (another Katia) was unsuccessfully betrothed to Peter the Great's grandson, Peter II, the last male Romanov. As a result of various intrigues, and the death of Peter II in 1730, Dolgorukov's family was banned to Siberia, where he died in 1734.

† Teplov sold his estate to Count Peter Zavadovsky, one of Catherine the Great's "favorites," who in turn "lost it" through debts to the Pole Count Josef Poniatowski. It was from him that Michael's wife, Princess Vera, bought it in 1844.

Soon, however, Michael followed in the footsteps of his ancestors with such precision that within a few years the dowry
of his wife, ironically nicknamed *"Princesse l'homme d'affaires,"*
was gone. Nevertheless, only because of his wife's energy, combined with her typical Ukrainian vigor, the large household
in some way managed to get along and even to "have an
honor"—to the surprise and envy of many (it was said at
the time that "neither the Dolgorukovs' rank nor position was
equal to such an honor")[13]—to entertain "lavishly" the Czar
himself when, in the summer of 1859, Alexander, after *les
Grandes Manoeuvres*, the first since the Crimean War, "deigned"
to stop overnight at Teplovka. The effort of the "provincial"
Dolgorukovs to impress "the world" was the last straw. Debts
piled up, and with the issuance of the great reforms of 1861,
when they lost all their serfs and therefore free labor, the
Dolgorukovs were totally ruined. The old prince died a few
years later from "anxiety," leaving behind him large debts
and a family of four sons and two daughters. To add to their
misfortune, the manor, with all its "priceless pictures and furniture," burned down and was eventually sold at auction to
satisfy the claims of the creditors.* Now the Dolgorukovs had
to face the cruel world the best way they could. But the old
Princess Vera was not a Wishnevsky and a Ukrainian in vain.
As soon as it was possible, she contacted St. Petersburg "connections" still fresh from the Czar's visit to Teplovka, with
the result that the unsold estates as well as the children were
placed, to "protect them from the creditors," under the imperial
guardianship. This was the usual procedure for all the classes,
especially for the children of nobles, and it therefore attracted
very little attention. At the same time, the two girls were
entered at the expense of the "Emperor's purse" (*i.e.,* his
private funds) as wards, or *pensionnaires*, at the Smolny Institute.† Now an entirely new world opened before Katia's
and Mouche's eyes. To them, "provincial" as they were, moving

---

* According to one version, the house was burned down by "discon-
tented peasants."

† Despite hardship, the energetic mother, in order to have a dowry
for her daughters, managed somehow to buy another "estate."

to St. Petersburg—to one of the most dazzling capitals of Europe—was an enchantment. Though life was certainly secluded, even somewhat rigid, at the institute, they had from time to time a chance to peek into the great, exciting, and mysterious world. The occasions that were especially anticipated most eagerly by all the girls were, of course, the imperial visits.

One day in April, 1865, an especially sad month for Czar Alexander, as we have seen, he visited the Smolny. The Smolianki always attracted his attention, and they were usually all "presented" to him. As their family names were pronounced— names of Great and Little Russians (Ukrainians), Polish, Cherkess, Baltics, Georgians, French, Finnish, and so on—the calling out of the Dolgorukovs brought to Alexander the memories of the last Teplovka visit. The Czar inquired, and as the girls made a deep curtsy to their Sovereign, he had an answer. Yes, they were the Teplovka Dolgorukov girls, whose family he had visited a few years earlier; he had had such a "delightful chat" with the eldest, then only 13 years old.* From that day in 1865 on, the Czar's visits to the Smolny became more and more frequent. The Emperor took a great interest in his "little charges" and often visited them at their school. But such an "unusual" interest of the Sovereign didn't create undue talks. After all, the imperial visits to Smolny had always taken place.†

Then suddenly, to the surprise of everyone, just a year before she was to graduate, Katia Dolgorukova I, as she was now styled to distinguished her from her younger sister, Mouche,

---

* Almost legendary, if not entirely mythical, is the story often told in several variations of their "first meeting" in Teplovka. Katia is usually portrayed as a ten-year-old girl. Actually she was thirteen in 1859 (see *Almanach de Gotha*, 1896 edition). Though contemporaries and various memoirists, including Katia's daughter[14] give 1857 as the year of the "first meeting," the Czar's visit to the South of Russia (the Poltava District) took place in the summer of 1859.[15]

† Once when Katia became ill, the Czar visited her in the institute hospital. "It was the first time," wrote a contemporary, "that the Czar could see Katia in the intimate atmosphere." On other occasions, Alexander would see Katia in the "Salon of Madame Leontiev," the Smolny directrice. Often "delicacies" would be delivered to Katia, brought by her "relative" actually a female "messenger" of the Czar. Her name was Barbara Shebeko, of whom more later.[16]

was, at the "request of her mother," withdrawn from Smolny, never again to return. A few days later Katia went to live with her elder brother, Prince Michael Dolgorukov (Jr.), a retired Chevalier Garde officer, then residing with his wife in a "very modest apartment" in the "very unfashionable" Basseynaya Street of St. Petersburg. His wife, another traditional heiress, a "charming Neapolitan," the former Marchesa Louisa Vulcano, Countess Cercemaggiore, did all she could to make Katia comfortable. So that Katia would not be "lonely," a relative by marriage, a spinster and also a former Smolianka, one named Barbara Shebeko, became her companion.

Katia's new life seemed "proper and natural" to outsiders. The explanation was that Katia, "due to health," was to leave for the South to stay with her mother "on their estate." Soon all the "talks" in the small and unimportant circle of the Dolgorukovs stopped. The event—leaving Smolny—after all was really not unusual. Nobody at this time even suspected that the real cause was the Czar alone.[17]

"Katia at 18," wrote a contemporary, "of medium height, with an elegant figure, her silky ivory skin [so fashionable in those days] and eyes of a frightened gazelle, her sensuous mouth and light chestnut tresses, always gay and cheerful, was an exquisite creature" (although her nephew, the late Count Boris Berg, thought that "her hands were not sufficiently fine").[18] It was not surprising that Alexander, middle-aged, "tired," and "lonely" as he was in 1865, succumbed to Katia with all the ardor of "a boy in love."[19]

In the fulfillment of his desire "to be with her all of the time," the Czar had actually the "help and guidance" of Katia's mother, the old Princess Vera Dolgorukov. "The Princess," wrote one of her relatives "certainly knew that Katia, her daughter, and the Czar began seeing each other." These rendezvous in public places at first were also known to the "charming" Neapolitan. But the go-between, the "trusted person" and the confidante, the one who "arranged" and "encouraged" these clandestine but platonic meetings, was Barbara Shebeko. Barbara, according to Katia's nephew, "understood only too well what this friendship [with the Czar] could mean to her and Katia."

Barbara, as well as Katia's mother, was aware "for selfish reasons" that at all costs the "plan" must be kept in great secrecy in order to avoid "notoriety." The liaison must not, they felt, "become known at the Imperial Court and St. Petersburg society." After all, competition for the Czar's favors was more than lively. Mademoiselle Shebeko went even further and repeatedly "reminded" the old Princess what her ancestor "once brought" to St. Petersburg.* At first these innocent rendezvous between the Czar and Katia, so skillfully managed by Barbara, took place in the Summer Garden, a beautiful place located "in walking distance from the Winter Palace." "The Emperor, my father," his and Katia's daughter wrote many years later, "used to come to the Summer Garden where these little walks became frequent occurrences. My father felt deeply drawn towards his beautiful little ward [both Dolgorukov girls remained as "wards of the state"] and despite the enormous difference in ages [he was forty-seven and Katia eighteen], looked upon his innocent companionship as the one pure thing in his life." Meanwhile these "little walks" in the Summer Garden (open to everyone "decently dressed," incidentally) continued but at first attracted little attention. The Czar frequently walked alone in the city and in those "peaceful years" used to chat with those he knew. His promenades from his residence at the Winter Palace to the nearby Letni Sad (Summer Garden) were an everyday occasion.

With time it was more and more difficult to keep secret these brief and "innocent" but regular meetings that had begun in the spring of 1865. It is true that the two were never alone, as both were always accompanied, the Czar by

---

* In 1731, Colonel Wishnevsky, the ancestor of the Princess, brought to St. Petersburg from his estate a young Ukrainian village shepherd and choirboy named Alexis Rozuma. The Empress Elizabeth, Peter the Great's daughter, was so "enamoured by his voice and looks" that she made him her "favorite." Soon he became Count Alexis Razumovsky, a more sonorous name then he bore before, and eventually even married, morganatically, the Empress "in a great secrecy." The marriage was never made official. He was extremely gifted, modest, and "universally" loved. It was his nephew the diplomat to whom Beethoven dedicated many of his works. A Razumovsky (a convert to Catholicism) branch of the family exists today only in Austria.[20]

an aide-de-camp and Katia by a "maid," the maid usually being Barbara. To Katia the unsophisticated, simple in a way and a provincial girl, the "clandestine" rendezvous with the "adored" Emperor, a demigod to many, arranged as if by chance amid a romantic background, were enchanting. The Italian marble and alabaster arbor in which the couple found refuge while their companions discreetly kept away was surrounded by a fountain in which swam "outlandish monsters"; "rare birds" were kept in aviaries in the shapes of Chinese pagodas; beautiful trees brought from distant parts of Russia and Europe and statues from Italy, Holland, and England completed the romantic scenery.

Soon the pathetic encounters, for obvious reasons, had to take place elsewhere. The nearby "Islands," or Ostrova—the Kammeny (immortalized by the Russian composer Anton Rubinstein), the Krestovsky and Yelaguine—these charming islands, formed by the branching of the Neva River, and the site of beautiful palaces and country homes, were their choice. There, "seated with Katia on the park bench," the Czar, wrote a contemporary, would "over and over repeat and declare his undying love, his sufferings and his passion" for Katia.

Yet for more than a year after Katia had left Smolny, despite family pressure,* her own victorious feelings of "conquest," and a tempting though difficult situation, Katia, brought up on traditional Russian principles of "maiden chastity and purity," remained "cold, adamant and even hostile." But how long could such an attitude last?

Many years later, Katia, then an old woman, answered the question herself: "How was I able to resist him for so long? How is it I did not love him sooner? I think that it was only the fact of seeing him so sad and distressed one day that [I] finally succumbed and our love triumphed."[21]

---

* In May of 1866, her mother died. It was Barbara Shebeko alone who relentlessly pursued her "plan."

"MY WIFE BEFORE GOD"
or "Delicious Reality"

As the new year, the year of 1866 dawned, Czar Alexander justifiably—despite certain criticisms—felt that five years after abolishing serfdom, he personally had accomplished a great deal. There is no doubt, and most historians admit it, that despite opposition from many quarters, especially from the "shortsighted" landlords, Alexander, with his power as an autocratic monarch, was the initiator of the "Great Reforms." His famous phrase that "serfdom must be better abolished from above than from below" is well known. Even Herzen, the most outspoken foe of Russian absolutism, exclaimed that the "name of Alexander II belongs to history. . . . The beginning of the emancipation of the peasants has been accomplished by him; future generations will not forget it."[1] To understand fully the "great achievements" of Alexander's reforms, "one has to consider," wrote a Western scholar, "the backwardness of Russia in the 1850's . . . [and] the absence of an organized public opinion. . . ." "To eradicate," he continued, "an ancient and entrenched agrarian system from such an extensive territory within the short span of four years must be regarded as a great achievement."[2] Moreover, groundwork begun in 1858 reached fruition, without a civil war, strife, or loss of life, on March 3 [February 19], 1861, two years before the Emancipation was proclaimed in the United States. Yet, as we have already learned, all this was "not enough," and dissatisfaction and "profound bitterness," mainly among radically inclined youths, "the longhaired angry young men"* of the day—the "nihilists," as they were called—began to be felt. The new phenomena of the *intelligentsia* and the "intelligent" arrived on the scene. To most of them, primitive materialists, as they were, "a good chemist," as Turgenev, coiner of the word *nihilist*, wrote "was 20 times as useful as any poet" and an "English Wash-basin" was progress. All of them atheists, disbelievers in legal marriages, accepting of no authority or traditions, most of the nihilists were in fact the precursors of Bolshevism and ancestors of the Marxian state in Russia.[3] Though nihilists believed "in nothing" (*nihil*), "there is no doubt," wrote an anonymous English contemporary, "that they were superstitious," for, as he continued, "an attempt [the first one] on the Czar's life was made on a lucky day for assassins, on the first anniversary of President Lincoln's death."†

On Monday, April 16, 1866, during the Easter holidays, the most revered days in Russia (Russian Easter fell on the eighth), the whole empire and the world learned, most with sorrow, others with glee, that an attempt "by a nihilist" was made on the life of the "Czar-Liberator" while he was "approaching the summer-garden on his daily walks."

The Czar was unhurt because a "newly-emancipated serf" by the name of Ossip Komissarov prevented the would-be assassin from killing the Czar. Meanwhile, the police tried, unsuccessfully at first, to establish the identity of the twenty-four-year-old nihilist, who eventually admitted to being one Dimitry Kara-

---

* Although in Russia it was now considered revolutionary or *avant-garde* for men to be longhaired and women to be close-cropped, in England at this time the wilder, more Byronic style of men's hair was no more fashionable and began to disappear. One of the first to follow the fashion was "Bertie," the Prince of Wales. On April 7, 1860, Queen Victoria wrote to her daughter, Victoria, ". . . he [Bertie] pastes his hair down to his head [*i.e.* parts it]. . . . That coiffure is really too hideous." Earlier, when he cut his hair short, she also complained that he "cut his hair away behind and divides it nearly in the middle in front. It is a frightful coiffure."[4]

† It was *almost* an anniversary. The attempt on the Czar's life took place on April 16, 1866. Actually, President Lincoln was shot on Good Friday, April 14, 1865, and expired the fifteenth.[5]

The words of Lincoln's assassin, "Sic semper tyrannus," were known in Moscow, wrote an historian.

kozov, a typical "intelligent" and a son of an "owner of a small property" in the Saratov District. At the same time, the government arrested thirty-five "accomplices," who, as one Soviet historian put it, "didn't face the trial like real revolutionaries."[6] All of them received mild punishments even though the trial disclosed that though Karakozov's attempt "was an act of an individual," they all belonged to a revolutionary society, "Inferno" ("Ad" in Russian), which had "branches throughout the Russian Empire, in Switzerland and in London."[*][†][7] Karakozov ("my offense is so monstrous") filed a petition for pardon and asked the monarch's forgiveness. The Czar answered that though he "personally had long since forgiven him," as a sovereign he had no right to do so. After a trial, Karakozov was hanged.

Meanwhile, "addresses" and "congratulations" to the Czar on surviving the assassination attempt had poured in from all corners of Russia, Europe, and Asia, but the American "message" was the outstanding one. Made public, "the unanimous" resolution of the U.S. House and Senate surprised the world for its contents

---

* Karakozov's attempt was followed by rioting in the villages because the peasants regarded the act "as a plot by the landlords against their own protector, the Czar, and not because they approved of it."[8] By popular subscription the public lavishly contributed for the construction of a chapel on the site of the attempt. It was destroyed by the Soviets after 1918.[9]

† The leading role of the "circle" was played by a merchant's son, the hunchbacked Nicholas Ishutin, one of the "ancestors" of Bolshevism and the cousin of Karakozov. According to a Soviet historian, Ishutin and Karakozov "occupied the flat [in Penza] where at one time Lenin's father lived. Yet, as Lenin's wife, Krupskaya, wrote later, the father was "rather indifferent" to political agitation. For him, Alexander II still remained the one "Czar-Liberator."[10] He even named both his sons after the Czar's children. The elder, Alexander—or Sasha for short—for the Czarevich, and Vladimir (Lenin to be) in honor of the next Grand Duke in line. (The later grandson, also Vladimir, is today the head of the Romanov family and the Pretender to the Throne of Russia. He resides in Madrid.)

David Shub, the author of *Lenin*, published in 1948, is convinced that Lenin's grandfather on his mother's side, named Blank, was Jewish. "But," asserts Shub, himself a Russian-Jewish *émigré* revolutionist, (in the United States since 1908), "communist dictators do not want that the peoples of the USSR to know that their god Lenin even for a quarter is a Jew." Actually this is still not a resolved problem. Shub's 1967 (reprint) biography of Lenin omits this discussion entirely.[11]

Other precursors of Bolshevism, writes Shub, aside from Ishutin, "were mainly Russians like Zaichnevsky, Tkachev, Nechaev and partly Bakunin and Tchernishevsky."

and subsequent action. "The Congress," read the joint resolution, "sends greetings to his Imperial Majesty and to the Russian Nation and congratulates the 20 million serfs upon the providential escape from danger of the Sovereign to whose head and heart they owe the blessings of their freedom." In addition, it was resolved to send a special envoy to carry the "Resolution." A squadron of three warships, of which *Miantonomoh* was the newest monitor, was chosen to proceed to Russia. "The act was unique in our history," wrote the official historian of the mission.[12]

The attempt on his life deeply affected Alexander. He became more tense, nervous, and restless and felt that his good deeds were not appreciated. Unfortunately for Russia and her people, the Karakozov case had negative repercussions. Dimitry Miliutin, the Minister of War, a "brilliant and highly educated" statesman, a man of "extremely democratic convictions," asserted[13] that "Karakozov's shot" put a halt on the effectiveness of many benevolent projects. . . . Everyone lost confidence [that more reforms were needed] and indeed all such undertakings were stopped, almost frozen in Russia and everywhere dissatisfaction developed. . . ."[14]

Summer of 1866 was approaching, and the imperial court, as was customary, moved to Peterhof. Located on the shores of the Baltic, sixteen miles from the capital, Peterhof, with a population of "7000 souls of both sexes," with its famous fountains, was a veritable Versailles of Russia, if not in some ways even more magnificent. That summer, in the fairyland surroundings, Alexander, still "sad and distressed," tried to relax and find greater freedom and leisure and less "protected" solitude. Two important events, aside from routine ones, were to take much of his time—the arrival of the large American delegation and the first visit to Russia of the *fiancée* of Alexander's "son and heir," the lovely and vivacious Dagmar, the Princess of Denmark,* whose sister Alexandra recently had become the Princess of Wales.

---

* On July 2, 1865, Grand Duke Alexander (Jr.), soon after the death of his elder brother Nicholas, was proclaimed the "lawful heir to the throne"—the Cesarevich. Dagmar was originally betrothed to Nicholas,

Almost simultaneously with the departure of the Czar's family to the shores of the Baltic, Katia's brother and his "charming Neapolitan" wife rented in Peterhof a modest *dacha*, built in an "attractive Gothic style" (more correctly a pseudo-Gothic style, then popular among middle-class house owners).* Their *dacha*, located not far from the main palace, in the so-called "Hare Reservation" (which was cut in half by the railroad), was pompously named the Beckman Villa after its owner. It was of course customary for many fashionables to follow the court during the summer months, but because the "Teplovka" Dolgorukovs were not of the "right circle," their migration didn't arouse undue speculation. Peterhof was open to "everyone" anyway.

Every July 13 [July 1 old style], the date of the marriage of the late Emperor Nicholas I,† "thousands of subjects of all classes" were admitted to the palace grounds and the parks surrounding it. On that Friday, July 13, 1866, throngs attended a ball, others listened to music or admired the "magnificent fireworks and illuminations" set off over an area of three miles! Many just strolled in the garden to view the *les tableaux vivantes* or to look at the cascading fountains. At dawn the "outing" was over and the tired but happy "guests of the Czar" returned to their homes.[15]

Meanwhile, late that night, the windows of the usually unoccupied, solitary, and isolated palace the Belvédère were aglow. The Belvédère,‡ situated in a sparsely populated park in Peterhof, about three miles from the main palace, was named appropriately Babyi Gon (Peasant Women's Run).§ The retreat,

---

who on his deathbed "asked" his brother to marry his fiancée. Dagmar was known later as the Empress Maria Feodorovna. She died in Denmark in 1928 as an exile from Russia. She was then eighty-one years old.

* The inevitable Barbara Shebeko followed them.

† Also the birthday of the Czarina Alexandra, the mother of the Czar.

‡ Some sixty years later, another "enchanting" place named Fort Belvédère, this time in England, made history too, when, in 1932, a "wholly improbable beginning" took place there, when an American couple by the name of Simpson received an "unexpected invitation" to spend a weekend from an Englishman known today as the Duke of Windsor.

§ It is very possible that Babyi Gon is a distorted name for the then fashionable English place Babbiecombe near the holiday sea resort of Torquay in Devon, England. In 1859, Torquay lost its reputation (see

a ten-year-old edifice, built in a "severe middle-Greek style" so popular in Europe in the 1850s rated rather poorly in comparison with the really beautiful buildings of Peterhof. "Richly furnished," the palace had the usual salon on the ground floor and boasted of a "moving armchair," or a lift. On the *bel-étage*, or the second floor, there were a few "private rooms," also "costly" furnished, and a bathroom completed the "modern comfort" of the place. What the retreat lacked in beauty, it gained by its seclusion and privacy. Surrounded by a park, with "antic ruins thrown here and there to complete the successfully achieved landscape," the Belvédère was an "enchanting" place.[16] In this palace, in one of the "private rooms," the "inevitable" happened between Alexander and Katia. On the very night of Friday the thirteenth, 1866, while the whole of Peterhof was celebrating, the "trembling" Katia "at last" succumbed to the charms of the aging Czar, himself "trembling" even more than Katia. "Today, alas!" cried Alexander, "I am not free; but at the first possibility I will marry Thou, for I consider Thou from now on and for always as my wife before God, *à demain. . . .*"*

During the entire summer, from that day on, "unforgettable" to both, the Belvédère became the secret *rendezvous* of the lovers.† But *à demain* was not always easy to accomplish. Busy and regulated as the Czar's life was, it was almost impossible to keep the "secret" from being known and—what was even more difficult—to find time for it.

Summer weeks in Peterhof were always busy, but the month of August of that year was, as if especially, filled with weddings,

---

Encyclopaedia Britannica, article on Torquay, 1961 edition). Earlier, however, it was the most favored place of Russian royalty and aristocracy.[17] I say possibly because another fashionable English resort of the last century, Vauxhall, also became a household word in Russia, when all the railroad stations were named Vokzal. This was due to the fact that the first Russian railroad built in 1837 between St. Petersburg and Czarskoye Selo with its terminal at Pavlovsk, ended in a public garden with a hall of entertainment, copied from the famous Vauxhall gardens in England. The name Vokzal has stuck to this day.[18] [19]

* This phrase, probably authentic in its substance, was subsequently repeated by Katia to Barbara Shebeko, who in turn told it to Katia's daughter.[20]

† We know also from the letters of the Czar that their "first" but "innocent" *tête-a-tête* took place on April 18 [30], 1866, in St. Petersburg, "two days after" the Czar's silver wedding anniversary.

receptions, and *fêtes*. Moreover, by the first week the first large official visit to Russia of "importance" by the "transatlantic friends," the Americans, was eagerly anticipated. What pleased the Russians most was the opportunity to extend to the Americans true Russian hospitality and thus repay them for the "magnificent" reception received by the Russian sailors in America in 1863.*

When, on August 6, the Americans finally arrived, they were for almost a whole month (an unusually long visit for any foreign delegation) lionized, feted, dined, wined, kissed, and finally tossed into the air *à la Russe* ("a peculiar Russian custom anything but agreeable but considered a mark of honor of highest character," wrote an American member of the delegation).[21] On August 8 the American delegation, headed by the Assistant Secretary of the Navy, the Honorable Gustavus Vasa Fox, was received by the Czar in Peterhof and presented to him the Resolution of the Congress. Czar Alexander, who, as one American noted, "speaks American," responded in a speech: "Tell them [the American people] how much I appreciate and with me the whole of Russia the testimonies of friendship they have given me, and how happy I will be to see the American Nation grow in strength and prosperity. . . ."†

The last function the Americans attended took place in the exclusive "English Club" of St. Petersburg, where a poem by Oliver Wendell Holmes was read, extolling the Russian-American "friendship." The "unforgettable" visit was soon at its end, and as one Russian *émigré* writer pointed out, the Russian-American relations "shifted [from now on] toward cooler and more practical attitudes."‡

---

* "The cordial reception which has been given to our [naval] squadron in the U.S. would never be effaced from my memory." (From Czar Alexander II's speech to the visiting Americans in 1866.) The Czar's statement alluded to the sudden and simultaneous appearance of two strong Russian naval squadrons at New York and San Francisco ports in the summer of 1863, when the fortunes of the North seemed at its most critical phase. The nation (the Union) went "wild with joy," and the five thousand Russian sailors ("Russian Saviors," "Russian Allies") in each port received a tumultuous reception.[22]

† The event was described in a cablegram, the first ever sent from Russia to the U.S. The cable service had just been opened.[23]

‡ At the dinner the entire speech of Prince Gorchakov, the eloquent but chatty Russian chancellor, was also cabled to the New York *Herald*

Meanwhile, Alexander once more could resume his "delightful" and more frequent *"têtes-a-têtes"* with his beloved.

Late at night, in Czarskoye Selo,'* on Saturday, August 26 [September 7], Alexander penned a four-page letter to Katia. This letter, as well as others that survived to our day and were never made public, illustrates a most tender and in a way tragic love affair. In these century-old *billets-doux*, as these missives were then called, one has an almost daily record of their passionate love, tribulations, jealousies, and quarrels. Unusual in its intensity, this liaison of the aging Czar was one of sorrow and repentance.

The letters of the Czar to Katia, invariably in French with occasional Russian words added here and there, were always written by hand in a beautifully even scroll on the imperial stationery bearing the raised family crest. The letters never bore salutations, neither were they signed—a custom that Katia, to preserve secrecy, also followed.

One simply marvels, knowing how busy the Czar was, that he found time, not only daily, but sometimes several times a day, to pen handwritten letters of several pages to his beloved. One should bear in mind that every day the Czar conducted a voluminous correspondence with various monarchs, statesmen, important functionaries, as well as numerous "royal relatives." He strictly followed the custom of his ancestors of not using a private secretary. Here is one of his letters to Katia:

Czarskoye Selo, Saturday, August 27 [Sept. 8],† 1866
at 11 in the evening

Still all saturated with the glow of our good sunshine, after the sweet moments we spent together this morning, I pick up

---

at the cost of seven thousand dollars. The thirteen-thousand-word oration was probably the most expensive "lend-lease" transaction of the nineteenth century.

* Alexander spent a few days there to prepare for the reception and ensuing marriage of Princess Dagmar to his son. Usually the court spent the latter part of the summer there.

† All dates are given according to both styles. The Czar, of course, used only the old style, unless abroad, when he used both styles simultaneously.

my pen again, dear friend of my soul, to thank you for the precious lines you began to write on Sunday the 21st [Sept. 2] and finished on Thursday the 25th [Sept. 6], and which only reached me this morning. Need I repeat to you that all your good words go straight to my heart, but that I am in despair over the fatigue imposed on you by having to rewrite them, after the bath the first ones took. At least may it not discourage you from continuing your diary and sending it to me every day, as you promised me. As to myself, while I will write to you every day, I will only send you my letters on Wednesdays and Saturdays. As we had the joy of seeing each other today and it happens to be a Saturday, I count on sending out this letter tomorrow. I hope, my well-beloved Angel, that you will find it to be a further proof of what I already repeated verbally to you this morning: that my true life is in you. Listen: I only wish you to feel loved, as I feel myself loved—*beyond the shadow of a doubt* [emphasis by the Czar]. In spite of this, or rather because of it, I must tell you all that is in my heart. Your habit of teasing me and of sometimes telling me *the exact opposite* of what *you think* and of what *you feel,* as it happened again this morning, pains and grieves me. It seems to me that by now you should know me sufficiently to understand how I love you, and all that you mean to me. Why then play a comedy with me, knowing very well that your pleasantries hurt me? I even find this tendency in your dear letters, in which, however, fortunately enough your true character gains the upper hand; which is also why, in spite of everything, they give me such intense pleasure. Do not be angry with me, dear Angel, for my frankness and see in it but a further proof of the true affection of your devoted friend, who knows not how to play a comedy with you, simply because he loves you so tenderly.

Before ending, allow me to thank you again for all the happiness you gave me this morning. I want you to know that such is the impression I carried away with me, and that I feel myself more than ever attached to you, my darling Imp.

I shall now live only in the hope of our meeting again and will try to delve patience and courage from your letters. Don't forget to give me sufficient notice, that is at least two days in advance, of your return to the city, and to let me know whether it will be on the 12th [Sept. 24] or some other day that we might meet again, so that I can make my arrangements accordingly. I embrace you, dear friend of my heart, very tenderly.

Christ be with you!

In the note I gave you in Peterhof on August 16 [28], it was I Corinthians 14 we were to read, thus today August the 27th [Sept. 8] it is II Corinthians 9 and so on.*

The second letter, written the next day, touches once more on jealousy but this time of a different kind. The usual lovers' quarrels are not so important. What is more ominous are the "ugly" rumors that no doubt reached Katia and "pained" her.

Czarskoye Selo, Sunday August 28 [Sept. 9], 1866
at 11 in the evening

As I promised you, dear friend, I start my diary [actually meaning correspondence] anew this evening, and you know that to chat with you, at least by writing, has become my only joy since, alas, we have been separated! I am still completely under the beneficial impression of our yesterday's meeting. At times it seems nothing but a delicious dream, yet it was a reality and *a delicious reality*, but one which, alas, passed only too quickly.

I have just reread and enjoyed your long dear letter received yesterday evening, and all your good words are a balm to my heart, which suffers no less than yours over our separation. But there is one part that still puzzles me: that in which you say that one of my letters from Moscow pained you, and that later something unpleasant happened to you because of me.

---

* Katia was more superstitious than religious. Alexander was both. According to the Orthodox teachings, Corinthian epistles were read daily, particularly beginning July 11, the name's day of Sts. Peter and Paul. It is probably that the Czar and Katia began reading the epistles the day their liaison began, *i.e.*, July 13, 1866.

You added that you wanted to explain it to me verbally on Saturday, but you said nothing about, and I admit that this worries me, because, as I told you more than once: I would like to avoid you any unpleasantness of any kind. Promise me, won't you, to tell me always frankly everything that is in your heart? Don't forget this, my beloved Angel, I entreat you.

I hope my letter of yesterday will have reached you by now and has given you at least a moment of sunshine.

This morning I took my early walk as usual, then went to Divine Service, then received people and worked. After 2 o'clock went for a drive in victoria and a walk at Pavlovsk [another residence of the Czar, about five miles from Czarskoye Selo], then went riding. Of course, I didn't miss seeing Mademoiselle Verpakhovski [the sister of the Guard officer then on the staff of Grand Duke Nicholas, the son of Constantine, the brother of the Czar] from afar, but happily only from afar; as to the pretty Madame Abashidze [née Gorlenko, the wife of a Georgian officer then serving at the Cossack Bodyguards of His Majesty] I found her at the spot she had indicated to me, but I did not even dismount from my horse and everything was limited to a few words of thanks on her part and polite phrases on mine. Such is the *exact truth*. I kept saying to myself: why, alas, am I no longer in Peterhof, where I had such an attractive objective, whereas here I roam about like a lost soul.*

You probably will again say: Oh, really? and yet that is how it was. Without you everything seems empty and sad. Both our oldest sons have happily returned from their voyage [Grand Dukes Alexander and Vladimir, then aged twenty-one and nineteen respectively—each almost Katia's age!]. In the evening we dined together and then went for a walk, and now I have just returned from a reception at which, as usual, all local society was present, and where my only distraction consists in a game of yeralash [an old-fashioned game of

---

* Katia must have been extremely jealous, possessive, and capricious. According to her nephew, she knew how "to play a comedy." Moreover, she was "very spoiled," mainly by the Czar, one should add.

cards, then rather popular in the provinces]. And now good night, darling Imp, I still have a lot of papers to read. Until tomorrow.

Monday, 29th, at midnight. It was on returning from the reception that I had the immense joy of getting your dear letter of the night before last, which made me happier than I can express, dear child and friend of my soul.

With their liaison in its third month, more and new troubles besieged the lovers. Katia began to fear that her younger sister Mouche (she was seventeen in 1866), who was still at the Smolny Institute and ready for her graduation the next spring, might suspect the "situation." With their mother dead, only her brother with his "scheming" Neapolitan wife and the ever present Barbara Shebeko were in the know. So Katia thought, perhaps not quite realizing that scores of people unknown to her not only suspected the "situation" but were well aware of it. It is doubtful that Katia suspected that her earlier and innocent *têtes-a-têtes* and subsequent nocturnal *rendezvous* in Peterhof were in a routine way recorded and therefore known to countless courtiers, guards, butlers, coachmen, and so on. On the other hand, at this time their "secret" was not yet "important." The court, after all, was accustomed to Alexander's escapades. What was more important, however, and what almost no one suspected and none knew, was that the Czar, this time, was really in love. It was there that the real trouble lay.

Czarskoye Selo, Tuesday September 6 [18], 1866
at 10 in the morning

I take advantage of the first free moment to thank you for your letter of Sunday, which I was agreeably surprised to receive already this morning. But while giving me pleasure, it also caused me *a lot of pain* [emphasis by the Czar], because you accuse me of something *which had never entered my mind.* How can you believe, dear friend of my heart, that in talking to you of your sister I could have ever thought that you confided to her the sentiments we feel for each other? I know you too well, and *have too great a confidence* in you, for such an idea to have ever entered my mind, I swear it. If this were the case, then I can perfectly understand that it would have grieved you, and that you would have the right to be angry with me.

Such a conjecture on your part hurts me all the more because it proves to me that you still do not really know me, if you deem me capable of having such ideas about you. In speaking about your sister, I merely wanted to say that I presumed her to possess that *women's instinct* which often leads them to discover things one does not tell them, but which they feel by intuition, particularly when it concerns a person whom they love. Please believe that I am speaking of you, not of myself. You see that I am dotting the "i's" for you, so that you should not be able to again misinterpret my words and thoughts. Confess, dear friend, that I am right in accusing you of having a bad disposition, as you always have the knack of giving a different meaning to my most innocent words. And with all this: Listen: I love you more than my soul, my Angel, and cannot be angry with you. *Oh, really?* you will say—but it is so, and I shall try to prove it to you on Saturday.

I am happy to have again forestalled your thoughts, in sending you the letter I wrote yesterday evening already this morning, instead of on Wednesday; and from now on I will send them out every two days, as you wish me to. May they only do you a little good, both *morally* and *physically*, for your state of continuous suffering grieves me deeply and worries me constantly; which will explain the impatience with which I wait for the moment when I will see you again, my child, my Angel, my ALL.

At 11:30 in the evening. Here I am happily back to my favorite occupation, that is writing to you, my naughty Imp, whom however I passionately love. I want you to know that in spite of all the unpleasant and unjust things you tell me, I cannot be angry with you, all the more so because most of the time it is mere teasing on your part, *of which you yourself do not believe a single word.* Thus it is with the irresistible charms of Mademoiselle Timanowski [?] to which you devote a whole half page of your last letter, and particularly with your allegation that *when I see such beings I forget everything else in the world*. You should have applied this to yourself, for it would have been more just, I mean as to the effect YOU produce on me.

Russian summers are short, particularly in St. Petersburg, and winter, as if skipping autumn, arrives quite suddenly and stays what seems forever. Peterhof and other summer places, as if by magic, are deserted by September. Katia was also back in St. Petersburg with her brother, the "guardian," in the unhospitable and shabby flat on Basseynaya Street. The Emperor and the Empress were busy meanwhile with the marriage of their son to Dagmar, who incidentally was two weeks younger than Katia!

Katia's letter that follows (one of the few we possess) shows clearly her mental and psychological state. It also shows her poor upbringing, the shortcomings of her education, her lack of culture and imagination.

Saturday, October 8 [20], 1866
at 3 o'clock

I am making use of the first free moment to chat a bit with you, my adored angel, for it has become my only consolation since having been separated from you, my friend. If you only knew how lonesome I am without you, I simply do not know what to do with myself for boredom, I keep yearning for you so that it is just unbearable. You ask me, dear friend, whether the proof of love I gave you the last time hurt me, no, my dear angel, on the contrary I am happy when I can give you the tiniest pleasure, for it is then that I forget all my pains; the only thing that torments me is that I cannot render you completely happy, for I see it is necessary to have as much will power as you do so as not to let oneself go. You think, my dear angel, that I neither see nor understand what goes on in you; I know that you love me truly, and that is why you do not forget *everything* in those moments. Forgive me my caprices, I will never have any again, the thought that I have grieved you tortures me night and day, it gives me pangs of conscience, and so I will only feel tranquil tomorrow after I have received your forgiveness for this letter. I know that you are not cross with me and that you have forgiven me already long ago, because you are good to me; but that is but one more reason to be remorseful. I confess that I am wicked, now it is my turn to say that I cannot understand how you can possibly love such a nasty creature, who so far has given you nothing but pain. I am sure that you must sometimes think so and say to yourself; why do I love her, she is not at all worthy of it. Confess, dear friend, that that is true and that it is a further proof of my knowing how to read what goes on in your good heart, which has now become mine. Today I feel well, but my foot hurts terribly, I was to stay in bed because I cannot walk, but as it bores me I did not follow the doctor's orders. I am waiting so impatiently for your letter which I should get at 5 o'clock. Yesterday I took a walk along Bolshaya Konnushennaya [Great Stables Street], I wanted to find out at all cost the house in which our confidant lives,* and I found it, it is the third house [belonging to Count Dimitry Cheremetev, a well-known and wealthy nobleman] from the corner turning to the Moika. Dear friend, I have again talked to my brother about the ball at the Institute† next week, he asked whether I wanted to go, and I said I would think about it. I have said nothing to my sister-in-law about your visit on Thursday,‡ she is not even expecting it. I know that if you tell her there is nothing wrong in my going to the Institute, she will not be so much against it. I must leave you, dear Angel, to send you this letter quickly, so that you get it this evening.

Yours forever, soul and body

Another winter went by, and the year of 1866, a fateful year for both lovers, was gone. But before it became a memory the "ugly" rumors, this time in the "right circles," began to be heard in St. Petersburg. Now it was impossible to evade them.

---

* It was the house where lived General A. M. Ryleev, great friend of the Czar and the "Commandant of the Imperial Household."[24]

† Katia wanted to go but was afraid to face "new" problems.

‡ The Czar again had begun to call at Katia's brother's flat.

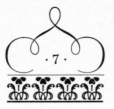

"MY ADORABLE IMP"

Weak as Alexander was, he made one important resolution—a pledge to marry Katia, which he was to fulfill "to the end of his life." But a resolution is not a fulfillment, and for Alexander especially in his position as a married man and as the Emperor of all the Russians, the Czar and Father of all his people and protector, if not the head of the Church, the present situation was an *impasse*.

The undated and incomplete letter of Alexander, written probably early in 1867, eloquently expresses his real feeling.

[We] involuntarily began to be drawn towards each other. All you tell me about the consequences of that meeting and of our first *tête-a-tête* on April 18 [1866] is also absolutely true, except that I could [as you claim] someday reproach you for your conduct on *July the first*. [July 13 new style. All emphases are the Czar's.] No, *that is impossible*, and you cannot seriously think it, because that was the day that laid the foundation of *our* actual happiness, and of the treasure we both carry in our hearts. What you go on to add is the exact truth—*for it was indeed I* and *not you* who was *the first* to let you feel the attachment I felt for you *by asking you to come to my place on April 18*, and you, my Angel, you merely wanted to heal the hurt you had dealt me that day by your reply. On July 1 both of us, as they say, became quits with each other. What makes me particularly happy now is that all your adorable words, my darling Imp, prove to me that you know me thoroughly and no longer doubt your true friend. Oh, really? *Thus,* and *nothing else.* And the conclusion is: It is *I who am yours forever, and you mine,* and we are both equally *happy to have given ourselves to the other for all our lives. So be it.*

Oh! what would I give to be able to prove to you at this moment the passion with which I love my adorable Imp. I would like to be home and to prove it to you there. Believe me, my Angel, that I feel myself loved and perfectly understand all that fills your heart, which is and always will be my possession. Should I need new proofs of your love, your adorable letters would each time supply a new testimony, but I need no further proof as from July 1st to December 1st [1866] you have unceasingly proved it every time we were together and believe me, my Angel, that those happy moments are so deeply engraved in *your* heart that they can never be erased and will go with it to the grave. I thank you beforehand for your dear [photographic] cards, which you promised me. Rest assure that I will give you my frank opinion as to how I like them. Thanks for giving me a description of your dresses. Oh! how they make my mouth water! How I yearn to get home and how I want you again—It is unbearable! This evening there is a ball at the English Embassy, which does not concern me, and in general I am glad not to have any obligations in view at present. Society is repulsive to me, and everywhere it seems empty and sad without you. I am only calm and happy when I get your charming letters and when I can write you. And in conclusion let me tell you some news: Listen—I love you madly.

Yours forever

The "clandestine" and frequent visits of the Czar at Michael Dolgorukov's flat now had to be explained to those in the know. The "secret" was out.

"Dear Princess," wrote Alexander to the "Neapolitan" Princess, totally unaware of Louisa's complicity in the matter:

> Your good letter has moved me deeply. I thank you from all my heart, and especially for being so kind as to treat me as a friend, a title to which I dare to aspire also in the future. If I took the liberty of asking permission to see you at least once again at your home, it was only so as to be able to ask your forgiveness verbally, for all the annoyances you had to bear with owing to me, and which worry me and make me more unhappy than I can say. What grieves me above all is that I harmed a person who is dear to us both, and whom I love more than my life. Forgive me for this avowal, but I cannot play a comedy with you who have always been so good and lenient to me, and who must have noticed the earnestness of my feelings for her. Your heart will also understand that she has become even dearer to me now, and that there is no sacrifice I would not be willing to make to ensure her tranquility and her happiness. Let me end these lines by forming the same wish as you do: that Heaven may some day grant me the happiness of being able to see you again at your home, as in the past, and without fear of Society. Please be certain, dear Princess, that nothing and nobody could change the devotion and the gratitude that I bear in my heart for you, for all the kindness you have shown me and above all for the true affection you have incessantly shown to her whom I would wish to see as happy as she is worthy to be.

> Your devoted friend
[SIGNED] *Alexander*

This time the "comedy" is played to perfection by Louisa. She was more guilty of spreading gossip than anyone else. Her nephew, Count Boris Berg, asserts in his (unpublished) memoirs that the "fact was well guarded" until Louisa told "in secret" about the "liaison" to her intimate friend, Prince Henry VII of Reuss, the Prussian minister in St. Petersburg. It was only natural that the Prince immediately reported the "new" situation to Berlin.[1]

The Czar's second letter illustrates Louisa's "game."

Dear Princess!

Forgive me for daring to disturb you once again by my writing. If I take upon myself to do so, it is because I fear that I displeased you by appearing at the theater yesterday evening. What makes me think this is the haste in which you left your box as soon as you caught sight of me on the opposite side.* In the name of Heaven do not be angry with me for this rash act, if it be one [which was quite involuntary on my part†], for which I reproach myself bitterly. Oh, please forgive me, I beg you, and plead my cause with dear Catherine, who I fear must also be angry with me. I would be [in despair†] inconsolable should you both bear me a grudge for it. Having learnt [from her†] that you like chocolate, allow me to offer you some and to add to it a little souvenir, which I am so bold as to beg you to accept from me. May it sometimes remind you of a friend who will remain thankful and devoted to you forever.

Sincerely yours
[SIGNED] *Alexander*

Soon the "diplomatic" correspondence stopped, as it was decided, in order to cut short the possible gossip and rumors, for Katia and the Dolgorukov couple to leave the cold and snowy capital "as soon as possible."[2] Nevertheless, their departure to Europe did not arouse any particular interest after all—the "Teplovka" Dolgorukovs were still relatively unknown in the "best of circles." Within a short time, the trio appeared in sunny Naples, the country of the birth of Louisa. There, in the former capital of the fallen Kingdom,‡ Louisa Dol-

---

* The Maryinsky and the Italian theaters were the usual places for the *rendezvous* of lovers who could not be seen publicly. For a perfect description of such a situation see Tolstoy's masterful chapter in *Anna Karenina* (Part V, Ch. 33).

† Crossed out in the original.

‡ The fiery little Kingdom of Two Sicilies ceased to exist when Garibaldi, after a "triumphal march," seized Naples in 1860 and "united it" to Italy. The royal family fled and became exiles.

gorukov, herself a local royalty, though *par la main gauche* created a furor. Born out of wedlock, but later legalized and "recognized" as the daughter of Prince Leopold de Bourbon, the "liberal" brother of the last king, the notorious "King Bomba," Louisa appropriately received the title of Marchese Vulcano with a "substantial settlement," according to the Neapolitan standard. Now, however, she arrived in Naples as the wife of an "immensely wealthy" Russian Prince, accompanied to top it all, by an unmarried but "rich" sister-in-law. (All Russian travelers up to 1917 were supposed to be "rich and noble," just as any post-World War I Americans were "all millionaires.") The reputation as "rich" Russians was certainly more than confirmed by their life in Naples. Many years later the wife of an Italian diplomat recalled the Dolgorukov *séjour* in Italy. "Scores of noble [and we should add impoverished] Neapolitans," she related, "sought the hand of the Russian Princess [Katia], who rejected the proposals of these handsome Italian Princes. Katia never danced at the numerous parties and balls she attended and appeared as if in a trance."[3] Renamed *"la princesse au bois dormant,"* the "sleeping princess," she suddenly departed. Her secret destination was Paris. It was June, 1867, one of the loveliest months in Europe, particularly in the French capital.

Yet, that summer was full of foreboding, and Europe seemed once more to be on the verge of another conflagration, this time between a dominant and aggressive Prussia and France.* Although in his personal sympathies Czar Alexander had been torn apart in the Seven Weeks' War, he always followed the "Russian line," never permitting himself to be influenced by "family ties." Indeed, the situation could perplex anyone. The Czar's mother was the sister of the King of Prussia, "the aggressor"; on the other hand, Alexander's wife was a Hessian, whose "Fatherland" was a year earlier "cruelly invaded" by the "hated"

---

* Only a year earlier, Italy, encouraged by Napoleon III and Prussia, had declared war on Austria and was thoroughly beaten. At the same time, Bavaria, Saxony, Baden, Hanover, Hessen, and Austria reluctantly lined up against Prussia and were in their turn, in the Seven Weeks' War, completely crushed.

Prussians. Alexander's son, the heir to the throne, was married to a Danish Princess, whose anti-Prussian sympathies were no secret. (In 1864, in a war with Prussia, Denmark had had to surrender the duchies of Schleswig, Holstein, and Lauenburg to Prussia and Austria.) It was natural that Napoleon III, the "upstart" Emperor, who was unable, it was said, to form correct judgments, sensed the Prussian danger and took immediate steps toward a project of a Franco-Russian alliance. The Exhibition Universelle, to be opened in Paris in the spring of 1867, was a perfect pretext for an invitation. The Czar promptly accepted it, only too happy to meet once more his beloved Katia. Early in June he arrived in Paris, was met by Napoleon III and escorted "in style" to the Élysée Palace, his residence, where, in the turbulent years of 1814–15, Alexander's ancestor the Emperor Alexander I also had stayed.*

Almost simultaneously Katia appeared in Paris and was installed in a "discreet and small hotel" in the Rue Basse du Rempart.[4] For the first time in six months, the lovers, who had once seen each other almost daily, were again together, and what was even more exciting, in Paris, the city of gaiety, love, and romance. Free, unobserved (so they thought), and "madly in love," the couple at last found "complete happiness." Daily (horseback riding in the *Bois* was their favorite relaxation) and sometimes nightly, whenever Alexander was free, Katia would drive to the Élysée Palace and through a "secret" garden gate would "discreetly" slip to Alexander's private apartment.† "Since the day when I began to love you," declared Alexander, "no other woman exists for me! During the whole year when you rejected me and later when you were in Naples, neither did I desire another woman nor approached one" (a statement from Barbara Shebeko, to whom Katia confided the "details").

---

* By 1867, Alexander was the only sovereign who had not paid a formal call on Napoleon III. When, in 1865, Alexander rushed to the deathbed of his son in Nice, Napoleon III met the Czar at the Paris railroad station for "barely ten minutes."[5] After all, the Crimean War was not quite forgotten by the Russians.

† Antoinette Poisson, better known as the Marquise de Pompadour, in her days occupied the same quarters.

But duties and obligations once more made themselves felt. When Alexander arrived in Paris (on June 1) a busy schedule awaited him and other sovereigns, including the kings and queens of Prussia and Belgium, the Sultan of Turkey, the Khedive of Egypt, and the portly Prince of Wales. Napoleon III had "arrived" at last. One Sunday, June 2, after a mass in the newly built Russian Church on Rue Daru, Alexander attended the races, followed in the evening by a state dinner and a ball at the Tuileries. There Empress Eugenie, perhaps with a hidden reason, "presented" to the Russian Czar all the beauties of the day—the Marquise de Gallifet, the Comtesse de Pourtales, Princesse d'Essling, the Duchesse de Bassano, to name only a few.* It was not recorded whether Alexander was amused or not. We know only that the next day, "relaxed and happy," he was present at the opera together with the rest of the sovereigns and their suites. The following day an event took place which was a foretaste of what was yet to come.

While sightseeing (there is no record that Alexander, unlike his predecessors, had ever been to Paris before) the Czar stopped at the Palais de Justice, where he was assailed by a French lawyer, Charles Thomas Floquet,† with a "loud" cry— "*Vive la Pologne, Monsieur!*"—reminding Alexander of the Polish uprising that was put down by Russia in 1863. Later that afternoon Alexander attended races at Longchamp. A witness reported that he had never seen such an "incongruous set of guests together." The King and Crown Prince of Prussia appeared "displeased," the Czar "seemed out of spirits" and talked to no one, even the Queen of Belgium, who sat next to him.

---

* The famous painting "Empress Eugenie and Her Ladies of the Court" by Franz Winterhalter (in the Musée de Compiègne) personifies the era.

† Floquet (1828–96), to whom the *Russian Encyclopaedia* of 1902 devotes more than a page and Larousse only three lines, took part in the *barricades* of 1848. In 1871 he was arrested in Paris as a *Communard*. A leftist member of the Chambres des Deputes, Floquet finally became a cabinet minister. Several times he tried unsuccessfully to "obtain pardon" from the Russian government. Finally, in 1888, he was "presented" to the Russian ambassador and peace was made. Later he was accused of taking part in the Panama "scandal" and was forced to resign. He died in obscurity in 1896.

"Only his sister," Marie, the Duchess of Leuchtenberg, "was the life of the party."[6]

If the Czar was not talkative at the races, he was certainly eloquent enough when he wrote a *billet-doux* to Katia at "half past 8 in the evening":

> Forgive me, dear friend, for bothering you again with my scribbling. I only want to tell you that when just now you asked me, when we were riding, where we could meet tomorrow, I quite forgot that tomorrow is our Ascension, so I shall go to Divine Service at our church at 11. So perhaps we could see each other there, at least from a distance, and then at the review. I love you madly, and our nice day makes me happy. Oh, how I love the Bois de Boulogne! You have driven me completely insane. I am happy to love you, and belong to you forever.

As he penned these lines, little did Alexander realize what destiny had in store for him. At the moment, as he himself confessed, the "Paris days were among the happiest" of his life—"an apotheosis" of his bliss. The next day, June 6, was the day for the "ordinary" Parisians to see the *"Czar de toute la Russie,"* since he was supposed to visit the Exhibition Universelle. Early that morning ("the day of Ascension" of the Russian calendar) Alexander attended the Russian Church services and afterwards proceeded to Longchamp for a military review. Returning through the Bois de Boulogne in their carriage (the Czar and Napoleon III occupied the first, with the Czarevich and the Czar's younger son Vladimir in the back seat), they were surrounded by an enormous and enthusiastic crowd. As a result the cortège was forced "to go at a walk." Suddenly a shot rang out: a man was seen firing at the Czar. The bullet went through the nostrils of the horse of the outrider and then passed between the two emperors, wounding a woman on the opposite side of the road. The man fired again, but this time the pistol burst in his hand, and he fell to the ground. "The horse's blood spurted all over the Russian princes," wrote the correspondent of the London *Daily Telegraph.* Napoleon III got up, waved his hat, and then said to the Czar "Sire, we have been under fire together." The second attempt on the life of the Czar had failed.*

Even though the Czar was pressed by many to cut short his stay and return to Russia, he refused (understandably) and "with restless activity" continued to visit "public institutions of Paris."†

Finally, on June 11, after ten "delirious days of bliss," Alexander departed for St. Petersburg‡ (he stopped to see his sister, the Queen of Württemberg, in Stuttgart), where, on his arrival, he was met by his ailing wife, the Empress, and the children. Meanwhile Katia sped directly home, but in a separate train.

---

* The would-be assassin, Anthony Berezovsky, was one of the many Polish refugees from the abortive uprising in Poland in 1863. The French government pensioned some of the poorer emigrants "to keep them quiet." (Some six hundred of these Poles were "enrolled" in the Communist army of the Paris Commune of 1871.)[7] Berezovsky was sentenced to life and hard labor and was transported to the French penal colony in New Caledonia. In 1906, at the age of sixty-nine, Berezovsky was amnestied. After spending almost forty years of his life on the island he decided to remain there, where he "bought himself a house and became a prosperous farmer." He died there at the threshold of World War I.[8]

† At the Louvre he bought a copy of a picture painted by a "young Pole" who had lost a leg, not in the "insurrection" against the Czar but by an "accident." "J'aime mieux cela," said the Czar as, the incident was closed.[9]

‡ Incidentally, Napoleon III completely failed in his efforts to form a Franco-Russian alliance. He finally "understood" that if he had to fight Prussia, he would have to do so alone.

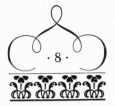

VA-ET-VIENT

When Katia and her brother and Louisa had departed for Naples in rather unexpected haste, Mouche, Katia's younger sister, remained alone in St. Petersburg.

It will be recalled that Marie, or Mouche, had continued her studies at Smolny when Katia left the Institute with "unusual suddenness." After graduation in the spring of 1867, with her mother and father dead, the seventeen-year-old orphan, "lonely" and "neglected," was more than "unhappy." For any girl, to be alone in a city is bad enough, but for Mouche, a girl without a position, money, or friends, it was even worse. The pitiful fifty rubles which she "inherited" after the liquidation of her mother's "estate," so badly mismanaged by Michael, was gone long ago. There were no suitors, as so often happened in such cases. In desperation she turned to her "nearest relative," to the sister of her younger brother's wife, none other than the spinster Vava Shebeko. Many years later, Mouche's son, Count Boris Berg, branded Vava, not without justification, as a woman who "should have been born at the Court of Borgia, where she would have found a suitable atmosphere."[1]

"Vava [Barbara Shebeko]" continued Count Berg, "knowing that Katia would be away almost all summer," hatched "a diabolic plan." Taking into consideration the "certain weakness" of the Emperor, Vava decided, now that the Czar was alone, lonely, and "free," to introduce him to Mouche, "who at that time just reached her 18 years." If Katia was a "sensuous" beauty, Mouche, two years her junior, had charm. With "ash blond hair and a remarkable coloring—a natural fresh complexion, slightly pensive eyes and a smile which simply captured everyone," Mouche, vivacious, gay, and what was even more important, clever, was a perfect but not a voluntary accessory to the "diabolic plot." Vava, as a contemporary witness asserted, understood only too well the advantages she would gain for herself from fulfillment of such a "plot." Therefore she worked fast. At first, everything went "according to her usual schedule": the innocent and routine *billets-doux* in French were exchanged (Vava dictating all the "answers"); then "inquiries" would be made. It seemed that another "victory" was forthcoming. Yet, unfortunately for Vava and happily for Katia, Alexander either had no wish to start a new adventure so "close" to the present or was true to his word that "no woman exists anymore for him." At any rate, summer came, and he left for Paris and his "beloved" Katia.*2 The "diabolic plot" was a complete failure.†

After his almost tragic visit to Paris, Alexander was back in St. Petersburg by the beginning of July. He remained in the capital while the Empress, whose health had somewhat improved, left for the Crimea to stay in her Livadia Palace.

The Czar meanwhile continued to pursue his busy and tedious schedule—visiting such towns as Vilno and Riga, stopping for a review of troops, meeting with high officials, and so on, and in

---

* Sensing a "failure," Vava promptly dispatched the "unhappy" Mouche to Kiev to stay with her brother, Vasilli Dolgorukov, married to Vava's sister Sophia. There, Mouche was to spend "two most unhappy years of her life," "almost until her marriage."

Many years later, a refugee Russian princess in Paris, a close friend of Mouche, confided to a friend: "They talked a lot, but it is not true that [Mouche] was ever a mistress of the Emperor. Vava did all in her power to make Mouche as such. I know what I am saying. Yet, unfounded rumors continued to persist during her lifetime." Mouche died in 1907, as the wife of Count George Berg. Vava died in Paris as a refugee in 1931. She was over ninety years of age.

† As Count Berg relates, what "saved" his mother from Vava's "monstrous" plan was the Czar's and Katia's visit to France in 1867 and their subsequent liaison.

"his spare time," continuing to see Katia. Their relations were now on a "permanent basis," and though rumors continued to flare here and there, they didn't seriously disturb the lives of the lovers. Came autumn, and Alexander, as was his custom, joined his family in the warm Crimea.

Livadia Palace was actually a private "Estate of His Majesty" situated at the southern shores of the Crimean peninsula, not far from the town of Yalta. The unpretentious small wooden structure, built by an Italian architect in the prevailing but ugly Victorian style of the day, was the residence. The Emperor's "personal" rooms were on the ground floor, the Empress's on the second; "they were simply, but comfortably furnished" and "adorned" with portraits of their relatives. To one of a group of American tourists from San Francisco by the name of Samuel L. Clemens, who visited Yalta and Livadia and was presented to the Czar in October of that year (1867), "the place was a vision of Sierras . . . [with] the tall, gray mountains that back [Yalta] . . . [and] bristling with pines—cloven with ravines—here and there a heavy rock . . . long straight streaks sweeping down. . . . All these were as like what one sees in the Sierras as if the one were a portrait of the other. . . ." The American tourists spent half an hour "idling through the palace, admiring the cozy apartments and the rich but eminently home-like appointments of the place. . . ." Then, wrote Mark Twain, "the Imperial Family bade our party a kind good-bye and proceeded to count the spoons. . . ."[3]

Alexander remained in Livadia until the latter part of November, when he returned to St. Petersburg, eager to see his Katia (at this period Katia did not follow the Czar to Livadia; a "very modest" house was purchased for her later in St. Petersburg).

On his return, Alexander was this time "disturbed" by "certain" rumors. Indeed, concealing the liaison became more and more difficult. Even Princess Louisa became "uncomfortable." She was trying to "make" St. Petersburg society, and the gossips hurt her efforts. One of Alexander's unsigned *billets-doux* to Louisa, which survives to this day, clearly shows their mutual anxiety.

November 24 [Dec. 6], 1867

You will understand my despair at having been capable of doing something unpleasant to her, and that just on the day before her name's day.* I who have only one single thought in my head, and that is to see her content and happy. May God preserve her and grant her all the happiness of which she is so worthy, and in which, as I know, you yourself are so sincerely interested.

Apparently Louisa's false "threats" had an effect, and in order to avoid "unnecessary" talk, Alexander decided to cut short the clandestine rendezvous, which were not a mystery to many. The two letters that Katia wrote within a day to the Czar are more than explicit. Katia, out of boredom, or lack of any interest in general, opens her heart:

Rec'd in St. P.
Jan. 3/15

Wednesday, January 3 [15], 1868
at 3 o'clock

Dear Angel!

I cannot refrain from writing you these few words, to ask whether you are going hunting to-morrow, so as to know what I should do. Oh, if you only knew how lonely I am without you, and since meeting you a little while ago I don't know what to do with myself, for you again proved to me that you prefer to go to the theater instead of meeting me on the Nevsky. Oh, how unhappy I am and my heart aches terribly. I cannot understand what pleasure you can find in going to see all those darlings at the theater who, judging by my way of thinking, ought to disgust you. I begged you not to go to the ball at the [Smolny] Institute this evening, but feel sure you will disobey me, so in the future I will never tell you my wishes again. I have again had some trouble and beg you to write me a few words to soothe this poor heart which loves you so much. I have a terrible headache that will force me to go to bed at 8

---

* Katia's name's day (St. Catherine, "the sufferess") fell always on November 24 old style, December 6 new style.

o'clock. Oh, how I would like to spend my life close to you, I do not know what to do with myself without you. Forgive me for writing to you on stationery with my crest, but I took the first sheet that came to hand and am hurrying to send you these few lines, so as to get a word in reply before 8 o'clock. I love you, and want you.

Rec'd in St. P.
Jan. 5/17

St. P., Thursday, January 4 [16]
at half-past 12 in the afternoon

The first thing I did on waking up was to ask about the temperature, and, alas, they told me it was 3 degrees above zero, which makes me sigh for we won't be able to see each other all day long, and that simply made my poor heart ache. You will understand that I cannot be in a good humour when I do not see you, I feel so sad that all the time I acted capriciously, furious that you went hunting. It is egotistical of me, but what do you want, I cannot breathe without you, I would have liked to see you or at least to have had the chance of meeting you out walking, and as if on purpose the weather decided otherwise, it hurts, it hurts so. I love you, my angel, and feel so sad. I had just finished dressing when Serge* came to ask me to go out for a walk with him, which I had to do because I had promised him to, but I confess I was in no humour to do it this morning, for my intention was to profit from my walk to have a chat with you; but as we so often are forced to act against one's will, I had to pretend to be very happy about it and we went out at 11, and having walked along the Morskaya to Saint Isaac's Square, we came home at noon, and I felt so sad I could not help bursting into tears. Oh, my angel, the thing is you do not understand how I love you and what it costs me not to see you, I feel so different when I am deprived of that joy; you do not feel as lonely as I do,

---

* Prince Serge Dolgorukov (1850?–98?), the younger brother of Katia. Never married, he had a son by a ballet dancer, who received the name of Alexandrov. During World War I, Alexandrov was officially "adopted" by Serge's brother Anatole and received, with the Czar's permission, the surname of Dolgorukov but without the title of prince.

and therefore you cannot understand it. You do not love me as passionately as I love you, oh, my angel, pity me, for I am so lonely! I feel well, my headache is better for I slept more or less well last night and dreamt of you all the time, my angel, my life, my happiness, my all. Oh, how I thought of you when I was out walking with my brother, I did not know what to do with myself because I so wanted to walk with you. Oh, how we would have enjoyed walking together or driving in a sleigh; if only we could do it without fear of gossip and slander, we would be an exemplary couple, and everybody would admire our mutual adoration, for there is nothing else like it in the whole world. I love you, angel mine, I only dream of you, I only have one thought in my head everywhere and always— and that is you, and I feel so absorbed by my love for you that I do not know what will become of me! Listen! I hope you will have good hunting in this pleasant weather, and that you will think of your poor Imp who only thinks of you; I feel you are as sad as I am because you cannot see me, so we have thus become a single being, feeling the same about everything. Oh, dear friend, I wish it were already tomorrow evening, to be able to throw myself into your arms and forget the whole world. I want to do bingerle with you, it is so sweet and cosy to stretch out next to my angel and to torment him.

At 4 o'clock. I love you, my angel, I am so lonely I just don't know what to do, you are my joy, and without you I am sad and lonely everywhere. After having written to you just now, I had lunch and then went out on foot for a little while, for I hate driving in a sleigh and only do it when I cannot meet you any other way. I went to see my sister [Mouche] whom I found in a sentimental mood, she declared she would not go to Kiev but would stay here at my brother Anatole's,* who is spending the winter here, because Basil† is curt and very nasty to her. You will understand, dear Angel, that I was more annoyed than pleased with this, so I could not refrain from trying to

---

* Anatole Dolgorukov (1845–1920s), Katia's "black sheep" brother, was married to a rich heiress, Maria Sinelnikov. More about him later.

† Basil Dolgorukov (1840–19?), another brother of Katia, married to Vava Shebeko's sister.

talk sense to her, advising her to leave for she will feel even less happy with the other brother [Anatole]. I foresee there will be endless incidents and comedies with her now, which is why I wanted to see her go, but unfortunately I did not succeed in convincing her. I returned home with a terrible headache and can hardly see what I am writing.

At half-past 7. I could not continue my chat with you, as my head felt dizzy and I could not see what I was writing, so I went to bed and only got up at 6 o'clock to have dinner with all of us together, and now I want to tell you I feel so sad and depressed because I have not seen you all day, that I do not know what to do with myself. I have the most terrible headaches, I cannot understand what causes them and do not have a single day without them, it is only when you are present that I suffer less from them, so it is you who know how to relieve my pains and to revive me, and how could I not be mad over your whole being, which I adore. So until tomorrow, if the weather is good I will go out at exactly 2 o'clock in the sleigh with Michel [the eldest brother, with whom Katia then stayed]; I shall drive around the Quay and the Nevsky and then go riding at the Manège, and at half-past 7 I will come to your place; please be punctual and be there before 8. I love you, I am terribly lonely, I just do not know what to do with myself. My thoughts are with you in the sleigh, you are probably on your way home from the hunt now. Oh, I love you. It hurts.

While the lovers, as usually happens, found their ways, Princess Louisa was not easily pacified. Here is the letter of the Czar-Autocrat to Princess Louisa:

St. P. March 7 [19], 1868

Dear Princess,

I beg you to forgive us for our rash acts, which have again caused us such unpleasantness, and above all do not blame dear Catherine, for if there is a culprit then it is I myself, not she. I promise you to be as reasonable and careful as [it is only*] possible, [but at least have some pity*] but you have such a kind heart and know the cult I bear for her and which

---

* Passages are crossed out in the original.

has become my life, you will have a little pity for us, and you will not be angry if by chance we sometimes meet—won't you? It is the only consolation that remains to us, since we are deprived of the happiness of seeing each other at your home.

You have seen, dear Princess, that I bowed to your will, since you demanded it for the good of dear Catherine, despite all the pain it caused me. I can only repeat to you that there is no sacrifice I would not be willing to make merely to know that she is happy, and to avoid misusing your friendship, on which I hope you will allow me to dare to rely in the future.

Oh, what would I give to be able to kiss your hands and tell you all that which overflows in my heart, and which I dare not trust to paper. Be also a little lenient with the uneven moods of the joy of the house, for you who know her as well as I do, you are aware that the bottom of her heart never changes, and that she never varies in her affection for those whom she really loves—as for you, who have always been her friend. I can assure you that she has never spoken to me about you otherwise than with gratitude for the truths and advice you have given her, for she is as persuaded as I am that they were dictated to you by your friendship towards her. So I can assure you that nobody is as sincerely attached to you as we both.

From Katia's letter that follows, it is evident that the rendez-vous continued to take place but no longer in the brother's flat. The lovers by this time began to meet "in your place," as Katia called a secret dwelling in the house of a devoted and loyal friend of Alexander, one General Alexander Ryleev, a relative of the revolutionary, the "Decembrist" Ryleev, who was hanged for his participation in the 1825 events. (See Chapter 2.)

Rec'd in St. P.
Mar. 11/23

Monday, March 11 [23], 1868
at 4 o'clock

I cannot understand what happened, why you did not pass through the Millionnaya [Street], where I waited for you,

expecting you to pass by, because as I was late owing to
Louisa, who forced me to receive the Troubetskoys [Prince
and Princess Troubetzkoy, probably friends of the Dolgoru-
kovs] just as I was about to go out, I was only able to get to
the Millionnaya at 2.25, I still kept hoping you would come
and I walked up and down four times but all for nothing, alas!
Oh, my angel, it is too much to have such bad luck as we do,
if only you could see the state I am in, you would certainly
pity me. I am writing these few lines to ask what you plan to
do this evening, for if you were free I could come at half-past
7, and we could console each other. Write me a few words in
reply. Oh, my angel, I fear I will go insane and I do not know
what will happen to me if we do not see each other this
evening. I love you, I love you, and am happy to love you. My
tears are stifling me.

But finally Princess Louisa won out. It was decided at this
"dangerous moment" to leave St. Petersburg "immediately." The
letters of the Czar to Louisa are worth recording *in toto:*

Dear Princess,

The kind words in your letter gave me real pleasure, for I
know that the wishes you express for your friend are as sincere
as the interest and affection that she feels for you. Thank you,
thank you from the bottom of my heart for calling me your
friend [emphases are the Czar's], a term I appreciate very
deeply indeed and which moved me more than I can express.
Alas, why can I only do it by writing? *The dear inquisitive
fairy* was not mistaken when she spoke to you about a new
photograph of me, I have commissioned her to give it to you
on behalf of that friend, whose life she has now become.* It
was from her that I learnt you are about to undertake a new
voyage and a new cure abroad. May it have a beneficial effect
on your health, and give us the consolation and joy of seeing
you return here in September, full of new vigor. This hope will
be the only solace I shall have during this sad period of

---

* A photograph of the Sovereign, particularly personally inscribed, was
a rarely given expression of highest esteem in old Russia.

separation, and I hope God will not remain deaf to the prayers of your most devoted

and thankful friend.

Z.S. [Czarskoye Selo] May 3 [15], 1868

Dear Princess,

On the eve of your departure, as alas I could not do it otherwise, I had to again resort to my pen to wish you a happy journey, complete success of your cures and *above all a happy and speedy return*. You know that it is *my life* that is leaving with you. This will explain to you what goes on in my bleeding heart, which can find no consolation in anything. I beg you on my knees, dear Princess, not to be angry with dear Catherine on account of our so very innocent meetings. One must really be very wicked indeed to throw stones at us for that. As though I did not meet with a hundred acquaintances every day, when out walking or driving. Why must we be the only ones who should not dare to see each other!—Forgive me for this cry of despair from a broken heart. You are her only support and only true friend. In the name of Heaven do not abandon her and be kind and lenient to *us*. I say *us*, for all you do for her is as though you were doing it for me as well. Have some pity on us, for our poor hearts are suffering more than we can express it to you, from the cruelty of society and this new separation, which I fear will bring us both to the grave. What distresses me is that I seem to notice that the mental side has already had a bad effect on dear Catherine's state of health, just when her physical condition had, thank God, so visibly improved after her return [to the fatherland*] to Petersburg. Oh, my God, what would I give to know that she is calm and happy! That has become the aim of my life. Forgive me the frankness of my words, but I can no longer keep from you all that is overflowing from my heart, which will remain devoted and grateful to you forever. May the Divine blessings [follow you*] be with you and yours, and bring you back [with the adored being who has become my life*] here safely. My

---

* The passages are crossed out in the original.

prayers will follow you everywhere. I kiss your dear hands and commend myself to your kind memories and friendship.

Your devoted friend

The hurried departure of Katia with her sister-in-law Louisa was well timed. As it was, Katia's presence in St. Petersburg in the spring of 1868 must have been embarrassing to many. Alexander's fiftieth birthday was just then being celebrated with a great deal of pomp and circumstance. In addition, his elder son's wife, the Cesarevna Marie, gave birth to a boy, the first born—an Emperor to be!* Yet at this stage very few, even among royal relatives, who knew Alexander as a weak, fickle and changeable man, considered this liaison "dangerous." "Embarrassing" yes, but not dangerous. After all, they said, the Empress is desperately ill, even the Czar needs a woman. What they still didn't know was what the "woman" in question really meant to their Czar.

We know very little about Katia and Louisa's trip abroad save to say that this time their journey took them to German spas, so fashionable in those years, especially to the upper-class Russians, whom Turgenev so vividly described in his "best seller" at the time, the novel *Smoke*. We also know, however, that at the end of July, Alexander left Russia for abroad to "join" the ailing Empress, who with all her younger children was staying with her relatives in Hesse. While the Empress took a "cure" in Friedrichshafen, in Württemberg, the Czar proceeded alone to Baden-Baden, where Katia was awaiting him.

Another year gone by, seemingly without any radical changes in the lives either of Europe, of Russia, of her royal family or for that matter of Katia. She apparently followed the same routine

---

* Following is how the American minister to St. Petersburg, Cassius Clay, reported the event to Washington by cable. The child in question was, of course, the last Czar of Russia, Nicholas II:

Mεy 19 & 23, 1868

On yesterday [sic] the Grand Duchess Marie H.I.H. the Cesarevna gave birth to a son, who has been named Nicolas; the Grand Duchess deservedly popular; and the regular succession to the Imperial Throne will no doubt be secure.

as a mistress of the Czar, yet conducted in an ostrich fashion, with the real "truth" supposedly hidden from her sister, brothers and friends. Another trip abroad, this time visiting Berlin, Frankfurt, and for "health" the German resorts of Wiesbaden and Schwalbach. Happily, a few telegraphs sent to Katia by the Czar survive to this day. They were usually addressed in Russian to "Her Highness Princess Ekaterina Mikhailovna Dolgorukova" but always using the Russian "Kniazhna," or the "unmarried" Princess, to distinguish her from the married one, or "Kniaghinia."

Zarskoye Selo,* May 17 [29], 1869

Berlin, Hotel Royal
Thank you for news sent from frontier and Berlin. Worried [your] cough continues. You know what supports me, as it does you. Will continue to write to Frankfurt until new instructions.

Zarskoye Selo, May 20 [June 1], 1869

Frankfurt, Hotel de Russie
Telegram from Frankfurt only received this morning. No letter yet. You will understand my sadness and where my thoughts are. Trust in God keeps me up.

Illinskoye,† June 17 [29], 1869

Wiesbaden
Today's letter still sent Wiesbaden, received indication too late, next will send to Schwalbach [a small health resort in Hessen]. Telegram of Saturday tranquillized me. Letters arrive punctually, my only consolation. You know where my thoughts are. May God support us.

Illinskoye, June 18 [July 1], 1869

Wiesbaden
Yesterday's telegram received evening. Worried by bloodletting and that letters are delayed. Beg you not to let yourself be

---

* The Czar's own spelling.
† Illinskoye, a private estate in Moscow province, bought by the Empress Marie in 1865.

discouraged. Think of the treasure which is our support. You know where all my thoughts are and whom I miss.

Illinskoye, June 20 [July 2], 1869

Wiesbaden

Yesterday's telegram received this morning. Answered immediately to one of Tuesday. Have just received letter of Saturday, which is true reflection of what I feel myself. Schwalbach address in letter does not coincide with telegram, please repeat. May God support and bless you. It is overflowing [with happiness].

Zarskoye Selo, June 25 [July 7], 1869

Schwalbach

Returned safely this morning. Will understand awful emptiness and what haunts me. Letters arrive regularly only consolation. May God support you and watch over you.

Zarskoye Selo, June 27 [July 9], 1869

Schwalbach

Thank you from all my heart for telegram and dear letters which give me life, received two together, last one of Monday. Despite emptiness and sadness, you know what keeps me up. May God return it to you. Beg you to send news of your health.

Krasnoye Selo, July 4 [16], 1869

Schwalbach

Received yesterday's telegram on my return this evening. The one of Tuesday was a veritable balm. Was sure both felt same gratitude towards God. Beg you to take care of your health and not go Sunday to Wiesbaden. You know what supports me and where thoughts are.

Zarskoye Selo, July 6 [18], 1869

Schwalbach

Thank you for following my advice, see in this new proof of treasure we carry in ourselves. Happy you could take up your treatment again. Understand perfectly where you would like to be and what keeps us up. It is overflowing.

Krasnoye Selo, July 9 [21], 1869

Schwalbach

Thank you for dear telegram, received yesterday, as well as letter 181. 180 not received. Feel that thoughts and wishes are same. Departure put off until 17/29. My trust in God keeps me up. May He watch over you.

Krasnoye Selo, July 12 [24], 1869

Schwalbach

Thank you for telegram received yesterday. Letter has not been found, yours arrive regularly and fill me with sunshine. It is overflowing. May God bestow His blessings on you.

Illinskoye, July 27 [Aug. 8], 1869

Schwalbach

Thank you for telegram of Thursday, received yesterday. Leaving this evening. Will conform to your indications. More than ever sad to hear you are not well. May God support you, and bless journey and return.

Livadia, September 2 [14], 1869

Received letter of 22/3 after this morning's telegram. Beg you to leave as you intended to. Am worried and impatient to see you again. Am writing to Berlin today.

Livadia, September 2 [14], 1869

If you leave Paris on Sept. 13/25, where address letters. More sad than ever. You will understand why. Have faith in God. Think of you.

Livadia, September 11 [23], 1869

Your 3 telegrams only received today brought me back to life. May God bless your return and our reunion.

By fall of 1869 the couple got back to St. Petersburg, and the usual routine once more began. As the year was nearing its inevitable end and the social season was in full swing, Alexander decided at last to set up Katia in her own quarters. One could only guess whether Louisa's "supervision" was too much for Katia or more privacy was wanted. The fact is that by early fall Katia moved from her bourgeois Peterhof *dacha*, not to the shabby, unfashionable Basseynaya flat, but to the most exclusive section of the city, the great Millionnaya Street (Millionaires' Row), within a stone's throw of the Czar's Winter and his brother's Marble Palace! The location of the "nest" couldn't have been more convenient for the lovers. If various daily duties and obligations kept Alexander from visiting Katia, now it was easy for him at least to "pass" before her windows.

The following letters from the Czar discuss a minor drama regarding an unhappy love affair of Katia's sister Mouche. Katia's real character can be clearly seen through the pages.

Tuesday, January 6 [18], 1870
at three-quarters past 11 in the evening.

Your answer to my letter of this evening reached me at quarter past ten, just as I got back to my room, having had a bath and taken my tea in a room next to the one in which the children [Alexander's children] were having fun, dancing in fancy dress.* I leave it to you, dear Dussia [endearing form of "Dousha," or "Soul"!] to judge the state of mind in which I appeared at the reception at half-past 8 and disappeared at 9 to go and take a bath. That conversation I had with Golitzine† seems to me to have been a bad dream, particularly

---

* January 6 [18] marked the great Russian holiday "the Blessing of the Waters." It was the beginning of the St. Petersburg season—dances, masquerades, and carnivals.

† Prince Michael Golitzine, A.D.C. to the Czar, thirty-seven-year-old would-be fiancé of Mouche. Eventually Mouche married a brilliant guardsman, Captain Emmanuel Meschersky, killed in the Russo-Turkish War of 1877. The widowed Mouche, more attractive than her sister, Katia, had many suitors. One of them was Prince Platon Obolensky, the future father of Colonel Serge Obolensky of New York. "In his early days," wrote Serge Obolensky, "Father [who eventually married a Nariskin] had been expected to marry Princess Yourievsky's younger sister, who later became Countess Berg. She was a very beautiful lady, and when she was with Father and I appeared he would say, 'Come on and click and say merci with your heels to someone who is nearly your auntie!' And he would roar with laughter." Little did this suitor imagine that his own son, Serge,

after all you told me yesterday and today about the step he
had taken, and which we certainly had the right to consider
decisive. I was so stunned the first moment that I thought I
hadn't understood the words he addressed to me as he came
into my room, where I was getting ready to clasp him to my
heart as a son, or as a beloved brother. I will give you the
details verbally tomorrow, it would be too long to write, and I
still have a pile of boring things to read through. What I fear
is that you will feel the counterblow even more than poor
Marie [Katia's sister] herself. I am so mad at her Mishechka
[would-be fiancé] that I could beat him. Oh, my God! What
will happen to her now? Provided they don't begin to gossip
about it around town. I plan to see Golitzine again tomorrow
morning, and to put it to his conscience not to say a word to
anybody, if he has a shred of honor left in him. I forgive you,
dear Dussia, with all my heart for your moments of bad temper
a little while ago, but I must admit they hurt me deeply and
were not worthy of our sacred cult, and I was sure that you
would regret them yourself.—Alas! I cannot continue, as I
must get back to my papers, while what I only want to do is
to go to bed. I feel quite low both physically and morally. God
have pity on us, and may He not forsake us! I feel more than
ever that *everything* for me is concentrated in *you*, my Angel,
and that it is *you* who are my life. I embrace you from the
bottom of my heart.

---

many years later, would marry the daughter of his intended bride's sister,
Katia. (She eventually married a Russian Balt, Count George Berg.) "When
Mouche returned from France to St. Petersburg," wrote a diarist, "she suddenly became the center of attention . . . carriages of most prominent people
stood before her house and there was no room for flowers sent by her
admirers."

Among other unsuccessful suitors were such "highly placed" personages
as General Prince Dimitry Sviatopolk-Mirsky, formerly deputy viceroy
of Caucasus; a hero of the War of 1877, General Michael Skobelev; and
the wealthy, illegitimate descendant of Catherine the Great, Count Alexis
Bobrinsky, a future member of the 3rd State Duma in 1907.

If one believes the 1887 version of Countess Levashov, her future
son-in-law Prince Leonid Wiazemsky was singled out by the Czar to
marry Mouche. "With his refusal," she relates, "he lost all of the Czar's
favor." Actually, he died in 1909 holding a high post as the head of
"The Imperial Appanage."

Wednesday, January 7/19, at quarter past 8 in the morning.
Good morning, dear Angel of my Soul, a great overwhelming
is with me and I yearn for you beyond all endurance. I hope
we will be able to meet at 2 and find ourselves in our dear nest
by 4 o'clock. May God not forsake us! I kiss you, my Dussia,
and am happy that you are mine, and I

Yours forever

Thursday, January 8 [20], 1870
at three-quarters past noon

Your dear letter No. 7 reached me at half-past 11 and filled
me with the glow of our sunshine. Yes, you are right, dear
Dussia, when you say that each of us is but the reflection of
the other, and that we are happy and proud to form but a
single being together, and to consider ourselves blessed before
God as man and wife. May He not refuse us His blessing, so
as to complete the only happiness we are still lacking! Now I
must go to the Academy [riding academy] and at half-past 2
I hope we will be able to meet despite the bad weather we are
having.

At half-past 11 in the evening. Returning from the ballet
at half-past 10 I passed in front of your windows, which were
already dark and I just yearned for you, particularly after our
conversation of a little while ago and our plans about my visit
to your place, which I hope we will be able to carry out some
day. To my great astonishment, I perceived Mishechka [Go-
litzine] sitting in the theater next to Serge [Katia's brother]
who was in his usual box. Michel [Katia's brother] made a
short appearance there also. As I had to read after I got home,
it is only now that I can resume our chat. We can truly say
that this was again a good day for us. Oh, I was so happy to
be able, as also yesterday, to kiss your hand at the promenade,
but I must admit that I was afraid you would catch cold
walking against the wind. You were such a darling that it
was simply unbearable. I regret having missed the moment
when your Mylord [the Czar's favorite dog] installed himself

in my sleigh. Oh, how sweet it was afterwards, when my little woman woke her repulsive fat one with a kiss, and when we clenched each other like cats and plunged in ecstasy to the verge of madness. This evening it was also so good to chat together, as we rested side by side. In a word, everything is sweet to us when we have the joy of being together, and therefore all the details of these precious moments do not cease to haunt me.

So as not to disturb those who like to go to the Opera on Mondays, the big ball has just been put off until Tuesday, which is all the same to us, all the more that as we are going out hunting tomorrow, there would not have been time to arrange for another shoot Wednesday. I have just read your dear letter of this morning again, with great pleasure, in every line of it I find the reflection of our hearts. I hope the pains in your side will disappear before tomorrow, and that you will spend a better night. May God watch over us and not withhold His blessing. I am going to bed now, clasping you tenderly to my heart, which only breathes for you, my ideal, my treasure, my all.

Friday, January 9 [21] at 8 in the morning. Good morning, dear Angel of my soul, I slept very well, and everything in me overflows more than ever. I hope we will be able to get some shooting today. I entreat you not to forget to put on a bashlyk [kind of a Caucasian warm scarf-muffler] when you go out in the sleigh or on foot in this awful wind, which seems to be as strong as yesterday. I love you madly, my Angel, and embrace you tenderly.

Yours forever, [Katia]

While all these love exchanges took place, the diplomatic chancelleries of Europe, in particular of Prussia and France, were more than busy, preparing once more a mutual folly, which not only changed the mood and the map of Europe but sowed seeds for a new and more devastating war with disastrous results no one could then foresee. The year of 1870 was here.

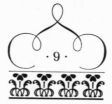

PRUSSIAN INTERLUDE

It will be recalled that as a result of his last meeting with Czar Alexander in Paris in the summer of 1867, Napoleon III "fully understood" that if he started a war against Prussia, he could not expect help from Russia. For Russia's own interest, the defeat of Prussia by France, with as a result a certain predominance of Catholic Austria—a traditional enemy of Slavdom—was not desirable. Neither was a complete annihilation of France to Russia's advantage. The policy chosen by Russia was neutrality, which she skillfully used to her advantage. It was not surprising therefore that both countries, Prussia and France, tried everything possible to bring the Czar of Russia to their side. Although Napoleon III failed in his first effort and made no further attempt, King William of Prussia, as a "relative" of Alexander and the "traditional friend," worked harder toward Russian "friendship." By May of 1870, Alexander, at the invitation of the King of Prussia, was in Berlin. Here is the first letter from Berlin which the Czar wrote to Katia, whom he was to meet "secretly" a week later in Ems.

Berlin, Friday May 1 [13], 1870
at 8 in the evening

After having sent out my letter to you a little while ago, I felt unbearably tired, so went to bed completely undressed to get some rest, sighing because I did not feel my adorable little wife at my side. She would have very quickly made me forget my weariness, as it happened to us more than once in our dear nest, and it would have been sweet to the verge of madness had we been *at home*. Oh, how I yearn to be back there. I see that the lack of our bingerles is already beginning to have its usual effect on you, and that those insupportable discharges of yours which had nearly completely disappeared last winter, have started again, and I am very distressed about it. Punch [one of the Czar's favorite dogs] was very flattered by your remembering him, and seemed to understand when I stroked him in your name; as to our two poor Mylords, I can imagine how lonely they are without us. Mine was as tender as could be, the day I left, as though he felt we were going to be separated.—At 5 o'clock I had to go to a big dinner at the King's, and returning from there at half-past 6 I had to go out again to show myself at the theater, where they were giving a ballet, but I only stayed a few minutes and here I am back again already and happy to chat with you, my ideal, my treasure, my All. Alas, I will have to be patient now for two days before I receive your next letter, for as I leave here Sunday at 10 in the morning, I will only arrive in Ems at 11 in the evening. I must leave you now, as I have papers to read and must write some tiresome letters.

At half-past 11 in the evening. I have just received your two telegrams of today, and am awfully worried to learn that you are not well and have to stay in bed. Perhaps it is only the effect of the vaccine, which sometimes brings on a fever. God grant it is nothing serious and that it will not prevent you from coming to Ems. As to the combination concerning Orloff,* I had decided on another one before I left Petersburg; and am waiting for the reply from the one

---

* Prince Nicholas A. Orlov, the son of Alexander II's mentor, was at that time Russian minister in Belgium, but in June, 1870, he was named ambassador to Great Britain, and later he was assigned in the same capacity to France, where he stayed until 1882. "The one in London" was the venerable diplomat Ambassador Baron, later Count Philip Brunnow, the chief architect of the abrogation of the humiliating Black Sea clauses of the Treaty of Paris of 1856.

who is in London and to whom I proposed Paris, having our friend in mind for London. Now it is time for sleep, I am unbearably tired. I embrace you, my Angel, from the depth of my heart.

Saturday, May 2 [14], at 9 in the morning. As I was so tired I slept fairly well, but woke up horribly worried by the knowledge that you are sick, and impatient to hear from you, hoping the news will be better than yesterday.

I love you, my darling little woman, and I yearn for you terribly. Oh God! Have pity on us and do not forsake us! I have just taken a short walk, in mild weather, and at 10 o'clock I have to attend a drill. According to your telegrams of yesterday, I have hopes of receiving a letter from you while I am still here; which being far away from you, my All, is my only consolation.

At 1 in the afternoon. I have returned from the drill, where we were caught in a terrific storm, which happily did not last long, and the sun dried us out quickly. We have just had lunch and I still have several visits to make. It is deathly dull and all I want is you and nothing else. I confess that I am anxious to get the impressions of our dear Mouche after her first days of marriage and the bingerles she must have gone through.* Oh! Oh! How dreadful! Has she had the courage to tell you about it?

At 4 in the afternoon. Alas, no letter, no telegram and it is time to send off my letter. I love you, dear Angel, and only breathe for you. I embrace you very tenderly

Yours forever

A week later, almost on the eve of the outbreak of the Franco-Prussian War, Alexander was again "taking waters" in Ems, which, as a result of the 1866 war—the Seven Weeks' War—

---

* Mouche was then married to the dashing guard officer Prince Emmanuel Meschersky, a relative by marriage of Prince N. A. Orlov, then the Russian minister in Brussels. Meschersky was the legation military attaché. It is evident that Katia and Mouche were trying to influence Alexander to name Orlov to a new and more important post in London.[1]

lost its relative independence as a part of Nassau Duchy and
was now simply Prussia's province of Hesse-Nassau.*² Probably
blissfully unaware of the impending "Ems Dispatch," Alexander,
now the fifty-two-year-old "tourist," continued his love letters
to Katia.

Wednesday, May 6 [18], 1870
at half-past 7 in the evening

Have only just got home, but I pick up my pen to tell
you, dear Angel of my soul, that first of all I thank God for
having given us the joy of meeting again. What I felt within
me you saw for yourself, just as I saw what was happening
to you. That was why we clenched each other like hungry
cats both in the morning and in the afternoon, and it was
sweet to the verge of madness, so that even now I still
want to squeal for joy and I am still saturated in all my
being. Oh what happiness to adore each other as we do,
and to just live for each other! We can be thankful to the
Lord for what we have. May He not forsake us in the future,
and not refuse us His blessing. You must have felt how my
heart pounded when I met you, when I was on horseback,
and how sad I was to part from you.

At quarter to 11, night. I have just finished my [card] game,
and am deathly tired, but before going to bed I want to
tell you again, my dear little wife, that I love you madly
and am happy to love you and to belong to you alone
forever. I hope you will have a good night's rest and I also.
Alas, why can't we go to bed together? I kiss and embrace
all my treasure passionately. I love you madly.

Thursday May 7 [19] at half-past 9 in the morning. Good
morning, dear Angel, I slept wonderfully thanks to you, my
ideal, my treasure, my All and I still feel saturated by our

---

* To Alexander the transformation of his "beloved" Nassau was not
too pleasant. His cousin, the Grand Duchess Elizabeth, the daughter
of his father's brother Michael, was until the 1866 war the reigning
Grand Duchess of Nassau, having been married in 1844 to Duke Adolph
of Nassau.

delirious bingerles of yesterday. Today it is just two years since your sad departure from Petersburg and one year since your first visit to Czarskoe Selo, where we spent the evening in the same rooms where I saw our dear Mouche after my return from Paris.

Just now as I returned from my walk I passed before your windows. You were probably still in bed and I wanted terribly to be there. I hope to meet you at 11, well rested and without a headache. I warn you that you will see me appear in a summer suit, light gray, with a pansy-colored tie and a straw hat. How horrible!* I am afraid it will frighten you. So until we meet again soon. In the meantime, I embrace you from the depth of my heart, and am happy that you are mine, and I

Yours forever

The Franco-Prussian War began on July 19, when France declared war on Prussia. Alexander as well as Katia were back in Russia by July, while the ill Empress visited her Hessian relatives.

Here is a letter Alexander wrote "at midnight" from the palace of Peterhof:

Sunday, June 22 [July 4], 1870
at midnight

It was again a good day for us, and I am happy we were able to spend such delicious moments at the Private Villa ["Private Villa of His Majesty"—a two-story dacha, built in the Renaissance style] and to enjoy our bingerles on a bed, as we had wanted so long to do. It was so sweet that I still feel like squealing for joy. We have had some bad luck recently with our meetings when out riding, but on the other hand this evening my heart just started pounding when I caught sight of you walking, and the hour we have just spent together at Ozierki [a small pavilion, located near

---

* Russian Military were not allowed to wear civilian clothes at any time except when abroad, Alexander simply loathed and disdained wearing civilian clothes.

the main palace of Peterhof] has left me with sweet memories, notwithstanding your moments of bad temper. Believe me, dear Dussia, I understand only too well what it costs you to have to be presented tomorrow and you do not have to explain it to me. But I wish you could also understand how painful it is to me to have to act against my own wishes so often, and to thereby arouse your dissatisfaction; if I do so it is merely out of precaution, and *always bearing you yourself in mind,* you in whom EVERYTHING is concentrated for me. That is why I insisted on your presentation, so that you should do as the others have to do, and as not to give people the chance of accusing you of lacking politeness. Neither you nor I pay much heed to society, and we both hate it equally, but since owing to our positions we have to show ourselves there from time to time, we however still have the pleasure of meeting each other there, and you know what effect those meetings have on us.* For the most important thing for us is to see each other as often as possible and that is why I do not want to let such occasions escape us, particularly when besides this we have the possibility of meeting in "tête-à-tête" and of exchanging our impressions. It is time for me to go to bed, and I only want to tell you that your dear letter of this morning, which I only received after Divine Service, produced its usual beneficial effect on me, and flooded me with our good sunshine. May God continue His goodness to us, and not forsake us in the future. I embrace you, my Angel, from the depth of my heart, which only breathes for you.

Monday, June 28 [July 10] at quarter to 10 in the morning. Good morning, dear Angel, I slept well, and my infirmity is back in order again, I only hope it won't start playing

---

* Katia was appointed a lady-in-waiting, in 1870, only because during Mouche's engagement to Prince Meschersky, the Czar had appointed her lady-in-waiting to the Empress. But inasmuch as the appointment of the younger unmarried sister in such cases properly did not precede that of the older one, Alexander had a good excuse to bestow on Katia the same rank of "lady-in-waiting to her Majesty, the Empress." Thus, with a lucky stroke, Katia could officially appear at all court functions.

tricks on me again as it did yesterday, as it affects my nerves so terribly. [Alexander's health failed in 1869, when he was over fifty. Asthma was his chief illness.] I am as happy as a child about meeting you again after Divine Service, and then at half-past 3 at the Windmill [a romantic spot in Peter-hof where a model of a real windmill contained "2 rooms in the attic tastefully appointed in a peasant style"]. I love you and am happy to love you. I kiss you tenderly.

Yours forever

Monday, June 29 [July 11], 1870
at quarter to 2 in the afternoon

Your dear letter reached me before Divine Service and filled me with sunshine, as also did our meeting in the Palace, when you seemed to me prettier than ever and I was so proud of my own, to whom nobody can be compared.

At midnight. I had no time to continue, because they were waiting for me to go for a walk—during which we had the good luck of meeting each other in the English Garden [a large and secluded park near the palace], and you must have felt, my Dussia, how my heart began pounding in my breast when I suddenly caught sight of you in the distance, just as it did in the evening near the Private Villa. You saw that I could not restrain myself and asked you: are there any sappers who frighten you? [Sappers Guard battalion, the favorite of Alexander, stationed during the summer months in Peterhof] which raised a lot of laughter when I told the joke after dinner. I would like to make Vava's [Vava Shebeko continued to chaperone Katia] gesture to ex-press to you how sweet I thought you looked in your outdoor costume, I just wanted to throw myself on you and forget everything.

The precious moments we spent together in the Windmill left me with the most delicious memories and you saw and felt that your husband had enjoyed his adorable little wife to the verge of delirium. In spite of the atrocious heat in the attic, we were very cosy up there, particularly when we clenched each other in our favorite light costumes. But I cannot conceal from you, dear little woman, that this evening you again hurt me badly, by the way in which you at the beginning tried to sulk and to pretend to accuse me of unwillingness and lack of haste in coming to meet you. I say *pretended*, because in reality I know you cannot think it sincerely. But what always pains me so much is that the least excitement brings on your fits of bad temper, which are not worthy of our sacred relationship. You are perfectly aware that I forget everything as soon as you again become a darling, that is your true self; therefore I have kept only the good impression of the moments we just spent together, and feel full of sunshine and more than ever in love with my naughty and adorable Imp, who in spite of everything remains my ideal, my treasure and my All. —So be it and nothing else. I ought to read some more, but must admit I feel very tired and so am going to bed, pressing you tenderly to my heart which only breathes for you. May God not forsake us!

Tuesday, June 30 [July 12], at half-past nine in the morning. Good morning, dear Angel, I slept very well and everything is overflowing in me more than ever. Today is four years since I first saw you in such an unexpected way, on arriving here [*i.e.*, July, 1866], and the 3 following years the contrast with the emptiness I felt that day was doubly painful to me, how after that could we not render thanks to God for having at last brought us together in this same place [an allusion to their first night in Peterhof on July 1 [13], 1866] where our hearts first understood each other so utterly that they since then form a single heart. After this you will understand, my adorable Imp, the impatience with which I await the moment of finding myself again in your arms at Olga's Island [a small and picturesque island in Peterhof, named in honor of Alexander's sister, the Grand Duchess Olga, at that time the Queen of Württemberg. A charming pavilion in "Italian style" dominated the island], which I hope will be no later than at quarter past 4, but I beg you once more not to sulk if by any chance I should against my will happen to be late. The puppies will be brought to you by the woman [*i.e.*, servant]. So until soon. I embrace you tenderly and am happy that you are mine, and I

Yours forever

At the very moment that Alexander was penning these touching words, the King of Prussia received the French Ambassador, Count Benedetti, in Ems. Two days later the famous "Ems Dispatch" made history.*

As the war was coming to the inevitable defeat of France, Russia realized only too well that a new and mighty but still a friendly power—the German Empire—was to be her neighbor. At the same time, the prestige of Russia and therefore of Alexander rose high in his own empire when Russia denounced the humiliating Black Sea clauses of the Treaty of Paris of 1856 which debarred Russia from becoming a naval power in that sea.†

The whole of Russia, to the dismay of England and Austria, rejoiced in the occasion. But Alexander, the monarch who received his nation's gratitude, by 1871 was ill and tired. Once more he traveled to Ems, his favorite spa, but this time he

---

* Karl Marx, then in exile, writing to a friend had this to say: "What the Prussian donkeys don't see is that the present [Franco-Prussian] war leads just as necessarily to war between Germany and Russia . . . and this war #2 will act as the wet-nurse of the inevitable Revolution in Russia."[3]

† Recently, another letter of the Czar to Katia was found. It is dated August 4 [16], 1870, and with it Alexander enclosed his minister's (Prussia did not rate then as a Great Power and therefore only ministers were accredited) report on the difficult situation of the French. The following is an excerpt from the letter:

". . . and I think before they enter [Paris] Napoleon [III] will not be an Emperor and it will be in Paris itself that the French will proclaim his fall and he will receive what he merits for all the unjust deeds towards us and to many others—excuse me, dear Doussia, for my impatience to leave you this evening, but you must understand that I can't be uninterested at all that is going on, still heavy in my heart the remembrance of Sebastopol [alluding to the Crimean War of 1854–55], which caused the death of my father [Emperor Nicholas I]. I see in all that as I told you, the hand of God who punishes the unjust."[4]

was joined by the Empress and their younger children. He purposely avoided staying in Berlin in order not to see "the entrance of the triumphant German troops." After a short cure in Ems, where Katia again joined him, staying at her own villa, they were back in Russia. The telegrams sent to Katia by the Czar clearly reflect his longing for his paramour.

Berlin, May 27 [June 8], 1871

To Petersburg

Arrived safely, not too tired. Received nothing [from Katia] at frontier, nothing here either. Am thinking of Mouche in the rooms which I occupy. You know what is going on in me.

Weimer, May 29 [June 10], 1871

To Petersburg

Safely arrived in Weimar, from where will send letter this evening. You know where my thoughts are and where I would like to find myself. Entreat you not to give way to discouragement.

Weimer, May 30 [June 11], 1871

To Petersburg

Thank you for telegram of yesterday. Will not fail to give information about villa in spa. You will understand with what feelings will see Ems again. May God grant us a happy reunion there. All my thoughts are with you.

Ems, May 31 [June 12], 1871

To Petersburg

Arrived here safely yesterday evening. You will understand with what feelings. Yesterday's telegram received this morning causes great pain. Assumptions are not worthy of you. Only received one letter in Berlin. The villa you wanted will be free [a two story villa, Petite Illusion, rented for Katia in Ems. The Czar lived across the river]. Will conform to your indications.

When Alexander returned to Russia, duty to inspect military preparedness again called him to take a trip to Caucasus, where he had not been since 1850. He traveled by the River Volga and stopped at Nizhni-Novgorod, Kazan, Simbirsk (a town that many years later would bear the name Ulianovsk in honor of a child just born there, Vladimir Ulianov, known later as Lenin), was "enthusiastically" received everywhere, and finally reached the Caspian Sea. Then, through the recently "pacified" North Caucasus, the Czar crossed the Great Caucasian Mountains and "in style" entered Tiflis, the capital of Georgia. By the middle of September he was in the Crimea, in his palace of Livadia. That the journey was more than successful was certainly proved by the loyalty of all Caucasian races, particularly the Moslems in the future Russo-Turkish War of 1877–78, when "very few" disturbances took place at that time. The Fifth Column of our days was not yet invented.

But for Alexander and Katia, the year of 1871 was more than noteworthy for personal reasons. For the first time, since their liaison began in 1866, Katia was expecting.

· 10 ·

BLESSED EVENTS

In the beginning of the winter, 1872, when the "season" really started, St. Petersburg was at the height of its gaiety. The court balls, which were usually given in January, were never so brilliant or so well attended. For Russia there were reasons for celebration. "The year that just ended [1871] no doubt will be one of the outstanding years of the second half of the 19th Century," wrote a Russian illustrated magazine. "For Western Europe," continued the article, "the year will be an era of a new order and a change of balance of power. For us, Russians, however the year passed was unforgettable, as it marked the end of humiliating conditions which the Paris Treaty imposed on Russia."[1] The theaters were crowded more than ever, for they had been enriched by many famous refugee actors and actresses who had fled from the bloody Paris *commune*. The celebrated Patti, Lucca, Pasca, Schneider and many others of lesser fame and lighter morals flocked to the richest, gayest, and most generous capital of Europe. "For that," philosophized the same illustrated, "we should thank Bismarck and the Communists. . . ."*

---

* Not only refugees flocked to St. Petersburg; many distinguished foreigners visited the city that year. Among them three notable Americans stopped in the capital of Russia and were received by the Czar. They were General William Tecumseh Sherman; the son of President Grant, Frederick Dent Grant; and the new U.S. minister to the Russian court,

The first court ball of the season in 1872 was given by their Majesties on January 21 [February 2] at the Winter Palace for 550 persons. That night the lady-in-waiting to Her Majesty, Princess Ekaterina Dolgorukova (Katia), whose new rank obliged her to be present, was significantly absent.

The indisputable fact that the *Favoritka* (Favorite: the word *mistress* [*soderzhanka*, or a kept woman, in Russian] was not used in polite society) of the Czar was pregnant didn't shock those who were in the know. After all, medical science then was not of the best. What did shock, frighten, and perturb many, however, was not so much the "event" or the age of the girl (that shocked some)* but the fact that the Emperor this time was "really in love" and what was even worse, in love with the "wrong person."

In his *Anna Karenina*, Leo Tolstoy masterfully characterized the attitude of society on Vronsky's love affair. "What also displeased her [Vronsky's mother]," wrote Tolstoy, "was, that according to everything she heard about the affair, it was not one of those brilliant, elegant worldly affairs . . . but some sort of desperate, Werther-like passion . . . that might involve him in some stupidity or other. . . ." In the case of the Czar, his "love affair" in addition was with an "outsider" and "provincial." To be forced to accept Katia in court circles, in the most exclusive, select, and snobbish court, was for the insiders more than distasteful. The mere fact that Katia was a "Princess" meant not very much. After all, weren't they the wrong Dolgorukovs,† so different from those one knew all one's life, the "real" Dolgorukys? What irritated the court circles even

---

Andrew Curtin. Former President Ulysses S. Grant visited St. Petersburg in the summer of 1878.

* The three eldest sons of the Czar were almost of the same age as Katia, namely twenty-eight, twenty-four, and twenty-two. The Cesarevna, the wife of the heir to the throne, was of the same age as Katia—twenty-three.

† The *Anna Karenina* Moscow princes Scherbatskys, though of aristocratic background, were considered "provincial" in St. Petersburg. Actually, the manners of Moscow society people, their speech, their entire mode of life—friendlier, warmer, more outspoken—differed from those of the more cold, cosmopolitan, snobbish, and reserved St. Petersburgers. The closest analogy in "grading" society in America would be the "smart

more were Katia's manners, indifferent, if not outright poor; her imperfect French, then an unpardonable sin; and finally her bad disposition, intense jealousy, and possessiveness—traits that even the Czar, no matter how much he was in love, could not help notice. All these, plus a total lack of tact, made Katia disliked by "most everyone" in St. Petersburg, and she became the object as if of "an official boycott." All "they" could hope for was that the imperial "passion" would end, and end soon.* This they were not to see. On the contrary. As the years went by, and her appointment as lady-in-waiting to Empress Marie was facilitated so that the Czar could meet his mistress in the open,† Katia began to be seen in the "right circles" more and more. It is beyond any doubt that the Empress knew all about Katia, but it is possible that she never realized what the girl really meant to her husband. One should also bear in mind that "keeping" a mistress was not only a Russian privilege. In those years, on the Continent as well as in England, a man of the world was not regarded as "smart" if he didn't have a "second establishment" of some kind. At any rate, the Empress was "aloof" to the affair, but she bore the isolation with fortitude and remarkable *chevalerie*, as we shall see later.

During the absence of the Empress, Alexander had clandestine meetings with Katia in his "private apartments" at the Winter Palace, and in May of 1872, while Marie was in Livadia, that household and the palace of Czarskoye Selo celebrated new

---

international set of New York" (St. Petersburg) compared with "old Boston" or "Philadelphia families" (Moscow).

* Incidentally, "nobody" in the "right circles" gave a thought to the fact that the Czar's brothers, the grand dukes Constantine and Nicholas, Sr., family men, had for many years kept mistresses, both actresses. Several children were born out of wedlock to both brothers. On the other hand, Alexander was "very severe" with his twenty-year-old son, Grand Duke Alexis, who fell in love with Alexandra Zhukovsky, a twenty-eight-year-old lady-in-waiting to his mother, eloped with her, and married her in Italy. The Czar did not recognize the marriage. Alexandra was the only daughter of his "beloved" tutor, the poet Vasilli Zhukovsky.

† In 1872 the popular St. Petersburg *Illustrated* significantly published the "Complete Genealogy" of the Dolgorukov family. Curiously enough, Katia's name was not even listed, though her parents were duly recorded! One must not forget that at this time anything referring to the imperial family was strictly censored.

arrivals. On May 9 in the latter residence, the Cesarevna gave birth to a son, her third, named George. Three days later, two days after Russian Easter Sunday, in the immense Winter Palace, Katia was delivered, "after terrible sufferings," of a boy, who with an inexplicable lack of humor also was named George.* Thus, almost to a day, Czar Alexander increased his family by two male members, a son and a grandson, and *La Grande Mademoiselle,* if there had been one, had thus ceased to exist.

The baptism of Katia's first child was secret. The baby received no family name and remained without a legal status for several years. Thanks to the short reminiscences of Katia's nurse, one Vera Borovikova, a simple but loyal peasant woman, we possess details that otherwise we would never have had.[2] According to Borovikova, the birth of the child was a "deep humiliation" to Katia. Now that she was a mother, the rank she held as an "unmarried maiden" lady-in-waiting was ridiculous. Moreover, confusion arose in addressing her. As we have seen, an unmarried princess is *Kniazhna,* a married one *Kniaghinia.* Katia, naturally, continued to be addressed as Mlle. Princess, or *Kniazhna.*

The Czar, however, Borovikova tells us, "simply adored the healthy beautiful child." Soon the baby, nicknamed Gogo (his three-day-older "nephew" George received the English nickname Georgie), was taken to a "discrete apartment" in the same house where resided Alexander's loyal and trustworthy friend, General Alexander Ryleev, "the Commandant Adjoint of the Imperial Headquarters." He was the godfather of Gogo and of Katia's subsequent children. In addition to Vera, a wet nurse

---

* The birth took place on a "simple divan," since the room didn't have a bed. An old soldier "informed" the Czar about the impending "event," and Alexander summoned the doctor. Sometimes a short note was exchanged. Here is one, which Katia kept undated and unsigned among her papers.

I wrote you at 7 *o'clock* to warn you that I had to go to the Service for the Dead, and that I proposed we should meet instead at 11 o'clock, but as our Confidant [Gen. Ryleev] was not at home I fear that my note did not reach you in time, so am writing you these lines in all haste. I love you and am happy to love you. Good-bye.

Yours forever [A]

and a "genteel maiden," a former classmate of Katia at Smolny by the name of Eiler, looked after the baby.

With the advent of summer, Gogo was moved to a *dacha* in Pavlovsk, then a residence of the Czar's brother Grand Duke Constantine, about a mile or so from Alexander's palace in Czarskoye Selo. Katia, however, occupied her own *dacha* in Czarskoye and took active part in the busy court functions and society life. As usual, during the month of July the court and the Czar moved to Peterhof, with the dutiful Katia following them. Once more she occupied her usual unpretentious *dacha* on the wrong side of the tracks.

On the sixth anniversary of the start of their love affair, Alexander penned the following touching letters:

Peterhof, Saturday July 1 [13], 1872
at three quarters past 11 at night

Our meeting just now and our two reunions in our dear Ozierki [one of the pavilions of Peterhof] have made me quite happy and I still feel full of our delirious bingerles. It was good to be able to exchange our congratulations in the way we love to do it, and I felt that we were haunted by the same precious memories. Thank you from the bottom of my heart, dear Dussia, for those that you gave me today, which gave me immense pleasure as all that comes from you my adored little wife, but I am grieved to have forgotten my little remembrance at Czarskoe Selo. Our drive in a "droshki" was also very pleasant, reminding me of those we took in preceding years. Alas, I must get back to my boring task, and I don't know when I will be able to get to bed. I embrace you, my Angel, from the bottom of my soul. I do not wish to end this day without telling you once again that I thank God for having inspired me six years ago with this sacred relationship for you, which has now become all my life. May God watch over us and preserve as from all new trouble!

Sunday, July 2 [14], at half-past 9 in the morning. Good morning, dear Angel, I only managed to get to bed at half past 1, but I slept well and dreamt of you, my adored little wife, and everything in me is overflowing again. This is a lovely morning, and I hope we can profit by it and take a walk along the left bank of the Babolovo Canal [a canal at the outskirts of Peterhof] where I will try to meet you not later than quarter past 3, and then afterwards again find ourselves in each other's arms.

I rejoice at the prospect of admiring you tonight at the wedding [of Captain of the Navy Dimitry Arseniev, A.D.C. to the Czar, and Barbara Skariatina], in a pretty gown, which charms me more and more each time. May God come to our aid and not forsake us. I still have a lot of things to do before Divine Service.

I embrace you, my Dussia, tenderly and am happy that you are mine, and I

Yours forever

A few days later the Czar, preoccupied with a forthcoming political meeting in Berlin, was interrupted by the arrival of foreign quests, reviews of the troops, and *Zoria* (or Retreat), a traditional bugle-call ceremony at sunset, at which the Czar, the court, and society were usually present. In addition, an unusually severe rainstorm broke out, which terrorized the superstitious population of the St. Petersburg area.

Wednesday, July 5 [17], 1872
at 3 in the afternoon

The review [in Krasnoye Selo, a few miles from Peterhof] passed off brilliantly and luckily was over before the rain, which started only after we had already got home, that is at quarter past 2, and now the thunder is rumbling, but I hope the weather will clear up by evening. As far as I can remember, in 1866 it rained continuously all through Retreat ceremony, at which I was so happy to see you present. If by any chance you again have a headache, but are coming out here in spite of it, I will be extremely worried for fear that this humidity might harm you.—I have been reading ever since the review and confess that I feel awfully tired, so I am going to try to get some sleep before dinner.

Quarter past 5 in the afternoon. I slept for about an hour, and on waking had the joy of receiving your letter, which as always flooded me with sunshine, and in which I found, more then ever, the reflection of our heart, which is happy to be but one single heart for the last six years. Oh, what it costs me to know that you are here and not to be able to fly to your side, my idol, my treasure, my All. I am in despair over this horrid thunderstorm which has started again as strong as before and this torrential rain, which has darkened my room to the point when I have to write with the lights on. If it goes on like this, the Retreat will have to be called off and postponed to tomorrow or the day after, but the weather can still change before 8 o'clock.

Three-quarters past 11 in the evening. Oh, how happy I was to see you at the Retreat, to have been able to shake hands with you and to see you enter my tent. My eyes must have expressed my feelings to you, as I read in yours that we were both overflowing, and we were just ready to forget everything and throw ourselves upon each other. I want you to know that I found you prettier than ever and that again I felt proud of my adored little wife, who is my idol, my treasure, my All.—I was also so pleased to see you in the theater, and so happy that afterwards we were able to spend at least a half-hour together, and kiss as we love to. I hope you will return safely and that you will not feel too tired. I still have a lot of business to finish before I go to bed. I embrace you, my Angel, from the depth of my heart, which is happy to love you and to belong to you forever.

Thursday, July 6 [18] at half-past noon. Good morning, dear Angel, I only got to bed at half-past 1 and I slept well, though somewhat restlessly.—I have just returned very satisfied with the maneuvers and must now get to work, which by no means is amusing, particularly since I do not have the hope of seeing you. May God watch over us and not forsake us! I love you and kiss you together with our dear Gogo very tenderly.

Yours forever

I only returned from the manuever at half-past 3, and could only get to bed at three-quarters past 3, so beg you to let me sleep until three-quarters past 4.

Thursday, July 6 [18], 1872
at 8 in the evening

After sending you my letter, I worked with two Ministers and wrote until half-past 2, when I went for a swim. We had dinner with guests at 3, after which I took an hour's rest, and I only got your dear letter at 6, just as I had to go to see the drill, and it was only on returning home just now that I had the joy of reading it. I found in it, more than ever, the complete reflection of our heart, which only lives for the sacred cult [relationship] that God inspired us with, and for which we do not cease to render thanks to Him. You will have seen from my letter how identical were our impressions of yesterday, when we felt prouder than ever to belong to each other, and to know that each of us was the life of the other.—We had a terrible downpour here yesterday also, as well as at dinner time, but the weather favored us during the drill, with which I was again perfectly satisfied.

At 11 in the evening. I had to interrupt my writing to get back to work, and only got to the theater around 9 [in Krasnoye Selo]. My eyes instinctively searched for you, and on the way back I walked a bit, sighing that we could not be together as we were yesterday. I feel you miss it as much as I do, and that we are both roaming about like lost souls. I have a lot of things to finish before I get to bed, but nevertheless I hope to be in bed not later than by 1 o'clock. Oh, what would I not give to find myself there with you, my adored little wife, my idol, my treasure, my all! May God not refuse us having that joy someday! I embrace you, Angel mine, from the bottom of my heart.

Friday, July 7 [19], at midday. Good morning, my Angel, having gone to bed at half-past 12 I slept very well, dreaming of you, my adored little wife. I have only just returned from attending the drill, with which I was entirely satisfied. It will again be a sad day for us, but what can one do? I foresee that tomorrow it will be impossible for me to leave here before 2, but at quarter past 3 I hope to join you at the Babolovo Canal, where we walk a bit, and then meet again in our dear little room. If your headache has not returned, I presume we will clench each other like mad cats, but if it has, we must absolutely be reasonable. Alas, now I must get back to my tiresome work. I embrace you, my Angel, with all my soul and am happy that you are mine, and I

Yours forever

May god not forsake us, and bestow His blessings on us.

Three days after Alexander penned these words, he attended the Officers' Steeplechase Races in Krasnoye—an outstanding social event of the season. If we believe Tolstoy, his hero Vronsky was one of the officers to take place in the race. What we know for certain is that the Czar was indeed displeased when he learned that many officers—among them Count Kutuzov, Prince Saxen-Altenbourg, and "three others"[3]—were "thrown off and hurt." We also know that Tolstoy had heard about this incident from his friend Prince Dimitry Obolensky, who shortly after the races joined the writer at Yasnaya Poliana. What we still don't know is whether Tolstoy, in describing the famous jealously scene between Karenin and Anna, had in mind the Czar and Katia.

By September, 1872, Alexander as well as Katia had departed for Berlin, where the momentous meeting of the "Three Emperors" was to take place.* The lovers traveled by separate

---

* The so-called "Drei Kaiser Bund"—"3 Emperors' League" (Russia, Austria, and Germany)—was eventually formed with the main aim of emphasizing "monarchial solidarity" against "subversive movements" and to "secure" for Germany support in the event of "trouble" with France. The league became a dead letter soon after the Berlin Congress of 1878,

trains and stayed in Berlin in different places: Alexander at the Russian Embassy, while Katia "descended" to the Hotel St. Petersburg, "a modest hostelry." Yet Katia was able, as a lady-in-waiting, to be present at all the official receptions taking place in connection with the Three Emperors' reunion.*

With the conclusion of festivities, Katia, who was from the beginning accompanied by Vava Shebeko and her loyal maid Vera (a former "serf girl" from Kostroma Province, the birthplace of the first Romanovs; she and Vava were constantly quarrelling, with Vava apparently "jealous" of Vera), received, as the maid wrote, "instructions" from the Czar to proceed to the Crimea, Katia's first such visit to the Holy of Holiest houses of the imperial family. Kuchak Sarai was the Tartar name for a very humble three-room "dwelling," situated less than a mile from the palace of Livadia and purchased by the Czar for Katia. She was "attended" there by an old soldier as a guard and a "very old woman by the name of Maria."

Two days after Katia's arrival to the Crimea, the maid Vera wrote, ". . . the Czar came to visit us." Every day at 4 P.M. he would arrive on horseback, accompanied by two cossacks. "He was always gay and kind," and "every morning" a man sent by General Ryleev would bring a letter from the Czar to Katia. Meanwhile, the still-ailing Empress remained in a specially built palace, Ereklik, situated in a pine tree forest, about two hundred feet above the Black Sea.

Despite his "relaxations," the Czar continued to work hard even in Livadia. Following are typical *billets-doux* exchanged by the lovers in the Crimea.

> My conference lasted until half-past 3. I am going out now to get some air, and will be back at about 4 o'clock.

---

in which Bismarck played the role of an "honest broker" and thus "displeased" Russia.

* Bismarck was somewhat blunt when he confided to the British ambassador that "for the first time in history the 3 Emperors sat down for dinner in the interest of peace. . . . I didn't give them a chance to say a word. The 3 imagined that they were much more of statesmen, than they really are."[4]

On Alexander's name's day, Katia received this message from him:

Livadia, August 30 [Sept. 11], 1872

Deeply touched and grateful for congratulations and wishes, which are mine also. May God bless return and reunion.

As usual, the missives bore no signatures.

Soon Alexander noticed that it was more than uncomfortable for the new family "group" (their son Gogo remained in St. Petersburg) to stay in his own house. He decided to buy a home from a "neighbor." It was renamed Biuk Sarai, also a Tartar name, meaning a Big Palace, and given to Katia. With a house in the Crimea, Katia became possessor of a "complete and duplicated" imperial residence, and from then on the regulated, monotonous life of a Russian sovereign was reflected in her life too.

"All winter," wrote Vera, "we lived in St. Petersburg, in spring we went to Germany, to Ems, where our Czar took a cure, so did the Kniazhna. From Ems we proceeded to Czarskoye Selo and at the end of August we would depart for the Crimea, the Emperor and the Empress to Livadia, and we to Biuk Sarai. There we remained 3 months, where the Czar . . . visited us daily, drinking tea and resting. . . ." The idyll lasted for a year until Katia was once more pregnant. Like the last time, her birth pangs were "terrible." Even the imperial *accoucheur*, the famous Dr. Anton Krasovsky, "tore his hair out, fearing a bad result," with the Czar, according to Vera, "more than in fear." Finally, despite all the anxieties, on November 7, 1873, in the Crimea, a girl, who was given the name of Olga, was born to Katia. At the same time, Vava Shebeko brought the little Gogo to the Crimea from St. Petersburg.

Following is a message that Katia sent to the Czar:

at 1 o'clock

Here is a letter from Vava [to you], brought by the courier who passed her on his way, and which I allowed myself to read. The dear little one is well, but very tired.

He will be able to get here at about 4 o'clock, but Vava prefers to stay at the hotel with him. She is so stubborn! Good-bye, I hope until 4 o'clock. I love you.

Yours forever

With the "family" rapidly increasing, it was more difficult than ever to hide the truth. Therefore a *secret de polichinelle* policy was devised, probably initiated and put into effect by Vava Shebeko. The children continued to live apart from their mother, and when a new baby was born, a whole new set of servants was hired. Shebeko became a "baroness," with Katia naïvely posing as the wife of a general, pretending that the children "belonged to others." "Despite the fact," wrote the maid, "that the English woman [the nurse] and Mademoiselle Eiler knew perfectly well whose children they were and who the Baroness and Madame la Generale really were, all servants, far from being stupid, continued to play the silly game."

While Katia was abroad, particularly in fashionable Ems, the "silly game" continued to be played, but in a different way. For instance, at their villa, Petite Illusion, the "family," with Katia at the head, was registered as "Frau Borovikov," Vera's family name. If Katia, accompanied by Vava Shebeko, took a carriage ride in the woods, they were "heavily veiled" in order that "nobody would recognize them," as Vera wrote. Yet "everyone" knew perfectly well who *les dames* really were. Since there was naturally more freedom abroad for the Czar, he, Vera tells us, "would come every morning to our villa and then go for a cure; he would return for the second time in the afternoon, bringing roses or violets to the Princess. . . . Then he would rest at the villa. . . ." To the Czar, life with Katia ("this immoral, sinful and pernicious liaison," as some called it) was "simply an enchanting change" from his usual complex existence. With Katia he reposed and became relaxed and sentimental.

In the Crimean, life was even simpler than abroad. While Vava Shebeko was away, the household was run by Vera "with the aid of only a one-legged old woman," who usually washed the dishes. Often a simple dinner, prepared by Vera, was served to the two lovers. Here are samples of messages sent by the Czar to Katia while in the Crimea.

Sebastopol, September 12 [24], 1873

Owing to bad weather we are returning by the land route [to Yalta]. I hope to be with you before 5 o'clock. Understand my impatience and where I am drawn to.

At three-quarters past 11. I am sending you the strawberries which I forgot just now and am utilizing the occasion to announce that I have managed to make arrangements so as to be able to dine with you, who are my idol, my treasure, my life. Be it thus and nothing else.—Good-bye until 3 o'clock [in the afternoon].

Yours forever

As winter came, duty once more brought Alexander, and with him Katia and the children, back to St. Petersburg, where new festivities awaited the Czar because of the forthcoming wedding of his only daugher, Maria, to Alfred the Duke of Edinburgh, the second son of Queen Victoria. Others who arrived at this time were Edward, Prince of Wales, and the Emperor of Austria, then on a state visit. The Empress was still abroad.*

---

* Returning to Russia from England at this time, because of the betrothal of his sister, were also Czarevich Alexander, with his wife, Marie. As the late Randolph S. Churchill tells us in the biography of his father, it was at the reception in honor of the Russian royal couple that Lord Randolph Churchill met his future American wife and the future mother of Winston Churchill, Jennie Jerome of Brooklyn, N.Y. It is amusing to speculate what would have happened to England if the Czarevich did not visit Britain and if the reception "from 3:30 to 7:30 P.M." on board the H.M.S. *Ariadne* on August 12, 1873, in Cowes did not take place.

Actually, Mr. Jerome was not greatly elated by the engagement of his daughter. "My daughter," he wrote to his future son-in-law, "although not a *Russian* Princess is an American and ranks precisely the same and you have doubtless seen the Russian settlement published claimed *everything* for the bride." The remark alluded to the generous Russian dowry given by the Czar to his daughter, Marie, amounting to two million (gold) rubles (about ten million dollars in American money today) with a stipulation that the capital was considered the bride's "property and the

Here is one of the few letters extant that Katia wrote to the Czar:

Rec'd. in Moscow
Jan. 26 [Feb. 7], 1874

Thursday, Jan. 24 [Feb. 5], 1874
at 1 o'clock in the afternoon

Good morning, dear Angel, I love you and everything in me is overflowing terribly. I again slept very badly and feel sad because we are not together [the Czar was in Moscow, entertaining the Prince of Wales]. My thoughts follow you into your study where we spent such happy moments, but now I feel so sad it is just unbearable. I do not know what to do with myself and everything in me aches. Oh, my God, when will we be able to never separate again, to be together everywhere and always, that is the dream of our lives. I have not yet received your telegram, and that makes me twice as sad. Oh, how lonely I feel, it is simply unbearable. I shall send you my telegram and then I have to make some very boring visits. I love you madly.

At 10 o'clock in the evening. I had to pay some bills, then decided to go and see the apartment which is to be rented on the Galernaya* and after that went for a walk. I made several visits without finding the people at home, and remained with the little one from quarter-past 4 to

---

income of 5% interest is for her separate and exclusive use and enjoyment." Marie became the Duchess of Edinburgh.

Incidentally, Jennie later became a close and "dear friend" of the Grand Duchess Marie and had "extensive correspondence with her throughout the years."[5]

* Galernaya No. 47 was Katia's apartment, a "gift" from the Czar. Though somewhat farther than her former residence from the Winter Palace, the new apartment was in a fashionable part of the city. The house extended up to the elegant English Quay. The neighbors included such illustrious names as princes Tenishevs, Paskevitches, counts Vorontzovs, Bobrinskys, and Grand Duke Vladimir, Alexander's son. Katia's new home was a far cry from Basseynaya, yet she still had no home of her own. The Galernaya house, despite aristocratic neighbors, was a so-called "income house," or in today's parlance an apartment house. The contract for the "rent" was made in the name of Katia's younger brother Michael.[6]

half-past 7. I had dinner with Gogo and then had to put my belongings in order, I have not been able to touch them ever since I moved in. Your good telegram reached me when I returned from my visits and filled me with sunshine, it is my only consolation when I am far away from you. Oh, I am so happy that you were pleased by the letter I wrote you that night, and I understand only too well how you are haunted, as I am, by the memories of the day-before-yesterday's ball,* and that you sigh when you miss seeing me in your rooms; it was so cosy there, and now I feel so sad that it is simply awful. I roam about like a lost soul, I feel a terrible weariness which I never felt in your presence, it is purely spiritual. I thank God you are feeling well and that you were able to rest in the railway car. It must have been a rest for you after all those festivities which are so enervating, especially for us who are only interested in ourselves and who only live for the feeling of belonging to each other and who have nothing in common with the rest of the world, and that is what bears us up. It is our treasure that helps you everywhere, so we have enough about which to be thankful to God, for having inspired us with this love that has become our life. Yes, He watches over us, and may He reunite us happily Monday at half-past 3, and bless your stay in Moscow. It overflows in me more than ever, and I feel more than ever what you mean to me. I cannot live without seeing you, everything is so empty that it is simply unbearable. The children are well; Gogo, who was very nervous today, cried when I told him you were not here. He is so sweet that one cannot but help adoring him. I feel that you are with us in thought, and that you are sad without us.

May God bestow His blessings on us. I love you and am

Yours forever

---

* The ball, on Jan. 22 [Feb. 3], took place at the palace of the Czar's brother, the Grand Duke Nicholas. Katia was present in her official capacity as a lady-in-waiting. The Czar, right after the ball, went to Moscow, where he remained four days. Katia followed him.

A rare 1832 engraving of the future Queen Victoria, when she was still styled as Alexandrina.

Marie, Princess of Hesse and the Rhine; daughter of Grand Duke Louis II of Hesse and the Rhine; wife of Emperor Alexander II of Russia.

Alexander II and his Empress-wife, Marie. A photo of 1872.

Emperor Alexander II hands to the Minister of Interior, Count Lanskoy, the Manifesto liberating the serfs, which he signed on February 19, 1861. Contemporary engraving.

ABOVE: *Portrait of 1890 of Countess Marie Berg, Katia's younger sister. (From the collection of her late son, Count Boris Berg.)*

LEFT: *Katia in 1866.*

RIGHT: *Katia in a uniform of "Smolianka".*

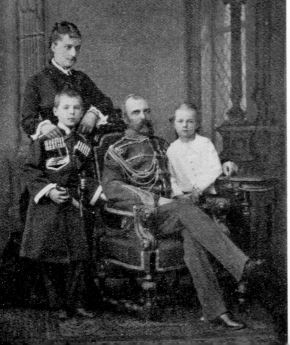

Alexander II's family:
(LEFT TO RIGHT) *Paul, Serge,*
Alexander II, Marie, Alexis,
Alexander III, his wife, Marie,
and their son, Nicholas—the
last Czar.
A photo of 1873.

Alexander II's "second
family"—*Katia, Gogo, and Olga*
A photo taken in 1880.

Katia in 1875.

Czar Alexander II with (LEFT TO RIGHT) *his son, Alexis, his daughter, Marie, and her husband, Albert, Duke of Edinburgh. (A photo taken at the time of their marriage in 1874.)*

Katia in 1880.

The surrender of Osman-Pasha, the Commander-in-Chief of the Turkish Army, in the War of 1877.
(Painting in the Winter Palace, N. Dmitriev-Orenburgsky.)

Count D.A. Miliutin,
the Minister of War.

The chapel erected on the spot of the
attempted assassination of Alexander II
near the Winter Palace in April, 1866.
The chapel was destroyed by the Reds.

Gogo and Olga. An oil painting by Constantine Makovsky made in the 1880's.

ABOVE LEFT: *General Aide-de-Camp Count A.V. Adlerberg 2nd, Minister of the Court.*

ABOVE RIGHT: *Oil painting of Czar Alexander II by Paul Bulow—about 1870. (From the collection of Mr. Henri Antoville.)*

RIGHT: *Alexander II's "liberal" brother, Grand Duke Constantine. (The oil painting was in the Naval College of St. Petersburg.)*

An artist's rendering of the scene of assassination. (An engraving that appeared in the Russian Illustrated Magazine on March 11, 1881.)

The Imperial coach (armored). Said to be a gift from Napoleon III.

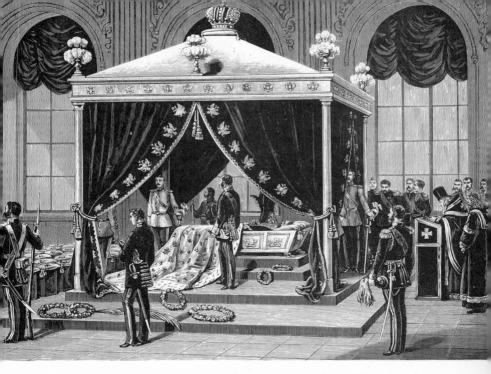

Funeral service at the Winter Palace. A contemporary illustration.

Emperor Alexander II on his deathbed. A contemporary photo engraving.

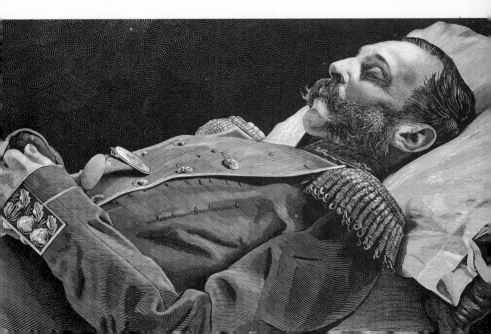

ABOVE:
BROTHERS OF ALEXANDER II.
Grand Duke Constantine   *Grand Duke Michael*
BELOW:
BROTHERS OF ALEXANDER III.
Grand Duke Vladimir   *Grand Duke Alexis*

Gogo in a Naval Guard
uniform. A photo of 1894.

Katia, Jr. A photo of 1883.

Family of the new
Emperor Alexander III.
(LEFT TO RIGHT) Nicholas
(the last Czar), George,
the Empress Marie, Olga,
Michael, Xenia, and
Alexander III. A photo
of 1892.

Katia, her daughter,
Katia, and the latter's
husband, Prince Serge
Obolensky, in Nice in
1921. (Collection of
Colonel Serge Obolensky.)

ABOVE AND RIGHT:
*Katia's and her
sister Marie's graves
in Nice.*

PRINCESSE
SERENISSIME
CATHERINE MICHAILOVNA
YOURIEVSKY
NÉE P^sse DOLGOROUKY
VEUVE
DE L'EMPEREUR
ALEXANDRE
1849-19??

ГРАФИНЯ
МАРІЯ МИХАЙЛОВНА
БЕРГЪ
Р???? КНЯЖНА

*"Church of the Blood,"
erected in St. Petersburg on
the spot of the Czar's
assassination in March 1881.
Photograph by Robert L.
Sammons. (Courtesy of
Town & Country magazine.)*

Here is the Czar's note to Katia, written at the same time as her letter:

> At 1 o'clock in the afternoon
> [in Moscow]

You are quite right in wanting to stop here for a day's rest, and I hope to see you at the Kremlin, but not before half-past 5.—I have so much more to do that my head is quite dizzy. Good-bye.

> Yours forever

By May, Alexander, alone this time, was once more off to stay with his sister Olga, the Queen of Württemberg, and to be present at the wedding of his niece, Grand Duchess Vera, daughter of Grand Duke Constantine, to the young Duke Eugene Württemberg. Here is the letter written from the capital of Württemberg.

> Stoudtgardt [sic], April 24 [May 6], 1874
> at 4 in the afternoon

Well, so here I am, having arrived safely after getting your nice telegram yesterday before I left Berlin, and that is my only consolation. They have just brought me the one you sent this morning.—Yes, I do feel that in spite of the sorrow of our separation, we both are also sustained by the treasure we bear in ourselves.—They have lodged me in the same rooms that I occupied in 1867 on my return from Paris, when I was so depressed at having left you after the ten days of bliss we spent there together, and at the prospect of only seeing you again in October. At least this time I hope God will reunite us within 16 days. [The lovers were to meet in Ems, after Alexander's visit to Queen Victoria in England, his first visit since his "enchantment" with her in 1839.] I forgot to tell you that I went to see Madame Oubril [the wife of the Russian ambassador to Germany] both on arriving in Berlin and before leaving there, she spoke to me with great affection about Mouche and even about you, my idol, my life.

At half-past 10 in the evening. We have since had a family dinner and a gala performance in honor of the betrothed which has just ended, and happily without a supper. They gave Wagner's opera Loongreen [sic], which I heard for the first time; there are some very beautiful parts, but I confess that towards the end I nearly fell soundly asleep. To get back to my quarters I had to pass through icy rooms owing to the cold outside, and as the temperature in the room in which I am writing to you is not above 12 degrees, I am freezing. I have put on my overcoat to try to get warm, but am nevertheless shivering. Oh, my Angel, I cannot bear it any longer, I do so yearn for you and would so like to be warmed by you, my adored little wife, and I feel more than ever that my whole life is in you.—May God continue to watch over us four, and bring us together again as soon as possible. I miss our dear Pupussia [Gogo] terribly, and keep thinking of all his sweet little mannerisms.—I still have some writing to do, but hope to get to bed before midnight.

I embrace you, my Dussia, from the bottom of my heart, which is happy to love you and to belong to you forever.

Thursday, April 25 [May 7], at 11 in the morning. Good morning, dear Angel, I slept well and went for an early walk with Mylord [one of his favorite dogs]. The weather was rather fresh. I had coffee at my sister's, and she kept me until now, as we thoroughly discussed everything that was of interest to her. I have just sent off my telegram and am impatiently waiting for yours, for it is my only consolation far away from you, my idol, my treasure, my life. For I am yours and only breathe for you. May God watch over us and grant us the joy of seeing each other soon!

At half-past 3 in the afternoon. This is the hour when we usually were together; so as I am free, it is a necessity for me to talk to you, be it only by writing. After lunch at my sister's, I had to make my visits and then went for a walk in the beautiful garden which belongs to the Castle, a thing I was never able to do since my departure from Petersburg. The weather has become somewhat milder, however as a precaution I wore my military greatcoat so as to cover my chest, which will prove to you, dear Dussia, that I do not neglect the duty of taking care of myself for the adored being whose property I am proud to be. [That year the Czar suffered from several severe attacks of asthma.] Good-bye, now I want to take a rest.

Because Alexander had at last a little more free time, his letters were more lengthy. The letter from Stuttgart continues:

At half-past 10 in the evening. After the family dinner at half-past 5, I went for a drive in a victoria all alone, and at 8 we gathered together for a reception at my sister's, where we began to by listening to the singing of the local Singverein and then I played cards; and now I am back again and happy to be able to resume my correspondence. I hope my letter from Berlin will have reached you by this evening and will have given you a bit of sunshine, by proving to you that everything in those rooms in which we spent so many happy moments together was full of memories of you. But you know, Angel mine, that everywhere and always I am constantly with you in thought. I hope our dear Pupussia still sometimes thinks of his Papa who adores him and who is sad without him, as well as without our dear Oly. May God keep them for us, and not forsake us in the future. I kiss you tenderly.

Friday, April 26 [May 8], at half-past 9 in the morning. Good morning, dear Angel of my heart, I slept well and dreamt of you, my treasure, my idol, my life. I dreamt that we were together, happily without any consequences. Today it is a year since we met in the evening, after the departure of the King of Prussia, at our dear Zarskoye Selo, where every corner of my rooms is full of tender memories for us. May God bring us safely back there, after we have the joy of meeting in Ems.—I have just taken my morning walk, the weather was milder, and had coffee with my sister.—I must get back to my papers, and my niece's wedding will take place at 1 o'clock.

At 3 in the afternoon. Here I am, back from the double Russian and Protestant ceremony, and everything went off very decently. You understand, dear Dussia, what my thoughts and prayers consisted of: that God should not refuse us the joy of one day going through the same ceremony! And here comes your telegram, which proves how well you guessed what was going on within me.—I am glad that my Berlin letter brought you a ray of sunshine, and I could not refrain from laughing when I read that you were entrusting your letter to Pounine, who is to join me at Amsterdam. I don't think that Emmanuel would be very flattered by that name, but I will be twice as happy to see him arrive.*

At half-past 7 in the evening. Since writing the above, I had a rest, and at 4 there was a family dinner, after which the newlyweds left for Friedrichshafen, where they will spend a few days before going to see the husband's parents in Silesia; and I went for a short drive in a victoria, and a walk, all alone, which always suits me best when I am away from you, my idol, my life. I have just got back and am happy to be able to chat with you, at least by writing, at the hour when we usually went to see our dear children, whom I miss terribly, as well as their adorable Mama. To console myself I keep looking at the dear locket with your portrait and that of our Angel Gogo—the one he used to love to open, crying: "Mama-Naya!" Oh, what a joy it will be to see you again at Ems!

At quarter past 10 in the evening. I have just this moment returned from a family reception, where I had my game of cards, and still have to do some writing, after which I hope to get to bed before midnight. Alas, why cannot we celebrate in honor of the newlywed couple, and clench to

---

* Prince Emmanuel Meschersky, Mouche's first husband, then the military attaché in the Russian legation of Brussels, Belgium. Meschersky probably accompanied the Czar to Amsterdam, whence the Czar proceeded to England. Pounine was probably taken from the name of a "fallen" character in Turgenev's short story "Punin and Baburin" written and published in 1874, in Paris. The allusion to Emmanuel is not clear.[7]

each other like hungry cats. But I confess that I do not envy the young husband!* I embrace you tenderly, Angel mine.

Saturday, April 27 [May 9] [1874]
at half-past 2 in the afternoon

Good morning, dear Angel, I had a terribly restless night and on wakening I had the joy of getting your dear letter of Tuesday, April 22 [May 4], which revived me and filled me with sunshine. But owing to my paper work and to the great review which was held at half-past 10, it was impossible for me to write you and that is all I can tell you at present, for I have to get back to my work and so will continue later on.

At three quarters past 4. It is only just now that I finished my work, and I must confess that I can't go on any more and am going to take a rest. All that you write about the sad story concerning my nephew and the conversations I had to have about him here have made me feel quite depressed.†—I hope that sleep, if I can get any, will calm me.

At 8 in the evening. I only slept for hardly half an hour, it did me a lot of good and at half-past 5 I had to go to my sister's for a family dinner, after which I had to talk to my sister, always on the same sad subject. It was only today, as we had agreed to, that my brother spoke to her

---

* Beauty was not one of the strong virtues of the young Grand Duchess Vera. Three years after her marriage she became a widow. Her twin daughters Olga († 1932) and Elsa († 1936,) married brothers, the princes of Schaumburg-Lippe.

† "The sad story," which echoed throughout the entire world, humiliated the Czar and his family. The twenty-four-year-old Grand Duke Nicholas, son of the Czar's brother Constantine and brother of Vera, the bride, "violently" fell in love with an American "world-famous adventuress," to say the least, one Harriet Blackford, née Ely, of Philadelphia. Forbidden to marry her, Nicholas resorted to a theft of his mother's jewels in order, after selling them, to elope with Harriet abroad. Harriet put the stolen jewels in the safekeeping of the American minister at the legation in St. Petersburg. Nicholas was arrested, proclaimed "insane," and banished to Turkestan and never forgiven. Harriet was arrested, then expelled to Belgium. She died penniless in Nice in 1886. The Grand Duke died in 1918. The American Minister, Marshall Jewell, was made to resign his post.[8]

about it, and she took it more calmly than could have been expected, saying that she had already felt it coming before he left.—As I had not taken any fresh air since the review, I have just had a drive and a walk, again all alone, in a very fresh and humid evening after the rain, dreaming of you, my adored Angel and of our dear children. Everything you write me about our dear Gogo has merely strengthened my desire to see him, together with his adorable Mama, and I hope God will grant us that happiness in 12 days, at Ems. You alone can understand the awful emptiness I feel when far away from you, my idol, my life, because you only share it too much yourself. It is so true that all my life is left in you, and yours in me. We want each other and nothing else and everything fades and disappears for us in the presence of that sacred cult which is our life.—I must leave you to go to a family reception at my sister's. At least I am happy not to have to mingle with society, for which I care but little.

At 10 in the evening. Here I am back again already, and I must write to catch the courier who will leave tomorrow morning. I count on sending you one other letter Tuesday evening from Flessingen, which I hope will still reach you in Petersburg, and then I will try to write you via the London mail, according to your indications, otherwise you would be without a letter for 9 days.—May God bless my stay in England,* your voyage and our reunion in Ems. I embrace you, my Angel, from all my soul.

Sunday, April 28 [May 10], at three-quarters past 9 in the morning. Good morning, dear Angel, I slept well and everything in me overflows with love and tenderness for you, my idol, my life. I read your dear letter of yesterday again, in which in every line I find the reflection of our heart. But I am as worried as you are over Michel's impudence of re-

---

* While in England, the Czar received an "insulting letter" from a Russian revolutionary residing in Europe. The letter mocked Alexander about "your theft-committing nephew." The whole story broke in English and European papers.[9]

turning to Petersburg; provided he does not become a source of some new kind of trouble for you.*—You indicate the Hôtel du Nord, instead of the Hôtel de Hollande, which is not on the list at all, and you do not say where it is. I suppose it must be in Cologne, instead of the Hôtel de Russie, but you will have time to let me know.—The day after tomorrow, on our Angel Gogo's birthday, you know where all my thoughts will be. May God keep him safely for us, and not forsake us in the future! I embrace all three of you from all my soul, and am happy that you are mine, and I

Yours forever

From the time of the Crimean War until 1874, asserted an English writer, when Queen Victoria's son, Alfred, married Alexander's daughter, England remained hostile to Russia. England's instinct for world power and her jealously of rivals were perhaps the dominating factors in this attitude. However, marriages of royal houses can do much to shift national sympathies. When, at twenty-one, Marie Alexandrovna, the Grand Duchess of Russia, was "sacrificed" at the altar of "cordial relationship," the Czar remarked: "It is for her happiness, but the light of my life is gone."† "The light" of the Czar's life, later to be the mother of Queen Marie of Roumania, was not as good-looking as her brothers. She was plump and brusque in her manners and talked about being "the daughter of the Czar of all the Russias." Actually she disliked the English, and their climate definitely did not agree with her. When the Prince of Wales heard that his brother was going to marry

---

* Katia's brother, the "black sheep" of the family, was usually in some "trouble," mostly concerning money and women.

† "The Junoesque Duchess," wrote Sir Henry Ponsonby, private secretary to Queen Victoria, "nurses herself which somewhat scandalizes prim English ladies." Yet of Marie's five children only one died by the age of twenty-five; the others Marie, Queen of Roumania; Victoria, Grand Duchess of Russia; and the wife of Grand Duke Cyril, the last Pretender, died in their sixties. One, Beatrice, the wife of Alfonso, Infante of Spain, is still alive. She was born in 1884![10] The Czar now intensely disliked Victoria, whom he called a "silly old fool," and his daughter Marie "discovered that the Queen drinks whisky, sometimes with water, generally without."

a Romanov, he was amused, even cynical. Victoria sent the Russian bride a sprig of myrtle and a prayer book. She also gave Alfred a prayer book—"a plain one." At this time it looked as if old animosities had died down—at least temporarily. As a token of a new friendship, several English towns returned to Russia the guns captured in the Crimean War. It may be added, however, that the city of Edinburgh itself did not relinquish its trophies. The Duke of Edinburgh might marry a Russian, but the guns remained on Carlton Hill. "Still it is possible that the Scots would have sent them back if the Russians had been willing to pay carriage."[11]

The Russians, not to be outdone by the English, promptly rechristened their newest frigate *Alexander Nevsky*, to *Herzog Edinbourgsky*.

The young royal couple had hardly had time to settle down when the Czar himself appeared in London. Victoria, his old flame, greeted him at the foot of the staircase of Windsor Castle; she drove him around; the Czar attended dinners, balls, and parties. Yet scarcely had he set foot back on Russian soil when he heard that the India Office had advised the British cabinet to order a naval demonstration in the Baltic, the reason—a Russian advance in Central Asia. (The Russian advance culminated in the conquest of the Khanates of Kokand, Bokhara and, Khiva.) The Czar pleaded that the advance had nothing to do with any "evil designs" on India, but all in vain. The encroachment of Russia into the heart of Asia is "a threat to India. . . . The advance must be stopped." It was not. Another deadlock, another complication. The prayer books (Marie's and "the plain one"), the returned guns, the renamed frigate— all were forgotten. At the moment it looked like the first of many storms to come. Yet in those days of gentlemen's diplomacy, everything worked out to a peaceful conclusion, with Disraeli reporting to the Queen that though the "Russians are as touchy as Yankees" they are nevertheless "reasonable."[12]

Though Victoria's farewell telegram to Alexander was to assure her former "love" that both "countries will remain on friendly, nay cordial terms," this greeting could not dispel the tide of political rivalry between Russia and England. As the "sick man" of Europe, as the Turks were then called, once more recovered, the "glowing mirage" of friendship "vanished in the twinkling of an eye."*[13]

---

* As one English historian acidly observed, the Czar's "health [in England] suffered under the strain of the hospitable attentions." Incidentally, the Queen at first refused to prolong the Czar's visit beyond the date that had been fixed by her. Disraeli interceded, however, and she complied.[14]

THE LAST CRUSADE

For Czar Alexander, the last two years of peace before war broke out in the Balkans in the spring of 1877 were far from easy. He tried at all costs to avoid war, for he knew only too well (the disastrous Crimean War was a good reminder) that no matter how war ends, it always brings upheaval and an increase of political unrest. "Of course," the Czar said to the Minister of War, D. A. Miliutin (on July 27, 1876), "if they will force us to fight, we'll do so but I personally mustn't give the smallest pretext toward a war. . . ."[1] And the British ambassador to St. Petersburg reported that the Russian government "was embarrassed" by the "movement" (for war), which forced the government and the nation to "a policy from which there was no means of recovery."[2] In addition, "difficulties" with his "secret family,"* as some called his "new" household, his failing health, several deaths in the Romanov family (in the 1870s Alexander lost his sister Marie,

---

* While in Europe the Czar stopped alone in Hesse, from where he sent the wire below:

Jugenheim, Hesse
June 14 [26], 1875

Mme. Danenberg [Katia's "cover" name]
Hotel de Tome, Berlin

Thank you for telegram and dear letter. Feel same emptiness as you do, after happy time. May God bless journey and return. Embrace you and little angel tenderly.

Alexander

his second son by Katia, his grandson Alexander, and a nephew—also named Alexander)—all these caused him to be anxious, nervous, and tense. Rumors circulated in Europe that he "seriously thought of abdicating" because of his health. The court doctor, Serge Botkin, who examined the Czar in June, 1876, found him "very exhausted," but with "no dangerous symptoms whatsoever."[3] Botkin felt, however, that the "exhaustion" might have been due partly to "excesses in sexual relations."[4] For Alexander the only possibility for "happiness" lay in the death of his wife. This he, as a Christian, even a pious man, let alone as the Czar of Russia, could not even "think" of. Yet this was exactly what he and his mistress wished and lived for. On the threshold of the new year of 1876 Alexander dispatched to Katia the following letters.

St. Petersburg
Wednesday, December 31, 1875 [Jan. 12, 1876]
at three quarters past 1 in the afternoon

Before going to see my sister [Alexander's eldest sister, Marie (1819–76), the widow of the Duke Maximilian Leuchtenberg and at this time the morganatic wife of Count Gregory Stroganov (1820–79), died on February 21, 1876], who thank God is slightly better, I only want to tell you that your good letter filled me with sunshine and that I keep ceaselessly thanking God for the happiness He has accorded me in you, my adored Angel, my idol, my treasure, my life. May he continue to watch over us, and not forsake us in the future.

At three-quarters past 10 in the evening. You must have felt my prayers during the Te Deum this evening [New Year's Eve church service] and you know what they contained. I thanked God from the very depth of my soul for all the happiness He granted us during this year that is about to end, and which I am sad to leave behind. May the one which is about to begin be as lucky for us. May God preserve you and our two little Angels, who are our joy, and may He bless your delivery and give you back all the happiness you have never ceased giving me for nearly ten years. Oh, how happy I was a short while ago when I was with you and our dear children, whose appetites and dispositions were both brilliant. But I was sad not to be able to bring them back and to be present at their going to bed. Dear Pupussia was as distressed as I was by it, and you saw how happy he was to look at the pictures spread out on my knees, which dear Oly wanted to look at also. Their tenderness to us is truly touching, and one cannot but adore them, as well as their dear little Mama, in whom all is concentrated for me. Now I will finish all I have to do, so as to be able to go to bed as soon as we have exchanged our New Year greetings.

At midnight. Just another word before I do go to bed. I am happy that we were able to exchange our New Year greetings as we like to do, and I hope it brings us luck. I embrace you, my Angel, from all my soul.

Thursday, Jan. 1 [13], 1876. I start a new day by congratulating you and wishing you all possible happiness, which I wish I could give you, and which is our dream. My heart overflows with love and tenderness for you, my adored Angel, and I can only think of the moment when I will be with you and our dear children again—I must get back to my work, and after Divine Service I shall go to make my visits. Luckily it is not so cold.—I embrace you from all my soul and am happy that you are mine, and I

Yours forever,

May God not forsake us, and bless us!

And from Katia to Alexander:

St. Petersburg
Wednesday, December 31, 1875 [Jan. 12, 1876]
at 4 o'clock in the afternoon

Our nice chats did me a lot of good, and I feel we are thinking about our angels, who are our joy, and that everything in us is overflowing more than ever. Yes, it is certainly rare to see a child be as tender to his parents as Gogo is, so I can well understand that you adore him and that you are happy to have such sweet children. I feel sure that your sister will get well, as she is already better. I find the Russian play very pretty, but it is boring that they are always too long. [Russian dramatic plays were, in the 1870s, not as popular or in fashion as the Italian opera and ballet. The Russian opera came into its own later on.] I would like to give birth as soon as possible [Katia's third child, Boris, was born on April 4, 1876], for I feel so heavy, but I am not grumbling, because it is my fault, and I confess I cannot be without your fountain, which I love so, and therefore after my six weeks are over I count on renewing my injections, for I can do nothing halfway. Oh, how I love you, you are my life, my happiness, my all, and everything for me is concentrated in you; therefore nothing can be compared to adoring each other as we do, and to be able to say to oneself that the adored being belongs to you alone, and to have nothing to reproach oneself for. I know you could never have been unfaithful to me, for you are too honest, and so you belong to me alone for 8 years now [since the "fatal" day in 1866*]. That is what makes you proud and raises you in your own eyes in every way. May God continue to watch over us, and may He bless my delivery, and preserve us as well as our children. Our hearts are full of gratitude to Him for all the happiness we

---

* It is reasonable to assume that during these eight years the Czar, remarkable for him, was faithful to Katia. "The gossips," stated Miliutin, "regarding Emperor's love adventures," were spread by "intrusive women themselves." Alexander was then fifty-eight years old.

However, in a 1968 article in the Paris magazine *Vozrozhdenie (Resurrection)* describing the life of the late Princess Maria Tenishev, born Piatkovsky, a White Russian exile hinted that she was the daughter of the Emperor Alexander II and was born in 1873.[5]

That the Czar, a great grandson of Catherine the Great, became a sensualist and an erotic, especially in his later years, there is no doubt. Baron Nicholas Wrangel († in 1915), a patron of the arts and an "attaché to the Ermitage staff," found a collection of erotica in Alexander's "private cabinet" at the Winter Palace. These pictures were pasted on the backs of "harmless" objects. A recent researcher claims that he has seen some of the *au naturel* pencil sketches of Katia made by the Czar which are now reposed in the museum of the Winter Palace. Actually, the Czar, who took up painting in his early days, was not a bad artist.[6]

have enjoyed this year. First of all for having blessed our
stay at Ems and then in Crimea, and I hope He will come to
our aid and bless us, for He knows how we miss His blessing.
I thank you again for everything, and do not forget that you
are my life and everything for me is concentrated in you. I
understand how you enjoy the presence of the children, and
their appetites, and Gogo's tenderness is truly touching. I hope
Oly's cough will not develop into something serious. This
awful cold makes me shiver, it is so enervating. I am happy
you sleep well now, and that Botkin is satisfied with your
condition. I feel everything is overflowing in us more than
ever, and that we are more than ever in love with each other.
I hope God will grant us a happy year and will preserve us
for each other's sake.

The same day the Czar replied:

at 7 o'clock in the evening

The children were in a very good mood just now, Gogo
delighted to play on your knees and listen to stories, and their
appetites at dinner were very good. I could see that you were
enjoying it all, and everything in us was overflowing more than
ever. I find the card and the letter from the Princess Charles
[Princess Charles of Prussia, born Marie, Princess Saxe-
Weimar, whose husband, the brother of Kaiser Wilhelm I,
visited St. Petersburg in November, 1875] priceless, and what
was also unconventional was the joy Vava [Shebeko] got out
of kissing your bingerles [?], which was big. I very well know
that no contact and no touch could produce any effect on it,
which it does only for me; and this should make you proud,
for it is "not a fish" only for me alone, as it has proved to you
many times in your escapades of bygone days, so if any other
woman were to touch it, it would not react. I love you, you
my joy, my All.

At 10 o'clock in the evening. Our nice evening left a lovely
impression on me. Gogo was so happy to look at the pictures
as he sat on your knees, and he was upset because we did not
go to put him to bed. I love our chats, and reading together,

and I hope you will have time to finish your papers and read your Gospel, so as to be able to go to bed after we have seen each other. I hope to meet you somewhere tomorrow. Thank you again, dear Angel, for all the happiness you gave me this year. May God give it back to you, and may He preserve you and bless us. I love you so terribly, my only consolation is you, so you can say to yourself that in all things you only give me joy. I am going to have tea and then I shall fly to you. It is such a sorrow to part with the year we spent so happily.

January 1 [13], 1876, at 1 o'clock in the morning. I congratulate you, dear adored angel, on the new year which has just begun, and wish you all the happiness possible. May God preserve you, and me and the children, and may He not abandon us, but bless us. I enjoyed our love-making madly, and am still all steeped in it. You are so tempting, it is impossible to resist! There is no word for this delirium. I felt that we were haunted by our children, and everything over-flowed more than ever.

At three-quarters past 11 in the morning. I congratulate you again, dear adored Angel, and wish you all possible happiness. May God reward you as you deserve to be, and may He preserve us and grant us what we pray to Him for. Please join me before the half-hour. I clasp you in my arms and embrace you, my angel, my all. May God bless our dear angels, and keep them from all sickness.

Yours forever

Alexander's hopes that the New Year would be as "lucky" as the past one were not realized. After several deaths within two months in his family, Alexander lost his third child by Katia within a week after he was born. (Boris was buried in Czarskoye Selo.) "How much sadness and tears," wrote the maid Vera. Also from her we learn the circumstances under which Boris was born. It is worthwhile to quote *in toto* the Russian maid's unaffected story: "Late at night," wrote Vera, "at our house in the Galernaya Street, the Kniazhna, feeling the impending birth of the child, woke me up. I always slept near her bedroom. She made me dress and said 'Let us drive to the [Winter] Palace to the Emperor. I must give birth there!' So we went out to take a cab and, as it happens, not one in sight! So we walked, poor serfs of God. As her pains got worse, Kniazhna would lean on my shoulder and say: 'Vera, please carry me, I can't go farther!' I was unable to do that, as Katia was big and tall, and I had no strength to hold her. Nevertheless, we limped somehow to the Senate [Square]. There we got a cab, and a lean, beaten up horse dragged us to the Palace. As I brought Kniazhna to the door [a private and secret entrance], an old grenadier [retired invalided soldiers composed a special platoon, "The Palace Grenadiers," for services at the imperial residences] took her from me and at once by a lift brought her to the restroom of the Czar. Meanwhile, I ran to the babushka [the usual name for a midwife] and sent her to the Palace and then drove to [Dr.] Krasovsky [the palace *accoucheur*]. While I was collecting them all God gave Kniazhna a son, Boris, and there was the Czar alone with the midwife arriving when it was all over. . . ." The father, the Czar was a "babushka," after all. For nine days Katia remained at the palace, with the Empress occupying the apartments on a floor below! Meanwhile, the child was taken to the Konnushennaya Street flat, where the children, separated from their mother, lived with their English and French governesses and Russian nurses and servants. Boris caught cold, and within less than a week he was dead.

Soon the old routine was repeated, and in the early spring the whole "family" was at Ems for a cure.* Autumn found them in Crimea. By early November the Czar and the Empress, who meanwhile had "amazingly recovered," returned to St. Petersburg, stopping on the way in Moscow.† There the Czar made a "stirring

---

* Alexander returned from Ems and visited Finland. This is his message:

Helsingfors, July 4 [16], 1876

Thank you for telegram and dear letter of day before yesterday, which did me lot of good. Except being tired I am quite well. Will telegraph tomorrow to say whether returning by sea or land and hour of arrival. My thoughts never leave you. Kiss you and children tenderly.

† The newspapers reported that the Empress returned from Crimea "in much better health." In 1876 she was particularly active, attending many events, had several talks with the Chancellor Prince Gorchakov, was present at state dinners, etc. During the year Russia was visited by Pedro, the

address" to the "cavaliers of St. George Cross" (Cavaliers of St. George Cross were officers recipient of the St. George Cross, the highest award for bravery in the old Russian Empire) assembled in the Kremlin in St. George Hall, so well known to many tourists of today. Here is the Czar's draft of the speech as written in his own handwriting. (It was found in Katia's archives.)

Moscow, October 29 [November 10], 1876

Thank you, Gentlemen, for the feelings you wished to express to me in connection with present political events. The latter have become clearer now, and therefore I am ready to accept your address, with pleasure. You already know that the Porte has submitted to my demands as to the immediate conclusion of an armistice, so as to put a stop to the useless massacre in Montenegro and Serbia, where unfortunately much Russian blood has also been spilled in defense of our brethren by faith and race. I know that the whole of Russia is with me in taking a most intense interest in their sufferings, but to me the true interests of Russia are dearer than anything else. That is why I have tried, and am continuing to try, to achieve by peaceful means a real improvement in the existence of the Christians inhabiting the Balkan peninsula. In the next few days conferences between the representatives of the Six Great Powers are to take place in Constantinople, to determine the conditions of peace. I deeply hope we will be able to reach general agreement. But if this is not attained, and I see that the other Powers are prepared to content themselves with new promises made by the Porte concerning improving conditions for the Christians, without any serious guarantees of these being carried out, then I am firmly decided to act independently, and I am sure that all Russia will respond to my call, when I consider it necessary and the honor of Russia demands it.* I am certain that Moscow will, as always, lead the way in this. May God help us to carry out our holy calling.

Emperor of Brazil, by the King of Denmark, and by the future King Humbert I of Italy, then Prince of Piedmont.

* That very day, the Emperor received by telegraph the contents of the speech by Lord Beaconsfield in which the latter had shown that England's "sympathy" was with Turkey.

By November the relations between Russia and Turkey deteriorated to such an extent that on November 13 the "preliminary" mobilization of the Russian army was proclaimed. Within a few months, even though Alexander did all he could to avert it, the Russian-Turkish war was an accomplished fact.* The Czar's letters addressed to Katia just prior to the declaration of war are particularly interesting.

St. Petersburg, Tuesday, December 12 [24], 1876
at noon

Extremely worried not to have received your letters, which is my daily bread, and because you let R. [General Ryleev] know that you had fallen sick. In the name of Heaven, give me news of your health so that I should know what has happened to you, and if I can still hope to see you in our nest [the Galernaya flat] or whether I can go to your place at about 4 o'clock. Please take pity on me, and do not forget that all my life is in you.

Yours forever

Tuesday, March 29 [Apr. 10], 1877†
at half-past 11 in the morning

Your nice letter did me a lot of good and I have kept the sweetest impression of the lovely hours we spent together, but I confess that the sad memories of last year brought tears to my eyes, although I tried to keep them back [a reference to the death of their son Boris]. May God preserve our two eldest

---

* A year before the actual declaration of war against Turkey (war was declared on Apr. 24, 1877), the Czar, who hated the war, said to his minister of war: "I can tell you only one thing, that I accept the war as impossible and I am absolutely sure we will evade it."[7]

† An anonymous person permitted Professor S. Konovalov of Oxford University, England, to reproduce in his Oxford Slavonic Papers nine letters exchanged by Czar Alexander II and Katia. The Czar's letters, written mostly in French, are dated between January 11 and 23, 1877, and June 20 and July 2, 1877. Three of Katia's letters, also mostly written in French, with many misspellings and errors in style, cover December 26, 1877, to January 7, 1878, December 27 and 28, 1877, and January 8 and 9, 1879. The letters record daily happenings and the Czar's observations on the progress of the war.[8]

dears, who are our joy and our consolation, and not refuse us His blessing in the future. Both of them were as tender as they could be with me. Dear Pupussia cannot bear to see me with my serious face, and his sweet smile always does me a lot of good. I have once again received a confirmation concerning the protocols, but not a word about sending an Ambassador, which will probably be also rejected, and about which we will learn tomorrow. Only then will we be able to fix the opening of hostilities and the publication of the Manifesto. [The Manifesto was issued on April 12 (24) in Kishinev, Bessarabia, marking the declaration of war against Turkey.] All this, I confess, pursues me like a nightmare. May God come to our aid. I love you, dear Angel, and feel more than ever that all my life is in you. I embrace you tenderly.

Wednesday, March 30 [Apr. 11], 1877
at 10 in the morning

Good morning, dear Angel of my soul, I slept well, but confess that this terrible anniversary of the day when our dear Boby [Boris] was taken from us makes me very sad. At the same time I feel that this terrible ordeal has become a fresh bond between us. We submitted without a murmur to the Divine Will, in the hope that His mercy would support us and would not be withdrawn from us in the future. I am going to have a very busy morning, and am impatiently waiting for the moment when I will see you and the dear children again; thank God they are well. I did not go for a walk because the weather is just as cold and unpleasant as yesterday and I will hold a decisive conference at half-past 11. [It was decided at the meeting to break relations with Turkey on April 12 (24).] May God come to our aid! I embrace you tenderly, and am happy that you are mine, and I

Yours forever

On April 19 the Czar left St. Petersburg and departed "for the front," in order to be "with his troops," ominously posed at the frontier of Roumania, then a Turkish dependency. On his way to the army, Alexander sent the following telegrams to Katia.

Korsovka [on the Warsaw Railroad line]
April 8 [20], 1877

More or less good night without cough. Awful weather. Snow-storm. Am feeling quite well. You know what supports me and where my thoughts are. Kiss you tenderly.

Kishinev, April 13 [25], 1877

Thank you for two letters received both together yesterday, they revived me. Am well. Weather is again rainy and cold. May God protect you. Kiss all of you tenderly.

The story of the Russian-Turkish war can be told here only briefly. The war, which started for their "brother Slavs" with tremendous enthusiasm on the part of the Russians, soon proved, for various reasons, neither triumphant nor easy. To begin with, the Russian army was in the midst of reorganization, and though the new military reforms brought certain results, it was too soon to expect the innovations to account for themselves fully. The crossing of the Balkans, in order to invade Turkey proper, took longer than expected and was costlier in human casualties. Not until December did the Turkish stronghold, Plevna, fall at the cost of heavy losses inflicted to the flower of the Russian army—its Guards. In the Caucasus, however, the Russian advance was speedier, and by the beginning of 1878 another Turkish strong-hold, the fortress Kars, surrendered to the Russians. Early in January the Russian army appeared within a few miles of the gates of Adrianople (in the European Turkey). The triumphal entry of the "infidels" to Constantinople, the capital of Turkey, was a matter of hours. But the Turks appealed for an armistice, which was quickly negotiated in the small town of San Stefano and by which Russia received all she asked from the Turks. With the British traditional opposition to Russia (which almost re-sulted then in a war between Great Britain and Russia), the San Stefano "gains" were put aside by a new international meeting, known since as the Berlin Congress, with Bismarck as an "honest broker." (Nevertheless, Russia obtained independence for Montenegro, Serbia, and Roumania, with part of Bulgaria becoming autonomous.) Russia, on her part, acquired the port of Batumo, and the fortresses of Kars and Ardahan in the Caucasus. All other Russian demands were drastically curtailed, with the result that a resentment against England and particularly Germany, with its "honest broker," spread throughout Russia. The popularity of the Czar suffered as well, a situation that the revolutionaries, as we shall see, took advantage of.

Let us return to the first days of the war. Here is the Czar's letter written on the day war was declared.

Kishinev, Tuesday, April 12 [24], 1877
at 1 in the afternoon

Good morning, dear Angel of my soul, I slept very well until 8 o'clock and on waking had the joy of getting your telegram of yesterday, which revived me. I am glad that mine reached you promptly. I began my day by taking a walk in the garden which belongs to the house, and the morning was at last milder and sunny. At 9 I went to the Cathedral, then to the review, where there was a Te Deum in presence of the troops, with reading of the Manifesto, which caused general enthusiasm. Emmanuel's [Prince Emmanuel Meschersky, Mouche's husband, volunteered and was serving with the Guard Artillery Brigade] battery was superb, as was all the rest and nobody will understand better than you how it pleased me. Then a Service for the Dead held in my room, for this sad anniversary of 12 years [of the death of his eldest son, Czarevich Nicholas, in Nice, in 1865]. Now here I am at last free again, and glad to be able to chat with you, who are my life. I hope to get your first letter later on in the day, because the courier, who was to arrive at 6 this morning, has been held up by an accident. We have already received news that the first troops have crossed the frontier successfully. May God come to our aid and bless our arms! The courier is about to leave, so it is time for me to end up by kissing you very tenderly, together with our two little Angels. Oh, how I miss you and feel that all my life is in you. Christ be with you.

Yours forever

Kishinev, April 14 [26], 1877

Thank you from my heart for dear letters and telegram of yesterday which touched me deeply. May God come to our aid. Weather still bad. Am feeling well. Kiss all of you tenderly.

By early May the Czar was back in St. Petersburg, having stopped in Moscow on the way and addressed "the nobles" in the historic St. George Hall. The Empress and "all of his other" family met him there. A witness found the Czar "greatly harassed and depressed." In St. Petersburg he was greeted with a welcome "which surpassed" all previous ones. "It was apparently spontaneous," wrote an Englishman present at the reception, "but the Emperor," he added, "looked very careworn and ill and anxiety produced by state of affairs is said to have aggravated the internal complaint from which he has suffered several years."⁹

This is what Alexander wrote Katia from Moscow:

Moscow, Saturday April 23 [May 5], 1877
at 11 in the evening

I have just returned from that reception, which was not at all amusing and to which I went chiefly to repay a courtesy, after all that Moscow was just given in connection with the War. As I drove there in a victoria with my son, without anybody recognizing us, I thought that I caught sight of you in the window [Katia met the Czar in Moscow at his request]. I want you to know that I have kept the best impression of the good moments we spent together, and was happy to see our dear children again, who were so sweet and tender with me. I only hope to God they did not catch cold and that you will bring them safely back to Petersburg. Alas, before going to bed I must finish at least part of the papers that are piled up on my table, as you saw, and I confess that that is what puts me out and tires me most on these voyages, especially on the return journeys. With all this I thank you from the bottom of my heart, dear Dussia, for having come here, because I know how to appreciate your love, and all the proofs of it that you give me touch me deeply. May God repay it to you! I embrace you from the bottom of your heart, which is happy to love you and to belong to you forever.

Sunday April 24 [May 6]
at 10 in the morning

Good morning, dear Angel of my soul, I could not get to bed before 1 o'clock, but slept very well until half-past 8, and everything in me overflows with love and tenderness for you, my idol, my treasure, my life. I regret we cannot see each other today, but what can one do? May God bring us back safely and may we be able to meet tomorrow at half-past 3, in our dear rooms. I still have a lot of matters to attend to before Divine Service, which will be held at three-quarters past 10, and at noon we must be at the railway station to go to Troitza [the famous monastery, now renamed the Zagorsk], returning here at 6 to start off again immediately. I love you, dear Angel, and kiss you and our dear children tenderly.

Yours forever

May God not forsake us, and not deny us His blessing!

About a month later the Czar was once more off to the "front." He stayed there alone for the remainder of the year. This was his longest period of separation from Katia.* The Czar continued to be dejected, lonely, and "not too well." As he had foreseen, the war was not going as favorably as had generally been expected. The terrible human losses added to his sadness. The letters that follow clearly reflect his anxieties.

Ploesti [Roumania], June 6 [18], 1877

Telegram of yesterday received this morning, as well as letter. Thank you from all my heart, feel revived and physically fit. We have had several successful encounters in Asia. Weather warmer. Hope the sty in your eye is cured. Kiss you tenderly.

---

* Some claimed that Katia "visited" the Czar for a "few days" in Kishinev in May, 1877. There is no evidence of such a visit in any of the materials on hand.

Zimnitza [Roumania], June 18 [30], 1866
at 10 in the morning

Good morning, dear Angel of my soul, I slept very well; to refresh myself, following Botkin's advice as I have no shower on getting up I am going to have water poured over me in the little tent placed just outside my house.* The heat is still the same, but yesterday evening and last night there was a real storm on the Danube, which will hold up the placing of the bridge. It is feared that some people were drowned.

At 1 in the afternoon. I have just received a telegram from Czarskoye Selo, so hope I will get one from you soon. Luckily nobody perished last night, although several lifeboats were capsized and a few pontoons sunk [on the Danube]. The wind has died down at last, and the construction of the bridge is advancing.

At half-past 3 in the afternoon. I went to inspect the building of the bridge, which they hope to finish by tomorrow, and then visited the wounded, of which only the most serious cases have been left here, the rest having been transported to Piatra, through which I passed the other day. This is our hour, when my thoughts are with you more than ever, my adored little wife, and with our dear children. May God grant us the joy of a speedy reunion. Now I am going to take a rest.

At 11 in the evening. After dinner I had a particularly good sleep, and on waking had the joy of receiving your dear long letter, which you finished on Saturday the 11/23, that is just 8 days ago. I immediately gave the enclosures to R. [General Ryleev] and Botkin, and both brought them back for me to read. I beg you not to worry about my health, nor about the danger I might be exposed to during the fighting. Rest assured, dear Dussia, that I in no way forget my duties. Tell dear

---

* The American military attaché to the Russian army, Lt. F. V. Greene, U.S. Army, in his *Sketches of Army Life in Russia*, gives a vivid description of the life led by the Czar in Turkey. "The Czar," wrote Greene, lived in an "ordinary Officers' tent," with the greatest simplicity ever imagined. The only luxury noticed by Greene were the servants who wore "crown livery of dark blue coat, embroidered with gold fringe."[10]

Pupussia that Papa thanks him very much indeed for his long letter, after reading which Papa always feels merrier, because he loves his own Pupussia very much indeed and kisses him tenderly, as well as Oly. And it is true that the dictations he writes are my joy. I hope that the treatment will finally do you some good, but I am distressed by the bad weather you are having. Here we had a thunderstorm which somewhat cooled the air. I had the four Guard officers who took such a brilliant part in the crossing of the Danube in to dinner with me. I ordered them back to me already on the day following the action, and today the soldiers are already standing guard at my door, and it is a pleasure to see their broadly smiling faces. Each of them killed from 3 to 5 Turks with his bayonet, and speak of it as nothing unusual. That miserable courier had brought me such a load of papers that I don't know how I will ever be able to go through all of them. Just as a start, Adlerberg [Minister of the Court] read merely the telegrams to me, from dinner to teatime and then until 11 o'clock. The telegrams from Vienna are rather satisfactory, but those from London are execrable. But what is strange is that in the Ministry itself the majority pronounces itself as being against war, which means nothing because it is that swine of a Beakensfield [sic] who decides everything according to what he has in his noddle. And so good night. I love you and kiss you very tenderly, and I feel more than ever that all my life is in you.

Zimnitza, June 21 [July 3], 1877

Thank you for telegram of yesterday received in the evening. Happy that mine are reaching you and that weather is better. Not a word of truth in what you found in the newspapers. Crossed to the other bank over the bridge. Found Emmanuel quite well. Heat is oppressive. His condition could not be better. Letter sent this morning.

Zimnitza, June 22 [July 4], 1877

Thank you for dear letter of 14th and telegram of yesterday, filled me with sunshine. (Yesterday's telegram was delayed.) Crossing of troops over the bridge continues. Cossacks had skirmishes and captured several Circassians. Very strong heat. Feel quite well. Kiss all of you tenderly.

Thursday, June 23 [July 5], 1877
at 10 in the morning

Good morning, dear Angel of my soul, in spite of the heat I slept fairly well, and everything in me overflows with love and tenderness for you, my adored little wife. Our advanced cavalry screen had a small engagement yesterday, in which the Turks and Circassians were thrown back without any losses on our side. It is time to get to work.

Three-quarters past 12 in the afternoon. I spent all the morning before and after lunch at work—first alone, then with Miliutin, Mezentzev and Adlerberg [Miliutin, the minister of war; Nicholas Mezentzev, the chief of the Gendarmes, an important post; Adlerberg, the Czar's childhood friend, General ADC to the Emperor and minister of the imperial court since 1872] and that at the sweat of my brow for you cannot imagine the heat we are suffering from here and the amount of dust we have to breathe, day and night. Everything is covered with it, even in the rooms.

Half-past 3 in the afternoon. I went on a tour of the various camps, with my nephew Henry [probably Prince Henry Battenberg, the son of Empress Marie's brother Alexander] and on my return had the pleasant surprise of finding your good letter, which you finished writing in the evening of the 16 [28], that is the day after the great day of the 15th, and I see that unfortunately you had not yet received my telegram announcing our victory. From the official report which is about to be published you will see that it was a complete one, and only cost us 830 casualties, of which 230 were killed. And we were afraid of losing at least 10,000 men. This wonderful achievement is certainly due to the wise dispositions taken by my brother and his Chief of Staff, and to the manner in which everything was prepared in secrecy. I alone was in the secret, neither my sons nor Miliutin knew anything about it. As a result I am getting letters and telegrams from everywhere, stating there is immense and general rejoicing at home, which is only natural after this long period of waiting which was as hard to bear for those far away as for those close at hand.—Dear Pupussia's dictation has again given me great pleasure, so please kiss him tenderly from me. Who is the little girl whose acquaintance he made on the net* which amuses him so much? I must admit that the delay of your reds makes me fear you are pregnant,† which would disrupt your treatment, and I also fear that if this is the case your agitation and involuntary worrying about your Mounka might do you harm. So I must admit that I would feel disturbed by it. I will continue later, as I want to go to bed now.

Half-past 7 in the evening. After dinner I went to see two unfortunate Bulgarians who had been horribly mutilated by the Turks, and whom our Cossacks found on the road from Nikopol to Systovo; they had just brought them to the Red Cross hospital which is only a hundred paces away from my house. I urged Wellesley [British military attaché]‡ who had dined with all my staff, to accompany me, and so be able to admire the work of their proteges. One of these poor fellows had just died, and his miserable wife was at his side. His head had been split by a cross-shaped saber cut; the other had three wounds and they hoped to save his life. His young pregnant wife had followed him. As I have just learned, the English fleet has received the order to proceed from Pyraeus to Bezika, probably to be as near as possible to the Dardanelles and Constantinople. ["To stem" the Russian advance and the eventual capture of Constantinople, the British moved their fleet close to the Turkish capital.]

---

* A sort of trampoline on the Peterhof Palace grounds.

† The last child, a daughter, Katia, Jr., was born on September 9 [21], 1878.

‡ This is what the Czar wrote to Katia: ". . . public opinion [according to the British military attaché] in England is against us. . . . They mean to stay neutral so long as the war did not run into the next year. I asked what was the reason. [Colonel] Wellesley [the military attaché] replied that the British government could in such a case no longer stand out against the public's wish to start a war against Russia.[11] What perfect logic!"

At half-past 8 in the evening. I had to break off my letter to
get to work with Miliutin and Mezentzev whereupon there
arrived Prince Imeretinsky [General Prince Alexander K.
Imeretinsky, then commander of an army division] of my suite
with details of the combat at Plevna, which lasted until late
into the night. The great blunder was that General Krudener
[General Baron Nicholas Krudener, then commander of the
army corps], while fully aware of the Turks' numerical
superiority, decided to attack them as he had been given the
order to do. Had he but taken upon himself the responsibility
of not carrying that order out, he would have spared a
thousand lives and avoided *a complete rout,* and *we must admit
that this is one indeed.* Luckily however the Turks did not
pursue the remnants of our brave troops, otherwise but few
would have escaped. This gave us the possibility of at least
reassembling those unfortunate remnants, and of saving all
our colors and cannon. But we will hardly be able to resume
the offensive before several weeks. Now the thing to do is to
prevent the Turks from marching on Systovo and cutting our
only communication line over the bridge. That is what my
brother will attend to before anything else. As to myself, for
the present I shall remain here, where I run no risks. On the
other hand, if I were to recross the Danube, it would have a
deplorable effect on the morale of the whole army. It is possible, however, that in a few days I might go to Tsarevitch [his
oldest son, Grand Duke Alexander] to be closer to the bridge.—
My Guard Squadron, which has taken part in all Gurko's
actions [General Joseph Gourko, then commander of the guard
cavalry division] and only lost 3 horses, returned here this
morning with several of the men wearing decorations. The
other day you asked me what is meant by a Saint George's
Cross, Second Class; well, there exist four classes of that Order
for enlisted men, the first being a silver cross like Emmanuel's,
the second the same cross with a bow on the ribbon, and the
third and fourth the same thing but with a gold cross; and all
may be worn together. Emmanuel's division did not take part
in the fighting at Plevna and is now holding Tyrnovo; it is to
be hoped that the Turks who are at Shoumla will not dare to
attack it.—In the meantime I had this morning received more

satisfactory news from London, as a consequence of Wellesley's reports. The language of the English had completely changed, and they were quite ready to use their influence on the Turks to make them ask for peace on any terms we would demand. Unfortunately, I fear that the Plevna disaster will cause them to change their tone again and will only render the Turks more arrogant.—Well, we shall see.—I went for my evening walk with Suvoroff [Prince Alexander Suvorov, general-inspector of the infantry, the grandson of the famous Suvorov], but I must say that our state of mind was far from rosy.—With all this my thoughts are with you more than ever, my adored Angel, and I know that nobody will understand your poor Mounka's sadness better than you.

At half-past 10 in the evening. I have just received your telegram of yesterday, and it did me a lot of good. Yes, I feel that your thoughts never leave me, just as mine are with you everywhere and always. I see that you are now having a cold spell, after only a few days of good weather. It is a pity, when one thinks that in Petersburg autumn usually begins with the month of August. Oh, how we will miss our dear Crimea and how I regret it on account of our dear children.—I kiss all of you from the bottom of my heart.

May God not forsake us, and bless us!

Yours forever

Camp at Pavlov, July 4 [16], 1877

After very sharp fighting yesterday, fortress of Nikopol surrendered unconditionally this morning at dawn. We have taken prisoner two Pashas and up to 6000 regular troops. Arrived here at 11 in the morning. Thank you for telegram of the 2nd, could not send you a telegram yesterday from the encampment. I am quite well and embrace all of you.

Belo, July 19 [31], 1877

Thank you for telegram of day before yesterday, received yesterday, and letter of 12th received this morning. Am well. Kiss all of you tenderly.

Belo, July 24 [Aug. 5], 1877

Telegram of 22nd received yesterday evening. Courier was delayed. I feel that our thoughts and prayers are the same on this day which was the anniversary of our Angel now in Heaven. May God watch over us and not abandon us. Am well. Nothing new.

At three-quarters past 10 in the evening. I had to talk with my brother again,* and then be amiable with the Prince of Roumania, who came to have tea with us in the large tent which serves as our dining room. According to the latest news received from the chief of the telegraph station at Gabrovo, it appears that there has been no further fighting at Shipka, and part of the Turkish troops have been observed withdrawing in the direction of Kazanlyk. God grant that this is confirmed. At my son's, there have only been insignificant skirmishes at the outposts and no movement from the direction of Plevna, which the Roumanian army will approach in a few days, menacing the Turks' line of retreat. And now good night. I love you, dear Angel, and kiss you very tenderly.

Wednesday, August 17 [29]
at three-quarters past 9 in the morning

Good morning, dear Angel of my soul, I slept more or less well and on waking had the consolation of getting your telegram, which always does me a lot of good. I must get back to my work, for which I will remain installed on my balcony. For the present there is nothing new.

At 3 in the afternoon. At last I am free, and happy to be able to resume my chat with you, my adored little wife, in whom all my life is concentrated. I have just taken leave of the Prince of Roumania, who is going to take command over his troops on our right, but will act only under the orders of

---

* Grand Duke Nicholas, commander-in-chief. He was a rather unfortunate choice for a supreme position. Disagreement between the brothers resulted in the dismissal (under the guise of "retiring") of the Grand Duke and eventual disgrace and oblivion.

my brother, and I also had a rather long conversation with Wellesley, from which I drew the conclusion: that the English Government is only showing more moderation, *for the time being*, because it hopes that after the bad luck we have had recently, we will not have time this year to march on Adrianople and Constantinople before winter. If on the contrary God grants us some guarantee that England will not declare war on us before the end of this year, despite the so-called good wishes for the success of our arms that he conveyed to me from that old madwoman of a Queen [Victoria of Great Britain] and he did not dare to deny it. I ended by telling him that it was not the time to talk of peace, but that when that time came, my duty toward Russia would be to bear in mind our true interests, which would only be just as all that England does is to put forward her own interests, which guide her policy.

At quarter past 8 in the evening. I took a rest until 6 and having put off dinner until 7 had time to take another walk, the temperature being much more bearable, before we went to table, and I count on doing this on other days also, following Botkin's advice. The band again played our dear organ waltz, which always reminds me of the winter in which our poor Boby was born, when we used to go to see the children every evening and watch them being put to bed. Oh, how I yearn to be with you, it's unbearable! This morning they announced the death of my childhood friend, Patkul [General Alexander V. Patkul, who accompanied the Czar to England in 1839. He was sixty years old at his death] and it made a very sad impression on me, as he was my age. I did not even know that he had been sick. Perhaps it was a sudden death, I am waiting for the details.

September 4 [16], 1877

It is exactly the same place where just a month ago I found that unfortunate 3rd Sharpshooter Brigade, which had so distinguished itself at Lovtcha and has now been decimated before Plevna, of the 4,000 men they were they now count only 1200. Their wounded, whom I visited today, are inconsolable over the death of their worthy chief, General Dobrovolsky[?], who in addition to being a brilliant officer had a charming family. Now I want to take a rest.

At half-past 10 in the evening. After dinner I had to write to Sacha [the Czarevich, the future Emperor Alexander III] and talk to Niki Dolgourouki [Prince Nicholas Dolgoruky, A.D.C. to the Czar and very distantly related to Katia], whom he had sent to me and whom I am sending back to him.—For the time being everything is calm on his side, and he has just been reinforced by the 26th Division, which arrived from Petersburg, and which is to serve as junction between his troops and those of Prince Shakhovskoy's [General Prince Alexis Shakhovskoy, commander of an army corps] 11th Army Corps, along the road from Osmanbazaar to Tyrnovo.—There is nothing new in front of Plevna either, where we are getting closer to the second great redoubt.—I am going to bed, and kiss you very tenderly.

Tuesday, September 5 [17], 1877
at 10 in the morning

Good morning, dear Angel of my soul, as I felt very tired yesterday I slept especially well and on waking I had the consolation of receiving your telegram of yesterday. God be praised that your head feels better, but the horrible weather you continue to have is quite distressing.—Last night we had a real hurricane, which is still continuing. The air has become much cooler, so I confess I am not displeased to be in a house, instead of my tent.—Nothing new at present.

At 2 in the afternoon. Thanks from the bottom of my heart, dear Dussia, for your good letter of the 30th, which reached me before lunch. All your good words, as well as dear Pupussia's dictation, did me a lot of good, but I confess that I cried like a child while reading them and I yearn for you so that it is unbearable. The little I was able to write you on the 29th and 30th will prove to you how much, in spite of all my responsibilities, our thoughts were the same, and it cannot be otherwise

when we form but a single being, both spiritual and physical.—
The rest will have to wait until later, as I must sort out my
papers, after having had a talk with my brother, who has just
arrived. Yesterday he again inspected our positions in front
of Plevna, where we are increasing our fortifications and
pushing our batteries forward, so that their action be more
effective.

At half-past 7 in the evening. At half-past 3 I again went to
visit the wounded and distributed presents to them; on returning I took some rest. As we were going in to dinner we
received a telegram from General Radetsky [General Theodore
Radetsky, then commander of an army corps—one of the
talented strategists of the war], announcing that the Turks had
attempted a new attack against Shipka last night at 3 o'clock,
but had been victoriously defeated after a combat that lasted
for 9 hours. Losses on both sides are high, and unfortunately
poor *Emmanuel* [Prince Meschersky "heroically died" in the
battle] is one of the victims. I am in despair and regret it from
the depth of my heart, for he was a noble character and in
him we lose a true friend; I am deeply distressed, *from all
points of view*, about poor Marie. I would much prefer her to
learn of it only through you, and therefore I hastened to send
you a telegram.—Here is what probably must be his last letter
to his wife, which R. [General Ryleev] received from him the
day before yesterday. Give it to her together with my letter. I
do not need to add anything, as we understand each other in
everything, and we have more than once discussed our fears,
should this ever happen. May God give her strength, and bring
her back to the right path. All those who knew him, my
brother to begin with, mourn him deeply and he certainly
was worthy of it. You will understand how after that it was
painful for me to attend the dinner, and all that followed,
when we drank to the health of the heroes of Shipka, who
certainly deserved it, but I must say I was not the only one
who had tears in his eyes. Oh, my God, come to our aid and
put a stop to this odious war, for the glory of Russia and the
good of the Christians! Such is the cry of my heart, that

nobody will understand better than you, my idol, my treasure, my life.—Now I must write to poor Mouche.

The "odious war" did not stop, and the Russian troops had the worst winter imaginable. The siege of the famous fortress Plevna, gallantly defended by the Turks, decimated the Russian ranks. It was only six months later, in December, 1877, that Plevna fell and Turkey was ready to treat for peace. But since Great Britain "advised" the Turks to continue the fight, the war dragged on. Czar Alexander remained all these critical months at the front. (He returned for a few days to St. Petersburg for the Christmas holidays.)

Occasional letters from his beloved lifted the Czar's depressed spirits. Here is one of the few of her letters extant. Undated, it was written probably in November.

At 4 in the afternoon

I did not either go out shopping or take a walk, as I felt very tired owing to the pains in my stomach, and have been with the children since 2 o'clock. Michel [Katia's "black sheep" brother, Michael, who was stationed in Orenburg, near the Ural Mountains] arrived from Orenburg and came to see us at 1 o'clock, and so as to get rid of him I took him back to the hotel, otherwise he would have kept me until 8. It is raining, and the humidity is terrible. I have just read again the dear letter I received from you yesterday. Your telegram is late, and I see mine are very often delayed also, which is most annoying. I am happy you like my warm stockings, you ought to wear them because your feet are always cold and you would do well to always wear woolen stockings. But those I sent you are even warmer, and you should wear them over yours when you have to stay out in the open watching the bombardments. We have already learned that the Sofia road has been occupied by our troops, and naturally this could not have happened without a combat, because the Turks have the habit of building fortifications everywhere. Happily God has blessed our Army and granted us some success. You did well to send Tuchkov [General Michael P. Tuchkov, A.D.C. general of the Czar] to find some hut for you to live in at Poradim, which as I am told is only 10 versts away from Plevna, so it will only take you about half an hour to get there, whereas Radonitsa was too far off, and in addition to the fatigue imposed on you by having to stay in one place all day long, it was tiring to spend more than an hour trotting back to Radonitsa, where you did not even have a hut. I well understand that you spent a restless night because my telegram was delayed, and besides that, you were anxiously waiting to know the result of the attack against the Turkish positions before Sofia. As though on purpose, our telegrams are always delayed just when we need them most. . . .

The Czar's telegrams follow:

Poradim, October 24 [Nov. 5], 1877

Arrived here safe at 3 o'clock. No telegram since the 21st. Great joy on seeing old and brave Guard comrades again, who had just covered themselves with glory. Otherwise nothing new. Weather clear, but cold. Am feeling quite well. Kiss all of you tenderly.

Petroshani, December 4 [16], 1877

Have just recrossed the Danube,* exactly five months later. Yesterday's telegram received this morning. Will spend night on train. Congratulate dear Vava on her anniversary [Vava Shebeko's birthday]. Am quite well.

By January, 1878, the nine months' war was over, but not the "war fever" in England. ("We don't want to fight, but by jingo, if we do, we've got the men, we've got the ships, we've got the money too.") The Czar returned to St. Petersburg and was warmly "acclaimed" by the population, but despite a victorious war he was more than anxious and "expected further complications with other Powers."†[12] Here is his own draft of his address to the guard officers in St. Petersburg:

---

* The Russian troops, by recrossing the Danube, virtually brought the war to a victorious conclusion.

† By February, 1878, the British fleet had begun to enter the Straits but returned when the Sultan, under Russian pressure, failed to give permission. The San Stefano Treaty resulting in the Berlin Congress finally averted the Russo-British clash.

Words I addressed to the officers
at the ceremony of Changing the Guard
on Sunday, January 22 [Feb. 3], 1878 [St. Petersburg]

I congratulate you, Gentlemen, on the conclusion of an armistice on such favorable conditions for us. We owe this to our glorious troops, who have proven that for our brave lads there is nothing impossible. However, this is not the end of the business by far, and we must remain prepared and on guard until we achieve a lasting peace worthy of Russia. May God help us in this.

Now that the war was over, Alexander had to tackle another delicate and purely a personal problem. It concerned legitimizing his children born out of wedlock—a problem complicated by the fact that Alexander's wife, the Empress, was still alive. If we recall, after the birth of Gogo, the Czar had not legalized the status of his first illegitimate child, merely baptizing him and giving him a Christian name. With the birth of his second child, Olga, and prospects of others to come, the question had had to be settled. Thus, in the spring of 1878, an imperial *ukaz*, signed by Alexander in Czarskoye Selo and directed to the empire's senate, was drawn but not then made public. (The *ukaz* was made public only after the death of Alexander II. It was published in the Official Journal of the Department of Heraldry on April 11 [23], 1890.) The paper stated that "His Majesty Emperor Alexander II graciously accorded to the minors George Alexandrovich [son of Alexander] and Olga Alexandrovna [daughter of Alexander] the rights of Hereditary Nobility with the family name of their Highnesses Prince and Princess Yourievsky." Katia, their mother, remained to be styled as Princess or Kniazhna [Mlle.] Dolgorukova. There was nothing unusual in this *ukaz*. The department of heraldry frequently received such imperial "wishes," dealing with numerous cases of "adoptions" (often a camouflage term for children born out of wedlock), "transmittals," or "elevations," to higher titles of Russian and even foreign subjects.[13] What was significant, however, was the granting by the Czar of the family name of Yourievsky, which hinted at Katia's "direct ancestor," (which was not) the illustrious Prince

Youri Dolgoruky, the founder of Moscow in 1147 and the forebear of the Rurik Dynasty.* Yet though she was a Dolgorukova, Katia was in no way a "direct descendant" of Youri. At the time of the *ukaz*, nobody in the know paid any attention to the "new" name of Yourievsky.† It became, as we will see, more significant later. Here is the Czar's letter on the subject:

Tuesday, April 25 [May 7], 1878
at three-quarters past 11 in the evening

I missed our meetings, and one must admit that the weather was hideous. I was happy, my adored little wife, to have been able, when I was with you again, to sign the ukaz concerning the children in your presence, and R. [General Ryleev] has already received the notification about it from Dolgourouki [General Prince Vladimir Dolgoruky, Moscow's Governor-General, in whose province the records of Katia's family were held. A very distant relative]. I confess that it is as though a stone had fallen from my heart, for the falsity of their position had been worrying me for a long time. May God keep them safely for us, and bless your pregnancy, and not forsake us in the future. Their humor was truly sparkling, and the vivacity of dear Pupussia is astonishing. God grant that the lack of news from London and Vienna be a good omen. I love you, dear Angel, and kiss you very tenderly.

Here is his next letter:

Wednesday, April 26 [May 8], [1878]
at 10 in the evening

Good morning, dear Angel of my soul, I slept very well, but on waking had the unpleasant surprise of finding every-

---

* This Youri was also named Dolgoruky, probably also for his long arms. He was not the direct ancestor of Katia, having been named three centuries before Katia's first "Dolgoruky" ancestor acquired the nickname and became the direct ancestor of Katia's branch of the family.[14]

In 1947 the Soviet Union, under Stalin, celebrated the eight hundredth anniversary of the founding of Moscow by Youri Dolgoruky. A statue to him was then erected in Moscow.

† Prince Alexis Lobanov-Rostovsky, amateur genealogist and eventually minister of foreign affairs, insisted in 1885 that it was Paul I's command

thing covered with snow, which is still falling, with the same wind as yesterday. It really makes me impatient! Of course, I did not go out and must get back to my work; at this moment they are deciding to send a long telegram from Totleben [General Edouard Todtleben, most able and famous military engineer], which I fear will not bring us anything good. Goodbye until midday, and after that until our usual hour. I embrace you tenderly, and am happy that you are mine, and I

Yours forever

As the rumblings of the guns ended on the battlefields of Turkey, Bulgaria, and Roumania, other noises, at first less deafening, began to be heard. Nihilism had come into full bloom.

---

in naming his wedlock daughter Yourieva, which gave the idea to Alexander II, his grandson, to bestow on his "new family" the name of Yourievsky. A rather doubtful version.

· 12 ·

"THE WILD BEAST"

While the "cold war" with England was still in progress, Katia gave birth to a child, this time in the Crimea, her fourth and last—a girl, whom she named Ekaterina, Katia for short.* The event took place in September, 1878, when the Czar was away. This is what he wrote to Katia:

> Saturday, December 9 [21], [1878]
> at three-quarters past 11 in the evening
> [St. Petersburg]

> The good moments we spent together have left me the sweetest impression. The dear children's humor was particularly sparkling, and they were enchanted to find their old toys again. You saw how dear Pupussia suddenly came to me and kissed me, with both his arms around my neck, and Oly of course had to imitate him. Their tenderness is my joy. May God keep them safely for us, as well as dear baby [Katia], and may He not forsake us in the future.—I confess that I have some misgivings about the fatigues of tomorrow, and above all about the Archbishop's Mass which will follow the christening. I love you, my dear Angel, and kiss you tenderly. I hope that at last you will spend a better night.

---

* In her later years Ekaterina for some reason claimed to have been born in St. Petersburg.[1] The nurse stated differently.

Sunday, December 10 [22], [1878]
at three-quarters past 9 in the morning

Good morning, dear Angel of my soul, I slept well and
everything in me overflows with love and tenderness for you.
Today it is exactly a year since my return from the war,
the result of which was the birth of our dear baby, exactly
9 months less a day, afterwards. Oh, oh, oh—did you see?
May God keep her for us, as well as our two dear eldest,
and continue to watch over us. I have to get back to my work.

I embrace you tenderly and am happy that you are mine,
and I

Yours forever

A few days later, Alexander gave a large dinner for "320
persons" mostly officers who had taken part in the last war.
Here is the Czar's speech, drawn by his own hand, which was
found among Katia's papers.

Words, I pronounced at the dinner of
December 19 [31], [1878]
[St. Petersburg]

When last year I considered it necessary to call the troops
of the Guard Corps to the theater of military operations, I
was convinced that my Guard, in the ranks of which I myself
began my service, and which later I had to command, as
Corps Commander and Commander-in-Chief, would not be
deficient in steadiness and courage, as compared to the other
troops of the Active Army, who already had had the occasion
to cover themselves with fresh glory in combat against the
enemy; in some of this fighting representatives of the Guards,
attached to my Convoy, had also taken part—notably at
the crossing of the Danube, and then in fighting at Tyrnovo
and Lovcha. [Bulgarian villages near Sofia, where during
a severe snowstorm on December 15 [27], 1877 the Russians
defeated the Turks. Today, on the anniversary of the glorious
battle of Tashkisseni [a Bulgarian village also in the vicinity
of Sofia], I am happy to repeat my heartfelt thanks to you
and to say that you entirely fulfilled my expectations. The
task that fell to the Guards and those Line units who worked

with them under the command of General J. Gurko [General Joseph Gourko, commander of a Cavalry Guard division] was by no means an easy one. You have proved that for the Russian soldier there is nothing impossible, and despite all the hardships which seemed unsurmountable, in wintertime, you were the first to cross the Balkans and exactly a year ago inflicted a crushing defeat on the Turkish troops defending the approaches to Sofia.

From the bottom of my grateful heart, I drink to the health of all Guards, and in particular of those who took part in the battle of Tashkisseni.

The year of 1879 came with Alexander and Katia's love affair still in full swing. While the Czar's *billets-doux* were more ardent then ever, he was even more than a lover. He was now a real *paterfamilias*, though his second family continued to occupy different quarters.

Here is what Alexander wrote to Katia:

> Monday, January 8 [20], 1879
> at three-quarters past 11 in the evening

I am still all saturated with our delirious bingerles of a little while ago. It was so good I wanted to cry out, and I slept so particularly well afterwards. The children's appetites were very good and their humor sparkling as always, but dear Pupussia was afraid I would make fun of his Hussar costume with the short pants. It's priceless how sensitive he is, and along with that the nice thing about the child is that he is real. May God develop in him all his good qualities and keep him for us, as well as his sisters, and may He not forsake us in the future. I love you, dear Angel, and kiss you tenderly.

> Tuesday, January 9 [21], [1879]
> at 10 in the morning

Good morning, dear Angel of my soul, I slept very well and everything in me overflows with love and tenderness for you. The weather is like yesterday, so I refrained from taking a walk. Botkin [the Court doctor] finds that Vava's

mother is in a serious condition, but not hopeless. It is time
to go to work. I embrace you tenderly, and am happy that
you are mine, and I

Yours forever

May God not forsake us, and bestow His blessing on us!

Tuesday, January 9 [21], [1879]
at midnight

I was so happy to have met you out walking, but one
must admit that the weather was awful. Our dinner was
not complete without dear Oly. God grant that her indis-
position does not develop into a serious illness. I was happy
to have been able to see her, as well as our dear baby,
who was sitting up so sweetly in her carriage, but afterwards
her cries were not natural. Let us hope that both will be
better tomorrow. It is so sad to see children sick, especially
if they are your own.—Our new novel promises to become
interesting. I love you, dear Angel, and kiss you tenderly.

Wednesday, January 10 [22], [1879]
at 10 in the morning

Good morning, dear Angel of my soul, I slept well. General Ryleev told me the children had slept calmly. God
grant they feel better. The cold is decreasing and there
is no wind at present. It is time to get to work. I embrace
you and am happy that you are mine, and I

Yours forever

May God not forsake us, and bestow His Blessings on us!

Wednesday, January 10 [22], [1879]
at quarter past midnight

I keep an excellent impression of the good day we had
together, but missed our dear Oly. God grant she gets
well quickly, as well as our dear baby. Dear Pupussia's humor
was as sparkling as ever, and he was so happy to have been
able to bring up the book with the engravings of Pavlovsk
[an imperial residence within a short distance from the

capital] from downstairs. His vivacity is astonishing. I only wish he were not so lazy with his lessons.—Our novel is most interesting and stirring. I love you, dear Angel, and kiss you very tenderly.

Thursday, January 11 [23], [1879]
at 10 in the morning

Good morning, dear Angel of my soul, I had some trouble in getting to sleep, but after that I slept well, and Botkin who has just examined me, was very satisfied with my lungs. The weather is clear but colder than yesterday and the wind seems to be stronger, which is very annoying. I will again have a very busy morning, and have to get back to work. According to R. [General Ryleev] the children slept well, and that is all I know so far. I embrace you tenderly, and am happy that you are mine, and I

Yours forever

May God not forsake us, and bestow His Blessing upon us!

Saturday, January 13 [25], [1879]
at quarter past midnight

I am so sorry that your stomach is again out of order, and that our delirious bingerles last night have given you pains. And I also want you to know that I found you particularly beautiful this evening, in your blue bedgown. The state of our poor Oly is beginning to worry me. God grant she is not incubating some serious illness, as Botkin seems to suspect. I hope you have not forgotten to have Gogo's bed changed to another room. The remarks he made were quite amusing, and the white cap, which brought on his tears when it was left behind, suited him very nicely! I love you, dear Angel, and kiss you tenderly. I hope we will sleep better than we did last night.

Sunday, January 14 [26], [1879]
at 10 in the morning

Good morning, dear Angel of my soul, I got off to sleep more or less quickly and slept well. I did not go for a walk as there is a wind and the temperature is 6 degrees. After the review I must attend a boring patriotic concert at the Nobility Hall, which they say will last for over 3 hours. But in any case I hope to join you at half-past 3.—I must get back to my work, and am waiting impatiently for news of Oly. God grant it will be satisfactory. I embrace you tenderly and am happy you are mine, and I

Yours forever

May God not forsake us, and bestow His Blessing on us!

Wednesday, February 21 [Mar. 5], [1879]
at three-quarters-past 11 in the evening

I was so happy to find that you no longer had a headache, when I came to kiss you this morning. After my so tiring mornings, it is a real physical and spiritual rest for me to be with you again, my adored little wife. I love our good chats, and to be woken up by the children's kisses, whose carefree gaiety always does me so much good. Oly now has quite a good appetite, but dear Pupussia was not feeling well. I hope his photographs will turn out to be good ones. Our new novel is becoming more and more interesting. I love you, dear Angel, and kiss you very tenderly.

Thursday, February 22 [Mar. 6], [1879]
at 10 in the morning

Good morning, dear Angel of my soul, God knows why, but I had a lot of trouble to fall asleep, but slept well after that. I did not go for a walk, as the weather is very unpleasant on account of the wind and of a kind of sleety rain, which produces an awful mush. I am again going to have a very busy morning. I embrace you tenderly and am happy that you are mine, and I

Yours forever

May God not forsake us, and bestow His Blessing on us!

Thursday, March 15 [27], [1879]
at midnight

Oh, how I love the good moments we spend together, and in which all our real life is concentrated! The presence of the dear children is my joy and their carefree gaiety does me such a lot of good, in the midst of all my worries. May God keep them safely for us and continue to watch over us! I hope that poor Mishechka [the "black sheep" brother Michael Dolgorukov] will get well again, and I fully share your fears. Our novel interests me greatly, and our reading together is a real rest for me. I love you, dear Angel, and kiss you tenderly.

Friday, March 16 [28], [1879]
at 10 in the morning

In spite of a small spell of coughing, I slept very well, and everything in me overflows with love and tenderness for you. I have not been out for a walk, as the temperature is 7 degrees; but the cold is already decreasing and I think the weather will become pleasant later on, if there is no wind. It is time to get to work now. I embrace you tenderly and am happy that you are mine, and I

Yours forever

May God not forsake us, and bestow His Blessing on us!

Sunday, March 18 [30], [1879]
at midnight

I am sorry that you had such a bad night, but happily your headache has decreased during the day. The good moments we spent together have left me the sweetest impression, and I was glad Oly was able to come—provided it didn't do her any harm, for one could see she did not feel well. Dear Pupussia's humor was as sparkling as ever, and he loves when I explain the pictures to him. I thank you for having read such a lot to me this evening, and at that read things that were not especially amusing, but however rather important, and I hope that the proposed measures will not fail to bring about results. I love you, my dear Angel, and kiss you tenderly.

Monday, March 19 [31], [1879]
at three-quarters-past 11 in the evening

I must confess than this morning's bulletin concerning our dear Oly [now six years old (born Nov. 7, 1873)] frightened me terribly, as did the doctor's fears of inflammation of the lungs. Measles are not amusing either, and would prevent her coming with us to Livadia. God grant it does not develop into something serious. As to dear Pupussia, it is but natural that the idea of sleeping with us pleased him. He had a good appetite at dinner, and his humor was sparkling. Our new novel promises to become interesting. I hope we will spend a better night than the last one. I love you, dear Angel, and kiss you very tenderly.

Tuesday, March 20 [Apr. 1], [1879]
at 10 in the morning

Good morning, dear Angel of my soul, I slept very well at the beginning of the night, but towards morning got very restless. I did not go for a walk as the weather is the same as yesterday, and am feverishly awaiting news of our dear Oly. God grant it will not be bad news.—I must get back to work, and I have a conference which will probably prevent me from coming to kiss you before noon. I embrace you tenderly, and am happy that you are mine, and I

Yours forever

May God not forsake us, and bestow His Blessing on us!

While Alexander prayed constantly for God not to forsake him or his "family," destiny ruled otherwise. Though the precursors of bolshevism and communism have today fairly faded into history, a very short outline of the revolutionary movement needs to be given here. Not long after the Karakozov attempt on the life of the Czar in 1866, more stringent police rules were established, and as a result the revolutionary movement in Russia was or seemed to be at a low ebb. Soon, however, young "intellectuals" of all classes and all professions—students, small office-holders, even junior officers of the army and navy—began to form various revolutionary groupings, at first without any organized program but always based on violent "eradication" of monarchy.* There was plenty of fuel for such groupings; only the leaders to ignite it were wanted. They were able in fact to overcome police inspection and rulings, thanks to a rather naïve and often lax method of police administrative actions. In the early 1870s the slogan "to the people," by which thousands of young men and women clad in peasant clothes (often looking like masqueraders rather than revolutionaries) invaded the countryside, "contacted" the peasants, and tried to convert them to socialism—which form the agitators were not sure themselves. These efforts, without violence at first, were on a whole a failure and resulted in many arrests and a dispersion of the movement. Often the peasants themselves delivered "the agitators" to the police.

The Russian-Turkish War somewhat abated the revolutionary activities, but as soon as peace was proclaimed, the smoldering fires began getting hot again.† Unrest in the capital soon was

---

* Even at the funeral of the Russian "people's" poet, but not the best, Nicholas Nekrasov, in January, 1879, young students made a political demonstration at his grave. In his eulogy, Dostoyevsky the famous author, placed Nekrasov where he certainly belonged—"after Pushkin and Lermontov" but was interrupted by students' shouts: "He is higher, higher!" Among the leaders of the students' demonstrators was the young George Plekhanov, the father of Russian Marxism and socialism, the mentor and finally the enemy of Lenin.

† While the war was still on in January 1878, a young "emancipated" girl,[2] of "noble family" by the name of Vera Zasulich, a follower of one of the most ruthless members of the party, Serge Nechaev (he murdered in cold blood his fellow party member Ivanov), attempted to assassinate General Feodor Trepov, the chief of police of St. Petersburg. To show the signs of the times, she was tried not as a "political" but as a common criminal. The case was tried publicly by a jury, and she was acquitted! The Zasulich *cause célébre* created the worst kind of publicity for the imperial regime. As the *Revue des Deux Mondes* wrote, Europe "forgot everything" for forty-eight hours, except to talk about the "new Moscovite Charlotte Corday." But Leo Tolstoy,[3] at that time, not quite as liberal as later, commenting on Zasulich's attempt, wrote this to his friend N. N.

followed in Kiev and Odessa, this time with political assassinations, kidnaping of officials, and other violences. At first the revolutionaries did not dare to attack the Emperor; after all, he still had a tremendous popularity, particularly among the peasants, as the "Czar-Liberator." But as the movement gathered more momentum and received organizational structure, with talented and energetic leaders, the plan was put into action to "get rid" of the Czar. The second attempt (the first was Karakozov's) on the life of the Czar was organized now by a revolutionary and terroristic group called the "People's Will." Meanwhile,[4] on March 25, 1879, an attempt on the life of General Drenteln, the new chief of gendarmes, and the head of the dreaded "Third Division" (political police), was made by a Jewish youth, Leon Mirsky, a member of another revolutionary group, "Land and Liberty." The attempt took place almost in the same spot, in the vicinity of the Summer Garden, where the Czar was shot at by Karakozov in 1866. (Incidentally, the Czar this time commuted the death sentence. Mirsky died peacefully in Soviet Russia in 1919!)

Less than a month later, also in Easter week, as in 1866, an "illegal" (i.e., a person who had no right, owing to revolutionary activities, to reside in the capital) by the name of Alexander Soloviev, "a retired civil employee," shot at the Czar with a revolver while the latter, unguarded, was taking his daily constitutional in the Palace Square. The Czar was unhurt and returned to the palace, where an enormous crowd awaited him with "thunderous hurrahs."[5]

Here are the Czar's own notes of his speech from the Winter Palace balcony, also found among Katia's papers.

Here is the substance of what I said, as far as I can remember:

I am deeply touched, and thank you from my heart for the feelings of devotion you have expressed to me. I can only regret that the occasion of this was so sad an event.

Strakhov: "This acquittal is nonsense and madness. This is the first sign of something not clear to us. But it is important. It looks like a forecoming of revolution!"[6]

God was gracious enough to spare me, for the third time, from certain death, and my heart is full of gratitude for His mercy. May He help me to continue serving Russia, and witness her happiness and peaceful evolution, as would be my wish. Thank you again.

April 2 [14], [1879]

On September 4, 1879 (almost exactly a year since Katia delivered her last child), another near-tragedy awaited the Czar. While he was returning from the Crimea, via Odessa (at that time the railroad ran to Odessa and not yet to Sebastopol) to St. Petersburg, attempts were made in two places to blow up his train. Fortunately for the Czar, all the undertakings of the revolutionaries failed.* However, for the third time, on December 1, while the imperial cortège was approaching Moscow, the would-be regicides blew up a whole train. But it was not the train in which the Czar was traveling. (Usually two similar trains of four or so cars—one for the Czar and the others for his suite—traveled within a half-hour of each other.) Luckily there were no casualties.

On arriving at Moscow the Czar addressed the population in these prophetic words (again the draft is in his own handwriting):

Moscow, November 20 [Dec. 2], [1879]

I am very happy to be able to repeat, in person, my heartfelt thanks to all the classes of Moscow for their charitable activities during the past war. Your noble example was followed by the whole of Russia. I hope that in the very near future a solidly based peace will be signed with Turkey. I thank you also for the feelings of devotion you expressed to me on the occasion of the sad events in

---

* The two main perpetrators of the crime were Sophia Perovskaya (of whom later) and Lev Hartmann, son of a German emigrant, who eventually settled in the U.S. (in 1880), where Lev died in 1909. He escaped to France and was arrested at the insistence of the Russian government while he was in Paris. But because of "public agitation" headed by Victor Hugo, he was not extradited.[7]

Petersburg and other localities of Russia [a reference to recent political terrorism and disturbances]. I fully believe in the sincerity of those feelings, and do not doubt that when I am not longer [alive] you will transfer them to my son and to his heir. I count on your collaboration to halt the erring youth from following the deadly path to which they are lured by evildoers. May God help us in this, and may He grant us the comfort of witnessing the gradual development of our dear Fatherland along peaceful and lawful paths. Only in that way can the future might of Russia be established, a might that is as dear to all of you as it is to myself.

The same day, the following statement was made public throughout Russia. Here is what the Czar said in Moscow to an assembled delegation:

Moscow, November 20 [Dec. 2], [1879]

On arriving in Moscow yesterday evening, I felt glad to have the opportunity to repeat to you personally my heartfelt thanks for the feelings of devotion expressed to me on the occasion of the sad event of April 2 [the attempt of Soloviev].

Similar declarations have reached me from all over Russia, and were of real comfort to me in the midst of my worries.

In the meantime, no later than yesterday evening God again saved me from danger that threatened me. The train which was following mine was wrecked by an explosion, just as it reached the limits of the city, but happily no one was hurt. This event is a further proof of the necessity of uprooting treason and consolidation of internal peace.

I therefore appeal to all loyal people, and especially to all fathers, to use their influence on enthusiastic youth, to try to guide them to the right path so that they should become useful to Russia by their actions. May God help us in this!

Three days after the railroad explosion the revolutionaries published an appeal demanding from the Czar the convocation of a "Constituent Assembly." Only then, they claimed, the Czar, "a reactionary and a repressor of liberty," will be "pardoned." The authorities were surprised and perplexed with the audacity of the revolutionists, all of whom they mistakenly named "nihilists" or sometimes "anarchists." Rumors claimed that their groups numbered in the thousands (actually, all in all, there were only a few hundred members).

Furthering the tragedy of these days for the Czar as he was being constantly haunted,* the Dolgorukova "affair" had come under criticism. Whispers began to be heard that "God's punishment" was the result of the "sinful" life the Czar led. The fact that the ailing Empress was still alive aggravated these grievances. Soon Alexander found himself isolated even from his closest circle, not excluding his sons. (Alexander, the Czarevich, and his wife, the Grand Duchess Marie, were the leaders in the "anti-Dolgorukova" party.) What also became a new subject for the gossips were the supposedly "weekly" visits of his "secret family" to the Winter Palace. "Rumors" had it that the Empress, while lying in her sickbed, could hear the children of Katia and her husband playing and "trampling" on the floor above.† On the other hand, we know from the reminiscence of the maid Vera that the children, Gogo and Olga, went "once" to the Palace, where "Papa" took them to "Aunty" (the Empress),‡8 who kissed them and blessed them, "while Aunty and Papa cried."

The new year of 1880 began with still another tragedy. On February 17 an attempt was made to kill the Czar and the entire Romanov family, assembled that night at the Winter Palace. A peasant's son, and a skillful carpenter, Stepan Khalturin, the founder of the "Moscow Workers' Union" and a member of the

---

* "What have these wretches got against me?" the Czar said at this time, "Why do they hunt me down like a beast?"

† This is one of these countless "they said" stories, which are hard to rely on.

‡ There is no doubt that Katia often stayed in the Winter Palace quarters, during the Empress's last years of illness. However, all the shorter stays were always more than secret and what is remarkable were little known outside. The "family" was permanently moved to the Palace in the early fall of 1880.

"People's Will," who in his youth planned to emigrate to America,[9] was the chief organizer of the attempt. Shortly before the event, Khalturin had secured a job as a carpenter at the Winter Palace. Because of this he was able to collect (gradually) a supply of explosives. He timed his attempt to kill the royal family on February 17, the day of a family dinner planned in honor of the Czar's brother-in-law, Prince Alexander of Hesse, the Empress's brother.* At exactly 6:20 P.M. that day a "tremendous explosion," heard even far away,[10] shook the palace. But the so-called Yellow Room where the Czar usually dined *en famille,* was only slightly damaged. Moreover, because of the lateness of his train (the Prince minus his morganatic wife, Julie Princess Battenberg, was coming from Germany), none of the intended victims was present in the dining room.† "God has saved me again," exclaimed the Czar the next day when he greeted German Ambassador von Schweinitz. To another witness, the Frenchman Vicomte de Vogüé, the Czar looked like a "ghost." "Never," he added, "have I seen him so pitiful, aged, played out, choked by a fit of asthmatic coughing at every word."[11]

In the meantime the "Executive Committee" of the People's Will party issued a statement, "condoning" the fact that the Czar escaped his death "to the misfortune of our country."[12] In their journal, secretly printed and distributed a month before the Winter Palace explosion, the terrorists had echoed the words of the Frenchman Edouard Vaillant, a member of the Paris Commune: "Society has only one obligation towards Monarchy: to put them to death."[13]

---

* Khalturin escaped but was caught in 1882 in an attempt to assassinate a general. He never disclosed his real identity and died on the scaffold under an assumed name. Only after the Revolution of 1917 were all the facts established.

† More than seventy casualties occurred among soldiers on guard duty that night. Eleven of them were killed outright. The Empress was not present and spent the entire night in her room. She was unaware of what had happened.

On February 5 [17] the Grand Duke Constantine, Jr., noted in his diary: "We are reliving the days of the Terror [of the French Revolution] with the difference, that the Parisians saw their enemies and we not only don't see them and don't know them but even haven't the slightest idea of their number—a complete panic."[14]

The palace explosion threw the population of St. Petersburg into a panic. Many of the well-to-do began to leave the capital. Rumors had it that on February 19 [March 3], the twenty-fifth anniversary of the Czar's reign, "several fires will be started in the city" and "three principal streets will be blown up."[15] Nothing that was predicted occurred, however; yet the next day another member of the People's Will party, the twenty-five-year-old converted Jew Hippolite Mlodecki, fired at—but failed to kill—Count Mikhail Loris-Melikov,* hero of the recent Russian-Turkish war and an outstanding military administrator. He had recently been appointed by the Czar, in view of "disturbances," to head "the Supreme Commission for the Maintenance of State Order and Public Peace" and became in fact a "dictator" with "unlimited power."[16]

Summer came and it seemed that the terror had abated. As the London *Times* reported, the measures of Count Loris-Melikov "had broken the spirit, if not the backbone, of the revolutionary monster."†[17] Once more, despite the attempt on the Czar's life, general anxiety, and even fear, Katia's life assumed the old routine. This is what she wrote the Czar during these troublesome months.

No. 122 St. P[etersburg]
[Received] May 7/19

Tuesday, May 6 [18], [1880]
at 4 o'clock in the afternoon

Oh, how I love you, dear adored Mounka, my life, my all, and what happiness it is to love each other as we do, and to only belong to the being you adore. I know

---

* In 1878 General Loris-Melikov, an Armenian by birth, received the title of Count, then a high honor, for his military exploits in the war of 1877–78. As an "outsider" and an Armenian in addition (a nationality usually referred to in ridicule on account of its predilection to commerce), he was snubbed by many of the St. Petersburg members of "The Spheres"— *i.e.*, by the society of the higher-ups. Yet he was particularly liked by the Czar (and Katia). A remarkable personality with vision and charm, and a real statesman, Loris-Melikov is awaiting his biographer.

† At the time these words were written, the terrorists had organized two more plots against the life of the Czar. Both attempts failed. Police were never aware of them.[18]

that this supports you, and that you never could have been unfaithful to me, because you are too honest. You are my all, may God watch over us and bestow his blessing on us. Gogo does not seem to be sick, his humor is sparkling. We were quite right in putting off our moving until Thursday, for the weather is awful. God grant it gets warm and that the children do not fall sick. For the present it is shivering cold outdoors, but we do not feel it in our good rooms, in which we feel so happy.

I am happy that you slept well last night, and that you get some sleep now. I am sure that the chapel will be deliciously [decorated]. Thank you for the money you gave me for this. I love our chats and all is well, may God reward you as you merit to be. I love you.

Wednesday, May 7 [19], [1880]
at 11 o'clock in the morning

Good morning, dear angel, I love you and everything in me is overflowing terribly. I slept well, and am only waiting for the moment of seeing you again. May God bless you and come to our aid. I love you.

Yours forever

No. 129 St. P[etersburg]
[Received] May 8/20

Wednesday, May 7 [19], [1880]
at half-past 4 in the afternoon

I can understand that this cold weather jars your nerves, and of course if tomorrow is not a really good day we will only move on Saturday, for what with this chilly weather the children would catch cold. Their summer place is very cold. Yes, the children's gaiety is good for us, they are always happy and have no worries. May God preserve them for us, and come to our aid! It is so good to be so much in love, and to belong only to the one you adore, and to have nothing to reproach oneself for. I know that this gives you support, and that you could never have been unfaithful to me.

You are my all. I am happy you slept well and that now you get some sleep.

I love our chats and all is well, for we are each other's life. As to Gogo, he shall be punished for his discourtesy, which is merely letting himself go from laziness, a thing I do not tolerate, particularly in a man. I love you, you are my life.

The same evening Katia dispatched several notes.

At 7 o'clock in the evening. Our dinner was very lively, and the children were in very good humor. I felt that everything was overflowing in me. I love you. May God bless you.

At 10 o'clock in the evening. Our novel is very interesting, and all is well. May God bless you and come to our aid! I love you.

On June 3 [May 22], 1880, Empress Marie, in the fifty-sixth year of her life, peacefully died in her sleep in the Winter Palace. That very morning the Czar himself told War Minister Miliutin that "no one was near her when she died."* With her death, a new page began for Alexander and Katia.[19] All that they so eagerly awaited for the last 14 years, yet had never openly acknowledged, had now become an established fact. At last they were "free."[20]

---

* The (London) *Graphic* of June 12, 1880, stated that the Czar [and Katia] was then in Czarskoye Selo and that "there was not even a nurse in the room."

A. A. Polovtzev, a State Secretary in 1880s and himself the son of a girl supposedly born out of wedlock by a Grand Duke, states a questionable version in his memoirs, recently published by the Soviets, that it was the Czar's brother, the liberal Constantine, who "hating" the Empress, "encouraged" his brother with his liaison and urged him to be away as much as possible.

"I forget the insult to the Empress,"—she was supposed to have said to her favorite lady-in-waiting, Countess Alexandra Tolstoy (the favorite "Aunt-Grandmother" of Leo Tolstoy), "but I cannot forget the torment inflicted on the wife."[21]

THE LAST PARADE

"*Morganatic*—a form of marriage which members of various royal families in Europe may contract with persons of inferior rank, and wherein the wife, if inferior, does not acquire the husband's rank, and the children do not succeed to the titles, fiefs, or entailed property of the parent of higher rank."—*Webster's Collegiate Dictionary* —Fifth Edition.

"The name 'morganatic' is derived from the medieval Latin *matrimonium ad morganaticam*, meaning 'marriage on the morning-gift' (in German *Morgengabe*), or the implication that this gift or dowry was all the bride was to get and that this 'morning' marriage, as a restricted one, should be 'celebrated quietly at an early hour.' "— *Encyclopaedia Britannica*, Vol. 15, 1967 Edition.

As soon as the mournful funeral chimes of the Sts. Peter and Paul Fortress, the burial place of the Romanovs, announced to the population of the capital that the Empress "had gone to a better world," Alexander began preparations for his marriage to Katia. As he himself later confided to War Minister Miliutin, the "justification for his decision" (to marry Katia) was based on "the debt of my conscience and my honor." As to the time, it must take place at the earliest possible moment, since "he could never be sure on any day that that day would not be his last on earth."[1]

The Czar also explained his motives in a letter dated October 20 [November 1], 1880, to his sister, Olga, the Queen of Württemberg, of whom he was very fond. ". . . I would never have married before a year of mourning" he wrote "if not for the dangerous time we live in and for the hazardous attempts I expose myself to daily which can actually and suddenly end my life. Therefore, I am anxious as soon as possible to secure the future of the object, which lived for me during the past fourteen years as well as for three of our children—happiness. Despite her youthfulness, Kniazhna Ekaterina Dolgorukova preferred to refuse all the pleasures and gaieties of society which means so much to a young woman of her age in order to devote her entire life to love and care for me. Therefore, she has a full right for my love, esteem, and my thankfulness. She literally saw no one except her only sister, and she never mixed herself in anything, despite many temptations. People had even shamelessly used her name without her even knowing it or getting her permission. She only lives for me and spent all her time in educating her own children. I can assure our family [meaning the imperial] that Ekaterina understands perfectly her position as a morganatic spouse and will never present demands contrary to my wishes as head of the family and a monarch. I only wish that the other members of [the imperial] family will remember it and will not force me to remind them about it."[2]

The correspondence between the lovers, before their marriage, is more than eloquent. Here is what Alexander wrote to Katia in a four-page letter:

No. 179 Z.S. [Czarskoye Selo]
[Received] June 27 [July 9]

Thursday, June 26 [July 8], [1880]
at half-past four in the afternoon

I know that you are enjoying the presence of the children, and you love our nice walks; you are right in saying that I treasure all our good habits and I will always treasure them, for I love you and all my life will be spent in loving you, for it is an adoration and an attachment that cannot decrease. It is so good to be so madly in love and to belong only to the one you love, and to have nothing to reproach oneself for. I know that you enjoy it. May God preserve us and bestow His blessings on us. As to Gogo's jealousy, it is but too natural, for he would like to be free in his movements and to run everywhere and be at liberty to see you all the time, and so I hope that all this will be granted him on May 23 [Empress's death anniversary] and that he will be able to enjoy it always. I am happy that you slept well last night, and that you get some sleep now. It was nice to have a walk a little while ago and to chat. I find that one should be more cautious in the choice of prison wardens,* for that will play us a bad trick someday. I love you, you are my life.

Monday, June 30 [July 12], [1880]
at midnight

I congratulate you again, dear adored angel, on this day when 14 years ago we became attached to each other forever. Since that day we have only given happiness to each other, and your heart knows how to appreciate all that you have done for me. May God preserve you, and bestow His blessing on us the 6th [July 6 (18), the date set for the wedding] and grant us many years of happiness. Thank you once again for everything, and do not forget that I have grown part of you forever. You must feel that everything is overflowing in me. We had a lovely walk together, and the children were in sparkling humor. But I am so sad not to have you beside me tonight. I love you, and am going to bed. I embrace you passionately, you are my all. I congratulate you once more.

Tuesday, July 1 [13], 1880, at 11 o'clock in the morning. Good morning, dear angel, I love you and everything in

---

* Probably a reference to the famous "Zasulich" case, which as we have seen was caused by an illegal punishment meted to a "political" by a prison warden. As a protest, Vera Zasulich, a young revolutionary, shot the St. Petersburg Chief of Police in 1878.

me is overflowing terribly. I congratulate you from all my heart on this birthday anniversary of our heart, and hope God will allow us to celebrate it for many more years to come. I am waiting for the moment to kiss you. I love you.

Yours forever

(A)

No. 184 Z.S.
July 2 [14]

Tuesday, July 1 [13], [1880]
at half-past 2 in the morning

I congratulate you from all my heart on this so dear anniversary, which is the most precious festivity that can exist, for nobody in the whole world can adore each other as we do, and behave as irreproachably as we, and therefore God will bless us for this and will grant us long years of happiness. May He keep all evildoers away from you, and come to our aid. Thank you again for all you have done for me during these 14 years which have passed only too quickly. I will never forget that day when we came back frenzied because we had seen each other, and *he* who *made his debut* by bursting! Oh! Oh! Oh! It is a real joy to be so mad, and to feel oneself so absorbed. I know that you enjoy it and that you feel happy. I am so sad not to have slept with you and not to have been able to congratulate you as soon as I woke up. I am only just waiting for the moment of seeing you again, and everything is overflowing in me. I love you.*

(A)

Katia's long letters eagerly express anticipation of the wedding day.

---

* This is the last letter of Alexander to Katia found among her papers. Whether there were more letters, after their marriage is difficult to ascertain.

No. 133 Z.S.
July 6 [18]

Saturday, July 5 [17], [1880]
at half-past 4 in the afternoon

I saw that you were worried yesterday to see me so nervous and ailing, but fortunately towards evening I felt much better, and today I have no complaints except that I feel weak after the pains I had last night. I am frenziedly waiting for tomorrow, and hope you will sign our document on Monday [probably an *Ukaz* legalizing the existing "family"] for then we will feel more at ease, and one of these days you will write the letter to your son, and I shall also *change my will.*

And then we will no longer have a stone on our hearts. May God watch over us, preserve and bless us. The children are in a sparkling humor, and it was nice to walk and chat at Pavlovsk. It is so good to be so mad and to only belong to the one you love, and to have nothing to reproach oneself for. Thank you again for all you have done for me during these 14 years of happiness. I want to express my gratitude to you in the last letter you will receive from me before we become *husband* and *wife before God and all men.*

(K)

Another letter, the same day, continues:

You must understand what will take place in me at the moment of being pronounced your wife, and what a joy it is to become the wife of the man you have madly loved for 14 years, and this gives us our only happiness on this earth! I will be so grateful to God for having fulfilled the dream of our lives, and for having regularized our position. At last we will be able to breathe freely. As to yourself, I thank you on my knees for all your noble conduct and for everything. May God allow me to prove all my gratitude to you. I am happy that you sleep well now and that you slept well last night. I love you, I am madly in love with you.

At 7 o'clock in the evening. Our dinner was very lively, and the children were in sparkling humor. I love you, you are my life, my all. May God bless you.

At half-past 11 in the evening. Our walk was very pleasant, I love our chats and all is well. Thank you from the bottom of my heart for the charming souvenir you gave me as a remembrance of tomorrow's event, I like it immensely. The day will be the happiest one of my life. Thank you for everything.

(K)

And do not forget that I am not the ungrateful kind. May God give you all the happiness you deserve. I embrace you passionately, you are my all. I love you.

Sunday, July 6 [18], 1880 [the wedding day*]
at half-past 10 in the morning

At last the long-awaited day is here, and I hope that in a few hours God will bestow His blessings on us and will preserve us. Thank you once again for everything, and do not forget that nobody in this world is as beloved as you are. Oh, how happy I will be in a few hours, you will become my protector in the eyes of the law, and nobody will be able to separate us, and we shall be *one* forever, as we have been for 14 years. I love you. Yours forever.

I am waiting for you to come and be kissed.

(K)

If we can believe Katia's maid Vera, "Kniazhna's wedding dress" was "made" more than a year before the Empress's death. Be it as it was, the dress with *fleurs d'orange*—a must for any Russian wedding—was ready to be used on the day of Katia's marriage, Sunday, July 18, 1880, only forty-six days after the Empress's death.† There was no end of indignations

---

* Alexander was the only Russian ruler who had married a Russian since Peter the Great, who of course was the first Emperor who did so.
† According to the Orthodox Church, the fortieth day of mourning was always observed with a special funeral service. A widower or widow had to wait at least a year to remarry.

when at first the rumor regarding the wedding reached "very limited" circles. At first, the marriage was kept secret from almost "everyone"; even the Czarevich was "not informed." The secret was so well kept, in fact, that the War Minister found out about it only a month after it had taken place,[3] and a high functionary noted in September that "the marriage most probably took place but nobody knows about it for sure, except those intimate persons who do not utter a word."*[4] The "dictator," Count Loris-Melikov, was notified only after the event. Even Count Adlerberg, perhaps the Czar's closest friend since childhood (when they had shared the same "wash-bowl together" and even addressed each other with the familiar "thou"), confessed to Miliutin after the death of the Czar (Miliutin was a most reliable diarist) that despite a "close and friendly relationship," the Czar "never discussed the ticklish problem with me and I pretended to know nothing about it."† "Finally," related Adlerberg, "40 days after the death of the Empress, the Emperor for the first time" decided to raise the "question." Even though Adlerberg hotly "argued" against the marriage in principle, adding that it was "indecent" to marry at all before a year had elapsed after the death of the Empress, the Czar, "pale, silent, disturbed, with shaken hands," was adamant. "Suddenly," continued Adlerberg, "the door opened and came in a woman with whom for the first time I found myself face to face" (meanwhile the Czar discreetly retired into another room). "A most violent" and lengthy scene then

---

* A. Polovtzev, whose diary was recently published in the Soviet Union, relates that Countess Sophie Bobrinsky, who was the daughter of Count Andrew Shouvalov and belonged to the "Court Set," was asked by the Czar "to give the bride away" but she refused, basing her refusal on the assumption that "she never had a close relationship with the Czar, which could not give him the right to make such a request."[5] One may question this version.

† Even as late as 1917, Count Vasilli Adlerberg, the grandnephew of the above, did not know all the details of this morganatic marriage! As he tells it: "This question was never discussed in our family."

This is not a surprising phenomenon for the days of no telephones, radio, or television. What is surprising is that the intimate relationship which existed between Franklin D. Roosevelt and Lucy Mercer Rutherfurd, while he was President of the U.S.A., became known only in 1968![6]

took place with Katia, who accused Adlerberg of "dissuading" the Czar. During "our conversation," the door opened and the Emperor "meekly" asked if he could enter. "No, leave us to end this conversation," Katia answered with "vehemence." "It would have been difficult to foresee" [for later years], continued Adlerberg, "to what extent [of trouble] this woman, insolent, and at the same time stupid and [mentally] undeveloped, could have led the Czar. Perhaps his martyr's death forestalled new and imprudent actions and saved his brilliant reign from an inglorious and humiliated finale."[7] "The story seemed to me so interesting," wrote Miliutin, "that I dared to put it in my diary. It is possible, that many years later a future historian will use it, as a priceless material for the epoch in which we live."* The thoughts expressed by Adlerberg, perhaps not quite an objective witness, were shared by many.

Another witness left us a description of an *intime* dinner.

"November 24 [Dec. 6] 1880 [recorded Bobrinsky† in his diary] on St. Catherine's Name's Day [when all Catherines in Russia celebrate their name's day (name's days are celebrated more than birthdays)] the city expected a Manifest to announce the [future] marriage of the Emperor with Kniazhna Dolgorukov. None appeared. Rumor also spread there will be a "Sortie" [imperial reception]. No "Sortie," [instead] the Emperor dined [at the Winter Palace tonight] at 7:00 P.M. with a small family circle. On his right he seated Princess Meschersky [Katia's widowed sister Mouche], on his left his wife, next to Katia, Gogo, the 8-year-old boy, then Mlle. Shebeko followed by little Meschersky [Leonilla, who survived the Revolution and died in France in the 1930s] and the little girl, Olga [Katia, Jr., was ill], then Grand Duke Alexis [the Czar Alexander II's

---

* The traditional attitude of those days that *"on n'épouse pas ses maîtresses"* (one does not marry his mistress) was strong as ever. Queen Victoria felt that the Czar "ought to have done it, but kept it secret."

† Count Alexis A. Bobrinsky (1852, died in France as an exile in 1927), a distinguished and loyal statesman (and a godson of Nicholas I), was at one time a member of the Duma and finally Minister of Agriculture until November, 1916.[8] He was the direct and eldest descendant of Catherine the Great by her *liaison* with Orlov.

youngest son] that is the whole *Rout*—all of which, they say, amused Grand Duke Alexis. At the dinner the Princess [Katia] was served first, then her sister and only then the Emperor, a protocol ordered personally by His Majesty. The appointments are magnificent, all in white satin and silk at exorbitant cost. As the marriage is not officially declared Princess Catherine has no right to Calling Cards, neither to bear Coat-of-Arms. Her [personal] laquais wear liveries with golden buttons only. Her future Coat-of-Arms is combination of Imperial Eagle [double] with a Griffin, also symbols it seems of the Romanov Arms. Wooing [by members of the Romanov family] is perpetual and zealous. The Grand Dukes Nicholas [Sr.] and Constantine [the Czar's brothers] are slavishly at the feet of Madame Catherine! Grand Duke Alexis [Katia's stepson, three years younger the she] holds himself with dignity, but is very polite. Their son [Gogo] is very badly brought up. When Princess Meschersky [his aunt] made a remark to him while he was speaking with Alexis he replied to her "I am not talking to you!" Princess Meschersky, red in the face, retorts, "How dare you talk to me like that? If I were your mother I would beat you for such an answer!"[*9]

None of the witnesses left traces of their impressions of the wedding.[†] We know, however, from the memoirs of Vera, that Katia was very "agitated" the morning of the wedding day. When she asked for a glass of water she inquired, "There is nothing in the water?" meaning was it free of poison. "Today," Katia said, "is a great day, do pray for me. We waited 16

---

* Count Boris Berg, Princess Meschersky's son, in commenting on these notes, writes that they were confirmed by his mother,[10] but he adds that it is possible that Bobrinsky was somewhat prejudiced toward "both sisters," which is explained perhaps by a "very assiduous but unsuccessful courting" by the former of his mother with a final refusal.

† An aide-de-camp of the Czar's brother, Captain V. Vonlarlarsky, in his memoirs, tells us how "embarrassed" he was when arriving on some mission at the Palace he was told immediately "to take off all the attributes of Grand Court Mourning [according to regulations the "Grand" called for black crepe for a year on the shoulder straps and on the *aiguillettes*] in order not to sadden His Majesty as today, 6 [18] of July, is the day of his espousal."[11]

years [the nurse added two more years] and how we suffered."*

The wedding took place in a small chapel (so-called military chapel) of the Czarskoye Selo Palace. The Czar wore a *Vengerka,* his favorite "Hungarian" blue jacket of the Guard Hussars, with Katia wearing the wedding dress ready "a year before." (Katia's nephew wrote, however, that she wore an "ordinary habit.") There were no outside guests. Only the Minister of the Court, Count Alexander Adlerberg, very reluctantly and as a "witness only" ("as a protest" Adlerberg "appeared in civilian full dress suit," instead of customary military uniform, even though the military were not allowed to wear civilian clothes except abroad); General Ryleev, "the confidant" of the Czar; and General Count Edouard Baranov, "his closest friends,"† served as crown bearers —a Russian custom at all weddings.¹² The ever present Vava Shebeko was Katia's only witness.

A priest, the Most Reverend Xenophont Nikolsky of the "Grand Cathedral of the Winter Palace," officiated. He signed an act that read, but was not made public:

> In the year of 1880 on 6 [18] July at 3 o'clock in the afternoon in the Czarskoye Selo Military Chapel, His Imperial Majesty the Emperor Alexander Nikolaevitch of all the Russias, has been graciously pleased to contract a second legitimate marriage with Kniazhna Ekaterina Mikhailovna Dolgorukova, the Lady-in-Waiting.‡

That very day and several days later, Katia dispatched several love notes to her husband. (At first the newlyweds

---

* Vera was "terrified" when Katia lost the wedding ring. "This is a very bad omen," wrote Vera, "it means loss of a husband."

† The grandnephew of Adlerberg and the grandnephew of Baranov, both exiles of the 1917 Russian Revolution, are now American citizens. General Alexander Ryleev (1830–1907) perhaps one of the most loyal friends the Czar ever had (it was rumored that he even petitioned the Czar at the request of the latter for a formal adoption of his illegitimate offspring). Later, the Czar apparently changed his mind and canceled the petition.¹³

‡ Curiously enough, the document in question does not mention the *new* name of the bride, usually bestowed by Emperors in morganatic marriages. However, she was from that day on addressed as "Princess Yourievskaya" with the appellation of her "Serene Highness." More about this later.

resided at Czarskoye Selo in separate quarters—the Czar at his palace, Katia with her children at a new *dacha* recently purchased by the Czar as a "gift.")[14] Here they are:

No. 189 Czarskoye Selo
[Received] July 7 [19]

Sunday, July 6 [18], [1880]
at quarter-past 5 in the afternoon

And so, now you are my adored husband before God and man, and you can rest assured there will never be a husband as greatly loved by his wife as you are, and always will be. May God render to you all the happiness you deserve, and may He also allow us to live long and enjoy our happiness, and may He bless the children. Of course, it is a stone that fell from our heart, and I shall never forget today's ceremony, which was so meek, I prayed so hard for you and us. Oh, what happiness to be your wife, it is a true consolation to adore each other as we do, and to belong only to the one whom you adore. Thank you for everything and for the blessing you bestowed on me this morning, and for the adorable ikon which will bring us luck.

Thank you also for the charming souvenir you gave me in memory of today, which I will treasure as a relic. Happily I am feeling well, and am not tired. The children were very pleased with the toys we gave them, and our walk was very pleasant, in a word the whole impression was delightful. I am happy you slept well last night, and that you sleep well now. Thank you for all the happiness you have given me for 14 years. I hope God will grant us many more years of happiness, and that He will come to our aid. I very well sensed how moved you were during the ceremony, and how happy you are now. I love you, you are my life, I cannot forget how excited you were as I was dressing.

I love you.

At half-past 11 in the evening. I thank God from the bottom of my heart for this delightful day and I feel so happy, may God preserve you, bless you in all you undertake and give back to you all you have done for me. I love you, and thank you for everything. Do not forget that you are my life. I feel so very happy!

Monday, July 7 [19], 1880, at 11 o'clock in the morning. Good morning, dear angel, I love you and everything in me is overflowing terribly. Oh, what a good night it was, and now I have awoke with my heart filled with gratitude towards God and yourself. Good-bye until 1 o'clock. I kiss my adored husband passionately.

Your adored wife (forever)

[K]

The very next day after these lines were written, her "adored" husband gave a small dinner in his palace, present at which were his son, Alexis, "recently returned" from London; his daughter, Marie, Duchess of Edinburgh; "The Dictator," Count Loris-Melikov; Miliutin; and a few others. Katia, the two-day bride, was absent. There was no mention of the wedding. In the meantime, Katia and Alexander continued to live apart.[15] The "little wife" was more than busy with her *billets-doux*. Here are a few:

Z.S.

Wednesday, July 9 [21], [1880]
at half-past 11 in the morning

I was certain that my adored husband would comfort his little wife who did not sleep well, because of her worrying about her adored Mounka. I love you terribly, you are my life, my all. Good-bye until 1 o'clock. May God bless you. You are my all. Thank you for everything.

Yours forever

Z.S.

Sunday, July 20 [Aug. 1], [1880]

Dear adored husband, please give orders to have your horse ready at Pavlovsk, for the weather is superb. I love you.

Your little wife forever

Morganatic marriages, particularly in Imperial Russia, were a disaster area. Nobody liked this institution except the pair in question, the royal relatives for obvious reasons, the relatives of the bride because close family relationships become constrained and restrained, also for obvious reasons. Courtiers and other minor officials and servants of a court are traditionally snobbish and resentful of a newcomer, an upstart far beneath them but from whom they must take orders. The upper classes, particularly select court circles—*i.e.*, those who are "admitted to the court," the upper society in general—even the upper and middle classes are to a large degree negatively predisposed.* The rank and file of the population, the lower strata— small merchants, peasants, including particularly the clergy, a strong influence on the people—feel that an unequal marriage of "one of their kind," to "the mighty Czar" is "no good and immoral." Finally, to the professional, amateur, and assorted revolutionists of Alexander's time, his morganatic marriage was a God-sent weapon to be used on the side of agitation and propaganda in order to topple the "rotten regime." In a word, one must agree that the Royal French Traditional formula of a *"maîtresse en titre"* institution is relatively sound.

August came, and as it was customary, the Czar was ready to leave Czarskoye Selo for Livadia in the Crimea. What had formerly been a relatively simple task now seemed more than difficult. Aside from the "extraordinary security measures" to be taken during the long travel to the south (as we have seen more than three attempts to blow up the Czar's train had been made by the terrorists), the problem of transporting the Czar's "new" and still "secret family" in the "same train" caused further complications.†

---

* Jealousy played a large part too. "Why is she the lucky one?"—it certainly was thought, if not said.[16]

† A group of terrorists, headed by Andrei Zheliabov (we'll hear more of him later), learned, probably from their own spies in the palace, that Alexander and Katia were planning to leave Czarskoye Selo on August 29 for the Crimea, "via St. Petersburg." On the basis of this knowledge the revolutionists placed four sacks, containing 250 pounds of dynamite, in the water under a bridge leading to the railroad station of Czarskoye

To begin with, when on Sunday, August 29, the imperial train left the St. Petersburg railroad station, the Czar and his "family" were not among those present. They boarded the train at Kolpino, a small station thirteen miles south of St. Petersburg. According to Vera, the Princess (she now used the title of Kniaghinia) arrived at Kolpino in a troika, the Emperor in a regular carriage. Katia, her two older children, and the ominpresent Vava Shebeko were placed in the Czar's "private" train; Vera, the maid, boarded train B with little Katia and a "French nurse" in St. Petersburg.* Both trains were "exactly alike" to "fool the plotters" and at each large station switched "places"—*i.e.*, A (the imperial train) was to follow B (reserved for the imperial suite) and then the reverse. Thousands of soldiers and peasants guarded the way in "unending chains throughout the whole road." The trains stopped neither at Moscow nor at "any large towns."

"When we [the suite of the Czar]," wrote the loyal Miliutin, "found out [that the "family" was also on the train] we were very surprised and somehow disturbed, fearing to be put in an awkward situation. However, everything went well without special inconvenience, except that we were placed in the different carriages as before, with the result that we couldn't pass the Czar's wagon in order to reach the dining room. Only Count Adlerberg, Count Loris-Melikov and General Ryleev, initiated in the secret of the marriage, were placed separately next to the women's wagon and the dining salon. The new spouse of the Czar, Princess Yourievskaya, with her two children not once left her car. We never saw her during the entire trip."[17] Neither had she left the train in Kharkov, where the Czar "attended manoeuvers," and reviewed the local troops. While waiting for the Czar, Katia, in her bold handwriting, filled six pages; here is her lengthy missive:

Selo. The plan fell through because one of the accomplices arrived late for the "appointment." The police were not aware of the new plot.[18]

* Count Loris-Melikov "unsuccessfully tried" to persuade the Czar not to take his new wife along, giving as a reason "countless warnings" received about "planned attempts" on the life of the Czar. "Here is a chance" Miliutin wrote ironically, "for a woman to show her self-denial and devotion . . . and occupy the same compartment in the Czar's train, in which about a year before traveled the late Empress."[19]

No. 192 Kharkov
[Received] in Tchuguyev*

Aug. 19 [31], [1880]
at 5 o'clock

I entreat you to let me know how you arrived and how you feel. I am as a lost soul, and am only waiting for tomorrow. I love you terribly, you are my life. I slept for a full hour from 3 to 4. I saw Baby [little Katia], who is well, but adores the chambermaids. I feel well, except for a strong cold, and my throat hurts. Gogo is very busy with his writing without anyone urging him to do it. He keeps asking whether Loris-Melikov follows you in a victoria, for he is afraid you will be attacked by brigands. I confess that I will only cease to worry when I see you again. May God preserve and bless you, and reward you as you deserve.

You are my life, my all. Write me a few words, for I am afraid you caught cold. I feel the strength of my love more than ever, and miss you so. The cossack has orders to wait for a reply. Tell them to give him something to eat. He is such a good man, he offered to carry the letter himself, with great joy. When I said that I would send one of his comrades, he said: "I will go and find out how they got there: we will be more reassured that way." I love you.

You are my life. Greetings to Loris-Melikov. I love you and it is so sad without you. May God bless you. Your Mounka who thinks of you all the time.

Your adored little wife†

In Livadia,‡ which they reached on the sixth day, new complications arose at once on account of the "new family."

---

* A small town near Kharkov, where the Czar also reviewed the troops.
† This is the last of Katia's letters that we possess. It is very possible that after their marriage, their habit of exchanging daily *billets-doux* ceased. At any rate, Katia's archives contained no more mutual correspondence.
‡ The Czar was the first Russian ruler to buy land in the Crimea. The thousand-acre estate included a palace, which he built, and a large

As it happened, the day of their arrival at Livadia on the third of the month was exactly the day the Empress had died three months earlier. Hardly had they put feet on the ground at Livadia (the party arrived at 6 A.M.) when a "liturgy for the repose of one's soul," in the presence of the Czar (Katia was not present) and his entire suite, took place. For the superstitious Russians the arrival of the "new family" to coincide with the liturgy was certainly not an auspicious omen.[20]

The Kniaghinia "descended" with her children to the "same quarters," formerly occupied by the late Empress. The next day Alexander at last "initiated" Count Miliutin* "in the secret of the marriage." "The Emperor explained to me the reasons for it," wrote Miliutin. "It is the debt of my conscience and my honor," said the Czar and, "very simply, naturally and without extra words presented me to the new 'Princess,' who after saying a few polite words immediately retired." Somewhat later, Miliutin noted that at the parade of "His Majesty's Bodyguard Cossacks" (on October 16) the Czar for the first time appeared publicly before the troops with his new spouse and children. The boy Gogo was even dressed in the cossack uniform of the Bodyguard. "The official apparition of Princess Yourievskaya made a painful impression on all of us. How sad and pitiful for him," ended Miliutin's diary entry[21] on that day.

As rumors spread that the Czar "evidently" wished to give his "new family" an "official position," life in Livadia became "unsupportable"[22] for most of the courtiers, with the exception, perhaps, of Count Loris-Melikov, "the outsider" and the "vile Armenian" (as some, envious of his rising career, called

---

vineyard (which gave an impetus to the launching of domestic champagne and wines). As a result, many members of the royal family and several noble families followed his example. Tracts of land were also "granted" by the Czar to various statesmen for their deeds.[23]

* For his deeds towards "reorganization of the army" and introducing universal conscription on a "democratic basis," Dimitri Miliutin, the liberal and the very capable Minister of War, was granted the title of "Count" on September 11, 1878, by the Czar. Miliutin was also responsible for abolishing corporal punishment in the army and navy—a measure which was an "innovation," unknown in Europe and even in the U.S.A.[24]

him), who was considered, not without justification, to be the "Princess's favorite."*

Happily for Miliutin and others of the Czar's entourage, the Czar and the "new family" left Livadia for St. Petersburg at the end of November. "Once more," wrote Miliutin, "extraordinary measures of security were taken. Aside from troops, which lined all the way from Simferopol [on the Black Sea], about 20,000 private inhabitants on foot and on horses, guarded the tracks." The Czar "almost nowhere" left the train, and while the entourage was stopping at the stations, "nobody" from "outside" was allowed to be on the platform. During the whole trip Count Loris-Melikov received "alarming" telegrams about the arrest of "suspicious characters" and of bombs planted here and there. Three days later the entourage was in the capital, where a Te Deum in the Winter Palace took place in the presence of those who had made the journey. No members of the imperial family except the Czar and his "new family" were present.

We already know that even though the marriage of Alexander and Katia had been "legalized" by a church ceremony, she "officially" still had no "name." Only on December 5 [17], 1880 was an imperial *ukaz* printed but not made public.†

By Imperial ukaz it is ordered to bestow on Kniazhna Ekaterina Mikhailovna Dolgorukova the family name of Yourievsky, with an appellation of Her Serene Highness.

No mention was made of the children or the marriage that had taken place six months before!

Regarding the creation of the name Yourievsky, several versions exist. In the opinion of the present writer, the version of Mouche, Katia's sister, is most plausible. According to

---

* The "conciliatory and liberal policies" of Loris-Melikov, perhaps one of the few real statesmen of the period, "aroused a storm of indignation in the ranks of the unemployed statesmen and the unrecognized saviours of the country"25 a Grand Duke wrote many years later.

† Many years ago, morality had its own rules. What should be noted, however, is that only after thirty years of social ostracism did the Duchess of Windsor meet Queen Elizabeth II, "under the trees along the mall," at the unveiling of a memorial plaque to the late Queen Mary in 1966.26

her, as told to her son, Count Boris Berg: "When [after Katia's marriage] they began to look for marriage links between the Dolgorukovs and the Romanovs they remembered that the first Romanov Czar, Michael, was married to Princess Maria Dolgoruky [who died without an issue]. Moreover, Michael was a direct descendant of a Boyar Youri Zakharin (died in 1503) whose descendants much later assumed the family name of Romanov [Michael's great grandfather's first name] all Youri's direct descendants. Hence, the Yourievsky name." The Yourievsky county near Moscow, originally one of the estates of the Romanovs existed until 1917. The coat-of-arms which was especially[27] created for Katia carried both symbols of the traditional crest of the Romanov family—the double eagle and the griffin. The device on the coat-of-arms read: "For Faith, the Czar and Motherland."

The news, shocking as it was to many, spread in wider circles and created a "furor." To many it was "unbelievable" that the Emperor, the Czar-Liberator, and Father of his people could, within a "few days" of becoming a widower, at his age (he was sixty-two) marry a "girl half his age" and, what was even worse, a "climber," an "outsider," and nonroyal.* The specter of the "Troubled Times" of 1612 arose in everybody's mind.†

The gossipers asserted that the "Princess" would be soon "proclaimed an Empress" with a large and sumptuous coronation to follow, all this while the legitimate heir to the throne, Alexander, Jr., and his eldest son, Nicholas, were more than alive! As a result, the relationship between the "new household" and the rest of the imperial family was at its lowest.‡ Every-

---

* Prior to Peter the Great, the Czars always married girls of "noble" but not necessarily royal birth. This invariably created jealousies and intrigues. Though Peter did not follow the custom (on his second marriage), he was the first monarch to enforce the foreign "Dynastic Marriages."

† "Troubled Times" or "Times of Troubles," was a period of unrest between 1598 to 1613 due to the extinction of the House of Rurik. The period ended with the election of the first Romanov to the Throne of Russia.

‡ As Count Berg noted there "was talk that the Cesarevna Marie planned to leave Russia for her native Denmark" if the rumors of Katia's

one in the "family" (except the "liberal" Grand Duke Constantine, the elder brother of the Czar), tried to pretend that the Czar's marriage "did not exist."* For cabinet ministers it was even more difficult. Finally it was decided that they all (the ministers) should "leave their names" (etiquette didn't allow "leaving cards"; each one had to sign his name in a special book) in the Winter Palace and thus pay his "respect to the new consort."

It was also rumored by the "enemies" of Loris-Melikov that it was he, who, in order to "obtain more power from the Czar," "planted" in Katia's head "the idea" of a coronation. One can be reasonably sure that Katia no doubt "cherished" the idea, but there are no facts on hand to confirm that plans were being made for such an extraordinary event. However, many years later Katia confided to her nephew Count Boris Berg that "Moscow archives were searched, regarding [the ritual of] the coronation of Catherine [the Livonian maidservant], the second wife of Peter the Great."† Katia also related to

---

coronation would be fulfilled. Rumors were so persistent that Count Loris-Melikov gave an order that the imperial yacht should be "out of order."[28] Actually, the Czarevich and his wife went to Livadia, where of course they ran into Katia, who was staying, "to their chagrin and humiliation" in the late Empress's palace.

* Grand Duke Alexander, the son of Alexander II's brother Michael, in his memoirs vividly describes some of the "family" dinners and receptions at which Katia made her appearance. One should read these memoirs with caution, as they have been "touched up," for in 1880 Alexander was only fourteen years old! But Miliutin, not Katia's friend, "noted that after dinners she always promptly retired."

A reliable memoirist, the old Elizabeth Narishkin, relates that at the "Great Fast Days" early in March of 1881, at a church ceremony, the Czarevich "shook Katia's hand but did not kiss it as the Czar had evidently expected. 'Sasha is a good son,' he cried [sic], 'but you have no heart!' The assembled Court trembled." All this, of course, could and probably did take place but not in the form described.[29]

What also enraged some of the Czar's relatives and members of the court was an order of his, to create, supposedly at the request of Katia, a Winter Garden in the palace, complete with hothouse flowers, fountains, and exotic blooms.[30] The room survived to the year of the Russian Revolution in 1917.

† Martha Skavronsky, or Empress Ekaterina Alexeyevna I, was baptized and received her patronimic in honor of her godfather and stepson, Alexis, the son of Peter the Great. She was crowned only in 1724, after having

her nephew that "once the Czar ordered the Empress's crown brought in" and he "himself placed this crown" on Katia's head to "see if any alterations would be necessary."[31]

It was also "remembered," that the Dolgorukys were "directly descended from the ancient Russian Rulers" and that the first wife of Czar Ivan the Terrible was Maria Dolgoruky, whom he ordered to be drowned the day after the wedding. The first Romanov, Czar Michael, was also married to Maria Dolgoruky, "the first Czarina of the Romanov Dynasty" (she died four months after the wedding "probably poisoned"). More than that, it was "recalled" that Peter II, the last male Romanov, "was betrothed" to another Dolgoruky also named Catherine (he died a day prior to the marriage). Finally, Katia's family claimed that their relative Michael Dolgorukov "had been also betrothed [but never married, as he was killed] to a sister of Alexander I, the conqueror of Napoleon" (a fact impossible to ascertain).

True as it might have been, one had to remember that the above Dolgorukys were more than distantly related to Katia's branch of the family, the Dolgorukovs of Teplovka. What somewhat refutes the allegations and "rumors" regarding the "crowning" is the contents of the last will drawn by the Czar in November, 1880, and addressed to his son and heir, the future Alexander III. In this document there is not a hint regarding the "future Empress." However, it is quite possible that Alexander, weak as he was, would have been able as an autocrat to "proclaim" Katia Empress, with his next heir, however, the Cesarevich Alexander and not Gogo.

---

married Peter publicly in 1712 and having lived with him since 1702. Moreover, the two little daughters were bridesmaids of their own mother's marriage in 1712! Their four daughters: the first died in 1703; Catherine, born in 1706 († 1708); Anna in 1708; and Elizabeth in 1709, until 1724 were actually "non-persons" and with their mother, known then as "Caterina Vasilievna," were not even listed in the official Court Calendar until 1724, the year Peter the Great died. It is ironic that Anna, later the Duchess of Holstein-Gottorp, became the progenitor of the Romanov Dynasty, since Peter's grandson, Peter II, the last Romanov male, betrothed to the Princess Catherine Dolgoruky, died in 1730. All this was openly published in a book in 1874 by the well-known and popular historian of the day Daniel L. Mordovtzev![32]

Grand Duke Alexander, writing in exile, had this to say about Katia:

In the winter of 1880–81, the members of the imperial household and the venerable leaders of St. Petersburg society were openly accusing Princess Yourievskaya of planning to entrust her favorite, General Loris-Melikov, with dictatorial powers and to bring about radical changes in the Constitution.

As is always the case, the women proved to be particularly merciless in their denunciation of Gogo's mother. Guided by hurt vanity and blinded by bitter jealousy they rushed from house to house repeating the wildest possible rumors and spreading poisonous calumny. It matters not that Princess Yourievskaya belonged to the old historical family of Dolgoroukys who traced their origin directly to Rurick, the Scandinavian conqueror of Russia. In fact, it made her situation more precarious, the insatiable gossipers dwelling with relish upon the fantastic tales of the imaginary feud between the Romanoffs and the Dolgoroukys. They talked of a peasant prophet who had predicted two hundred years ago that swift death would befall any Romanoff marrying a Dolgorouky. They quoted the tragic end of Emperor Peter II to lend strength to this crazy theory. Did he not die on the day set for his wedding to the young Princess Nathaly Dolgorouky? Was it not significant that the best of physicians failed to save this only son of Peter the Great?[33]

There was another story that the Czar, upon learning that one of the society ladies, the witty Princess Maria Vorontzov, born Princess Troubetzkoy, was criticizing him for such a "sudden marriage," scolded her: *"Il parait, princesse,"* he said, *"qu'il faut être sur ses gardes avec vous, que vous avez la langue bien pendu?"* and received an answer: *"Oui, Sire, mais elle est trop courte. Elle ne touche jamais le palais."* (A play on words. "Palais," palace, sounds like "palais," palate, the roof of the mouth.)[34]

It was also rumored that Grand Duke Constantine, the Czar's favorite brother, "kissed" Katia's hand and thus made the heir, the Cesarevich Alexander, an enemy from that moment on.* To make matters worse, criticism of the Czar was heard even among lower classes. A reliable diarist noted that several policemen reported that "simple people" (*i.e.* peasants and workers), promenading in the Summer Garden (near the Winter Palace), were overheard calling Katia "a *mamselle*"— in Russian parlance a "hussy." Other reports, gathered from conversations of the "lower classes," stated that "the devil forced the Czar to fool around with a girl and now God will forsake him." On the other hand, it was also noted that some of those few peasants who knew about the marriage (censorship of course prevented the "news" from being largely known), expressed their opinion on the subject in a different fashion: "How is it to be without a housewife?" they said. "Mother Czaritza died, nothing else to do for him, but to get another one."[35] It was not surprising that the Czar, who undoubtedly felt and even knew that the attitude of most of the people was negative, became "bitter, disillusioned and melancholic." When he heard of someone speaking badly of him, he exclaimed: "Strange, I don't remember even having done him a favor; why then shall he hate me?"[36]

On the other hand, one has to admit, the "situation" was aggravated by a tactless, somewhat brusque, and not a very clever attitude on the part of Katia herself.† It is true of course that to "win friends" in Katia's new position was difficult, if not completely impossible. Those who knew her assert that

---

* Upon his accession Alexander III instantly dismissed Constantine, who in the capacity of the General-Admiral was one of the ablest members of the imperial family. Alexander III, himself a "model family man," "intensely" disliked Constantine for his "liberalism" and "libertinism" as well. He considered him to be a "Freemason"—then "a great sin" in Russia. He simply "couldn't stand" the fact that his uncle also had "another family"—a ballet dancer with whom the Grand Duke lived "almost openly." Several of his illegitimate children received the names of "Constantinov."[37] The *pince-nez* he wore also was considered an attribute of a "liberal."

† Elizabeth Narishkin, one of the ladies of the court who survived to our days and died in France as a refugee just before World War II, in her memoirs describes Katia as "an ignorant" with "no idea of the manners and custom of high society," given to "constant tactlessness," which shocked the court "again and again. She had no self-control."[38]

Katia "never read anything," neither books, magazines, nor newspapers. "Her knowledge," wrote her sister-in-law, "is all she has heard from her[39] very small circle of friends," headed of course by Vava Shebeko. Morever, her extreme jealousy, usually unfounded, her possessiveness and pettiness, made her a difficult personality all around.*

One of her friends, perhaps not so much by choice as by necessity, was the Czar's favorite at the moment, Count Loris-Melikov. Here is his note to Katia.

> I most earnestly request Your Serene Highness to extricate me from a difficult situation.—In reporting to the Emperor that I was free for the game of cards this evening, I completely forgot that today there is a meeting at Count Valouyev's [Count Peter Valuev was a cabinet minister] to discuss press matters, at half-past 8 in the evening. Therefore I could only come at 10 o'clock, that is when you will already be sitting around the tea table. Be so good as to inform me whether I can do this, or would it better to ask Valouyev to cancel the meeting.

> Saturday   Your deeply devoted
>   M. Loris-Melikov

While in Livadia the Czar, who had no illusions that he was not constantly facing danger, decided to draw up a last will "confiding" his new family to his son and heir, Alexander, "Sasha." Here is this unusual document, made public only by the Soviets. It is dated November 9 [21], 1880, from Livadia.

---

* It was said that the Czar, to refute criticism, exclaimed "Why if my ancestors were allowed [to have mistresses] am I not?" Though his reasoning had grounds, the comparison had not. The mistress *en titre* of Czar Alexander I (he had several) *"la belle Narishkin,"* of a polonized family but a descendant of Rurik-born Princess Maria Sviatopolk-Czetwertyn-ska († 1854) was a married woman very rich and apparently discreet. Barbara Nelidov, the mistress of Nicholas I, was the personification of discretion. Incidentally, contrary to his ancestry, Alexander III was an *"Odnolub,"*—one who faithfully loved one at one time, which trait he certainly kept all his life—with his son Nicholas II fully adopting the vocation.[40]

Dearest Sasha,

In case of my death I confide to you my wife and children of mine [by Katia]. . . . My wife received no inheritance whatsoever and therefore, all that she owns now is her own, with her relatives having no rights or claims to it in any shape or form. For security's sake she has willed everything to me. . . . [The letter also mentioned that the house that Katia owned on the English Quay and Galernaya Street 47–48, the *dacha* in Czarskoye Selo, Peterhof, and two more *dachas* in the Crimea—"are all hers too."]

My wife's capital [continued the letter], until our marriage will be officially proclaimed [it never was in his lifetime], is in my name. . . . All objects, which she gave me, must after my death be returned to her. I wish that in this case [*i.e.*, his death] the living quarters in the Winter Palace should be reserved for her and her children. . . . these are my last wishes, which, I am certain, will be fulfilled by you conscientiously.

God bless you for all your care! Don't forget and pray for the soul of your sincere and tenderly loving Pa.

Alexander[*41]

Moreover, as early as September 5 [17], 1880, the Czar drew up a paper in Livadia attesting that the Minister of the Court, Count Adlerberg, "has deposited" a sum of more than 3,302,910 gold rubles (an enormous sum at that time, equal to at least $30 million today) at the state bank in the name of "Princess Catherine Yourievsky and her children. For her alone to use this capital, during my lifetime or after my death."[42]

Only after their return from the Crimea, did Alexander move permanently his whole "new family" to the Winter

---

* The Grand Duke and his wife, the Czarevna Maria Feodorovna, arrived at Livadia on October 7 [19]. Their relations with Katia, according to Miliutin, "were said to be cold and straight-laced."[43] E. Narishkin, a fairly[44] reliable diarist, tells us that Alexander "had no idea" that Katia lived in the palace and not in her "villa." "Had I known it," said Maria, "I [would have] taken another [boat] back."

Palace. Their bedroom adjoined the cabinet *de travaille* (the study) of the Czar; below that floor was Alexander's "resting room." A small elevator connected the floors. The Czar arose daily at seven in the morning. "The Princess, who loved to sleep," usually woke up at eleven o'clock. Staying at the palace, the children, as the maid Vera tells us, had a "great deal of fun," with their father arranging "costume parties," to which the children of the Czarevich were often brought to play with their "stepuncle" and "stepaunts," several years their juniors. (The oldest of the Czarevich's children, Nicholas, the last Czar to be, was twelve in 1880, while Gogo, his "stepuncle," was only eight years old!)

Although Alexander, now that he was "legally" married, had more "troubles" than ever before, his "Premier" and the man of the hour, Count Loris-Melikov, had "successfully," so he himself thought, brought "pacification" to the troubled empire. The pacification plan consisted of a policy to satisfy "the loyal elements" among the "liberals," for which purpose two commissions were proposed to prepare new legislation, one to deal with administrative and the other with financial matters. For the first time in the history of Russia, a commission would include men of "liberal professions"—members of *zemstvo* (local self-government), "learned men," and publicists. Though "the plan" was not radical, for the autocratic Russia, Loris-Melikov's reforms, as one English historian has put it, "paved the way for a peaceful transition from autocracy to a semi-constitutional monarchy."*[45]

In the meantime, while these "constitutional plans" were being developed, the struggle against the "nihilists" as it again seemed to the police and, therefore, to the higher-ups, including the Czar, was "successfully accomplished." Actually, "the nihilists," or the members of the terrorist group of the People's Will party, as we know now, were not at all interested in the

---

* It was asserted at the time but doubtful that Alexander Abaza, "the liberal" Minister of Finance, through "flattery and other means," had the ear of Katia in the hope that she would use her influence on the Czar, to put into effect the reforms of which Abaza claimed to be the originator.[46]

preservation of the monarchy, in any shape or form. The reforms, given from "above," were exactly what they didn't cherish. What they wanted was "the overthrow of the autocracy, through a popular rising preceded by a series of terrorist acts."[*][47]

One of the most ruthless revolutionaries of that time was Pyotr Tkachev, one of the earliest Russian followers of Karl Marx and later the disciple of the no less ruthless Nechaev.[48] Many years later (in 1902) Tkachev's doctrine "to impose the new order on the people by force" received the greatest accolade from his spiritual grandson Lenin, who wrote that the Tkachev "plan,"[49] which he then "prepared" and "preached," was "majestic." Dostoyevsky, "the prophet of the coming revolution," who preceded the Czar by a month to his grave, wrote in February, 1881, to Suvorin, the well-known newspaper publisher, that in his future novel, even "pure Alesha [Karamazov] will kill the Czar." It wasn't surprising that to most of the revolutionists the "reforms" were not only unwelcome but actually a hindrance.

Although on the surface there appeared to be a lull, actually the situation was more than ominous. The arrests of some conspirators (in many cases through the "defections" of several party members), their deportation and exile, led the surviving revolutionists to prepare this time for a certain and last coup— the assassination of the Czar-Liberator. On December 2, one day before the Czar's arrival at St. Petersburg from the Crimea (the "party men" were fully informed of Alexander's traveling schedules), the terrorist group in the capital decided to act without a delay.[†] The die was cast.

---

[*] Russia was not the only country to be infected with revolutionary unrest. All Europe and even the U.S. felt the impact of the "trend." As one American author wrote: "1877 was a crucial year, and one in which America came close to class warfare." "What do you think of the workers of the U.S.?" wrote Karl Marx to Engels: "A nice sauce is being stirred over there."[50] In 1872, attempts were made to assassinate Queen Victoria, Kaiser Wilhelm I, and King Amadeo of Spain. The Spanish Republic was proclaimed in 1873 and lasted for two years!

[†] It should be stressed that the terrorist group throughout the whole of Russia amounted to not more than a few hundred. Owing to many "attempts," political assassinations, etc., it was "felt" that there were "many, many thousands" of them. In the final phase "less than 40

The same day, the terrorists rented under the guise of a cheese shop a "three room front basement" on the Malaya Sadovaya Street, frequently passed by the Czar on his weekly carriage promenades. It was planned to dynamite the street (they began to build an underground passage) or to toss the bombs into the Monarch's vehicle.*

March came, and though the "soul of the party," Andrei Zheliabov, was arrested, the twenty-eight-year-old Sophia Perovskaya, his mistress, remained as a "strong personality" behind the party. Of "a noble[51] but poor family" (she had descended from the brother of the famous Gregory Razumovsky, "the simple cossack" who, it was "assumed," had married morganatically the Empress Elizabeth, the daughter of Peter the Great). Perovskaya, the daughter of the former governor of St. Petersburg (incidentally he was not persecuted for the deeds of his daughter but died from a "broken heart" in 1887), was more than indispensable for the intended plan of assassination.

While some of the conspirators were progressing in their work (boring a passage under the street), others were at the same time assigned to assassinate the Czar in the open. Sunday, March 13, 1881, was chosen as "the day."

On that very Sunday the Emperor was in "excellent spirit." Count Peter Valuev, one of the "liberal" members of the cabinet, noted in his diary that he hadn't seen his Sovereign

---

persons" were engaged.[52] As one of the participants wrote later: "14 of us gathered [in June 1879 to make preparations for a regicide]. This was practically all our forces, which spread so much fear in the autocratic government of the 100 million people of Russia."[53]

* It is amazing that the police, despite many informers among the revolutionaries, were unaware of the underground passage, on which the terrorists worked for four months! Moreover, just two days before the assassination of the Czar, the police, "being suspicious," visited the house in question under the guise of a routine "sanitary" inspection! The excavation was not discovered, even though the "shop" was full of barrels filled with earth from the passage. It is curious to add that as early as 1879, the Odessa Governor General Todtleben wired the St. Petersburg Gendarmerie that he "received information that the terrorists have a plan of mining Malaya Sadovaya in view of the Czar's frequent trips to the *Manège.*" Nothing was done about it! By an irony of fate, the phony "cheese" house was actually built in the eighteenth century for Alexis Razumovsky, the very ancestor of Sophia Perovskaya![54]

"look so well in a long time."*⁵⁵ As a matter of fact, the day before, after the Czar attended a Lenten service (Russian Easter fell on April 23) and had taken Communion, he was informed that one of the revolutionary ringleaders, whom we have already mentioned, Andrei Zheliabov had been seized and arrested. This was reassuring news to the Czar. Now that the brain and the soul of the "nihilists" was in custody, the Czar felt he was safe. Nevertheless, Count Loris-Melikov, who arrived at the palace around noon, pleaded with Alexander not to leave the imperial residence.† The Czar, who was to attend a trooping of the colors at the nearby *Manège* (a routine Sunday event), refused not to go. Aside from the fact that Alexander "loved" this specific parade—"*Razvod*," as it was called in Russian—that Sunday his young nephew, Grand Duke Dimitry, (shot by the Soviets in Petrograd in 1919), the son of his "favorite" brother, Constantine, was to take part in the parade for the first time as an "aide-de-camp to His Majesty." Moreover, it was argued that with the leader of the "nihilists" arrested, they would have to abandon their plans.

The Czar, after brushing aside Loris-Melikov's pleas, asked his "Premier," as the latter was nicknamed, to submit to him that very morning for his signature the project of the manifesto,

---

* We also have the testimony of the Reverend Basil Bazhanov, the Czar's confessor, that on Sunday, March 13, Alexander, "happy as never before," told him he had "made peace with my sons and they forgave me for my marriage; thus a complete reconciliation took place, that's why I am so happy." The statement is difficult to confirm.⁵⁶

If one can trust Katia, there is an intimate story which she told to Dr. Serge Botkin (in Biarritz in 1887), the Czar's most favored and famous practitioner, which may explain the Czar's "excellent spirit" this day. According to her version, the sixty-three-year-old Czar, on the fatal day of March 13, before departing for the parade, entered Katia's apartment and "in a moment of passion threw her on a couch and took her *en hussard,—i.e.,* roughly."⁵⁷ We also learn that this "story" left such an unpleasant impression on the celebrated physician that he decided not to see her again.

† However Count Loris-Melikov related in 1884 in Nice, France, to Prince Dimitry Obolensky that "he never pleaded with the Czar because if he knew there was a danger I would simply never let him [the Emperor be present at the *Manège*], for that I had a force and authority." "The assertion" that Katia and Count Loris-Melikov "tried to persuade" the Czar "not to go" is simply "an invention," concluded the memoirist.⁵⁸

which was to be "published soon."* The manifesto in question, rather still a "project," dealt with the mild concessions of summoning representatives "of various classes" to "render service" to the State Council. (Rumors had spread, that the manifesto was a "constitutional project." Actually it was not. However, one must admit that it was the first step toward more progressive government.) As the Czar "certified" the "project," "with his signature,"[59] he dismissed[60] Loris-Melikov and turning to the two of his oldest sons, the Czarevich Alexander and Vladimir, who were present at this historical event, exclaimed: "I have approved the report of my Minister of Interior [Loris-Melikov], though I must admit that this measure is the first step toward constitution."† With these words, Alexander "in an uncommonly good humor," and attired in the uniform of his "beloved" Guard Sappers‡ embraced Katia and his "Yourievsky children" and at exactly "quarter to one" was off to the *Manège*.§ That very hour, the regicides, working in several

---

* The official but secret report to the new Czar read: "On March 1 [13] at 12:30 in the afternoon, the Emperor [orally] approved the drawn project of Government Communication, and ordered that before it is printed in the Government Messenger [in other words, made public] it should be heard at the meeting of the Council of Ministers, to be called on March 4 [16], [1881]."[61]

† In August, 1880, the Czar had received a letter from his eighty-three-year-old uncle, Kaiser Wilhelm I of Germany, with a "well wishing" advice, based on "many years of experience" of a "relative and a friend" not to grant a constitution to Russia. Alexander "ordered" an answer to be drafted in which he stated that he "had no intention, now or later, while he is alive, to grant the constitution. He will not make this mistake."[62] Wilhelm outlived his nephew by eight years, dying peacefully in 1888.

‡ The Guard Sappers was the regiment, if we recall, that guarded "the little Sasha" the tragic December day of 1825. The same regiment "kept watch" in Peterhof near the Belvédère Palace, the place of Alexander's and Katia's "fatal" rendezvous in 1866. Eventually, the Czar was buried in the uniform of this regiment.

§ On the way he called on the oldest of all the ladies-in-waiting of his late wife, the spinster Countess Antonina Bludov (1812–91), the "confidante" of the late Empress and the daughter of the famous statesman and "emancipator" Dimitri Bludov. She, however, was extremely conservative, if not outright "retrograde" and "chauvinist."[63] In addition there were 179 simple "Frauleins" or ladies-in-waiting at the court, and she was the senior of the three "Kammer-Frauleins."[64] It was her *jour-de-fête*, or name's day. The countess resided at the palace out of "goodness of the Emperor."

groups, were waiting for the Czar's carriage at various squares, streets, and canals of St. Petersburg.

When the parade at the *Manège* was over (it had lasted about forty minutes; the Czar was particularly "gracious"), Alexander, in his closed two-seater coach (said to be a gift from Napoleon III and "thoroughly bomb proof"), departed for the Winter Palace. On the way he stopped to call on his cousin, the Grand Duchess Catherine, the daughter of his father's brother Michael.* He was accompanied that day by only six mounted Terek cossacks. Another cossack sat upon the coachman's box. Three open small sleighs, with Colonel Adrian Dvorzhitsky, the district *"policemeister,"* and two officers of the Gendarmerie followed the imperial cortège.

As the procession approached the Ekaterinsky Canal† and the Czar's carriage entered the quay of the same name, a thick-set youth in a fur hat (the nineteen-year-old student Nicholas Rysakov) threw his first bomb between the legs of the Czar's horses—the eighth attempt on Alexander's life. It was two fifteen in the afternoon. A loud explosion "with a blue tint of smoke" combined with a spray of snow, glass, splinters, and stones. In the confusion that followed, one could see first casualties: a cossack and a passing boy (a butcher's delivery boy) and a few other passersby lay on the ground groaning. The Czar himself was not hurt, but "dazed." His carriage, however, was "somewhat shattered."‡ He alighted

---

* This visit to his cousin spelled Alexander's doom. He didn't return by the Malaya Sadovaya Street, which, though mined, was safe, due to poor workmanship by the regicides, but made the above stop and thus had to take the "Ekaterinsky" Canal Quay route home. This gave the terrorists time to take new positions.[65]

† Curiously enough, the name of Ekaterina, or Catherine, played an uncanny role that day. The Czar said the last "good-bye" to Katia and his daughter, Katia, Jr., called on his cousin Catherine, and met his doom on Catherine Canal Quay!

‡ Alexander I. Solzhenitsyn, the Soviet author, in his semifictional novel *The First Circle*, states that some parts of Alexander's carriage of that day were for some reason kept by Mathilde Kschessinska (the well-known ballerina now living in Paris) in her house in St. Petersburg. On Stalin's order, they were removed in 1937, the year of the twentieth anniversary of the 1917 Revolution. This was, of course, the house which Lenin had "appropriated" since his return to Russia in 1917 and which

from it and walked right up to Rysakov, who was in the meantime "seized by passersby sailors and police" and inquired his
assailant's name and, as some related later, "wagged a finger"
at him. Still others asserted that the Czar, in answer to a
question whether he was wounded, pointed out the dying
butcher's boy and said: "I am not. Thank God, but he . . ."
whereas Rysakov muttered: "Isn't it too early to thank God?"*
A moment later the Czar approached the wounded cossack
and after a few words of "encouragement," went to the pit
formed by the explosion. As he was ready to leave the scene
of violence, a young man (he was the twenty-five-year-old
Ignaty Grinevetsky, a former engineering student and the
second bomb thrower) was leaning "only a few steps away,"
against the railing of the canal. In his hand he carried a small
parcel. A "second later," and there was another "loud explosion." When the smoke dispersed, a terrifying scene presented itself: On the bloodstained, almost "black snow," in-
termingled with splinters, stones, and clothing lay a number
of people moaning. The Czar, bareheaded (he had lost his
hat in the second explosion), with his Sapper Guard uniform
in shreds, seemed mortally wounded. The eighth attempt on
his life had succeeded. One of his legs was torn away, the
other completely smashed. The assassin himself had been blown

---

became one of the "museums of the Revolution." The Soviet author states
that suspicious Stalin also ordered removed at once from the exhibit
the blown-up photos of Perovskaya and Zheliabov with a streamer: "Kill
the Tyrant!" The coach itself was on exhibition in the "Imperial Stable
Museum" in St. Petersburg since 1881.[66]

* When arrested, Rysakov began to inform on his comrades, with the
result that several "important accomplices" were apprehended.[67] William
Henry Chamberlain wrote in *The Russian Enigma*,[68] discussing the
Kirov assassination in the 1930s, that "it is difficult to imagine the fury
that the assassination of a prominent official excites in the governing
group of a totalitarian dictatorship or the ferocious reprisals it excites.
Many high functionaries of the Tsarist Regime were assassinated without
bringing down retribution on any one except the perpetrators of the
killings. Even when Czar Alexander II was murdered, only 5 persons,
all indisputably connected with the plot which led to his assassination,
were put to death."[69] The Minister of Justice was Dimitry Nabokov, the
grandfather of the author of *Lolita*.

apart by his own weapon.* The shattered body of Alexander was taken in the small open sleigh of Colonel Dvorzhitsky,† who was also wounded, to the Winter Palace. "Home to die— it's cold," were the last words of the Czar.

As the sad procession approached the Winter Palace, crowds of people, who had heard the explosions, assembled in front of it.‡ At the palace, the two "court doctors, both Jewish, who were on duty, Marcus and Kogan,[70] tried a "blood transfusion,"§ a primitive operation as it was then, but without avail. Oxygen was then administered. "I was among the witnesses,"¶ wrote Miliutin, "of the Emperor's agony when he lay with shattered legs on a campbed . . . while Princess Yourievsky [in a semi-hysterical state] . . . and the Cesarevich held the head of the sufferer. Despite all the efforts to prolong his life, his breathing stopped. . . . It was 3:35 in the afternoon. . . ."‖[71]

As was customary, a pronouncement of the death of the Sovereign was made from the balcony of the palace by a

---

* Ironically, another of the bomb throwers, Ivan Yemelianov, probably "on impulse," helped to put the shattered body of the Czar in the sleigh. While he was doing this a bomb wrapped in a newspaper was all this time under his arm![72]

Twenty-year-old Yemelianov, a trade-school graduate and a cabinet-maker, had studied abroad on grant from Baron Horatio Ginsburg, the great Russian-Jewish philanthropist and an "admirer" of Alexander II.[73]

† The nephew of Colonel Dvorzhitsky, former Commander of the Russian Imperial Navy, George Dvorzhitsky, is now residing in the U.S.A. and is one of Directors of "The Russian Imperial Association of Russian Imperial Naval Officers in America."

‡ "There was tens of thousands of people, all kneeling bare-headed in the snow. I thought the sight of those serried thousands kneeling bare-headed, praying for the soul of their Emperor, a strangely moving and beautiful spectacle," wrote the secretary of the British Embassy, Lord Frederic Hamilton.[74]

§ As early as 1874, blood transfusions were "successfully" practiced in St. Petersburg City Prison by a Swiss doctor Russell.[75]

¶ Vera, the maid, also "saw" in the room the "terror stricken," Vava Shebeko and the widowed Princess Meschersky, Katia's sister. All the members of the imperial family, including the thirteen-year-old Nicholas, the last Czar to be of Russia, assembled in the room of the dying Czar. He could "never outlive" the "horrible day," Nicholas II wrote ten years later.[76] (*See his diary entry Sept. 12/24/1891*)

‖ The clock on the Czar's table was stopped at three thirty-five and remained so until the Revolution of 1917. The bloodstained campbed, on which Alexander always slept, was never removed from the palace.

senior general. This time the duty fell on the "aide-de-camp general to His Imperial Majesty, His Serene Highness Prince Alexander Italiisky, Count Souvorov Rimniksky,"[77] in short, "the lethargic," to say the least, grandson of the famous Suvorov.* As the General appeared on the balcony, he shouted, to the multitude of people assembled below: *"Sa Majesté L'Empereur est mort!"* Few people could hear his voice, let alone understand his French words. Far more eloquent than his shouting was the lowering of the imperial standard at 3:35 P.M.

Symbolically, as the French words faded in the immense square, the era of "benevolent western liberalism," initiated by Alexander, the Czar-Liberator, was at is end.† There began a new epoch—an epoch of inevitable reaction and "true Russian nationalism."[78]

---

* The great Suvorov received the title of a Prince for his victories in Italy in 1799 and was made a Count for his conquest in 1789 of Rimniki, or Rymnik—then a Turkish town.

† Thirty-six years later, exactly on the day and almost on the hour of Alexander's death, the revolution that broke out in 1917 in St. Petersburg (renamed Petrograd in 1914) overthrew the imperial government and with it the 304-year-old Romanov Dynasty.

POST-MORTEM

Quite a few witnesses (mostly men) left to us their striking but not always accurate impressions of the fatal March day on which Emperor Alexander II was assassinated.* However, no expression was more vivid, with full emotion yet factual accuracy, than that of Elizabeth Narishkin, born Princess Kourakin, one of the senior

---

* To Queen Victoria, on whose life were made no less than eight attempts of assassination, Alexander's death gave "a thrill of ineffable horror," and as Miliutin noted in his diary the Russian[1] people and the press, "except the extreme left radical socialists, expressed their deep horror." In Paris the Senate and the Assembly closed their meetings, and, as he added, "from Berlin and London we received lots of expressions of sympathy, not only from the Court, but from people and their Parliaments. Only the Austrian Reichstadt felt it was not necessary to express a statement at the moment." (It is possible to assume that as a result of this, Russia had her revenge. In 1889 when Archduke Rudolph committed suicide, the Russian Court did not cancel a ball which was planned that week. Instead all lady guests were requested to wear black gowns. This, the wise statesman Pobedonostzev called "sacrilegious.") In far away America the United States Senate passed a unanimous resolution denouncing the assassin, and the New York State Assembly ordered the flags of the state to be flown half-mast. American newspapers wrote tributes to the "White Czar." But one New York paper also reported that "nearly a dozen members of the Société des Réfugies de la Commune met on Houston Street to arrange the commemoration of the 10th anniversary of the Commune in Paris. They also drank beer and discussed the assassination of the Czar, which they highly approved. . . ." That same evening in Washington, the Russian minister was obliged to give members of the Diplomatic Corps "a good lecture," because they had attended a dance instead of the memorial service for the Czar.[2]

ladies of the last Czar's Court.* That very day, Madame Narishkin entertained for luncheon at her home her son Anatoly's childhood friends and playmates, the fourteen-year-old Grand Duke Nicholas, the future and the last Emperor of Russia, and his cousin Prince Peter Oldenburg (who was later to marry Nicholas's sister Olga).† All three, born in 1868, were planning to ice skate with another cousin, the fifteen-year-old Grand Duke Alexander. Meanwhile, the young group began to sing to the piano accompaniment of the hostess with the result that the noise of the explosion of a few streets away was not heard by them. "As the dreadful news was brought to me," wrote Madame Narishkin, "I ordered my carriage at once and drove to the Winter Palace. I had to make my way on foot through a surging crowd of people before I reached the door of the Palace. I found it closed and guarded. It was only by way of a detour through the apartments of the Countess Bludov [Court Lady] that I was able to penetrate into a corridor close to the Imperial apartments.

"Suddenly [Father] Beliaev appeared. His face was wet with tears and, hurrying past us, he cried that the Emperor was dead. We stepped nearer to the door of the death chamber, behind which all the members of the Imperial Family pressed timidly and awe-stricken about the body of the Czar. All the Ministers of State and the members of the Emperor's suite stood in the corridor; there hung his blood-soaked cloak, and from a side-room they led a wounded Cossack who had just been bandaged. The excitement was indescribable. Everyone expressed a conjecture, told of conspiracies, names were mentioned, uprisings were feared, and the question arose: Have we enough military protection in St. Petersburg?

"Suddenly [Prince] Ivan Mikhailovich Golitzine appeared and announced in passing:

---

* Her diary, smuggled from Soviet Russia by René Fülöp-Miller in the 1930's was later, with many errors in translation, published in the U.S.A. The same year she died as a penniless refugee in Paris at the age of 90. "With her death," wrote Fülöp-Miller, "one of the most fascinating personalities of Old Russia has gone forever."

† Anatoly, who remained the loyal and steadfast friend of Nicholas, was present at the tragic abdication of his "playmate" in Pskov on March 15, 1917.

" 'Tomorrow we'll have a formal reception.'

" 'Reception?' I asked. 'You mean a funeral service.'

" 'No, a ceremonial reception anent the accession to the crown of his Majesty the Emperor Alexander III. Ladies in formal court dress. Gentlemen in gala uniform, but no mourning!'

"I shall never forget the 'ceremonial reception' on March 2, 1881. When their newly made Majesties appeared, all broke into cries of 'Hurrah!' Only a few paces beyond lay the mutilated body of the Czar, over which the physicians were working in an effort to restore it to something near human resemblance, so that it might be shown to the people. . . ."[3]

Ten years later, usually reserved and emotionally controlled Czarevich Nicholas remembered the tragic event, an event which, as he noted in his diary, he could "not re-live again."[4] There is another not too factual recollection of this day, left to us by the Baroness Sophie Buxhoeveden, the young lady-in-waiting to the last Czarina who voluntarily decided to follow the Imperial Family into Siberian exile and miraculously escaped with her life.* "As I was walking [in 1913]," wrote the Baroness, "in the park with the young Grand Duchess [Olga] we met the Emperor; he joined us, the talk reverting to the Court servant Kondratiev who was ill. 'He was one of the men who carried up my grandfather just before he died,' he said. It was the only time I have ever heard the Emperor speak of Alexander II's assassination. Not touching at all on the dastardly murder of the old Emperor by a bomb thrown by a nihilist in the streets of St. Petersburg, Nicholas II quietly and sadly gave his account of the death-bed scene to his daughter [Olga]. 'We were at lunch in the Anitchkov Palace [which contradicts Narishkin's version], my brother and I,' he said, 'when a frightened servant ran in.† "A misfortune has befallen the Emperor," he said. "The Cesarevich (Alexander III) has given orders that the Grand Duke Nicholas Alexandrovitch is to go immediately to the Winter Palace. He must take the first conveyance at hand. No time is to be lost."'

---

* This somewhat contradicts Madame E. Narishkin's story.

† A palace servant confirmed in 1892 that he was present at that time and "from the moment he was brought into the Palace [until he died] the Czar did not utter a single word."

General Danilov [the tutor] and we two hurried downstairs, and got into a Court carriage which was waiting for somebody. We drove down the Nevsky at top speed to the Winter Palace. As we went up the stairs I saw pale faces everywhere. On the carpet there were deep red stains. My grandfather was bleeding to death from his terrible wounds as he was carried upstairs. In his study I found my parents. Near the windows stood uncles and aunts. No one spoke. My grandfather was lying on the narrow camp-bed he always slept in. He was covered by the military cloak he used as a dressing-gown. His face was deadly pale. There were small wounds all over it. His eyes were closed. My father led me up to the bed. 'Papa,' he said, raising his voice, 'your sunshine is here.' I saw the flicker of an eyelid. Grandfather's blue eyes opened, and he tried to smile. He moved a finger, but he could not lift his hand or say the words he wanted, but he knew me. Father Bajenov came and administered the last sacraments. We all knelt, and the Emperor passed away. 'It was the will of God,' said Nicholas II quietly. '*Tak Gospodou ougodno bylo.*' He walked on silently. There was no repining, no violent words about the assassins. Submission to the will of God was his whole creed, and his trust in the Divine Wisdom that ordained events gave Nicholas II that almost superhuman calm which never failed him in the times of his worst danger."[*5]

Grand Duke Alexander, then fifteen years old, gave his own version of the tragic day:

"Thousands of people were already surrounding the Palace," he wrote. "The women cried hysterically. We entered by the side door. There was no need to ask questions: large drops of black blood showed us the way up the marble steps of the stairs and then along a corridor into the study of the Emperor. Our father stood at the door giving orders to a group of officials. He had to lift mother in his arms. She had fainted on seeing him alive.

"The Emperor lay on the couch near the desk. He was unconscious. Three doctors were fussing around but science was

---

[*] Whether this is a reliable rendering of the conversation is, of course, difficult to ascertain. At any rate, it is the only one supposedly coming from the lips of Nicholas, except for his short diary entry of the event, ten years later.

obviously helpless. It was a question of minutes. He presented a terrific sight, his right leg torn off, his left leg shattered, innumerable wounds all over his head and face. One eye was shut, the other expressionless.

"Every instant members of the imperial family came in. The room was packed. I clung to the arm of Nicky [the future Nicholas II], deathly pale in his blue sailor's suit. His mother, stunned by the catastrophe, was still holding a pair of skates in her trembling hands. I recognized the heir apparent by his broad shoulders; he was looking out of the window.

"Princess Yourievskaya burst in half-dressed. Something or perhaps some overzealous guard had detained her. She fell flat on the couch over the body of the Czar, kissing his hands and screaming: 'Sasha, Sasha!' It was unbearable. The Grand Duchess began to sob aloud.

"The agony lasted forty-five minutes. Not a detail of this scene could ever be forgotten by those who witnessed it. I am the only one left [he wrote in 1932], all the others are dead, nine having been shot by the Bolsheviks thirty-seven years later. . . ."

As the impact of the shock subsided, it was decided to embalm the body at once. "It was midnight," wrote the State Secretary, Egor Peretz, a reliable witness,* when the Count Adlerberg who was present at the embalming in the study of the Emperor came out to see me [to give instructions for further arrangements and there] appeared a lady in deep mourning, all in tears. This was Princess Yourievskaya. Upon learning that the body was being embalmed she withdrew."

Now that the first act of the tragedy was over, the interminable funeral mass and services began—"twice a day, seven days in succession," wrote Grand Duke Alexander. "Shadows of tall candles, chanting priests. Beautiful singing of a mammoth choir."[6]

Miliutin, who was one of the first to reach the Winter Palace and to be present at the "death-agony" and was more than shocked at what he saw ("The soul-tearing shrieks of Princess

---

* Peretz (1833–99), a son of a Jewish tax collector, had risen to a very high position in Old Russia. He was the brother of Gregory Peretz, who was implicated in the December Revolt of 1825. Neither this nor his being a Jew in any way hindered his career.

Yourievskaya resounded through the room," wrote a witness), left us also a mournful description of removing, the next day, the body from the study room, where the Czar expired, to the Winter Palace Church. "The body was put into the coffin," he wrote, "and carried to the Church by members of the Imperial Family. The pitiable Princess Yourievskaya could not suppress her hysterics and was taken into another room."

Perhaps this was just as well, for at that moment, according to an established strict etiquette (proper for a morganatic spouse and not out of spite) Katia became a sort of nonperson,* not a single newspaper, not one of various official bulletins issued, ever mentioned the existence of the widow of the Czar or her three children. Katia was, of course, present at all the services but was always the last, after the members of the "family" present, to kiss, according to the Orthodox custom, the forehead of the deceased. She was also "the last to follow the coffin," wrote Peretz.†[7]

On the seventh day, as was the custom, the Czar's coffin was carried in a procession across the frozen Neva to the Peter and

---

* A story that at the services her stepdaughter, the new Empress, took "Princess Yourievsky's hand and made her walk beside her saying " 'There is no rank here, only unhappy women,' " is probably a fantasy.

† Count Bobrinsky recorded that "separate arrangements" at the funeral were made for the Princess. He wrote in his diary on March 8 [20] that "to the right of the entrance of the Fortress Church, a small tent [palatka] was especially built for Princess Yourievsky [to rest in between services] similar to the one [on the left] for the Grand Dukes. There she is seated, pale as a wax church candle with her shortsighted eyes with the expressions of sufferings and numbness."

Another funeral in this "style" but much more humiliating—and "disgraceful," in the words of one Italian historian—took place a third of a century later in 1914, when the heir to the Austrian-Hungarian throne, Archduke Francis Ferdinand and his morganatic spouse were buried in Vienna. Arranged by Prince Montenuovo, himself the morganatic grandson of Empress Marie-Louise of France and her lover, Count Adam Albert von Neipperg, the funeral, "in accordance with his Majesty's instructions," stipulated that "nobody should be present at the station to receive the bodies," that the Duchess's funeral should take place at a different time than that of her husband, and that in the chapel the coffins should stand at a different level and be different in size and finish. A pair of white gloves and a black fan were put on the coffins, reminding of her "subordinate station." No wreaths were sent by the imperial family, and no members of foreign royalty were invited. Katia's treatment was more humane and less degrading.[8]

Paul Fortress for burial. "The ceremony of transferring the body," wrote Peretz, ". . . into the fortress was executed more than carelessly. There was no order in the procession, with many of the officials talking and following the coffin not in pairs as it is usually done, but in small groups—some of them even smoking. Those who carried [the Czar's] decorations did it unceremoniously, holding the cushion, for instance, in their arms. Yet it was not even too cold. . . ." This statement is confirmed by Lord Frederic Hamilton, secretary of the British Embassy, who wrote that the "procession sounded very grand on paper . . . but it was spoiled by lack of attention to details. The distances were kept irregularly and many of the officials wore ordinary civilian great-coats over their uniforms which did not enhance the effect of the cortege."[9] There is no doubt that the liberal and benevolent regime of the late Czar permitted many to become slovenly.*

As the "family" departed from the church, "Princess Yourievsky," wrote a witness, "stepped forward and followed by the ever present Barbara Shebeko, approached the coffin to give a traditional farewell kiss to her husband. On March 19, the Princess made her last farewell accompanied by her only son, the ten year old child, dressed in a sailor suit." "As she knelt by the mortal remains . . ." wrote Katia's daughter much later,[10] "she gently placed in his hands her wonderful plaits of hair she had just cut off."† Now it was all over. The Princess, who had known the Czar intimately for fifteen years and who was married to him for only seven months and three weeks, began a new life as the morganatic widow of the "Czar-Liberator" which was to

---

* The last funeral service, most moving of Russian Orthodox rituals, which lasted for hours, was over.

† There is no reason to doubt the story, but one should stress that the above custom usually was not a must among the upper classes, let alone among members of the imperial family. This custom prevailed more among the peasants and less among the middle classes. Katia, who was generally addicted to morbidity, also kept a shattered finger of the Czar, brought to her by a soldier who found it after the assassination. Eventually she carried the finger to France. Today it reposes in a special case in the Russian Cathedral of Nice, France.

Yet we learn that the lovely young Duchess de Morny, born Princess Sophia Troubetzkoy, the widow of Napoleon III's illegitimate brother, Auguste, at the latter's funeral in Paris in 1865, "impulsively snipped short her ash blond hair and placed the shorn locks between Auguste's hands."[11]

last for forty-one years, outlasting the Romanov Dynasty by five years.

In describing the events which took place after the accession of the new Czar, scores of writers (not all commendable)* stress that Princess Yourievsky and her family were, "the next day," after the assassination unceremoniously and rudely evicted by her stepson, Alexander III, from the Winter Palace. As the story goes, the unfortunate morganatic spouse had to leave Russia "at once" for Europe, where ever after she lived "in deep retirement." The facts do not correspond to this legend. We know today, for certain, that the Yourievsky *ménage* left the Winter Palace for an entirely different cause. Alexander III and particularly his wife, the Empress Marie, simply "adored" the small and "cozy" Anichkov Palace and were loath, after the accession, to change their fifteen-year habitat and move, as was the custom, to the immense Winter Palace. But secret police disclosures, based on "confessions" of Rysakov (the first unsuccessful bomb-throwing regicide) of a plot to kill the new Czar, led to the arrest of other conspirators at their concealed lodgings (from where the bombs were delivered to the assassins) rented by Hessia Helfman, the only Jewish regicide in the group, and forced the Czar, as a security measure, to leave the "cozy" Palace.

(During the altercations with the police, one of the conspirators committed suicide and all others were arrested but not before three police officers were gravely wounded. This was only the beginning of the arrests:† many of the revolutionaries later became informants.)

---

* Numerous "revelations" published in the 1920s, such as *Confessions of the Czarina* or *Behind the Veil at the Russian Court*, supposed to be written by a "person in the know," a Count Vasilli, but actually authored by Madame Catherine Kolb, an adventurous wife of the engineer and a former divorcée of Prince Watslav [Wilhelm] Radziwill of Vienna, were responsible for these "authentic" stories. Princess Bibesco's romanticized version of "Katia" based partly on another work of a Russian "expert," the last ambassador to Imperial Russia, Maurice Paléologue, whose *Le Roman Tragique de l'Empereur Alexandre II*, written for uncritical French audiences, for the sake of "romance," was noted for its deviation from historic truths.[12]

† It should be noted that on March 11, *i.e.*, two days *before* the assassination of the Czar, two leading conspirators, Trigony and Zheliabov, had been arrested.

"As I went," Miliutin wrote in his diary on March 15, "to the Winter Palace for a Funeral Mass, I ran into Count Loris-Melikov who related all the circumstances regarding the new arrests. He also stated that although he tried to persuade the late Emperor not to leave the Palace for four days, he was unsuccessful." "Now Loris," added Miliutin, "tries to persuade the new Emperor not to needlessly risk his life and decided to prevail on him to move to the Winter Palace in order not to traverse the Nevsky Prospect several times daily and by the same route."[13] Apparently the plea was successful, for the new Czar moved his entire family on March 17, *i.e.*, four days after the assassination. But not for long. Immediately after the burial of his father, the new Czar openly moved his family back to the Anichkov Palace, and in the beginning of April settled for the spring season—this time without any previous public announcement—in Gatchina, his most favored surburban residence.*

Meanwhile, Katia, to whom, as we know, her husband, just three months before his death, had willed not only a resident dwelling in St. Petersburg but also *dachas* in Peterhof, Czarkoye Selo, and two in Crimea, had to make a decision inasmuch as the Czar had stipulated that after his death Katia and her children could retain "the apartments" in the Winter Palace especially decorated for her "unless she, herself, would wish to move into her own house." She had a choice to make, but apparently "her house," the large "income bringing house"—*i.e.*, a rental-apartment dwelling—was not sufficiently in style for her status.†
Within a short time a suitable *osobniak*,‡ the sumptuous Petit Palais Rose, the Small Pink Palace (so named because the whole front of the house was covered with a pink Olonetz

---

* This move was interpreted by the critics of the regime and liberals as the Czar's cowardice; yet one must assert that Alexander, judging from reports of many witnesses, including Count Witte, was more than fearless.

† For an idea of the value of such a house: the one which belonged to Count Arthur Cassini (grandfather of the New York Cassini brothers) on Palais Quais in St. Petersburg was priced at 280,000 golden rubles or the equivalent of about $3 million today.[14]

‡ The simple "mortals" in Old Russia, *i.e.*, anyone outside of the members of the Imperial Family, were not supposed to possess "a palace." *Osobniak* means "a separate house," closest to the French *hôtel particulier*.

marble* from the north of Russia, including a "rose" staircase),
was presented to her by order of the new Emperor. Katia's new
osobniak—a two-story dwelling, with an unhappy past and, as
we will see, an unhappy finale, stood on a large tract of land
surrounded by a garden adjoining the Neva's "Gagarinsky" em-
bankment (later renamed "French Quais" to please the Franco-
Russian Alliance) not far from the Winter Palace. It was
originally built in the 1850s by the famous Maecenes of the day,
the dilettante writer Count Gregory A. Kushelev-Bezborodko
(1832–76), an heir to two large fortunes, who in his turn married
an immensely rich and beautiful heiress, Eudoxie Basilevsky, the
daughter of the self-made Siberian gold prospector. Named the
Small Pink Palace to distinguish it from the enormous Marble
Palace,† then the property of Alexander II's brother, the liberal
Grand Duke Constantine, Katia's imposing new domicile, at
Gagarinsky Street Number 3, was originally the scene of many
extravagant parties, the extravagance being supplied primarily
by Eudoxie.‡ Because of the death of Eudoxie's first and then her
second husband, the grandson of the illustrious General Suvorov,
the parties ceased but primarily because of her more than
generous "support" of the budding Monte Carlo Casino. Eudoxie
lived to the ripe age of eighty-eight, dying penniless as a
refugee in Monte Carlo in 1923, the place she was one of the
first to enrich and make famous.

Soon the small Marble Palace had been sold and become the
property of Grand Duke Nicholas, the son of Grand Duke

---

* Olonetz was famous for its pink marble, in a way competing with
the Carrara one.

† The large Marble Palace was built in 1785 and "presented" by
Catherine the Great to Count Gregory Orlov to mark his "retirement"
as a "favorite." Orlov reciprocated with the famous diamond, known
today as the "Orlov Diamond," which until this day enchances the
imperial scepter and is displayed in the Moscow Kremlin. Later, the palace
housed another favorite of Empress Catherine the Great—Stanislav Poniatowski, the last elected King of Poland. Eventually, the palace became the
property of Grand Duke Constantine and with his passing of his son,
Constantine, Jr., who became the last owner of the palace before the
Revolution of 1917.

‡ The last to bear the title Princess of Italy (Countess Suvorov Rymnik,
now Rimmicu in Roumania)—such were the titles bestowed on the family
of the famous Suvorov for his victories.

Constantine, the Czar's brother and owner of the big Marble Palace. The young Grand Duke's infatuation with an American demimondaine, one Hattie Ely of Philadelphia, whom we have already met, ended more than tragically.* He was banished in the 1870s to Turkestan, where he died in 1918 (but not forgetting beforehand to send a telegraph to Kerensky, congratulating his fellow Turkestanian† on the March Revolution of 1917).

The possession of the palace reverted to the imperial *Appanage* (Crown Domains, *i.e.*, crown lands), where it remained, un-occupied, until March of 1881, when Katia, through the generosity of her imperial stepson, took possession of it. "The building," wrote a Russian many years later, "was a magnificent affair of granite, and an almost overwhelming quantity of marble, both inside and out. The house may have been from the eighteenth century, but it is more probable that it was built in the last century. I was too young and unschooled to know anything then about architectural styles; to me it was all grand and marvelous, something out of an elaborate fairytale. The smooth, rich marble fascinated me—great marble fireplaces and swirling ornaments. There was a great deal of carved wooden panelling, and floors were inlaid with ebony and mother-of-pearl. The whole effect was grandiose and magnificent. There was an enormous ballroom with panelled walls of white silk with gilded moldings and upholstered in white satin. There were crystal chandeliers. At the end of the ballroom was its only window, little less than a whole wall of glass. At the other end two great arches gave on to a smaller room, a salon, in yellow silk, with a ceiling of pleated silk, delicious enough to make one's mouth water, especially at my impressionable age. Between the two arches, back to back, each room had its fireplace, one of white and the other of pink marble. These fireplaces were for me a source of endless wonder,

---

* The Grand Duke once more defied the rules of the game when, as an exile in the city of Orenburg in the 1880s, he married, without the consent of the imperial house, the daughter of the Provincial Police Chief named Dreyer. By irony of fate, Katia, who was Nicholas's stepaunt, be-came also his relative, as her "black sheep" brother, Michael Dolgorukov, Jr., the retired naval officer, later married Sophie, the other daughter of the Police Chief!

† Kerensky grew up in Turkestan.[15]

because the expanse of wall between the arches, above the mantelpiece, instead of being inset with the customary tall mirror, was filled with thick glass, so that you could see from one room into another. We used to climb up on the mantelpieces and make faces at each other through this glass. But where the smoke from the fires went to has always remained a mystery to me."[16]

Outside, at the entrance, topping the canopy, Katia, the new owner, installed an impressive symbol of semiroyalty—a princely crown, made of black wrought-iron instead of the usual gilt, apparently to denote a touch of mourning, resting on a tasseled cushion. It certainly reminded passersby and visitors of the morganatic, yet exalted, status of the new mistress of the imposing residence.

However, Katia really was on her own, alone face to face with a hostile Russia, if not the world. With the assassination of the Emperor, all kinds of rumors floated in the capital. One was that the new Czar had an ugly quarrel with Katia and expelled her from the palace. "Reliable witnesses" described the scene with her stepson, of almost the same age (Katia, thirty-five, the Czar, thirty-six, and the new Empress, thirty-four) of throwing a heavy *presse-papier* in her face. As her nephew Count Berg relates, ". . . nothing of the sort took place. Yet there were some grounds for these false rumors."* We have already seen Katia's difficult position for the fourteen years while she was a mistress and later a morganatic spouse. Now that she had become a *ci-devant* (a has-been), a woman of no importance, with her supporter and confidant, Count Loris-Melikov, soon to become another *ci-devant*, and soon to be dismissed, tongues of her "former friends" and enemies unloosened. On March 18, Pobedonostzev, the "evil statesman," in a letter which actually set a new course for a new policy, wrote to the new Czar: ". . . if [Loris] will sing again

---

* A letter from Emperor Alexander III to Princess Yourievsky illustrates their actual relationship. On August 6, 1881, he wrote:

> Going through my late father's papers from his study in Livadia I have found a whole package of Gogo's drawings; I am sending them to you as I am sure they will remain for you and for dear Gogo an always precious remembrance of happy times.
>
> A

Such letters are not written by an enemy.

sirenic songs that one must calm down, continue the liberal course and yield to the so-called public opinion then, Oh, Your Majesty, in the name of God, do not believe. Do not listen. This will be the ruin, ruin of Russia and yours. This is clear as day. . . . The insane villains, who destroyed your parent will not be satisfied by concessions, and will only become more furious. One can abate them and tear out the evil seeds only with a death struggle with iron and blood. . . . Do not keep [as a premier] Count Loris-Melikov. I don't trust him. He is a juggler. . . . If you will give in, he will lead you and Russia to perdition. He could only put through liberal projects. . . . He is not a Russian patriot. See, Your Majesty, that he does not try to possess your will. Do not lose time.*

"Good God," wrote the same "evil statesman" to a woman correspondent in early March of 1881, "how I pity the new Sovereign. . . . I am afraid that he won't have the will power [to withstand the liberal encroachments]. Who will lead him? I fancy so far that this juggler, Loris-Melikov. Right now, at all symptoms, he enmeshes him, as he holds the keys and is his Security Protector. . . . Yesterday, a simple man came to me in tears exclaiming—'For God's sake, tell the Czar that first of all one must expel from here [St. Petersburg] Constantine [the elder and "liberal" late Czar's brother, who sported the *pince-nez*] and Princess Yourievskaya.'"[17] But the Czar, though he yielded to his Counsellor regarding the new political policy, did not follow the advice about Katia. We also know that Alexander III, a month after the tragic day (actually only on April 22) conferred with Loris and gave him instructions regarding the future transfer of the Yourievsky family from the Winter Palace† and

---

* Emperor Wilhelm I, the eighty-four-year-old granduncle of the Czar, also came up with a counsel. Although he did not reject the benefit of "assembling the representatives of the people," he suggested that the Czar act "cautiously" not to grant "all voting rights" and not to let the Parliament rule the country. He warned of "unlimited freedom of words" (*i.e.*, press) but felt that "equal[18] religious rights" should be given.

† It is difficult to ascertain, but it is feasible, that the two households for a while "co-existed" under one roof of the immense Winter Palace, which had literally thousands of rooms. We know that in March the new Czar occupied the corner part which overlooked the Neva and the

discussed "the disposition of the 3 million, 400 thousand rubles [in gold] which the Princess decided to deposit in the Imperial State Bank [of Russia] in the name of her three children."* The colossal sums which Katia inherited, so to say, did not surprise those in the know. Traditionally, the heads of the imperial family were always generous, even to morganatic spouses and illicit offspring.†

Meanwhile, as a result of Katia's marriage, the new Czar, "perturbed" as he was by his father's example and his uncles' secret families,‡ decided to regularize the situation involving the

---

Admiralty. Katia's "apartments" were a floor above, on the other side of the palace. We know that at the end of May (15–27) Katia still resided at the Winter Palace, because, as Count Miliutin noted in his diary, he "called on the Princess at the Winter Palace and signed the book [for visitors]."

* As we saw originally, Czar Alexander on September 17, 1880, deposited in Katia's name government bonds in the amount of 3,302,910 rubles. When she took complete possession of the funds eight months later, their worth had risen to 3,400,000 gold rubles!

† Although morganatic marriages in Russia, like everyhwere else and even now, were more than scorned, the descendants of such marriages and even children out of wedlock were always more than fairly treated. Their status was in time legalized, titles were bestowed on the morganatic spouses and their children, and always suitable financial provisions were made. To cite only a few morganatic marriages of later years, one should mention the Zarnekaus (morganatic descendants of the Prince of Oldenburg) and the Belevskys (morganatic descendants of Grand Duke Alexis, the brother of Alexander III). More than curious is the case of Katenka, the mother of Mimi, the governess's daughter so vividly described in Leo Tolstoy's semifictionalized *Boyhood*. There is no doubt, as family documents have recently brought to light, that Mimi was a child of a "very high member of the Romanov family, perhaps even of Nicholas I." The descendants very reluctantly disclosed that the imperial family "always took care of them until the Revolution of 1917."

The case of Nicholas V. Isakov (1821–91) is more than illuminating. A natural son of an "unknown lady" and of Emperor Alexander I, the baby, for legality's sake, received his family name and patrimony from one Vasilli Isakov, a minor court employee. Gifted as he was, Isakov, even though he was, so to say, the "Czar's first cousin," reached an important position in the state and in time, as a natural son of an emperor, received a legacy of 2 million gold rubles and an estate of almost 10,000 acres in Kiev Province. His daughter married Count Alexander Adlerberg's nephew. Count Vasilli Adlerberg of New York, who is their son, learned about "the story" only after the Revolution.[19]

‡ It was an open secret that both brothers of Alexander II, the Grand Duke Constantine, Sr., and Nicholas, Jr., both married, had not only

problem of acquiring "Imperial titles as a result of morganatic marriages." Eventually, the "Regulations" governing the imperial family, established in 1797 by Paul I, when the "family" consisted of only five members (against twenty-three in 1881), with the help of the instigator of the reform, the new Minister of the Court, Count H. I. Vorontzov-Dashkov, were changed and became law in 1886. The new law, much resented by most of the Romanovs, stated that only the children of an emperor and later, grandchildren, were allowed the appellation of "Grand Dukes" or "Grand Duchesses" with the title of the "Imperial Highness." Other descendants bore the titles of Princes or Princesses of Imperial Blood or "Their Highnesses." A generation below, *i.e.*, the great-great-great grandsons and granddaughters received the titles of "Their Serene Highnesses" Princes and Princesses, with the exception of the eldest son, permitted to be styled as "Highness." These descendants were allowed to marry nonroyalty provided they received the Czar's approval. Aside from the above changes, the new law, of course, reduced the amount of the allowances due each member, which also met many protests by the Romanovs. This law was followed in June, 1889, by another *ukaz* forbidding the male members of the family to marry persons of other religions except Greek Orthdox (or the brides had to be converted), and finally, twelve years after Alexander II's death, *i.e.*, in 1893, a new law was issued categorically forbidding morganatic mar-riages*—about which Grand Duke Michael, Alexander II's

---

mistresses of long standing but several growing "natural" children. "They [the Grand Dukes] imitate their elder brother," Miliutin wrote in his diary.

* Up to 1870, morganatic marriages were not frequent with the Romanovs. Aside from Peter I, the brother of Alexander I, Grand Duke Constantine contracted a marriage with a Polish woman, Alexander II's sister Maria married a Count Stroganov, and the Czar's son Alexis, a daughter of the poet Zhukovsky. After the 1890s the morganatic marriages, often without the permission of the Czar and despite forbidding laws, were more than frequent. In 1891, Grand Duke Michael, Jr., "ran away" with the "commoner" Countess Torby, followed by a Duke Leuchtenberg and by two Oldenburg Princes. During the last reign, morganatic marriages accelerated. Thus, Grand Dukes Paul and Michael, uncle and brother of Nicholas II, contracted marriages with "commoners" without ever re-ceiving permission to do so. (So did Prince Gabriel, the grandson of

brother, in a conversation with a friend, exclaimed: ". . . my children [six sons] can't marry except Orthodox and of equal stations. Where then would they find such fiancées? Or should they put a bullet in their head?" His brother, Nicholas, Sr., was even more explicit, complaining that the new "law dooms Grand Dukes to bachelorhood, with all the troubles resulting from it. . . ."[20]

But to return to Katia, as we have seen, she was not in a hurry to vacate the Winter Palace; neither was the Czar pressing her. Her daughter's "earliest recollection" (if one can trust her memory) "of St. Petersburg [was] in going with my brother and sister to play with our half-brother, the Emperor Alexander III's children . . ." (*i.e.*, the future Nicholas II and others). "I well remember," she wrote, "the huge enjoyments and shrills of laughter accompanied this game and the amusement of the Emperor who seemed a playful and kind Goliath among all the romping children. . . ." But the halfbrother-Emperor, wrote Katia's daughter, granted to her mother the privilege of moving from "my father's private apartment in the Winter Palace all the furniture, books and decorations."* "There was [a replica, as the bloodstained bed remained in the palace] his simple soldier's bed, so narrow and severe, his many decorations, even the clothes in which he was assassinated, pitifully torn, like his body, by a madman's bomb.

"These rooms, with their precious and beloved relics, became a place to which Russians made a solemn pilgrimage. I can see

---

Constantine and Alexander II's brother, who tells us that he "secretly married" a "Commoner" in 1912.) The three unequal marriages before 1917 which, however, received imperial approval were: in 1911 of Princess Tatiana to Prince Constantine Bagration-Moukhransky; in 1914, Princess Irina to Prince Felix Yusupov; and in 1916, Grand Duchess Olga, the sister of the Czar, to Captain Nicholas Kulikovsky. Times have changed.

* Katia also received the bloodstained uniform with all the decorations, and the underclothes which the Czar wore on that fatal day; a cross, several ikons, the gold wedding ring which was almost flat-ended as a result of the bomb explosion, and his eyeglasses. After Katia's death all these relics were given to the Russian Cathedral of Nice, where they repose to this day. A torn stump of Alexander's finger which was found after the assassination was given to Katia, as we have seen. It also is today preserved in the Russian Cathedral of Nice.

them filing sadly and reverently past these living reminders of an Emperor they had loved so well. There was a private chapel inside the Palace; the altar was hand-painted white marble, the most beautiful and wonderful work imaginable."

Many years later, in 1933, Katia Jr.'s brother-in-law,* Prince Vladimir Bariatinsky, residing in Paris, published in a local Russian newspaper a page of his own reminiscences under the title "Princess Yourievsky." A scion of a famous and wealthy family, Vladimir considered himself an esthete (he married in Russia the famous actress Lydia Yavorskaya—a *mésalliance* which produced quite a scandal) and was rather critical of Katia's taste in interior decor. "My brother, Alexander," he wrote, "then married to Katia, Jr. and who disliked his mother-in-law, possessed extremely good taste combined with a bit of biting sarcasm" and was more than curious to see the house which his mother-in-law decorated. "The decor," wrote Vladimir, "my brother described as a mournful style of Louis Philippe, *i.e.* extremely bourgeois, except the arrangement of the library." But even this room shocked one, remembered Vladimir as "over some of the armchairs, with forbidding ribbons were seen silver plaques with an inscription: 'Removed from the Winter Palace Study of the Emperor.' Vladimir also related that in a small private chapel hung "a frightening oil painting" by the fashionable artist Constantine Makovsky, depicting "the Czar in a coffin showing the smaller details of his wounds on the dead face!!"† Generally, very little of interest transpired behind the thick Olonetz marble walls before Katia and her family finally departed for Paris. But if everything seemed as "usual" at Gagarinsky Number 3, her life had changed.

---

* In 1901, Katia, Jr. married, in Biarritz, Captain of the Guards Prince Alexander V. Bariatinsky. He suddenly died in Florence in 1910 after a stormy life. His extravagant *ménage à trois* with the famous Italian Opera singer, "the most beautiful woman in the world," Lina Cavalieri, no doubt ill-affected both his income and his health. In 1916, Katia married Prince Serge Obolensky, now of New York City.

† Constantine Makovsky (1839–1915) made many portraits of Alexander II and of his "second family." The painting depicting the Czar in his coffin was also Makovsky's work. He also made sketches at the trial of the regicides. They are now in the Leningrad Museum of the Revolution.

Although she had lost the status of "almost an Empress" and was blamed for all that had "happened," she had one compensation. She was more than financially affluent. But though not a spendthrift, in money matters Katia was something worse. She was utterly, as many of her friends attested, devoid of any financial acumen. Never well off in her early life (we have even seen her in straitened circumstances), now, in 1881, at thirty-five years of age, Katia, was more than a rich woman. But with her three small children (Gogo was nine, Olga was eight, and Katia, Jr., three), her younger sister Mouche, with a husband who was not wealthy, and her three brothers with their numerous marriages, escapades, (mainly financial), and divorces, she now had responsibilities.* The 3,400,000 rubles in gold which were now her own were worth at that time about $1,700,000—or in terms of today's purchasing power, about $17 million. This capital at a conservative calculation of 5 per cent annual interest brought her yearly income to almost $1 million in today's terms.† One should also add to the monetary income the jewelry given to Katia, including at least three diamond tiaras, or diadems, pearl necklaces, and other precious stones—as well as, of course, to use a modern term, real estate. In short, a fabulous fortune considering that in the 1880s an average family could live well on an income of $50 per month.

One should also remember that Katia, since her childhood,

---

* One of Katia's brothers, Michael, if we remember, the ex-sailor who married the Chief of Police's daughter, was always in debt. While the Czar (his brother-in-law!) was alive, Count Loris-Melikov, at the Czar's request, guaranteed a debt of Michael's of 50,000 rubles in gold (equivalent to a half million dollars today). When ten years later, in 1889, the debt was not returned, the guarantee had to be honored by the new Czar. As Miliutin tells us, Michael, aside from his *affaires de coeur* and gambling, also indulged in intrigues, trying to unseat in Turkestan the hero of the day, General Skobelev; in that, as states the memoirist, he was successful.[21]

† The income, was divided as follows: Katia and her children received a yearly income of 200,000 gold rubles, equal to today's rate of one million dollars; 100,000 rubles went to her, with Gogo receiving 40,000 and the two sisters equally 30,000 rubles each. All of these sums were, of course, free of any taxes, charges and deductions. Considering that the Dowager Empress's the (widow's) annual income, according to the State Law was set at 300,000 rubles, Katia's income, as morganatic spouse of an Emperor, was not too exorbitant.

youth, and even during her fourteen-year liaison with the Czar, was forced to lead rather a secluded and later, up to the 1880s, even a clandestine life with practically no social life, precluding cash expenditures. "During the 14 years [of her liaison] my aunt," wrote Berg, "lived far away from society and amusement. She never went out and practically no one saw her or knew her, except her immediate family, but even they had a rather distant relationship." Count A. V. Adlerberg, the former playmate and "the closest friend" of the Czar, confided to Count Miliutin in May, 1881, that the Emperor "until the very death of the Empress, continually evaded all conversations with me regarding Princess Dolgorukov and I was never before acquainted with her." Miliutin himself noted in his diary that even he who reported to the Czar "almost every week and sometimes oftener" learned about the "positive existence of the Princess" only in August, 1880,* *i.e.* after Katia's wedding, and then only through Count Loris-Melikov.

As a result of the "hush-hush" policy, all kinds of rumors flew, very often devoid of any truth, all of which did not make Katia a popular figure (Count Witte's† insinuations that Katia took "appropriate kickbacks" were more than unfair).[22] "She was," lamented Katia's nephew, "considered an *intrigante* who was set to capture the heart and to be crowned and gain the confidence of the Sovereign for her own interest. No one was on her side and not a person would say a nice word [that is, of course, mainly before her marriage]. Only the Czar stood for her against anyone around." As Count Adlerberg opened his heart to Miliutin in May, 1881: ". . . he [Adlerberg] was sure that his official position at the Court [as a Minister of the Court] and despite a friendly, almost brother to brother relationship with the Emperor, had become impossible, if not unbearable." "Even if there weren't the catastrophe of March 1," Adlerberg told Miliutin, "I nevertheless [because of the Czar's intention of crowning Katia] would

---

* In his diary, recorded almost daily from 1873, there is one casual mention of Katia in 1876, but as the Soviet editor points out, this paragraph had been added in 1900.

† Count Serge Witte, (1849–1915), one of the greatest Russian statesmen, yet a vain, gossipy and spiteful man.

not now [*i.e.* in May, 1881] be the Minister of the Court. The late Sovereign was entirely in the hands of Princess Yourievsky, who brought the Czar to extreme recklessness and dishonor. . . ." If one takes into consideration Adlerberg's resentment of the past, his position under a new Czar was now "unbearable" because the new Czar without foundation (as a result of false rumors, the price of secrecy) "never forgot" that Adlerberg was "present" at the wedding, though, as we have seen, wearing civilian clothes to underline if not his protest, at least his non-official attendance.* The sixty-three-year-old Count Adlerberg had continuously occupied his post from 1872 (superseding his aged father, who died in 1884 at the age of ninety-three), but was rather brusquely dismissed by the new Czar on August 29, 1881.†

At any rate, with the new policy of surrounding the court with "true Russian people" (Count Hillarion I. Vorontzov-Dashkov was to be appointed) Adlerberg's retirement (he never complained publicly about the treatment he received) had been a

---

* If one believes certain memoirists, Alexander III also had a grudge against Adlerberg for "rudely" preventing, while he was not the heir to the throne (his elder brother was still alive), his intended morganatic marriage to his mother's maid-of-honor, the young Princess Marie Meschersky (1844–68), who was promptly bethrothed to the very rich Paul Demidov and died in childbirth the same year of 1868.

† To use Adlerberg's own words, he was "harshly, almost rudely, even shamefully dismissed"; "*c'est la fin de Dynastie Adlerberg,*" he exclaimed. The family, who had faithfully served the court since the end of the eighteenth century, was through. There is no doubt, as we have seen, that the chief cause of the dismissal was the erroneous assumption by the new Czar and his spouse that Adlerberg was in collusion with Katia. Moreover, after his dismissal an inquest was ordered regarding the financial state of the Ministry of the Court with the result that everything was found in perfect order. Shortly, he was appointed to the State Council (highest office in the empire), and when it was found out that Adlerberg had personal debts in the amount of over one million rubles, the new Czar gave an order to settle the debts which the new minister was "boasting that he bought them out at half price." When Adlerberg died in 1889, "his widow petitioned for a pension and tried to sell her husband's collection of snuff-boxes." However, the house, which housed the Ministry and which was valued at 3.5 million golden rubles in 1910, had been willed by Alexander II to Adlerberg, but the latter's widow (who incidentally lacked the tact her husband possessed) declined the gift. She died fairly forgotten to the world in 1910.

question of time.* It is well known that under both Adlerbergs' administration of the imperial court, actually a gigantic organization, covering the Crown Domains, including the gold and platinum mines, forests, theaters, stables, etc., effected economies up to the 1880s amounting to almost 7,400 million gold rubles.

Naturally all these changes, or as they were then labeled "the new course," could not but harm Katia's new status, in which even her new wealth was of no avail. She realized only too well that as "almost an Empress" and a widow of the beloved "Czar-Liberator," she should not and could not remain in Russia any longer. Just like Chekhov's cry of *The Three Sisters* a decade later, "to Moscow, to Moscow!" became Katia's obsession. Plans to leave St. Petersburg for "abroad" were made almost at once. But it was a whole year before the large *ménage* departed for France.† The date of departure was Katia's tactful gesture: the Yourievsky household made their exodus, not before a memorial mass, conducted at the St. Peter and St. Paul Cathedral, a year later to mark the anniversary of her husband's death on March 1 [13], 1882. Naturally, the whole Royal Family attended, and she was present, again in the capacity of a "nonperson."

Now Katia was ready to move her large and cumbersome family, which in those days was not an easy thing. Aside from Katia's immediate family of three small children (from three to nine years of age) tradition in force for centuries called for her to be accompanied by a tutor (for Gogo), a governess, a doctor, nurses (for the girls), Russian cooks and assistants, footmen, a guard, maids and coachmen—a total of twenty, excluding of course Katia's *grise éminence*, the ever present Barbara Shebeko. Three dogs "the Mops," the pugs, beloved by her, completed the

---

* In April, General Ryleev, "the most trustful man of the Czar's secret family," to use the words of Miliutin, was also dismissed.

† As she was virtually a has-been and a "nonperson" (all newspapers, publications and public notices continued to keep a complete silence on her existence), Katia's status naturally changed overnight. A memoirist believes that one trivial incident made her speed her departure for abroad. He cites a case which "deeply humiliated and offended her": Katia was once refused the use of the so-called "Czar's Room," actually a waiting room in principal railroad stations and reserved for high administration and government people. Naturally Czars had rarely used these rooms, but by a tradition the name stuck.[23]

exodus. All of them, including the household staff, had to be equipped with European clothes,* so different from Russian ones, and servants' liveries to match the colors of the newly designed Yourievsky coat-of-arms had to be ordered. To top it all, the caravan was to be escorted by a Colonel Emelian Dolinsky, especially assigned by the new Minister of the Court to "look after the Princess." Lastly, if not of most importance, a country, a city, and a house had to be selected. The choice fell on Paris, where for centuries *les Princes Russes* and in a lesser degree *les Princesses Russes* with their fabulous *train de vie*—extravagant spending—were more than famous. Though France was traditionally a "free-thinking country," with several revolutions in the eighteenth century to her credit, she was more than courting Imperial Russia, to whom she looked as an eventual ally in her future reckoning with Germany, while not forgetting the help that Alexander II had extended her in the defeat of 1871.† Katia knew only too well that no Frenchman ever forgot the intercession, though unsuccessful, of her husband with his uncle Wilhelm I, during and after the War of 1870. In fact, a few days before Sedan, in a letter to King Wilhelm I, the Czar entreated him not to impose on France "a humiliating peace." Later, in a letter, he also vainly implored the King to reduce the five-billion-franc (or $1-billion) contribution, which was also refused by the victors. (The reply, a copy of which Alexander sent to the Empress Eugenie, was delivered by her in 1919 to Clemenceau, who read

---

* A Russian diplomat, assigned to the London Embassy, relates his meeting with the Dowager Empress Marie who arrived in the spring of 1912 for a visit with her sister, Queen Alexandra. "We were at the station," he wrote, "to meet her. The King, the Queen and several Ministers were also present. The whole group was elegant in frock coats and silk hats. The Russian guests who arrived on the train looked as if they had come from the North Pole. The Empress Dowager in an old-fashioned fur coat, the lady-in-waiting in a pre-historic coat, rushing about and looking for the Empress Dowager's dog, which had disappeared at the last moment—it was so typically Russian that it reminded me of my dear Moscow. And to say that royalty was not human!"[24]

† Although the Czar could not sympathize with the French Government (after all, France had invaded Russia twice in his memory—in 1812 and 1854), his intercessions were simply based on realistic policy for his country, to which a strong and a united Germany would be a menace.[25] See page 143.

the contents of it to the German Peace Delegation, thus defeating their claim in reducing "excessive" French contributions).*

April came, and the semiroyal exodus (naturally in several *salon-wagons* usually reserved for minor royalty and high-placed bureaucrats) boarded the Nord Express and within a few days, after changing trains at the German frontier, disembarked in Paris. Soon the household settled in a *hôtel* while waiting to purchase a *hôtel particulier, i.e.,* another private domicile, while the ever present Barbara Shebeko was dispatched by Katia to Switzerland in order to prepare accommodations for a "future visit to this country." "Soon," wrote Vera, the maid, "our entire family, not forgetting the three pugs [we will hear more about them later] arrived in Switzerland where Shebeko met us."

The not too edifying characterization and role of Barbara Shebeko must be briefly told here.

Barbara Shebeko, or Vava, as she was always called by Katia, was an enigmatic woman. A spinster all her life, older than Katia by six years, she was "well born" and well connected.† As we have seen, Vava, from her early days of involvement in Katia's liaison (she was one of the few who knew about it) to the death of Katia was her constant companion, confidante, and to others an *éminence grise*. "My aunt," wrote Count Boris Berg—perhaps not a very objective witness—"possessing a soft heart, rather a meek character was absolutely devoid of greediness, [but] all her

---

* Although at that time France was not yet "an ally of Russia," (the Franco-Russian Alliance was a decade away), sympathy for the "Moscovites" was more than felt. Peter I. Tchaikovsky, then a relatively unknown composer in Europe, who, as he confessed many times, "simply hated [visits]" to Europe, was more than elated with the reception he received in Paris in 1882. "The ovation I received," he wrote to a friend, "has nothing to do with my personality [read admiration for his talent], but because in my person they are honoring the Russian music and Russian art. . . ."

† "Vava," born in 1840, was a daughter of a Russianized Pole—a minor official in the Mogilev Province. (A "Shebeka," says the Russian Encyclopedia of 1903, was a "light 3-mast ship" used in the Mediterranean in the former days by the Corsairs.) Vava's older brother, General Nicholas Shebeko, was at that time (in the 1880s) the Assistant Minister of Interior, and "the Chief of the Corps of Gendarmes." Her elder sister, Sophia, was the wife of Katia's brother, Vasilli, who died in Nice in 1910, thus Vava was Katia's sister-in-law.

life she was under a spell of someone and once in a while under an influence of several. This is why Vava found in her suitable material for fulfillment of her designs [to bring her together with the Czar] and as a result she carried out all of her errands, was the most trustful person and adviser. From the start she transmitted all their letters, managed all the rendezvous with the Czar and actually was involved in all the intimate encounters. Later, all the money problems were Vava's responsibility as my aunt on principle never discussed these matters with the Czar.

"At the same time, Vava loved money and was prone to mix in various [business] affairs which very often were attributed to my Aunt, who had nothing to do with it and probably knew nothing about them."*

Count Berg goes even further by asserting that Vava "though not a mistress of the Czar in the full meaning of the word, tried everything [unsuccessfully] to be one. This was confirmed to me by my cousin Katia Bariatinsky (Katia, Jr.)," he wrote. Yet Count Berg maintains that Vava "who was tied by fate to Katia and their interest coincided therefore had to be loyal to her." "This woman," he wrote vehemently, "with her resolute character, was devoid of any moral attributes and in order to achieve her aim would stop at nothing. She should rather have been born in the era of Renaissance at the Court of Borgias or Medicis. . . . She was an atheist and rather republican than a monarchist in her views. Some [like the nurse Vera, who also hated her] considered her a revolutionary but I think she became one since the reign of Alexander III. . . ." If the simple woman, Vera, disliked, to say the least, the bossing Vava, Count Boris Berg's harsh characterization is justified by a personal feeling,† as Vava did everything in her power to "bring together" Mouche with the Czar. As Count Berg stated, Vava's "machinations" began, not only because Mouche was younger and more beautiful (which many attested she was) "but because Katia's liaison with the Czar at

---

* As Count A. A. Bobrinsky recorded in his diary on November 24 [Dec. 6], 1880, "One feels hidden but powerful and at the same time meddling influence of Mlle. Shebeko. She uses her position for her own advantage."

† Yet Katia, Jr., wrote that she considers Vava "my oldest friend—the faithful and devoted companion of my Mother's girlhood. . . ."

first did not produce children" (it is true that their first child, Gogo, was born to Katia only in 1872, six years after the first encounter). Count Berg, without mentioning the sources, also asserts that Vava pointed out to Katia the example of her very distant relative the "cousin-aunt" Princess Alexandra Dolgoruky, "whose liaison, despite a serious and lasting infatuation [mutual] with the Czar, was abruptly terminated due to her not being able to produce children."

As we have already seen, Vava after a long illness, ended her life in Paris in 1931 at the age of eighty. As her friend Princess Valentina Golitzine remembered what gave her "a *coup de grace* was the theft of all her possessions while she was ill, for what she lived all her life. . . ."*

But to return to Switzerland in the 1880s. Switzerland at that time was seething with Russian political *émigrés*, "dissatisfied students" and with "dedicated" or simply professional revolutionaries. It was even reported that in Zurich they were making bombs for their use in Russia. The neutral country, always a haven for countless Russian "rebels," at one time harbored the famous anarchist Bakunin, who in the 1870s represented Karl Marx in the "General Council" of Switzerland, Serge Nechaev, a precursor of Bolsheviks, "whose slogan was "Our Task Is Total, Terrible, Universal and Merciless Destruction," now in Geneva, also sheltered the famous revolutionary Vera Zasulich, who, after her sensational trial took part once more in a street scuffle and was rearrested but a few days later fled abroad.† If Vera was a

---

* The last Ambassador of France to Imperial Russia, Maurice Paleologue, was in 1923 the author of a rather superficial work, based on Katia's liaison with the Czar, entitled *Le Roman Tragique de l'Empereur Alexander II*. All the materials in the book including some letters were supposedly sold by Vava to the Ambassador. Eventually all Vava's "archives, including the Czar's and Katia's letters were sold at various auctions in France.

† As one American historian wrote: "Vera Zasulich became the heroine of the hour, admired even in the Salons [after acquittal] and . . . according to the *Revue des Deux Mondes* for forty-eight hours Europe forgot everything to talk only of the new Judith, the Muscovite Charlotte Corday. . . ." Oscar Wilde added his talent as the author of an unsuccessful play *Vera* shown in England in 1880 and produced in New York in 1883 with the protagonist based partly on the above *heroine*. Vera returned to Russia and died there in 1912, a foe of Bolshevism.

veritable star of yesterday, there were many more Russian "stars," men and women, then living in Switzerland. In Zurich the university recorded scores of former Russian students, expelled for political agitation at home. In the scholastic year 1872–73 alone, more than 140 young Russian girls registered at the Zurich University. The rostrum of Russian revolutionaries then residing in Switzerland reads like a Revolutionary *Almanach de Gotha*. Lavrov; Tkachev, "the first Bolshevik," "the magnificent one," in the words of Lenin (Tkachev, who died insane in 1885, advocated complete ruthlessness and the seizure of power by a small body acting in the name of the people); Plekhanov, the father of the Social-Democracy (in 1883 he founded in Geneva the first Russian Socialist Democratic organization); Axelrod; Deutsch— to name only a few luminaries—all more or less in sympathy with the assassination of Alexander II—lived there. "The haughty evil upstart, Barbara Shebeko," wrote Vera the maid, "left us shortly to go to Montreux where scores of [Russian] Revolutionaries lived. What she wanted to do there was unknown to me, but as I understand it she was against the Czar's family, as even the Princess [Katia] was in a quandry [sic] noting her frequent absences." In fact, something else less violent was in the offing. The Princess, meagerly informed politically, piqued as she was by the new Czar's policy, who she wrongly believed had "let the Russian people down by taking away what her husband promised" (*i.e.*, granting on March 13, 1881, the Constitution, which as we know now was not approved or decided upon by the late Czar), resolved to issue a pamphlet and "tell for once the whole truth."*

---

* Here is Katia's rather naive *cri de coeur* regarding the March events:

(*"Continuation of my Memoirs which are deposited in the Bank of London"*)

"When the Emperor wanted to grant a Constitution, in the year 1879, [sic!] the Emperor William wrote him a letter begging him not to grant constitutional liberty, as this would be a misfortune for Russia. That old man was not writing what he thought, but what was dictated to him by the infamous Bismarck. That horrible man only wanted Russia's ruin, and was never at rest when she prospered—for this disturbed his plans, of course. However, the Emperor at once understood what was behind the beautiful advice of his uncle, and naturally did not follow it, and had taken the decision to do all he could for his country, as he proved on the day of his death by signing the first steps towards a Constitution.

This decision, which points heavily to Shebeko's influence, certainly could not improve Katia's relationship with her reigning stepson. It looked as though Katia followed the example of her countrymen revolutionaries, who, as exiles, took advantage of the "free press" to publish often biased, controversial, revolutionary articles and books containing assertions not always bordering on fact. The brochure, issued in Geneva and Paris in 1882 under a provocative title, *"Alexandre II. Détails inédits sur sa vie intime et sa mort,"* by a heretofore unknown author "Victor Laferté," immediately provoked in Russia a wave of protests. It looked as if, under the pseudonym of "Laferté," the author was her Serene Highness Princess Ekaterina Yourievsky herself, the morganatic widow of Emperor Alexander II!

The booklet, covering the last three days of the Czar's life and his activities for the period, including alleged conversations he had with Katia, tried to prove that on the morning of the day he was assassinated the Czar not only "initialled and approved the Constitution" but "even ordered it to be made public the next day." More than that, the brochure also related an improbable story that after granting the Constitution the Czar had decided to abdicate in favor of his son (*i.e.,* Alexander III) and leave

---

This act was never made public, it was carefully hidden away, for the policy suddenly changed and everything the Emperor had done was abolished, but his memory shall never fade.

"All the uniforms were changed, and everything that was reminiscent of the period of the Sovereign who was the Saviour of Russia was discarded, even that which was sacred to him was ill-treated; finally, one went towards the most sad issue, and nothing good came of it.

"All the most horrible, dirty and vicious sentiments became the fashion. Never is a good example given in high quarters, never are those who commit infamies shamed, and so there is complete demoralization. One wishes, everywhere and in everything, to delete that angel who, by his noble conduct and his principles, used to put a stop to the wicked trends in this world. He could never let pass a single case of dishonest conduct, without taking the defense of the offended, and severely punishing or reprimanding the one who was acting dishonestly. Such cases were punished by his long-lasting coldness; and this was what deterred them in many circumstances. On the other hand, no noble and honest deed passed unnoticed in his eyes, and what good works were addressed to them in return for it, and how he always rewarded them."[26]

Note: "The memoirs" apparently were never finished and eventually disappeared.

Russia "for a warmer climate." The polemical tone of the booklet, which even a recent Soviet historian dubbed as "based on
low-grade sources," with many intimate details of the Czar's
life and a rather flattering description of Katia herself and her
"ally" Count Loris-Melikov, revealed the real author.*

"This outstanding Minister" (Loris-Melikov), stated Laferté,
"understood only too well what a zealous and a beneficial ally he
had in the person of the Princess, the wife of the Sovereign." The
brochure, according to Count Berg, was probably conceived in
Russia, but he thought it was actually written by Barbara Shebeko
in cooperation with a "second rate Russian author and poet," a
descendant of a French *émigré*, one Nicholas P. Gendre (1818–
95) "with whose daughter Barbara was very friendly."

Within a few months a reply from Russia was forthcoming.
Under a French title *"Quelques mots sur la brochure de Monsieur
V. Laferté"* and under the anonymous authorship of *"par un
Russe du grand monde,"* it was published in 1882 in Baden-
Baden.† At first it was thought that the reply was written by
Alexander A. Vassilchikov (1832–90), a loyal court dignitary and
the director of the Hermitage Museum,* but it was soon disclosed
that the real author was no less than the venerable Countess
Alexandra Tolstoy, the aunt, "the perpetual protectress" at the
Imperial Court of her rebellious nephew, Leo Tolstoy,§ and an

---

* Miliutin, not especially a friend of Katia's or new Czar's (he was
dismissed in June, 1881), thought the pamphlet was "unskillfully written
by a boastful woman [*i.e.*, Katia] or almost under her dictation and
probably with the aid of people close to her. . . . [It] tries to show her as
an *ange-gardien* of the late Czar-martyr in order to assure a future position
for her son. . . . It is remarkable," his diary entry ends, "that the brochure
never mentions the late Empress."27

† Apparently there were also editions issued in Basel and Paris.

‡ Ironically, it was Vassilchikov's daughter, Maria, who in 1915, in
the midst of World War I, arriving from Austria, brought a letter to the
Empress Alexandra from her brother the Grand Duke of Hesse, and with
it not only compromised the guiltless Imperial couple but created false
rumors by accusing the Empress of starting separate peace negotiations.
Actually neither the Czar nor the Czarina even received Maria. She was
arrested and exiled into the interior for the duration of the war. But
the harm was done.

§ Named by Leo Tolstoy as "The Aunt Grandmother" or "Aunt-
Babushka."

intimate of the late Empress and a great favorite of the new Czar. The fifteen-page reply, written in "bold and emphatic language," to quote General Miliutin, condemned "the unknown author," meaning, Katia, of course, "who dared to publish intimate conversations with the Czar, which actually were not even true." Though the new brochure was of course not addressed to Katia, it was full of hostile remarks directed at her. The reply, though criticizing the morganatic marriage of the Czar, was closed with a sacramental phrase: "The marriage," the Countess wrote, "was unfortunately incontestable." Soon the tempest in the tea pot subsided but with the result that the Princess was forbidden by the new Sovereign to reenter Russia.*

Meanwhile, Katia returned to Paris, stopping at first at the Hôtel Clermont-Tonnère on the Rue Las Cases, to assume, as she thought, the place in society due her as a widow of an emperor. In that she was not mistaken. What was more difficult for Katia to achieve in Russia, with one of the most snobbish societies in

---

* Although in the early days Katia and her entourage never ceased to talk of their eighteenth-century "illustrious" Dolgoruky or Dolgorukov ancestors, they hardly mentioned the black sheep, including Katia's grandfather the Siberian exile, so harshly criticized by a fellow exile, the famous revolutionary Alexander Herzen. But another Dorgorukov much later gave more trouble to the government than any other of that family since the eighteenth century. This was Prince Peter V. Dolgorukov (1816–68) Katia's distant kin (their mutual ancestor was born in 1675), who after publishing in Russia several volumes listing titled and noble families of the Russian Empire, emigrated to Europe in 1859, where under the pseudonym of Comte Almagro he published various books critical of Russia's political structure and its society. Ordered home, he refused and as a result was considered "expelled." There is no doubt that with the publication of the Laferté brochure, many remembered their Dolgorukov kin's political escapades in Europe, all of which certainly did not help Katia in winning popularity in high spheres of Russia.

Another Dolgoruky, a grandniece of Alexandra, "the platonic" friend of Alexander II, this time a White Russian exile in England, Sophia (Sofka) Dolgoruky Zinovieff-Skipwith, "horrified family and former friends" after World War II by joining the British Communist Party and becoming the secretary of the Chelsea Branch in London. Though Sofka eventually "ceased to be a card-holding member of the party" and resigned from the party, the former Princess Dolgoruky, as she wrote in her 1968 book, "still considered myself to be a Communist" and because of this was regarded by her family and foes as the "black sheep, the class traitor [and] the pariah. . . ."[28]

Europe, *i.e.* to be accepted, seemed to her much easier in France. As financial problems did not exist for Katia, a *hôtel particulier,* or the fashionable 52 Avenue Kléber in Paris, was in time purchased. Soon Katia inaugurated a veritable "salon," where luminaries of the day gathered under the large oil portrait of the Czar surrounded by his Yourievsky family. Although Russians in general and upper classes in particular neither understood nor liked publicity, the fledgling art which then was called self-advertising, or *"Samo-Reklama,"* was considered not *"comme il faut"* but *"mauvais genre,"* but the morganatic widow of Czar of all the Russias apparently was not against it. *Figaro Illustré,* a popular picture magazine of the day, devoted two pages to Katia "whose Yourievsky Princely title," as the publication stated, "belonged to the Romanovs" and whose "at home" with another full-page with sketches and the names of her guests was featured. The rapturous author of the article informed his readers that among *"tout Paris"* at the "salon of Princess Yourievsky, who is usually assisted by her beautiful sister, Countess Berg, one sees such famous persons as Her Imperial Highness Princess Mathilde . . ." (1820–1909).*

Other guests—the diplomat with the name of the Suez Canal to his credit, Vicomte Ferdinand de Lesseps and whose "Panama" scandal had not yet made a headline; writers Alexander Dumas, the young Ernest Renan, Jules Claretie, Camille Doucet, the well-known French dramatist and secretary of the French Academy, the Marshal of France and Senator Certain Canrobert, "the hero of Wars in Crimea and Algiers," the young but already famous actor Ernest Coquelin, the baker's son from Boulogne, to mention a few—were the *habitués* of Katia's new salon.

"Tout Paris," concluded the reporter of this enthusiastic article, "met the Princess [who had reached her thirty-fifth year] with her beautiful but enigmatic face semi-covered with a halo of eternal black crepe which even improved her appearance," to

---

* Her marriage and subsequent scandalous divorce, settled by an "enormous alimony" ordered and forced by the Czar Nicholas I, from the immensely rich but irresponsible Russian, Anatole Demidov, had been more than the talk of the town years back. Meanwhile, Mathilde had a penchant for young artists, among whom the current one was "a minor poet," a youth by the name of Popelin. Mathilde had claimed that she was "destined" to marry the future Alexander II![29]

whom, concluded the article, (hopefully at this time) the "Princesses Woronzoff, Kourakin, Lobanoff, Troubetzkoi and other Russian *grande-dames* frequently paid their respects." But what one could not help noticing was the absence from the list of her guests of any representative of the old Faubourg St. Germain aristocracy. No less conspicuous was the absence of the Russian Ambassador, General Prince Nicholas Orlov, the son, if we remember, of the man who took the young Czarevich to Europe in 1838 and whose wife was born a Princess Troubetzkoy.

Neither the members of the Russian Embassy bearing such well-known names as (counts) Kapnist and Mourariev; (princes) Cantacuzene and Sayn-Wittgenstein; as well as Narishkin, Fredericks, nor others of the embassy paid Katia their respect. The Laferté brochure no doubt was still remembered. But within a few years this incident was forgotten. The "first swallow" to pay "his respect" was her stepson of the same age, the oldest brother of the present Czar, handsome Grand Duke Vladimir, with his wife, both reputed to be the leaders of the smart, if not the "fast," set of St. Petersburg. Soon after, "the Beau Brummel" of the Romanovs, the Grand Duke Alexis, the younger brother of the above and whose love marriage was so scorned by his father, a sailor and a *bon vivant*, who according to the description of his nephew, "was hopelessly spoiled by women, particularly of Washington, D.C." and whose frequent Paris escapades coined for many years the phrase *"la tournée des Grand Ducs,"* also paid his respects.* The two visits, aside from somewhat improving Katia's status and reputation, particularly in Russia, had another significance. Gogo, who had now reached his adolescence and was a spoiled, capricious, and pampered boy, brought up mostly among women, was to join the Imperial Navy, the head of which was now his half-brother "the General-Admiral" Alexis, who had recently replaced the rudely dismissed "liberal" Grand Duke Constantine.† Alexis was in time followed by his sister, the Grand

---

* To this day, Maxim's *maître d'hôtel* in Paris proudly points to a table and to a faded couch supposedly the preferred seat of *"Son Altesse Imperiale Le Grand Duc Alexis."*

† Although the political views of Constantine were mildly "liberal" (he was prophesied to be a *franc-maçon*—a deadly sin in Old Russia), his dismissal by his nephew, the new Czar, was also explained by his "loose" life, as he kept for many years a "second home," the mistress of

Duchess Marie, now the Duchess of Edinburgh, with whom, we are told, Katia, the stepmother, was on "excellent terms." Somewhat later both Grand Duchess Marie and Anastasia (the wife of Vladimir and the daughter of Michael) made their *obeissance, i.e.,* called on her.

The ice was broken. Soon the "well placed" Russians began to call on the widowed Katia and her *hôtel* resounded as in old days at home with loud Russian conversations, laughter, and even gaiety. As the time went on, Katia, who still resided at the imposing 52 Avenue Kléber, decided to purchase a large country house in Neuilly sur Seine, which in the 1890s was considered a suburb of Paris. The new "country" home at 1 Boulevard des Sablons, was surrounded by a large park, with "services"—stables and garden cottages discreetly hidden in back—a place fit for a widow of an Emperor. "As one entered through the vestibule of her private residence [in Neuilly]," the critical Prince Bariatinsky wrote in later years, "one was struck by a large portrait of Emperor Alexander II. The *Laquais* in black liveries with golden *epaulettes* handed me a book to sign [a custom usually reserved for members of royal families] instead of leaving calling cards. . . . 'Don't forget,' my brother admonished me, 'to address her as *Votre Altesse, elle y tient* [she was particular about it].' Every morning at eleven o'clock," Bariatinsky tells us, "the large iron gates would open and a carriage with the *'son Altesse'* and with one of her numerous dogs, driven by a pair of restless black thoroughbreds, presided by an enormous Russian coachman [for some reason Russian tradition decreed that coachmen had to be large specimens of manhood. Even their overcoats were proportionately stuffed to increase their "importance"] with a liveried outrider, will majestically go for a ride. Passersby would turn to look, *les agents de Police* will salute *L'Imperatrice Veuve* as the locals, not well versed in the genealogical voyages, dubbed her. . . ."[30]

---

which was a ballet dancer who bore him many children. Later the male children received the names Messrs. Konstantinov. One should stress that Alexander III was more than an exemplary husband and family man, and unlike his inheritance, was an *odnolub, i.e.,* a man who loves one woman only. As we have already seen, he was to change the laws of the Imperial Family regarding morganatic marriages.

Now that Gogo had reached his twentieth year (he never went to a regular school; his elementary education Gogo received home with specially hired teachers, among whom a Frenchman, Monsieur Constantine de Tour, was the most important but least effective).* He, as any other Russian subject to the Czar, had to enter military service. Katia's choice† was the Imperial Navy, which was headed, as we have seen, by Gogo's half-brother, the *"bon vivant"* General-Admiral Grand Duke Alexis. Very reluctantly Alexis admitted Gogo, who, "without any preliminary examination," appeared one day in 1893 in the Russian naval uniform of a *Junker* (the lowest grade of a navy volunteer), ready to sail with the squadron to New York. The squadron's mission was to express the Russian Emperor's gratitude to President Cleveland for the help extended by the American nation during the partial Russian famine of the past year. The person chosen to deliver the Sovereign's message was the twenty-seven-year-old Grand Duke Alexander. (He became well known in America, particularly after the Revolution of 1917, for his lectures and books.)‡[31]

At the same time, the world's Columbian Exposition in Chicago, celebrating with a year's delay Columbus's discovery of America, welcomed warships of other nations, culminating in a brilliant international naval review of the Hudson. Though in his memoirs Grand Duke Alexander devoted few pages to his American visit, he had not once mentioned Gogo, his first cousin. It was true that there was a difference in the two young men's status. While the Grand Duke, with a rank of only lieutenant, and A.D.C. to the Emperor represented the Czar nominally (the squadron, consisting of Russia's newest battleship,

---

* De Tour was recommended by Vava Shebeko. He stayed with Katia until his death from a heart attack on learning he had lost all his savings in Russia in the 1917 Revolution.

† One of Gogo's shipmates thought that the only reason Gogo joined the navy was "because he loved to sail small boats on the Riviera. . . ."

‡ New Yorkers, Washingtonians, and particularly Philadelphians were the first to send "a ship with flour to Russia." Among them were Colonel A. J. Drexel, Jr., and a Dr. Biddle. As a gesture of appreciation, these men received costly Russian gifts. If the Russian visit to America, unlike the 1863 demonstration, left hardly a trace in history, the squadron's Toulon visit in October, 1893, cemented the Franco-Russian Alliance, which certainly made more than history.[32]

Emperor Nicholas I, and two new cruisers was commanded, of course, by an admiral), Gogo's rank was the lowest of the low. But this was not all. While the young Grand Duke was prominently mentioned and described in the American press (after all, he was the third Romanov since the visit of "Uncle Alexis,"* in the 1870s to pay respect to America, with the Russians still popular, particularly since the Russian naval visit of 1863 during the Civil War) and was constantly feted officially and socially, about Gogo the American press kept a silence (one of the New York papers briefly mentioned that the morganatic son of Emperor Alexander Prince George served aboard the cruiser *Rynda*, atrociously misspelling the Yourievsky name! Luckily, we have vivid descriptions of the "non-person Prince" from a friendly shipmate, written four decades later.†

"Just before our Squadron left the Greek ports of the Mediterranean, a young man of nineteen or twenty, a [naval] Junker," D. Nikitin related, "joined our battleship *[Emperor Nicholas I]*.‡ The Naval Uniform [the Junkers wore regular ratings uniforms with an open collar] *à l'enfant* did not harmonize with his rather large and corpulent body. He spoke a stumbling Russian, always looking for words, as he was brought up in France. His manner of talking through the nose, which was then affected by officers in some of the Guard Regiments, did not please us. One could not say that at the first meeting he charmed us. He received a separate cabin, despite the fact that our Lieutenants doubled up in one. Special instructions apparently were sent from the Naval Staff [from St. Petersburg] how to treat this 'person'. We also noticed that in Greece, Queen Olga, the daughter of Grand Duke Constantine and whom we called "Our Mother Queen," when visiting the ship, was very friendly with him and asked how his

---

* Alexis was the first Romanov visitor in 1870–71. This sojourn was followed by another visit to the United States, with his cousin, Grand Duke Constantine, Jr., in 1876.

† The shipmate, then a young lieutenant junior grade, Dimitry Nikitin, who died as a refugee with a rank of admiral in the 1950s in Seattle, Washington.

‡ The Russian Mediterranean Naval Squadron of the 1890s, to the "delight" of France and the "suspicions" of Great Britain, was then a permanent fixture in this region.

mother was, who was then living somewhere on the Riviera Coast. . . . Soon we found out that the mysterious Junker was George Alexandrovitch, His Serene Highness Prince Yourievsky, son of the Emperor Alexander II by his morganatic spouse, born Princess Dulgorukova." D. Nikitin goes on to relate that none of his shipmates understood why Gogo ever joined the navy.

Though he received from eight hundred to a thousand francs monthly from his mother (a very large sum, considering that the salary of the midshipman was less than three hundred francs a month), he was always short of cash and repeatedly borrowed money from a fellow officer.* When he stayed in the service for about half a year and was supposed, with the rest of the Junkers, to take examinations, he flunked, but soon "Our Admiral . . ." wrote Nikitin, "received confidential instructions from the Naval Staff to 'examine him until he passes.' . . . Later on, Gogo now an officer, while sailing in home waters of the Baltic, went AWOL. This was too much. A Court Martial was in the offing, which nobody could afford to institute. He was quietly dismissed and transferred to the Hussar Guards Regiment with a lowest officer's rank of a Cornet." If reminiscences of good old days become sometimes blurred and not always charitable, it will be worthwhile to cite a letter written to Gogo's mother by the Grand Duke Alexis, Gogo's forty-two-year-old half-brother, then the head of the Navy, about the "Naval Junker."

Saturday, December 24, 1893 [Jan. 5, 1894]
St. Petersburg

Dear Princess, as I have already cabled you, I granted leave to Gogo, but only for your sake. He himself, of course, had not earned it, and unfortunately I must again repeat that I am extremely dissatisfied with his services.

Both when on duty and on board during cruises he simply does not want to do anything at all; neither advice, nor the example of others have any effect whatever on him. Laziness, untidiness, and total lack of self esteem make him

---

* Nikitin recollects Gogo's escapades on the Riviera when, during the *Carnaval*, Gogo used to throw handfuls of gold coins, the *Louis d'or* at girls.

the laughing stock of his comrades and draw upon him the dissatisfaction of his superiors, who do not know what to do with him. Today I gave him a severe reprimand, and have ordered his superior, that is the Commander of the Ship, to punish him severely for every misdemeanor! Perhaps that will have some effect. I am writing you all this, because I am afraid that Gogo will hide the truth from you, all the more as he is past-master at inventing excuses and talking himself out of trouble. It seems to me he would do better to transfer to land service, for he will never make a good sailor! It is very unpleasant for me to have to write you all this, but what can I do.

I send you my best wishes for the New Year, and trust that you and the children are well.

Heartily yours,
Alexis

Gogo's naval career was over.

As the nineteenth century was slowly nearing its inevitable end, Katia's life also changed. On November 1, 1894, her stepson, the Emperor Alexander III, died in his forty-ninth year, and his son, the twenty-six-year-old Nicholas, to be known as Nicholas II, ascended to the throne. As was customary on a new accession, several *mylosty* (graceful favors) were granted to many of the people of all classes of the immense Empire. The new reign also affected Katia's status. She was from now at least allowed to be listed in the *Almanach de Gotha*, which, though not an official publication, had at that time incomparably more than now an authoritative stamp. Although this first listing in the 1896 edition was incomplete in its data* (she was listed as "*épouse*

---

* Unexplained mystery surrounds the *Almanach's* five various "listings" for the "Yourievsky" name for the years of 1896, 1904, 1911, 1923, and finally *Gotha's* last peace edition of 1939. While Katia's birth year in the 1896 to 1911 editions is listed only as "*née à 1846*," the 1911 edition for the first time adds "*née à Moscow . . . 1846*." The 1923 and 1939 editions list her as "*née à Moscow 2 Novembre 1847*," making her suddenly a year younger, the date which is also repeated on her tombstone in Nice. This writer is inclined to believe that the year 1847 is correct. This can be explained. For a public airing, prior to the Russian Revolution of 1917,

morganatique de l'Empereur, Alexandre II de Russie . . ."), it gave her, at least outside Russia, a much better standing, even though correctly she was listed, as a morganatic person, in the third (III), the least important, part, reserved for nonroyal princes' families. However, it should be stressed that very few Russian princely families, actually out of traditional disdain (it was not *"comme il faut"* of upper-class Russians to be listed: "We are well known, we do not need to be listed," they would say), inserted their names in the *Almanach*.* Meanwhile, with her new "recognition," Katia continued to lead a life in Europe which she thought was equal to her status. Serge Obolensky, "her favorite son-in-law" (since 1916) but who knew her in Europe when he was still a young boy, left us his prewar recollections of Katia. "There was quite a large Russian colony in Biarritz [in the early 1900s]," he wrote, "and a number of people had villas and spent much of their time there. Princess Yourievsky, the widow of Emperor Alexander II, and her sister, Countess Marie Berg, and Princess [Tatiana] Gagarin† and Countess ["Betsy"] Shouval-

---

of the difference in ages of the monarch and his morganatic spouse (twenty-nine years younger, if 1847 is correct), a reduction even by a year somewhat lessened the disparity. Inasmuch as the Russians were proverbially lax in genealogy, Katia's father's and mother's dates were never given until the *Gotha* reached its untimely "death" in 1944 during World War II, with all the archives seized by the invading Soviets. Another case of mystery is the birth of Katia's daughter, Katia, Jr. while her birthplace in all the editions is listed as *"née à St. Petersburg 9 Septembre 1878,"* the funeral notices in England, where she died in 1960 and was buried, are recorded as "Born 9/22 [sic] September, 1880." Moreover, as her nurse, Vera, wrote in her memoirs, Katia, Jr., was born in Crimea.

* Such old and well-known (historically) princely names of Russian and Georgian descent as Bariatinsky, Obolensky, Bagration, Eristovs, Orbeliani, Belosselsky-Belozersky, Dolgoruky, Cantacuzene and Kourakin, Troubetzkoy, to name only a very few, were never listed in any of the *Almanachs de Gotha* up to 1918. After the Revolution of 1917 when large Russian *émigrés* groups appeared in Europe, "nonlisting" led to many "misunderstandings." As a result, some Russian families submitted their names. The last edition of the *Gotha* listed altogether only about a dozen or so titled Russian families.

† Katia also apparently knew many "rich Americans." We learn about it from the memoirs of Countess Marguerite Cassini, the daughter of the first Russian ambassador to the United States in 1898 (prior to this year Russia was represented only by ministers. Ambassadors at that time were accredited only to the "Great Powers," less than ten in all). "In America,"

off were all great friends of my father. They were more or less permanent residents abroad, often related, united by common friendships or family, always meeting for lunch and holding dinner parties and bridge parties, for they all played bridge with a passion. In those days, Princess Yourievsky was still attended by a staff of twenty or so. Besides the house that Alexander II had given her in St. Petersburg, she had a house in Paris, the Biarritz Villa, and in the very center of Nice, a big three-story villa of gleaming white marble that looked like an old-fashioned town-hall converted into an elaborate residence—the last two properties were bought after her exile from Russia. Dressed in long, flowing mauve dresses, very dignified and gracious, she looked exactly like what she was, the widow of one of Russia's greatest rulers. Officially, she was addressed as Serene Highness. . . ."

Toward the end of the nineteenth century, when her daughters were grown up, Katia, like any other mother, had to give a thought to finding them suitable husbands. The first to go, as Russian tradition insisted, was the eldest, the twenty-two-year-old Olga, who, in Nice in May, 1895, married a young German two years her senior who was, as herself, a "product" of a morganatic marriage. He was Count George Nicholas von Merenberg, the only son of *Son Altesse Serenissime Prince Nicholas Wilhelm of Nassau*, who in London in 1868 made a mistake by marrying morganatically a Russian divorcée. Although today practically nobody remembers the divorcée of the former Duchy of Nassau (if one "counts out" Nassau, Bahamas, and Nassau County, L.I., N.Y.) and its confusing history,* the Russian divorcée, the simple "mortal," bore more than a famous name: she was the only daughter of the greatest poet of Russia, Alexander Pushkin.†

To Katia, Olga's choice of a husband, though he was relatively

---

Katia advised the young Marguerite, "you'll find most educated people as cultured, charming and well-bred as any of our oldest families. I pride myself on their friendship."[33]

* The Duchy lost its independence in 1866, when she sided in the 7 weeks war with Prussia's enemies and was annexed by her to become just a "Wiesbaden District of the Province of Hesse-Nassau."

† Curiously enough, their daughter contracted also a morganatic marriage with the Grand Duke Michael, Jr. of Russia. This "grievous marriage"

moneyless and the son of a morganatic marriage, was pleasing enough. One can doubt that the name of Pushkin was even mentioned in connection with the marriage.*

Five years later, another marriage took place in Katia's family. This time it was that of her son and heir, the unsuccessful mariner Gogo, now twenty-eight years of age, a dashing young officer of the Hussars, one of the most expensive regiments in which to serve and in which the Czarevich Nicholas, now the Czar, earlier had taken his military apprenticeship.† Gogo, whose innumerable *"tournées des grand-ducs"* in Paris in the style of his much older half-brothers, the Grand Dukes Alexis and Vladimir, and later his cousins Cyril and Boris came to an end, depleting his health and purse (in that order), finally proposed to and was accepted by the lovely seventeen-year-old Countess Alexandra (Sasha) Zarnekau, also the issue of a morganatic marriage.‡ The marriage, which took place in Nice at the height

---

—in the words of his father, "contracted" by the Grand Duke in San Remo in 1891, without a family approval—brought the wrath of the new Czar, who not only refused to approve the marriage but forbade the pair to return to Russia. The bride, the former Princess Sophie von Merenberg, was created by the Duchy of Luxembourg Countess Torby and had several children of which one, Nadejda, married in 1916 the Marquess of Milford-Haven (Battenberg) a Queen Victoria descendant, thus transmitting to their children the blood of Pushkin, as well as the blood of an Ethiopian slave, Pushkin's ancestor on his mother's side.

* It is very possible and even plausible that Vava "arranged" Olga's marriage with Count Merenberg, as she was distantly related to him through her brother's marriage to the cousin of the Countess Merenberg, Pushkin's daughter.

† The uniforms which each officer had to buy, some trimmed with sables, came to about 6000 golden rubles or $60,000 per today's purchasing value. Each officer's horses were also an additional expense.

‡ "Sasha" Zarnekau was the daughter of the grandson of Paul I, Prince Constantine Oldenburg (1850–1906) and his morganatic spouse of 1882, "a Georgian beauty," widow of Prince Dadiani, born Agrafena Djaparidze. Thus Gogo and Sasha Zarnekau were related, with Gogo being the uncle of his wife! The Zarnekau title was "bestowed" on Agrafena and her descendants by the Grand Ducal House of Oldenburg in Germany in 1882. The German Duke of Oldenburg, as a result of his marriage in 1809 to the daughter of Paul I, stayed in Russia, where he died in 1812. All his descendants remained in Russia and became, through marriage, part of the Imperial Family. Their loyalty to Russia and their achievements in the country of their births were above reproach. Their direct descendants are today in France.

of the "season" in February, 1900, brought to the Riviera once more all of what was then considered "*tout l'Europe*" and "all of Russia. . . ."

After a honeymoon, the young couple returned to St. Petersburg and "settled" for a while in the Gagarinsky Number 3 *osobniak*, which from then on belonged to Gogo as its rightful owner. Within a year in Nice a son, whom his parents also imaginatively named Alexander, was born. He was Katia's and Czar Alexander II's first grandson.

Hardly had the excitement subsided when in October, 1901, the engagement of the far more beautiful, talented, and vivacious of Katia's daughters—she sang, played the piano, and was an excellent horseback rider—was announced. Katia, Jr., was to marry the dashing cavalry guardsman, the handsome, immensely rich Prince Alexander Bariatinsky, a scion of a famous family of achievements and of illustrious ancestry and as we have seen, famous for his liaison with Lina Cavalieri. This time, to be different, the marriage took place in Katia's other home in Biarritz, where the whole ritual in the presence of royal and nonroyal international nomads (the word was then cosmopolitan) was once more repeated. Now Katia a widow for twenty years with all her children married, and by the standards of the day an old woman at fifty-four years of age, was alone.* Yet she was more than busy: she had to run two homes in Paris and Neuilly, two more on the Mediterrenean coast, as well as two in St. Petersburg, not counting several *dachas* in Russia. All this needed human help, and there was no lack of it. "They," were always on hand, living, quarreling, eating and drinking at the expense of the "Princess." Aside from the ever present "*l'éminence grise*," Vava Shebeko, "the group" included Katia's family doctor, no less ubiquitous a Dr. Lubimov (whose name gossips always linked romantically with the Czar's widow) and the innumerable men and women of various services still on the payroll after more than a quarter of a century abroad. The household comprised a Russian coachman (replaced later by a chauffeur), Russian chef,

---

* However, her nephew Count Berg hinted that a doctor Lubimov, who, as Katia, Jr., wrote, "followed my mother in her voluntary exile," was more than her physician. What happened to him later is uncertain.[34]

assorted numbers of *laquais* and footmen, chief maid, parlor maids, and even the former children's maid, Vera (on the retired list), secretaries, and last but not least several pet pugs. Katia also had to take some financial care of her children and their growing families. In addition, Katia's brother's "behavior" brought her further worries. (We will hear about this later.) Yet Katia's uneventful life, to use the phrase of Queen Victoria, of "busy idleness" and sometimes of joyless "frivolity," was soon to come to an end. . . .

By April, 1902, Katia, getting older, felt she should draw up a will, which was made in Russian and in French. This is what she wrote to her brother, Anatole:

[On Cover]

In Russian: Open immediately after my death.
In French: Open immediately after my death and transmit
          to Prince Anatole Dolgoroukov.

[Letter]

Nice, April 1/13 1902

My dear friend, Anatole, I turn to you with the request to act as executor of my Will. I esteem you so much and value you so deeply and my confidence in you is so great that I know you will carry out my wishes as a sacred mission.

Everything I left in my Will to [blank] must be left to *Signal* [a dog] and give orders for Sasha Vinogradoff [maid] to receive for her maintenance and the maintenance of Signal, what I have stipulated. She is to receive (40) forty thousand roubles, and two thousand roubles a year for Signal's maintenance and her own. He must see me when I am lying in the coffin, and he must not be driven away from me, he must know that they will take me to the church and where they will take me to in Zarskoye [Selo]. He must lay on the same armchair in the same room. Be good to him tell them to bring him to you so that he should not feel sad. He loves you. If Sasha does not return in time he must be left with Maria, my chambermaid, until Sasha's return. Sasha left an envelope with papers and a packet with me they must be returned to her. My chambermaid Maria is to be given three thousand roubles, and five hundred roubles a year. The dogs must receive for their maintenance 25 roubles a month each. A man must be kept to look after them, I would like Julien [footman] to stay with them, and then a woman to look after them.

I love you from all my heart and thank you for your friendship. I embrace you, and am sorry to part with you.

Your loving sister,
Catherine

In her own handwriting, Katia also left instructions for her safe, where she kept all the jewelry she had received since she had married the Czar.

Before touching the handle, one must press a string at the bottom of the central square with the tip of the key, then introduce the key. Before turning the key, the figures must be placed as follows:

9   No
8   A

Or:

e   n
g   a

then turn the handle to the right, so that it will open twice, and at the same time the key will turn twice.

The safe in my town house opens as follows:

One must turn the lion to the right so as to be able to introduce the key, and after turning the latter once, the square with the letters will open. The letters should be placed as follows:

J   B
b   c

To close both safes, the key must be turned twice and then mix the combination, but do not touch the figures before locking the lock, as otherwise the safe would have to be broken open.

At the same time, she made a separate will, leaving a fairly large sum to her maid, Alexandra (Alexandrine or Sasha) Vinogradov, her latest *protégée*, whom everyone in her entourage intensely disliked.* In fact, this will was drawn mostly for the benefit of Katia's dogs.†

[On cover:] (undated)
>Immediately after my death give this letter to Alexandrine Vinogradov.

[Letter:]
>Dear Sasha, I am leaving Signal to you, you look after him and never leave him alone. I have left you a packet with forty (40) thousand francs for him [about 10,000 golden rubles or at today's value about $50,000], so that he should never lack anything. Both of you live on this money. You must see me in my coffin and you must be near me and know where I am buried. Take him for walks and when you travel take a separate compartment. I entrust him to you and am convinced that you will take care of him.
>I bless you.
>
>Princess Yurievskaya

---

* "This uneducated woman" wrote Count Berg, "had so well studied the character of her Barinia [mistress] that she got completely in her confidence and exerted on my aunt a strong influence. Actually, she with all her soul—hated all of us so-called upper classes but cleverly hid her feelings in order to achieve her aims, which sometimes ran contrary to the wishes of my aunt. She knew all the secrets and it was very difficult for all of us to get rid of her. We gave her a nickname, 'Sasha-Velikaya' or 'Sasha the Great.'"

† Katia, as we have seen, had a great predilection for dogs, especially the pug-nosed types. In Nice she purchased part of a lot which she named "Le Puff," where all her canine friends were buried. Each grave had a tombstone with an appropriate plaque. Curiously enough, an American society woman, originally a Philadelphia Biddle, Cordelia Robertson, also a great lover of dogs, has today a similar burial ground (for eleven dogs) on her estate in Southampton, L.I. Earlier, Catherine the Great installed for her dead dogs in Czarkoye Selo a granite pyramid memorial named "The Egyptian." Apparently, it is an old occupation. Only recently New York papers announced that Kay Francis, the actress, "left in 1967 an estate valued at more than $1 million, the bulk going to the Seeing Eye, Inc. of Morristown, N.J., an institution for training guide dogs for the blind" and in Chicago in 1968 Mrs. Margaret Montgomery left $15,000 to her five surviving cats.[35]

Two years after the will was drawn, Russia experienced her first serious upheaval since the early nineteenth century, the days of the Decembrist revolt. The unfortunate Russo-Japanese War culminated in 1905 in a nationwide revolutionary upheaval with thousands of officials wounded or assassinated, including Katia's stepson, Grand Duke Serge, the second Romanov to be killed by a revolutionary. The events of 1905, which Lenin called a "dress rehearsal," probably made Katia, like many others, ponder the future of her country. At the same time, coincidentally with "the new times" in Russia, Katia's family also suffered reverses.*

In 1907, in Nice, Katia's younger sister, Marie, now Countess Georges Berg, died and was buried there, and now her closest family link, aside from her own children, had been severed. A year later, in 1908, Sasha, Gogo's fiery Georgian wife, sought a divorce to remarry the same year the dashing Leo V. Narishkin. More misfortunes plagued Katia. Hardly had two years passed since Gogo's divorce, when the young Prince Bariatinsky, Katia, Jr.'s, husband, "exhausted" from the life he had led, suddenly died in Florence in 1910. This was followed by Katia's brother's (Vasilli's) death in Nice the same month (February) and year. Three years later, just at the threshold of World War I, Gogo, at the age of forty-one, also "exhausted," died in Germany from kidney disease, the same malignancy which took the life of his stepbrother, Czar Alexander III, at forty-nine. One could imagine Katia's grief at losing her only son, on whom earlier she had pinned so many (never fulfilled) hopes.

The great war and the beginning of the end of Katia's world was just eleven months away. Yet few people were prepared to face, let alone even to be aware of, the impending catastrophe

---

* Katia's and Gogo's names come up at this time for a different reason. A German Consul reported from Russia that "there is talk among the Guards [officers of St. Petersburg Regiments] of replacing Czar Nicholas II and his wife by Gogo and his mother, Princess Dolgorovsky!" [Sic!] The same source reported that already during Alexander II's reign "there had been talk in Paris of putting Prince Yourievsky on the Throne"! This ludicrous report, dated February 24, 1906, survived in the files of the German Foreign Office and was discovered by Professor Sidney Harcave who used this "rumor" in his interesting book *The Years of the Golden Cockerel.*[36]

and the close of an era. The years 1913 and 1914 were not only years of brilliant royal dynastic celebrations (the Romanovs' tricentennial, the Kaiser's fifty-fourth jubilee, the "Hohenzollern Year," and others) but also the era of artistic and technological sensations—the birth of futurism; the "discovery" by Europe of the Russian ballets and operas; fabulous and sumptuous parties; the blossoming of fashions; the use of the automobile, the radio, the airplane; and the popularity of the tango, a dance which for the first time in the history of mankind brought dancing couples—"the right ones"—into close physical proximity.

Owing to the "exorbitant" speed of transportation,* traveling was more frequent than ever. Katia, Jr., who had made her home in Paris, never for a long time stayed in one place the last few years before the "Déluge." "We used to spend several months in Biarritz, the Riviera and Italy and visiting [occasionally] St. Petersburg," she wrote. "I always travelled with my little pet cow, who supplied my baby boys with milk—and favorite horses and of course the dogs. . . ." However, her mother, who did not complicate her frequent voyages by transporting a pet cow, also traveled in a private railroad car of "Compagnie Internationale des Wagons-Lits" with all of her *retenues*, including the Russian chef, who always had "freshly cooked Russian style bread with hot Russian style *cotelettes* baked in it" on hand for the Princess and her guests. "Princess Yourievsky," wrote Serge Obolensky, "subconsciously expected French people to treat her as the widow of the Emperor of Russia. She always traveled from Paris to Biarritz in her private railway carriage attached to the fast night train, alone except for her dog and her servants. Princess Catherine [Katia, Jr., Obolensky's wife] once told me many years later, that on one occasion a commercial traveler got

---

* In these years, for instance, one could reach Paris from Vladivostok on the Pacific Coast, a distance of more than six thousand miles, in less than eleven days! The Trans-Siberian Express, a marvel of the century, offered (in a Paris booklet) "a palace of luxury . . . a restaurant, salon and a lounge car in Louis XVI decor with an adjacent smoking room in vivid Chinese style." A church car, "an ambulatory basilica," was attached to the train in addition to a "gymnasium, equipped with exercise dumbbells and a stationary bicycle." All this for only seventy-five dollars in gold for first-class passage.[37]

into Princess Yourievsky's private car by mistake and made himself comfortable. The old Princess was horrified to discover a stranger sprawled out on her cushions and imperiously ordered him to leave. He protested that he had bought a ticket. She said she owned the whole car. He thought she was crazy. Finally the matter was straightened out but it left Princess Yourievsky badly shaken."[38]

Katia's last visit to St. Petersburg took place in the spring of 1912, just before the outbreak of World War I, exactly thirty-one years after she had become a widow, in a city which in the past witnessed her "downfall," her rise, and her tragedy.

What prompted Katia once more to return to the country of her birth is not clear. However, her nephew, Count Berg, asserts that the real reason for her last visits (she had visited Russia since the accession of Nicholas II) to St. Petersburg was to petition her step-grandson, Czar Nicholas II, "in view of the size of her family for a double increase in her allowance." At this time, Katia was almost in her seventies (recently she had fallen gravely ill and had had an operation), with several grandchildren in existence, and their annual allowance of 100,000 gold rubles, established in 1881, was apparently not large enough. Countess Olga von Merenberg, the eldest daughter, had a son, George, born in Hanover in 1897, and a daughter, also named Olga, born in Wiesbaden a year later. Katia, Jr., by her marriage to Prince Alexander Bariatinsky, had two boys, now orphans, Andrew and Alexander, both born before 1910. Finally, Gogo, by his only marriage, to Sasha Zarnekau, had a son, also named Alexander, born in 1900. Thus by 1914 a total of seven persons, including three orphans, descendants of Alexander II and Katia, lived in Europe—all of them more or less financially dependent on Katia, in addition, of course, to her four brothers, constantly in need of financial support for themselves and sometimes for their "second families."

Katia, apparently was not present at the dedication of the "Church of the Blood" erected exactly on the blood spot where Emperor Alexander II had been murdered in 1881. The church construction, which began in October, 1883, was finished only in 1907. "The big new Church of the Resurrection . . ." wrote

Joseph C. Grew, then secretary of the American Embassy in St. Petersburg (the church was consecrated on September 1, 1907) "represented some of the most imposing scenes I have ever witnessed. . . ."

A St. Petersburg society magazine, *Town and Country (Stolitza i Usadba)*, which was entirely devoted to "*Mondanites*" and which issued its first number on December 28, 1913, published a short notice on Katia's "recovery from an illness" and even featured her photograph, perhaps the only likeness of her ever made public in Russia.

After this short visit in St. Petersburg, Katia returned to France just when war came and everything changed overnight. *La Belle Epoque* was over. . . .

In Russia probably nobody now had the time to worry about the "Yourievsky petition." Yet neither Katia, nor any other loyal Russians in their own country or stranded abroad, ever thought of transferring their capital from the "unsafe" Russia to the "safe" banks of Europe.* On the contrary, Katia invested quite a sum in Russian Imperial Bonds, which became worthless within three years! No one could foresee the total collapse of Russia within less than three years. While Russia's currency was still sound and the Empire still powerful, Katia's allowance continued to arrive regularly. But this was not Katia's worry. Now the "dividends" on her being an international "nomad" had to be paid out. With one daughter married to a German reserve officer who had a son of military age, (who fought on the French Front), with the other daughter stranded in Germany, Katia, though not royalty, went through all the griefs, sorrows, and anxieties that members of many European royal houses understood only too well in their now divided loyalty to their country of adoption. Luckily for Katia, the German government, in those "*chevaleresque*" days,

---

* As a rare exception one should cite the case of the celebrated statesman Count Witte, who in the midst of the war (he was the most prominent if not the only one of importance to advocate peace with Germany) on January 25 [February 7], 1915, wrote to Mendelsohn, the Berlin banker, asking him to transfer his (Witte's) Russian funds to a neutral country in the name of his wife. Nothing came of it as "the friendly banker" thought the deal will "compromise Witte completely." Witte died a few weeks later.

in deference to Merenberg's Russian mother (poet Pushkin's daughter who died in Cannes in 1913) and Russian wife, the Czar's aunt, transferred him to a Red Cross unit taking care of "War *Prisonniers* Camp" in Germany, with the proviso that he would not serve on the Russian Front, though as we have seen his son was sent to the Western Front. Katia, Jr., the widow with two boys, was stranded in Germany and had a hard time in reaching Russia, traveling to the frontier in a "filthy cow wagon— good enough [in the words of the Germans] for filthy Russians."

Meanwhile, Katia was not idle in Paris. As a widow of an emperor, and a subject of the new Czar, an ally of France, her duty was to help the cause. She at once, at her expense, volunteered to maintain a hospital for wounded Allied soldiers, with her ex-daughter-in-law, now Madame "Sasha" (Alexandra) Narishkin to help her. As the war, which was to last "just a few months" (the belief of most of the statesmen and generals of all the warring countries), took more and more lives with the aid of perfected instruments of death, gruesome news from Russia, though often distorted and exaggerated, reached Katia.* But nobody, least of all Katia, could even dream that by March, 1917, an era would end, not only for Russia but for the whole of mankind.†

The 1917 Revolution, which ended the three-hundred-year-old Romanov Dynasty naturally, at the same time, fundamentally changed Katia's life once more. With the abdication of the Czar the Imperial Domains were all sequestered, proclaimed the property of the people; and all the payments to the *pensionnaires*

---

* The news gladdened Katia, when in November of 1916 she received word that her widowed daughter, Katia, Jr., married in Yalta, Crimea, a Cavalry Officer of the Chevalier Garde Regiment, Prince Serge Obolensky-Neledinsky-Meletsky, then on leave "recovering from shell-shock"—(now a well known personality in the U.S.A.). Katia, Jr., who in the beginning of the war turned her country estate into a hospital, herself became a registered nurse. The pair who had not seen each other since "childhood days in Biarritz" met again in Yalta at a charity bazaar at which Katia, possessing a wonderful voice (she studied with Reszke in Milan) gave a recital, accompanied by a "young, frail looking pianist, one Dimitri Tiomkin," who in a few years was to become a Hollywood celebrity.

† During this period, Katia also received the sad news that her other brother, Michael, died in Russia in 1915.

(Katia's pay came not from the state but from the Imperial Domains) of the Czar stopped, and though the new regime recognized private property it was difficult to receive funds from Russia. For the first time since Katia could remember, money problems really frightened her.* Complete silence from her two daughters, one, Katia, Jr., in Revolutionary Russia (there were rumors that Katia, Jr., and her husband had both been shot) and the other one, Olga, in an enemy country, almost drove her to despair.† To make it worse, within less than nine months, the so-called liberal, but impotent, government of Kerensky fell or was seized in early November by Lenin and his Bolshevik cohorts, who made their headquarters in the Smolny Institute, the very school for "Maidens of Noble Birth" where more than half a century earlier Katia was a student.

One can imagine Katia's reaction to this news. The exclusive Smolny, founded more than 150 years before, where she had spent her youth and where as a *mademoiselle* she had met her fate, was now desecrated. "As we returned to Smolny for studies [after November 1917]" wrote a former *institutka*, "we felt that the page of history is turned over and that something new, rough and dirty began. . . ."

Finally, the separate Peace Treaty with the Germans, signed by the Reds at Brest-Litovsk in March, 1918, made even more difficulties for the Russians in France. Overnight, the Russian sacrifices were forgotten. *"Les Braves Russes"* of 1914–16 became

---

* During the war of 1914–18 it was strictly forbidden to correspond with anyone, even closest relatives, in the enemy countries. Royalty, particularly, had to heed the rule. Corresponding with enemy relatives was one of the gravest, but, in fact, false and unfounded, accusations, against the Empress Alexandra of Russia, which led her and her family to their dooms.

† One should add that the myth of "Romanov's millions" in British hands still persists. The last Czar's funds were all kept in Russian state banks with the British funds transferred early in the 1900s. All the government funds in German and Austrian banks were transferred to Russia in July, 1914. It is true, of course, that the Russian Imperial Government in 1915 and 1916 transferred many millions in gold bullion to England and less to France, but all these funds were sent to cover the purchase of munitions. After the Revolution of 1917 all these sums were sequestered by the Allies.

"*Les salles Russes les traîtres*".* Numerous Russian officers stationed in Paris were ordered, to escape possible insults, to wear civilian clothes. All this could not but exacerbate the worries of the already despondent Katia. One could readily imagine with what grief she received confirmation of the assassination of the Imperial Family† (their deaths were denied by many, including the Red government, which led to the wholesale appearance of false pretenders).

By July, 1918, Katia, to her horror, had learned that aside from the Imperial Family a kin of hers, General Prince Vasilli Dolgorukov, one of the few former courtiers who had volunteered to follow the Czar's family into their Siberian exile, had also been executed.

---

* "The Miracle of Marne" in September, 1914, could not doubtlessly be achieved without Russian sacrifice. In desperation, Russia, by invading East Prussia with two unprepared armies, forced Germany to transfer from France almost 4½ corps (about 250,000 men)—actually 2½ corps were sent from the western to the eastern front—which were sorely missed at the Battle of the Marne and were, in the words of General Ludendorff the deciding factor in losing the war!

It is significant that several years after the Russian Revolution of 1917 when the old Russian Government was generally condemned and criticized not only by her successors, the Bolsheviks, but even by her former Allies, Sir Edward Grey, former Secretary of Foreign Affairs, had this to say about the desperate moments (prior to the Marne) "when the only hope of saving the Allies," he wrote, "was for Russia to attack once and at all cost." "Let it never be forgotten," he added, "that it was the energy and tremendous sacrifices with which Russia made this advance that *saved* the Allies in the autumn of 1914." It should be added that in 1915, Russia "shipped" to France several army brigades who fought throughout the war on the Western and Salonica fronts.

"It is extraordinary," wrote an English historian, "that a scholar of the standing of Langer [Professor W. L. Langer of Harvard] could write in 1929: 'No one appears to have discovered what concrete advantages the alliance brought to France. . . . The alliance was from start to finish a Russian instrument which operated to Russia's advantage almost exclusively. . . .' Yet it would be unfair to blame the eminent American historian when the French people themselves seem unable even in 1950 to understand that it was Russia's action which saved them in 1914 and doomed them in 1940."[39]

† Out of sixty-three members of the Romanov family of 1917, seventeen —six of them females—were executed or killed during the Red Terror years. Thirty-five have died since. Eleven (all born before 1917) are still alive.

The Allied victory in November, 1918, did not help the Russians in France. At the Victory Parade in Paris, at which every Allied country was represented, including even Siam, Cuba, Honduras (all of which had entered the conflict only since July, 1917, with Honduras a year later, and whose blood casualties amounted to nothing versus Russia's total of more than nine million casualties), Russia was significantly absent. To Katia the decline of the Russian prestige, which had stood so high so many years, must have been most humiliating.* As the Russian Revolution progressed deeper and deeper, countless Russian refugees from Soviet paradise appeared on the European scenes. This was something new for Europe to see—destitute Russians—a specie heretofore unknown. Eventually, Katia's daughter, Katia, Jr., with her new husband and two boys by her previous marriage, with great difficulties managed to escape Russia and arrived in France practically without any means.† The life which "the Princess" led at her villa in Nice was, in comparison with what they went through, a veritable paradise. At the same time, a rumor spread among Katia's friends and relatives that she, before the war, had transferred "colossal" funds to England, which was not true at all. Now, in the 1920s, all that remained for Katia was, aside from jewelry, her Villa Georges in Nice (her other possessions and the houses in Paris, Neuilly, and Biarritz had been disposed of at a loss over the years). If it had been "difficult" for Katia to live under the old Czarist days with more than generous subsidies, now it seemed virtually impossible, yet she continued to live "the old way," spending the last funds and finally selling

---

* In his memoirs Grand Duke Alexander relates the humiliation he received in Paris in 1919 when he, the first cousin of the Czar, who was "the originator of Franco-Russian Alliance," in vain tried to be received by Clemenceau, then the Premier. "Nobody cared," he wrote, "that the former Russian Empire had fought on the side of the Allies. . . . Monsieur Le President [said a secretary] would like very much to see you and to talk to you . . . but he is so crowded with work at the present moment . . ." A thing, of course, impossible to take place in the former years.

† Only after the Armistice Katia received word that her daughter, Olga, her German husband and both their children all survived. So had (after an escape from Russia) her brother, "the naughty Anatole" who with his latest wife, the Odessa born Jewess named Stephanie Kumbo appeared once more at the threshold of Katia's Villa in Nice.

her jewels at a loss,* to support her numerous relatives and still keeping on her payroll a really unnecessary retinue.†

Meanwhile, Katia, Jr., who with her husband had moved to England, where she tried to earn her living by singing, described in her book the last visits to her mother in Nice:

"After deciding to make my home in England, and settling in London," she wrote, "I spent the summer months and the early winter ones with my mother in France, who lived only for these visits from me. They brought the sunshine back to her, she always said. The war had broken her terribly; not only the changed circumstances (for she, too, suffered heavy losses), but the terrific anxiety she suffered concerning my fate during the revolution had aged her prematurely. For over a year (during my difficult pilgrimage to Russia) I had been unable to send her any news, and it was only on my arrival in Switzerland that I had been able to let her know I was alive. The only news concerning me before had been the information my dear mother received that I had been shot, together with my husband. My presence always did her good, and though each time I stayed with her I found her still more broken in health and in spirits, she said it made all the difference having me, and while I was with her she really seemed, and the doctors said, to improve. What grieved her terribly was, besides the knowledge of the tragedy of my married life, was the fact that she knew the hard struggle I made to earn my living, and was powerless to help.

---

* All the jewelry, including the *pièce-de-resistance*, an emerald necklace of great value, all given to Katia by the Czar, were sold for a song.

Other articles which belonged to the Czar and were eventually sold at an auction in Paris in the 1930s comprised a New Testament, given by him to Katia with the following inscription: *"D'un être qui t'aime de toute son aime et de tout son coeur et qui t'a consacré sa vie. 24 Decembre 1877."* It went for 11,000 francs. A small ikon with an inscription in French by the Czar, "To remit to Princess Dolgorukov the Ikon of Christ the Savior, which is always with me," went for 3000 francs. A *"necessaire"* went for 2,100 francs. Finally, a saber with an inscription "for bravery" marked "Fabrica Toledo ano de 1868" brought 1,700 francs.

† A Mr. Markov, who for some years was Katia's secretary, apparently got hold of "certain diaries" of Alexander II which he tried to publish. A law suit to stop the publication by Katia, Jr., and her sister, Olga, was unsuccessful. However, no extracts from the "diaries" ever appeared in print and their whereabouts are unknown to this day.

My beloved mother was heartbroken at the thought of being unable to provide me with the means of existence. All of her fortune had gone with the revolution in Russia, and her remaining possessions were sold one by one, to enable her to live. She always hoped that things would right themselves in Russia, and that I should live through better times—for like the older generation, she could not quite get used to changed circumstances. In February, 1922, my dear mother, after much suffering, passed peacefully away. Her loss has left a cruel blank in my life that nothing can ever replace. I try to feel reconciled to God's will, and at times can rejoice that all her sorrows are over, but I miss her so—her death has indeed left me alone, for wherever she was meant home to me, and I could go to her for comfort."

The tragedy of her country—the dissolution of the Empire, the desecration of the past, and the condemnation of all that once was revered and esteemed in Russia with the numerous violent deaths of her friends and relatives—was the last straw. When she died in 1922, she had outlived the Empire and its dynasty by five years.

Her passing during the depressing postwar years attracted little attention in Europe and none in Russia, by now named the Union of Soviet Socialist Republics. "Her death on February 4, 1922, in Nice," read the obituary in the local French paper, "greatly moved aristocratic Russians, now residing on the Côte d'Azur. Her [Serene] Highness who lived in Nice some 40 years . . . possessed a golden heart, opened to all misfortunes, as her charitable character was well known." The funeral cortege after leaving the mortuary slowly moved to the Russian Cathedral on the Boulevard of Nicholas Czarevitch.* Among the wreaths which were placed on the coffin, one could see, aside from the family ones, one from the Russian Consul and its personnel [France recognized the Soviets only in October, 1924]. Among those present were: Her [Imperial] Highness Grand Duchess Anastasia [the daughter of the Grand Duke Michael, brother of Alexander II]; the Grand Duke Andre [the son of Alexander III's brother Vladimir]; the Countess of Merenberg, the daughter

---

* Named after her stepson, who had died in 1864 in Nice.

of the illustrious defunct, Prince Alexander Yourievsky; her grandson, Prince Anatole Dolgoruky [Dolgorukov]; her brother, her niece, and others. . . .[*] Others present were the [nameless] Russian Consul, Monsieur Broca, the *Préfecture* Councillor and a delegation from the local Mayor, as well as a delegation from Jeanne d'Arc Association with a flag. The Service was officiated by Archbishop Protopopov, assisted by Archbishops Selivanov and Troitzky. The Archdeacon Pobedonostzev [sic!]† assisted them. . . . The burial took place in *Cimitière Caucade*. . . ."‡

As she lay buried in faraway France, her small Rose Palace in Russia was also slowly dying. A sixteen-year-old Russian, son of an Officer of the Guards, Igor Schwezoff (now in the United States), stranded in Petrograd during the Revolution, joined a private ballet school in 1920, which was then housed in "the small palace of Princess Yourievskaya in the Gagarinskaya Oulitza," left us this story:

"The place which now became a Ballet School was unoccupied and falling into ruin from neglect. . . . The dining room was in a state of hopeless ruin, having been destroyed by the rain which came in through the broken glass roof for several years. Pictures, furniture, inlaid floor were all in a pitiful state. One or two panes had been covered with cardboard, in a feeble attempt to shut out the elements. Glass was impossible to get, and nearly all the windows in Petrograd were broken—the splinters of glass left in gaping panes, or roughly stopped up with rags, cardboard or wood."[40]

A more gruesome picture reached us a few years later. On February 24, 1926, a Russian newspaper in Paris reported that "the *osobniak* of Princess Yurevskaya, the morganatic spouse of

---

* Apparently Katia, Jr., then Princess Serge Obolensky, was either unnoticed by the reporter or was away on her singing tour and was not able to come in time. Her husband Serge, as he himself relates in his book, was en route from Australia to Italy.

† Probably either a relative or namesake of the famous statesman, Katia's foe in the 1880s.

‡ She was buried in the Russian Nicholas Cemetery, located outside the city of Nice, where scores of Russian exiles found the place of their last rest. The mausoleum, built for her sister Marie, now holds the graves of both sisters, Countess Marie Berg's and Katia's.

Alexander II, is nearing a complete destruction. In the White Grand Ballroom on the parquet floor of black ebony wood with mother-of-pearl incrustations, one can see piles of snow-drifts. Through the broken glass roof, the snow also covered other rooms and there is no possibility to penetrate into them. The snow, no doubt, will destroy the four valuable sculptures by N. S. Pimenov [well-known Russian sculptor, 1812–64]. . . ."

Her Serene Highness, Princess Ekaterina Mikhailovna Yourievskaya—the morganatic spouse of Emperor Alexander II of all the Russias, a woman who was "an adorable imp," a "beloved angel," and "a wife before God" to one, was "an unscrupulous, strongly willed, impudent, stupid, scheming and greedy adventurous person" to others and "a woman in love, loyal, gay, charitable, talented, generous" to many of her friends—was no more. Although in the words of the Czar's last minister of court, Katia was "a brazen and at the same time stupid and mentally undeveloped woman [and] only the death of a martyr perhaps prevented imprudent acts [*i.e.*, of crowning her] of the Czar and saved the brilliant reign from a dishonorable finale," Count Berg, her nephew, felt that people who harshly criticized Katia "hardly knew her," for to him she "was simply a girl who fell in love with the Czar and who, since her meeting him had fought the temptation in all her powers, until their mutual infatuation reached a point which conquered all the obstacles. With her unusually deep love, self-sacrifice, devotion, and also with absolute uninterest [in material things] she touched the Czar's heart. Moreover, she took great care in watching his health . . . and with this she even brought him closer to her. One should not forget that she sacrificed everything she had— her reputation, denied herself all social life and amusements which in turn [ironically] brought on her general censure. She went nowhere and lived only in the expectation of meeting the Czar and this lasted 15 years. . . .

"Alexander II loved Ekaterina Mikhailovna for her gaiety and sincerity. Only with her he found rest from all of his preoccupations and anxieties. With the years his feeling [during the liaison] towards her deepened until he married her, despite the opposition of the entire Imperial Family. . . ." In the words of another author, that Katia gave the Czar "peace, comfort and pleasure he no longer enjoyed elsewhere is beyond doubt. She gave him much more. . . ."[41]

Her husband, Alexander II, the "Czar-Liberator," Emperor and Autocrat of all the Russias, of Moscow, Kiev, Vladimir, Novgorod, Czar of Kazan, Astrakhan, Poland, Siberia, Kherson of Tavrida, of Georgia, Grand Duke of Finland, etc., etc., etc.,* died at the age of sixty-three, thus exceeding by several years the age of any Russian monarch before or after. Kluchevsky, the celebrated Russian historian, who was not a particular admirer of the monarchistic regime and who in 1904 predicted that "the son [Grand Duke Alexis, who was born that year] of the Emperor will not reign" in his speech on the fiftieth anniversary of the "Liberation of the Serfs" in 1911, stated that "in our past there is no other event equally important by its significance. Centuries will pass and hardly we will ever see another public act which influenced so many spheres of our life." Indeed, though his untimely death actually stopped the reforms (for which he is always unjustly blamed by modern historians), Alexander II was the monarch who, in the face of bitter opposition, liberated millions of serfs ahead of Lincoln's emancipation of the Negroes, modernized Russia after her defeat in the Crimean War, instituted a great program in educational institutions,† reformed the Russian courts; created institutions of local self-governments, put through the "industrial Revolution" without undue human losses, in foreign affairs repudiated the Provisions of the Treaty of Paris (1856) forbidding Russia to maintain her navy in the Black Sea,

---

* The Czar's titles had three forms—complete, abbreviated (used here), and short. Countries are listed according to their "incorporation" or "acquisition" into the Russian Empire.

† During Alexander's reign, i.e., for twenty-six years, 59,000 lower schools were opened, or over 2,000 schools yearly. As one author stated: "The tempo of school openings and lower education during the Great Reform multiplied by 2000 times in comparison with past history of Russia. . . ."[42]

One should bear in mind that preliminary censorship was abolished entirely as of April 6, 1865, and instead a system of warnings and fines, modeled on the Regulations of Napoleon III, was introduced. One should also note that Alexander was the first Czar to grant many privileges to the Jews, which is attested in an article by Abraham Yarmolinsky in the "Universal Jewish Encyclopedia" of 1939.

supported vanquished France against the newly formed Reich, liberated Bulgaria through a war with Turkey (1877–78), reclaimed Bessarabia, recovered for Transcaucasia (Georgia) her lost Provinces (1878), and in the Far East founded the Port of Vladivostok (1860), acquired the Island of Sakhalin from Japan in 1875 (without a war) and Maritime Province from China in 1858.

Yet, unlike the past and present Soviet rulers, who while alive allowed statues, cities, towns, villages, hamlets, and ships to be created or named and renamed in their honor *ad nauseam,** Alexander, had never allowed himself to be an object of "a personality cult,† to use a modern term. In that modesty he was following his uncle Alexander I—after liberation from Napoleon, the "antichrist"—to whom members of the Senate, Holy Synod, and the State Council wanted to erect a monument in St. Petersburg, honoring him as "Alexander the Blessed . . . the magnanimous restorer of the Powers in Europe." They received his reply that though he appreciated their request, to accept it would set an example for his subjects "contrary to the sentiments of moderation and the spirit of humility."

Though every monument to the "Czar-Liberator" has been destroyed since 1917 in Soviet Russia, the statues to him in Helsinki (formerly Helsingfors)‡ in Finland and in Sofia in Bulgaria not only stand untouched but are revered by the population—an act of remarkable expression of appreciation of the Monarch's deeds, taking into consideration the semisatellite status of these countries in the past and present.§

---

* As one writer pointed out: ". . . in due course [after the assassination of Kirov in 1934] 80 cities and villages would be named after Kirov, only one less than Stalin had named after himself."[43]

† As a matter of fact, Alexander II shunned the appellation of "Liberator" given him the first time by the famous Russian exile and revolutionary Alexander Herzen when the latter heard about the plans for the liberation of the serfs in 1857. Professor Pushkarev noted that the appellation "Liberator" was officially not frequently used during Alexander II's reign and became a household word only later.[44]

‡ The Russian Cathedral erected by Alexander II in 1868 still stands in all its glory (with regular services) in Helsingfors and is to this day a tourist attraction.

§ Strange as it may seem, there was no large monument to Alexander II in St. Petersburg (there was one unveiled in 1898 in Moscow). Many

As late as 1956 an American educator who visited Leningrad observed that the "Church of the Blood" was closed and "though not used as a Museum [as were other Churches] now is a storage place for theatrical scenery. . . ." Still later (in 1966) another, this time an anonymous "White" Russian (American) tourist wrote that "all the windows of the 'Church of the Blood' where the Czar-Liberator was killed were broken—in general a tearful picture."* Still another witness described this Church when he visited Leningrad in the 1960s as "very neglected . . . all the doors are broken and simply boarded, interior is probably all ruined . . . yet by the large Crucifix, which stands outside the Church the perpetual groups of supplicants bring flowers and kneel before the only remains of the ruined Church. . . ." "To the foreign tourists," asserted another witness, "one does not tell in whose memory the Church is consecrated." Yet in its Number 7 issue for 1960 the Soviet magazine *Zvezda (The Star)*, an organ of the "Union of Writers," debating and condemning religion in Russia, had this to say about the Church of the Blood: "Near the church," wrote a correspondent, "one sees scenes nonsensical for our times. Some woman, prostrated on the ground, with her

---

projects were submitted but none was accepted. (Yet the monument to Alexander III was dedicated with grand pomp in St. Petersburg in 1909.)

* Not only did many of the old monuments disappear from various causes during the years of the Revolution—famine, terror, wars and blockades—but most of the streets, squares, and lanes were renamed to "forget the past." Thus the street next to the Winter Palace, formerly Millionnaya (street of the millionaires) now is renamed Khalturin Street "in honor" of the man who tried to blow up the entire Imperial Family in 1880 and instead managed to kill about forty simple soldiers. The Mikhailovsky Street, which led the Czar to his death, is now Brodsky Street (named in honor of Isaak Izrailevich Brodsky, 1883–1939, who specialized in "Social-Realism" art by painting official portraits of Lenin, Trotsky, Stalin, and Voroshilov). The Zheliabov Street, which is named after the regicide of 1881, was Bolshaya Konnushennaya Street (Large Stable Street) where in the apartment of General Ryleev, Katia and her children were secretly harbored. "The Malaya Sadovaya #14," Harrison E. Salisbury, wrote in 1961 "where the regicides set up a cheese shop and where they made their bombs, is a bakery now. . . . There is no sign or placard to indicate what happened here. . . ." Finally, the latest "immortalization" by the Soviets, was naming a spot on the moon "Kibalchich," in "honor" of the man, who prepared the bomb, which killed the Czar. He was at the same time "absorbed" in designing a flying machine.[45]

front close to the stone steps [leading to the Church] and with other women praying with frenzy and time to time kissing the mosaic image of the Crucified Christ. . . ."

"Why," wrote another Western correspondent in 1960, "do people go for their prayers and kneeling not into the open Churches [in Leningrad] but in this 'Temple of the Blood' and why do they cover this desecrated place with flowers? Before the Revolution [of 1917] flowers were not brought here. It is clear that this place became a symbol of spilled Russian blood of victims of the Soviet Regime which flows and still flows. . . ."[46]

THE END OF THE BEGINNING

It might be of interest to give a short description on the fate of morganatic descendants of Emperor Alexander II and of Katia's immediate blood relations.

As we know, the Czar had by Katia three children who survived him (one boy, Boris, died in infancy)—Gogo, born in 1872; Olga, born in 1873; and Katia, Jr., born in 1878. Gogo, who died in Marbourg in Germany in 1913, left by his former wife, Countess Alexandra (Sasha) Zarnekau, an only son, Alexander, born in 1900 in Nice.° During his mother's divorce, remarriage, and once more a divorce,† the child was looked after at first by his Georgian grandmother, the morganatic widow of Prince Constantine Oldenburg, the Countess Agrafena (or Agrippinna) Zarnekau (died 1927) and later by Katia, his paternal grand-

---

° According to the memoirs of the second wife of Katia's brother Anatole, a work which is full of errors and distorted facts, Gogo, before his marriage, as a result of his liaison with a well-known gypsy singer of St. Petersburg, Anna I. Massalsky, fathered two children, who were named George and Olga Massalsky. According to Anatole, Gogo met the singer in the famous Moscow Cabaret-Restaurant Samarkand, where he was taken by his cousin Michael Dolgorukov, "the Gay Sailor." Both the children and mother eventually escaped Russia during the Revolution and settled in France.[1]

† "Sasha" died in Paris in 1957 at the age of seventy-four. Divorced in July, 1908, she remarried Lev V. Narishkin, Gogo's fellow guard and Hussar officer, in October of the same year. She divorced him a few years later.

mother, who sent young Alexander to an English school. With the outbreak of the 1914 war, Alexander was once more returned to live with his Yourievsky grandmother in France. The 1917 Revolution in Russia and the breakup of the Empire changed, together with that of countless other Russians, the life of the Yourievsky heir. Alexander, along with the rest of the Russian *émigrés*, sought employment, which he found in England. By 1930, "without revealing his identity," Alexander worked for a steel mill. Through the war years he remained in England, and in 1957 in Paris he married a young Swiss girl, Ursula Anne Marie, the daughter of Dr. Thomas Beer de Gruneck, whom he met while she was collecting material on the Russian Imperial Family. In December, 1961, they had a son, who was named Georges, undoubtedly in honor of Gogo Yourievsky, the child's grandfather. Today they live in a small town in Switzerland in a "Villa Georges" (the name of Katia's Villa in Nice) and divide their time among European capitals.

Fate was no less kind to Olga Yourievsky, Katia's oldest daughter. If we recall, in 1895 Olga married a German, Count George von Merenberg, the brother of Countess de Torby, and had a son, George, Jr., born in 1897, and a daughter, Olga, Jr., born a year later. Olga, Katia's daughter, died in 1925 in Wiesbaden, Germany, at the age of fifty-two, and her widowed husband, then a "retired Captain of Prussian Landwehr Cavalry," survived her by twenty-three years, dying in 1948.* Their son, George, Jr., another grandson of Alexander II—and to give his full name, Count George Michael Alexander von Merenberg—as we have seen was drafted in the last years of World War I but was commissioned a lieutenant in deference to his illustrious Russian relative (like his father) on the Western Front, was made a war prisoner, and spent the rest of the hostilities in a camp in Brittany. In 1926 in Germany, he married a Hungarian but divorced her two years later. During World War II he married again, this time a German, Miss Elizabeth Muller-Uri, and had a child in 1941, a girl, the great-granddaughter of the Czar

---

* In 1937 he visited New York and was feted by a local Russian colony as "a grandson of the poet Pushkin," which he certainly was. He made a second marriage in 1930. His wife died in 1942 and left no issue.

Alexander II, named Elizabeth Clothilde. In 1965 she married a Dr. Martin Karl Wilhelm von Rintelen of Wiesbaden, and they are so far childless. Young George Merenberg's sister, Olga, by a twist of fate, married in 1923 Count Michael Loris-Melikov, the grandson of Alexander II's and Katia's "confidant, almost a Premier and her *protégé*," Count Michael Loris-Melikov! In 1926 they had a son, who was named Alexander, no doubt in honor of his famous namesake and great-grandfather. At present the family resides in Argentina.*

Finally, the last and the youngest daughter of the Czar and Katia, Katia, Jr., outlived her brother, Gogo, and sister Olga. Thus she was the last of Katia's children to die. Fate was not very kind to Katia. We have already noted that by her marriage to Prince Alexander Bariatinsky, she had two sons, Andrew born in 1902 and Alexander born in 1904. A young widow since 1910, if we remember, she was stranded on her Bavarian estate at the opening of hostilities in 1914 and after a "nightmare journey" was able to reach Russia. There, working in an army hospital (she also lent her country house for a hospital) as a "sister of mercy" (a registered war nurse), Katia in 1916 met her second husband-to-be, the young lieutenant of the Chevalier Guards, Prince Serge Obolensky Neledinsky-Meletsky, who was then recovering in Crimea from shell shock.

In October of that year, just a few months before the Revolution, Katia, Jr., and Serge were married in Yalta, Crimea.† They both left their memoirs, vividly describing their life during the war days, the outbreak of the Revolution, Bolshevism, their

---

* The above genealogical information is derived from *Debrett* of 1967. All their names are listed under "The Royal Family" listing as "living descendants of King George II," as a result of Hanover intermarriages of Nassaus, Oldenburgs, and, of course, the Romanov dynasties.

† General A. I. Spiridovich, then the Administrative Chief of the City (*Gradonachalnik*), writes in his memoirs that he "received a wire from the Czar's headquarters informing him that the Sovereign will not be able to give the bride away. Instead the Grand Duke Nicholas (the historian and 'liberal' member of the Romanov house, shot by the Reds in 1919) will represent the Emperor. 'I,' wrote the General, 'was also commissioned to buy an Icon . . . with which the Grand Duke was to bless the bride in the name of His Majesty.'" General Spiridovich died in New York in the 1950s.

escape and their eventual settling in England with their two sons. After her divorce from Obolensky in 1923, Katia became, as she wrote "a professional singer," an occupation which she took "most seriously" with a *repertoire* consisting of about two hundred songs, ranging from old classical masters to ultramodern composers "singing in English, French, Italian and Russian." With such personalities as Melba, Queen Alexandra, the King and Queen of Spain, and other members of European royalty helping her with her concerts, she, the daughter of the Czar, was able, as she relates in her memoirs, "to earn a livelihood."*²

As her years went and the horrors of the Second World War were to follow (she remained all this time in England), Katia's health declined and she had to stop working.† Soon she was removed to a nursing home, where she "peacefully died" three days before Christmas in 1959 at the age of eighty-one, the last of the Czar and Katia's children.‡ A reporter present at the Anglican funeral and the interment which took place in St. Peter's Church§ in North Hayling Island, near Portsmouth, left us his impressions of the sad event.¶

---

* After the death of her mother in 1922, the Villa Georges in Nice, all that was left, and a "few remaining possessions," brought in only 600,000 francs—equal to about $24,000 at that time. This sum was divided "among my sister," wrote Katia, "myself and one nephew—our brother George's only child." However, Katia's share "never reached" her, for during her first marriage she signed papers making her "responsible for some debts of my first husband. . . ."

† Her former husband, now the American Army Colonel Serge Obolensky, continued all these years to help her financially. Though, as he wrote, "their marriage was 'a wartime delusion' they 'had been and always would be friends.'"

‡ She "left an estate of £1420 and a mortgaged freehold bungalow . . . on the Naval Road [on the] Hayling Islands."³

§ "At one time," as she wrote in her memoirs, she "almost embraced Catholicism" but apparently remained Russian Orthodox. This religion permits an intercommunion with the High Anglican Church.

¶ RUSSIAN PRINCESS LAID TO REST AT HAYLING
A simple, but very unusual, funeral took place at the little church of St. Peter, North Hayling, on Tuesday.
An 84-year-old [sic] Russian princess, Catherine Yourievsky, whose father, Alexander II, had been assassinated, and who had walked for miles without food during the Revolution, suffering great hardship, was laid to rest in this green English churchyard.
It was a strangely moving picture as Prince Alexander Yourievsky,

The passing of the last daughter of the Czar-Liberator, who more than a century earlier had courted Queen Victoria and who by his love marriage created a furor, did not create a sensation in England and was not even mentioned in Soviet Russia (Russian *émigrés* newspapers published short obituaries). A simple granite slab at the English Cemetery in Southsea reads:

> Here rests in God
> Princess Catherine Yourievsky, daughter of the
> Czar Alexander II of Russia.
> Born September 9/21 1878
> Died December 9/22 1959

Neither of her Bariatinsky sons, who, in the words of the step-father, "went through unstable periods in their lives," could be present at the funeral. The older, Andrew, after an unsuccessful marriage to a Russian *émigré* girl, virtually vanished while living in France in the 1930s. His only child by this marriage, *i.e.*, great-great-granddaughter of Czar Alexander II, Madeleine Bariatinsky, is today an announcer on the French National Radio. Apparently she is unmarried.

The younger Bariatinsky son, Alexander, the grandson of the Czar-Liberator, is today an American citizen (naturalized under the name of Barry), has been married and divorced (without issue), and served in the U.S. Army during World War II. As a

---

nephew of Princess Catherine, daughter of the Emperor of All the Russias, watched the coffin being lowered into the earth under the dripping trees on this stormy December day, writes a County Press correspondent.

Here was a story stranger than fiction—a daughter of an Emperor, an exile, a relative of our own Duchess of Kent, being buried with only one of her kin at her graveside and about twenty other mourners.

As her nephew, Prince Alexander, shook hands with Press representatives, and thanked us courteously for attending, I felt that this was not really happening in an English churchyard. . . .

The mourners included Prince Alexander Yourievsky, Mrs. Smithers, the Rev. L. G. Shotlander, Mrs. E. Russell (Matron of Wray House), Mr. E. Russell, Sister Morley, Dr. D. A. Broughton, Mrs. C. E. Hochstetler, Nurse Howell, Mrs. Grant-Ferguson, Mrs. Joan Smith, Mrs. Hertfield, Mrs. Spring, Mr. and Mrs. F. Cleeve, Miss Morley, Mrs. K. A. Lingard, Miss Rouse, Mrs. Northcott and Mrs. Frankly and Mrs. H. Willey, also representing Mrs. Phipps and Lieut. Armstrong.

war veteran he was a patient in one of the Veterans' Administration's hospitals. He now resides in the West.

Thus, the Czar and Katia's surviving descendants are dispersed throughout the world—all born in different countries and all bearing passports of different countries.

In conclusion, a few lines on the fate of Katia's brother may be given. Though of all Katia's brothers (there were four) Anatole, who outlived them all, gave his sister the most trouble and though he was the "black sheep of the family," as he certainly was, Katia was more than devoted to him.* Handsome, three times married to rich women and twice divorced (with three daughters), Anatole, owing to his sister's position, had an easy life at least before the 1917 Revolution. Appointed in the 1870s by his brother-in-law, the Czar, as a "Gentleman of the Imperial Chambers" *(Kammer-Junker)*, purely an honorary function and the lowest rank in the exclusive court ladder, he never attained any important position in the Empire.† It was his third marriage which created a scandal, estranged him from his relatives and friends, when, at the age of almost seventy, he married one Stephanie Broyde "a divorcée or a widow of Jewish origin with an uncertain past," born in Odessa in 1878 and thus about thirty years his junior. "There is no doubt," wrote Count Boris Berg with tongue in cheek, "that the marriage was *un marriage de convenance* for both." Stephanie, had previously been married to an Egyptian or Italian named Kumbo or Cumbodi, by whom she had two daughters. Residing in Petrograd during the war, the new Princess Dolgorukov, now actually the morganatic sister-in-law of the late Czar-Liberator, apparently became one of Rasputin's followers. An American historian and biographer of

---

* She, of course, was devoted mostly to her younger sister, Mouche, Countess George Berg, who died suddenly in Nice at the age of fifty-eight. Her husband died in Switzerland in 1918. Their only son, Count Boris Berg, died in New York in 1953, where his widow still resides.

† He was never promoted from this honorary rank, which he held until the Revolution of 1917. His civil grade never reached higher than a rank of a lieutenant-colonel. In all the "Court Calendars," a kind of Social Register for the officials of the Empire, he is always listed as the "Senior Associate for the Committee of taking care of the poor"—again purely an honorary position without pay and without responsibilities. He has been decorated with only two of the lowest orders.

Rasputin characterized her as follows: "a beautiful Princess Dolgorukaia [sic!], a lady of Spanish [sic!] origin, whose formal marriage with a Russian aristocrat had made it possible for her to carry through profitable transactions and at the same time to exploit the saint's human weakness for [her] own purposes" . . . in which . . . "the beautiful Princess [was] particularly skillful at this game."*4 This statement is also confirmed by the "Police Secret External Observation Report."† This was written for December 14, 1915: "Rasputin with Princess Dolgorukova arrived in an automobile to the Hotel Astoria, where she was living and stayed there until early morning hours. . . ." Another entry on December 20, 1915 [January 2, 1916], states: "Princess Dolgorukova's car called for Rasputin today and he proceeded to a private room in the Hotel Astoria. . . . Rasputin remained [there with others] until 6 A.M." A footnote by the Police Agent in December, 1915, reads: "Princess Dolgorukova, Stefania Semenovna, 38 years of age, wife of the Kammer-Junker of the Imperial Court Address, Morskaya (Street) #39/12 [Hotel Astoria]."5

When the Revolution broke out in March, 1917, in Petrograd and all the Cabinet Ministers were arrested, the new Revolutionary government was more than interested in discrediting the old regime. Naturally, the deeds of Rasputin and his followers were of particular interest. On March 18, 1917, the arrested former Minister of the Interior, Alexis N. Khvostov, testified before the judges that among frequent callers on Rasputin "was a sort of suspicious adventuress, who resided in the Astoria Hotel and who bought a title by marrying a Prince Dolgorukov. . . ." This was confirmed by "reports which were burned" (so he thought).6 No less emphatic was the former Minister of Agriculture,

---

* Such persons as Stephanie helped create the legend that Rasputin's "lady-admirers" were "all Princesses, Countesses and other aristocratic persons." Actually, police reports for 1915–16 indicate that most of the women he "brought" home "were of very low origin; mostly prostitutes, courtesans, maid-servants, and some honorary burgesses."

† In 1915–16, Rasputin was guarded, observed, surveyed, and spied on twenty-four hours a day by at least three different secret agencies of the government. Some of the reports were published after the 1917 Revolution.

Alexander H. Naumov, who on April 8/21, 1917, also stated that on January 22/February 4, 1916, "Rasputin called on me, received a very cool reception and later went to Czarskoye (Selo, *i.e.*, to the palace) to complain on me. He was accompanied by Princess Dolgorukova in her automobile. . . ."[7] How Stephanie attempted to do "business" through Rasputin is vividly and with humor described by one Moshe Novomeysky, born in Siberia, and who became a "Palestinian Potash millionaire" and died in Paris in 1961. The adventurous life of the Dolgorukov couple came suddenly to an end with the Revolution of 1917.[8] However, in February, 1918, both were able to escape Russia and its terror through Finland and settle in France, where they could depend on the bounty of Anatole's sister. Anatole died shortly after Katia's passing in 1922, and Stephanie, with her two married daughters by a previous marriage, appeared in the 1930s in New York, where she died in 1954 at the age of seventy-six.[*] The Manhattan Telephone Directory still lists her in 1970 as "Dolgorouky [*sic!*] Stephanie, Princess."

There is not much one can say about the other three brothers. We have already noted that one of them, the unmarried one who died young, Serge, fathered a son by a ballerina of the Maryinsky Theater of St. Petersburg, who as an illegitimate received a surname of Alexandrov (the family name of his mother). Michael or Misha Alexandrov (so named in honor of his godfather, Michael, Katia's brother), became himself a very successful ballet dancer, with the result that the famous Anna Pavlova took him on her triumphal tour through European capitals. While in

---

[*] While in France she published, in 1926, in French, under the authorship of "Princess Stephanie Dolgorouky" [sic] her memoirs entitled *La Russie Avant le Debacle*—a jumble of gossip, chatter, and attempts to analyze Russian history. No details of her past or of her marriage are given. The book raised unfavorable criticism, to say the least, among the Russian *émigrés* and in the White Russian press of Europe. It is interesting to point out that Stephanie, who probably could not even imagine that the Soviets would publish (in 1924) police reports on Rasputin's "visits," rather harshly ("a drunkard made a saint," she wrote) criticized him in her memoirs as well as in her previous book, *La Revolution Aristocratique en Russie*. "Rasputin," she wrote in her memoirs, "this Siberian marauder, a former criminal, who helped to rock the ship of Russia with its 180 million passengers was very much in vogue. . . .!"[9]

France he stayed in Nice with his "aunt" Katia Yourievsky. Just before World War I, Misha, if we believe Stephanie, petitioned Czar Nicholas II for a Dolgorukov surname and through family "pull" received permission to use the Dolgorukov name, but *sans* the title.[10]

Katia, as we know, stayed in her early days with her elder brother, Michael, and his Neapolitan wife. Michael bore also an honorary court title of "Stable Master" *(Staalmeister)* and was the one next to Anatole to cause Katia the most trouble. A gay blade, always in debt, but to whom the Czar, his brother-in-law, had "always shown a great sympathy," Michael, using his "connections," did more harm to Katia's reputation than anyone else. (We have already seen the rumors that were spread about Katia and her "deals.") *

The State Secretary, A. A. Polovtsov, in his diary entry on June 26 [July 8], 1889, wrote that "Michael Dolgorukov, the brother of Princess Yourievsky, made a debt amounting to a quarter of a million golden rubles," a colossal sum at the time and was unable to pay it. As a result, the creditor, a certain Zubkov, appealed to Count Vorontzov, the Minister of the Court, stating that "the late Emperor, through Count Loris-Melikov, authorized to repay the debt and only his death stopped the deal."[11]

In the end, with "the help" of the Empress and Countess Vorontzov-Dashkov, who learned about "and became sorry" for Michael, the debt was fully paid. Michael died before the end of the century, leaving a "restless" but also "gay" son named Michael, who at first joined the Imperial Navy, then resigned it to serve in the civil service. His marriage, which we have already

---

* Much later, the celebrated statesman but petty, jealous of power, and snobbish Count Serge Witte, a man of modest background but always proud to remember that his "maternal grandmother was a Princess Dolgorukov," as we have seen, repeated the gossip that hinted at Katia's "speculations" and bribes she was supposed to have taken. It is curious that Witte's Dolgorukov ancestry cannot be traced in any genealogical books on the family. His grandmother should have been listed in the official records of the "Russian Nobility" of the Dolgorukov family. In the genealogy published and edited by his own "relative," Prince Peter Dolgorukov in 1854, Witte's grandmother's name is also missing!

noted, to the sister of the morganatic spouse of "dishonored" Grand Duke Nicholas (son of the "liberal" Constantine) and a daughter of a provincial police chief at the time, created a mild sensation but made him also the brother-in-law of a Grand Duke. As Katia's nephew, he became an honorary Chamberlain of the Court. He died in 1915, leaving a son and two daughters, who were able to escape Russia after the Revolution and settled in France.[12]

Katia's second brother, Vasilli or Basil, did not distinguish himself in any way, except that he contracted a convenient marriage with Sophia, a sister of *"la grise éminence,"* Barbara Shebeko. In the end he attained, aside from being an honorary *Kammer-Junker* of the Court, the modest post of vice-governor of Vitebsk Province, known today more for the birthplace of a famous painter and the first "Art Commissar" of the Bolshevik Government in this city, Marc Chagall. When Sofia died, Basil, in a typical Dolgorukov fashion, managed to marry a younger lady and before dying willed "his fortune" from his first wife, to the last one, despite the fact that he already had a son and a daughter. He died in Nice in 1917.[13]

As Katia's brothers and their wives and their descendants fade speedily into history, one can close this chapter and this book. . . .

Sic transit gloria mundi

Source Notes

Preface

1. Sedykh, pp. 51–56.

2. As told to the author by Prince Orlov.

CHAPTER 1, *The Overture*

1. Nicolson, *Congress of Vienna*, pp. 162, 289.
2. Aronson, *Defiant Dynasty*, pp. xiii, 23.
3. *New York Times*, Oct. 7, 1969.
4. Blanch, p. 23.
5. McClellan, pp. 86–106.
6. Dugan, pp. 282, 306.
7. Kallistov, pp. 11–12.
8. Nagengast, pp. 302–15.
9. Von Richter, "Yesche ob . . ."
10. Minister, pp. 7–10.
11. Von Richter, see all three titles.
12. Their letter of May 6, 1959, to the author.
13. *New York Times*, May 29, 1968.
14. Hyde, p. 87.
15. Hyde, p. 93.
16. Pope-Hennessy, U., p. 13.
17. Thompson, p. 421.
18. Creston, p. 45.
19. Creston, p. 46.
20. Creston, pp. 66–69.
21. Gernsheim, pp. 2–3.

CHAPTER 2, *Alexander*

1. Harcave, p. 69.
2. Pope-Hennessy, U., pp. 36–40.
3. De Grunwald, *Tsar Nicholas I*, p. 13.
4. De Grunwald, *Tsar Nicholas I*, p. 24.
5. Graham, p. 13.
6. Smirnova, p. 201.
7. Told to the author by Count V. A. Adlerberg.
8. Zhukovsky, p. xliii.
9. Zaitzev, p. 204.
10. Berg archives; Savin, pp. 57–116.
11. Smirnova, p. 414.

12. Smirnova, p. 202.
13. Berg archives; Savin, pp. 57–116.
14. De Cuistine, p. 68.
15. Struve, p. 139.
16. De Diesbach, pp. 347–48.
17. Aronson, *Defiant Dynasty*, pp. 31–151.

18. Nicolson, *King George the Fifth*, p. 308.
19. Berg archives.
20. *Russkaya Starina.*
21. Almedingen, p. 60; Berg, p. 17; *Genealogisches*, p. 384; Mosse, p. 34.
22. Duff, p. 138.
23. Witte, *Vospominaya*, I, 204.

CHAPTER 3, *Alexandrina*

1. Hyde, p. 216.
2. Creston, p. 312.
3. Berg archives.
4. De Grunwald, *Tsar Nicholas I*, p. 144.
5. Berg, pp. 13–17; Creston, pp. 353ff.
6. De Grunwald, *Le Tsar Alexandre II*, p. 194.
7. Yourievich.
8. Creston, p. 355.
9. Creston, p. 353.

10. Creston, p. 355.
11. Athlone, p. 87.
12. Pope-Hennessy, J., p. 14.
13. Creston, p. 361; Longford, p. 126.
14. Told to author by Count V. A. Adlerberg.
15. Bolitho, p. 383; Longford, p. 129; Duff, p. 168.
16. Eyeck, pp. 13ff.
17. De Grunwald, *Tsar Nicholas I*, p. 198.

CHAPTER 4, *Intermezzo*

1. Tyutchev, p. 84.
2. Berg archives.
3. De Grunwald, *Le Tsar Alexandre II*, p. 201.
4. Berg archives.
5. De Grunwald, *Le Tsar Alexandre II*, pp. 142–50.
6. Berg archives.
7. Tyutchev, p. 77.
8. Tyutchev, pp. 78ff.
9. Tyutchev, pp. 78ff.
10. Tyutchev, pp. 85ff.
11. Connell, p. 11.
12. Berg archives; Olga.

13. Tyutchev, pp. 91ff; Berg archives.
14. Tyutchev, pp. 91ff; Berg archives.
15. Graham, p. 70.
16. De Grunwald, *Tsar Nicholas I*, pp. 210–12.
17. Berg archives.
18. Berg archives.
19. Blanch, p. 204.
20. Mosse, p. 45.
21. Mosse, p. 44.
22. Berg archives.

CHAPTER 5, *The Czar-Liberator*

1. Mosse, p. 125.
2. Kucherov, p. 296.
3. Mosse, p. 129.
4. Mosse, p. 133.
5. Bailey, *The Conspirators*, p. 63.
6. Tarsaïdzé, *Czars and Presidents*, p. 149.
7. Woldman, p. 262.
8. *Russian Encyclopaedia*, XIX, 203.
9. Berg archives.
10. Polyakov, p. 80; Troyat, *Tolstoy*, p. 437.
11. Berg archives.
12. Gersten, p. 129.
13. Berg archives.
14. Yourievsky, p. 2.
15. Tatischev, I, 254.
16. Berg archives.
17. Berg archives.
18. Berg archives.
19. Berg archives.
20. Soloveytchik, p. 29.
21. Berg archives.

CHAPTER 6, *"My Wife Before God"* OR *"Delicious Reality"*

1. Laserson, p. 224.
2. Laserson, p. 223.
3. Mirsky, p. 42.
4. Fulford, pp. 205, 208.
5. *Life of Alexander II*, p. 182.
6. Gernet, II, 357.
7. *Life of Alexander II*, p. 183.
8. Schapiro, p. 2.
9. Harcave, p. 202.
10. Kondakov, p. 24.
11. Schub, p. 33; *Noviy Zhurnal*, pp. 287–91.
12. Loubat, p. 21; Tarsaïdzé, *Czars and Presidents*, pp. 248–55.
13. Miliutin, I, 35–37; Mosse, p. 82.
14. Laserson, p. 181.
15. Geiroth, pp. 50–57.
16. Geiroth, pp. 104–6; Windsor, pp. 169, 192.
17. Smirnova, p. 186.
18. Hamilton, p. 195.
19. Tarsaïdzé, *Czars and Presidents*, p. 292.
20. Yourievsky, p. 4.
21. Loubat, pp. 88, 113; Laserson, p. 188.
22. Tarsaïdzé, *Czars and Presidents*, pp. 181–222.
23. Laserson, p. 195; Tarsaïdzé, *Czars and Presidents*, p. 252.
24. Miliutin, IV, 47.

CHAPTER 7, *"My Adorable Imp"*

1. Berg archives.
2. Berg archives.
3. Berg archives; Dolgorouky, p. 93.

4. Paleologue, p. 57.
5. *Life of Alexander II*, p. 190.
6. *Life of Alexander II*, p. 153.

7. *Life of Alexander II*, p. 190.
8. Berg archives.
9. *Life of Alexander II*, p. 190.

CHAPTER 8, *Va-et-vient*

1. Berg archives.
2. Berg archives.

3. Twain, p. 390.

CHAPTER 9, *Prussian Interlude*

1. Berg archives.
2. *Encyclopaedia Britannica* (1967 edition), XVI, 42.

3. Trotsky, p. 435.
4. De Grunwald, *Le Tsar Alesandre II*, p. 260.

CHAPTER 10, *Blessed Events*

1. *Vsemirnaya Illustratzia*, I (1872), 2.
2. Borovikova, pp. 50–87.
3. *Vsemirnaya Illustratzia*, II (1872), 42.
4. Potemkin, II, 13.
5. Churchill, pp. 17–20.
6. Berg archives.
7. Berg archives.

8. Kane, p. i; Tarsaïdzé, *Czars and Presidents*, pp. 315–18.
9. *Vpered*.
10. Longford, pp. 371–391.
11. Graham, pp. 173–75.
12. Bolitho, p. 271.
13. Lee, I, 284.
14. Gernsheim, p. 154.

CHAPTER 11, *The Last Crusade*

1. Miliutin, II, 58.
2. Graham, p. 198.
3. Miliutin, II, 51; De Grunwald, *Tsar Nicholas I*, p. 216.
4. Miliutin, II, 51; De Grunwald, *Tsar Nicholas I*, p. 216.
5. De Klapie.

6. Berg archives.
7. Miliutin, II, 34.
8. Konovalov.
9. *Life of Alexander II*, p. 291.
10. Greene, p. 5.
11. Paleologue, p. 51.
12. Miliutin, III, 18, 42.
13. *Russian Nobility*, p. 1.
14. Dolgorukov, I, 56.

Chapter 12, *"The Wild Beast"*

1. *Almanach de Gotha* (1911), p. 512.
2. Yarmolinsky, p. 160.
3. De Grunwald, *Tsar Nicholas I*, pp. 313, 384.
4. Yarmolinsky, p. 222.
5. Miliutin, III, 134.
6. Tolstoy's letter to N. N. Strakhov, quoted in Troyat, *Tolstoy*, pp. 384, 385.
7. Yarmolinsky, p. 296.
8. Borovikova, p. 68.
9. Yarmolinsky, p. 257.
10. Miliutin, III, 212.
11. Yarmolinsky, p. 261.
12. Yarmolinsky, p. 260.
13. Yarmolinsky, p. 257.
14. Zaionchkovski, p. 148.
15. Miliutin, III, 217.
16. Miliutin, III, 217.
17. Yarmolinsky, p. 263.
18. Yarmolinsky, p. 263.
19. Miliutin, III, 251.
20. Polovtsov, *Dnevnik Gosudarstvenovo . . .* , I, 189; II, 147–48.
21. De Diesbach, p. 316.

Chapter 13, *The Last Parade*

1. Graham, p. 300; Miliutin, III, 269.
2. Berg archives.
3. Miliutin, III, 265.
4. Perets, p. 11.
5. Polovtsov, II, 429.
6. Daniels.
7. Miliutin, IV, 79.
8. Berg archives.
9. Berg archives.
10. Berg archives.
11. Vonlarlarsky, p. 102.
12. As told to the author by Count V. A. Adlerberg.
13. Berg archives.
14. Perets, p. 158.
15. Miliutin, III, 259.
16. Alexander, p. 52.
17. Miliutin, III, 269.
18. Yarmolinsky, p. 270.
19. Miliutin, III, 269.
20. Miliutin, III, 270.
21. Miliutin, III, 275, 278.
22. Alexander, p. 52.
23. Harcave, p. 216.
24. Mosse, p. 98.
25. Alexander, p. 53.
26. *New York Times,* June 8, 1966.
27. *Boyare Romanovi . . .*
28. Narishkin-Kurakin, p. 70; Berg archives.
29. Narishkin-Kurakin, p. 70.
30. As told to the author by Count V. A. Adlerberg.
31. Berg archives.
32. Mordovtsev, p. 170.
33. Berg archives; Graham, p. 304. Alexander, pp. 51–52.
34. Volkonsky, p. 185.
35. Perets, p. 22.
36. Mosse, p. 163.

37. Miliutin, IV, 85–87.
38. Narishkin-Kurakin, p. 69.
39. Berg archives.
40. Berg archives.
41. Perets, p. 159.
42. Paleologue, p. 206; De Grunwald, *Le Tsar Alesandre II*, pp. 327–28.
43. Miliutin, III, 278.
44. Narishkin-Kurakin, pp. 67–68.
45. Mosse, p. 170.
46. Mosse, p. 170.
47. Bruce, p. 34.
48. Weeks, p. 3.
49. Weeks, p. 3.
50. Bruce, p. 34.
51. Asheshov, p. 6.
52. Yarmolinsky, p. 274.
53. Morosov, II, 420.
54. Yarmolinsky, p. 274.
55. Yarmolinsky, p. 277.
56. Obolensky, D., p. 18.
57. De Grunwald, *Le Tsar Alesandre II*, pp. 364–87.

58. Obolensky, D., p. 18.
59. Miliutin, IV, 62.
60. Miliutin, IV, 63.
61. Gotie, p. 256.
62. Miliutin, III, 266.
63. Tyutchev, p. 205; Narishkin-Kurakin, p. 72.
64. *Pridvorny Kalendar* (1877).
65. Yarmolinsky, p. 278.
66. Solzhenitsyn, p. 108.
67. Yarmolinsky, p. 283.
68. Chamberlin, p. 212.
69. Berg archives.
70. *Istoricheski, Vestnik.*
71. Obolensky, D., p. 18; Miliutin, IV, 25.
72. Yarmolinsky, p. 281.
73. Sliozberg, p. 59.
74. Hamilton, p. 159.
75. Berg archives.
76. *Nicholas II*, p. 42.
77. Miliutin, I, 126.
78. Miliutin, IV, 63.

CHAPTER 14, *Post-Mortem*

1. Longford, p. 444.
2. Polovtsov, II, 150; Tarsaidze, *Czars and Presidents*, p. 306.
3. Narishkin-Kurakin, pp. 74ff.
4. *Nicholas II*, . . . Sept. 12, 1891.
5. Buxhoeveden, pp. 316–17.
6. Alexander, pp. 59ff.
7. Perets, p. 24.
8. Albertini, p. 117.
9. Hamilton, p. 159.
10. Yourievsky, p. 5.

11. Pflaum, p. 254; Milyutin, IV, 30.
12. Almedingen, p. 345; Roberts.
13. Miliutin, IV, 28.
14. Polovtsov, II, 442.
15. Benson, p. 64; Tarsaïdzé, *Czars and Presidents*, p. 316; Kane.
16. Schwezoff, pp. 122–23.
17. Zaionchkovski, pp. 324–25.
18. Zaionchkovski, pp. 324–25.

19. Frichero; Berg archives. Tarsaïdzé archives.
20. Polovtsov, II, 209, 412.
21. Polovtsov, II, 214.
22. Witte, *Vospominanya*, pp. 286–88.
23. Berg archives.
24. Abrikossow, p. 12.
25. Aubry, p. 332; De Grunwald, *Le Tsar Alexandre II*, p. 260.
26. Berg archives.
27. Miliutin, IV, 137.
28. Skipwith, pp. 276–77.
29. Richardson, pp. 5, 41, 131.
30. Berg archives.
31. Alexander, pp. 122ff.
32. Reeves, p. 107.
33. Cassini, p. 94.
34. Yourievsky, p. 10; Berg archives.
35. *New York Times*, Dec. 19,
1968; *New York Post*, Dec. 14, 1968.
36. Harcave, p. 349.
37. Westwood, p. 122.
38. Obolensky, S., p. 42.
39. Grey, II, 183; Seton-Watson, p. 182.
40. Schwezoff, pp. 122–24.
41. Berg: Almendingen, p. 259.
42. *Novoye Russkoye Slovo*, Aug. 27, 1968.
43. Bailey, G., p. 169.
44. Letter by him to the author.
45. Salisbury, p. 177; Yarmolinsky, p. 285; *New York Times*, July 21, 1969.
46. Letter of May 4, 1968, of Dr. C. E. Kany to the author; *Novoye Russkoye Slovo*, Sept. 26, 1960.

CHAPTER 15, *The End of the Beginning*

1. Dolgorouky, pp. 229, 251.
2. Yourievsky, pp. 29, 100, 114, 235.
3. Obolensky, S., pp. 236–37.
4. Fülöp-Miller, pp. 108, 148, 197–212.
5. *Krasny Arkhiv*, p. 281.
6. *Padenie Czarskogo Rezhima*, I, 61, 78–79.
7. *Padenie Czarskogo Rezhima*, I, 437.
8. *Novoye Russkoye Slovo*, April 6, 1961.
9. Dolgorouky, p. 262.
10. Dolgorouky, pp. 205–11.
11. Polovtsov, II, 214.
12. Berg archives.
13. Berg archives.

Bibliography

Abrikossow, Dimitri. *Revelations of a Russian Diplomat.* Edited by George Alexander Lensen. Seattle: University of Washington Press, 1964.

Albertini, Luigi. *The Origins of the War of 1914.* Vol. II. London: Oxford University Press, 1952.

Alexander, Grand Duke of Russia. *Once a Grand Duke.* New York: Farrar & Rinehart, Inc., 1932.

Alice, Grand Duchess of Hesse, Princess of Great Britain and Ireland. Biographical Sketch and Letters. London: John Murray, 1884.

Almedingen, E. M. *The Emperor Alexander II.* London: Bodley Head, 1962.

Alville. *La Vie en Suisse de S.A.I. La Grande-Duchesse Anna Feodorovna.* Lausanne: Libraire F. Rouge 7 Cie S.A., 1942.

Aronson, Theodore. *Defiant Dynasty. The Coburgs of Belgium.* New York: Bobbs-Merrill Co., Inc., 1968.

————. *Royal Vendetta.* New York: Bobbs-Merrill Co., Inc., 1966.

Asheshov, N. *Sophia Perovskaya.* St. Petersburg: Gosudarstvenoe Izdanie (Government Publication), 1921.

Athlone, Her Royal Highness Princess Alice, Countess of Athlone. *For My Grandchildren.* New York: World Publishing Co., 1966.

Aubry, Octave. *Eugenie—Empress of French.* Philadelphia: J. B. Lippincott, 1931.

Bailey, Geoffrey. *The Conspirators.* New York: Harper & Bros., 1960.

Bailey, Thomas A. *America Faces Russia.* Ithaca, N.Y.: Cornell University Press, 1950.

Benson, Stella. *Pull Devil, Pull Baker.* Literary Guild, 1933.

Berg, Count Boris G. Personal archives.

————. "Svatovstvo Czesarevicha Aleksandra Nikolaevicha Perepiska Czarskoi Semyi" ["The Engagement of Czarevitch Alexander Nickolaevich/the future Emperor Alexander II/Through the

Correspondence with His Family"]. *Novik* II, 34 (1942), 13–18.

Bibesco, Princess. *Katia.* J'ai lu, aux Editions Ditis, 1938.

Blanch, Lesley. *The Sabres of Paradise.* New York: Viking Press, 1960.

Bolitho, Hector. *Reign of Queen Victoria.* New York: Macmillan Co., 1948.

Borovikova, Vera. "Domashnie Zapiski" ["Home Notes"]. *Na Chuzhoy Storone [On the Alien Side]* IV, v (1924). Berlin and Prague.

Boyare Romanovi i votsapenie Mikhaila Feodorovicha [The Boyars Romanov and the Accession to the Throne of Michael Feodorovich]. St. Petersburg: Gosudarstvenaya Tipografiya [State Publication], 1913.

Bruce, Robert V. *1877: Year of Violence.* New York: Bobbs-Merrill Co., Inc., 1959.

Burton, Jean. *Hey-day of a Wizard.* New York: Alfred A. Knopf, 1944.

Buxhoeveden, Baroness Sophie. *Before the Storm.* London: Macmillan Co., 1938.

Byrnes, Robert F. "Pobedonostsev on the Role of Changes in History." *The Russian Review* XXVI, 3 (1967), 231–50.

Carr, Edward Hallett. *Studies in Revolution.* London: Macmillan & Co., Ltd., 1950.

Cassini, Countess Marguerite. *Never a Dull Moment.* New York: Harper & Bros., 1956.

Chamberlin, William Henry. "The Jacobin Ancestry of Soviet Communism." *The Russian Review* XVII, 4 (1958), 251–57.

Churchill, Randolph S. *Winston S. Churchill. Youth, 1874–1900.* Vol. I. Boston: Houghton Mifflin Co., 1966.

Connell, Brian. *Manifest Destiny.* London: Cassell & Co., Ltd., 1953.

Cookridge, E. H. *From Battenberg to Mountbatten.* New York: John Day Co., 1966.

Creston, Dormer. *The Youthful Queen Victoria.* New York: G. P. Putnam's Sons, 1952.

Daniels, Jonathan. *Washington Quadrille—The Dance Beside the Documents.* New York: Doubleday & Co., Inc., 1968.

De Cuistine, Marquis. *Lettres de Russie.* Paris: Les Editions de la Nouvelle France, 1946.

De Diesbach, Ghislain. *Secrets of the Gotha.* New York: Meredith Press, 1968.

De Grunwald, Constantin. *Le Tsar Alexandre II et Son Temps.* Paris: Berger-Levrault, 1963.

———. *Tsar Nicholas I.* New York: Macmillan Co., 1955.

De Klapie, Olga. "Knyaginya Maria Tenisheva" ["Princess Maria

Tenisheva"]. *Vozrojdenie [Renaissance]* No. 194 (1968), 75–97. Paris.

Delderfield, R. F. *The Golden Millstones.* New York: Harper & Row, 1964.

De Stoeckl, Agnes. *Not All Vanity.* London: John Murray, 1951.

Dolgorouky, Princess Stéphanie. *La Russie Avant la Débacle.* Paris: Eugène Figuière, Éditeur, 1926.

Dolgorukov, Prince Peter. *Rossiskaya Rodoslovnaya Kniga [Russian Genealogical Book].* Vols. I–IV. St. Petersburg, 1856.

Duff, David. *Hessian Tapestry.* London: Frederick Muller, Ltd., 1967.

Dugan, James. *The Great Mutiny.* New York: G. P. Putnam's Sons, 1965.

Ehrenkrook, Hans Friedrich (ed.). *Genealogisches Handbuch des Adels.* Band 6. Gluksburg/Ostsee: Verlag von C. A. Starke, 1953.

Elets, Yu. *Russkaya Eskadra vo Frantsii [The Russian Squadron in France].* Varshavski Uchebni Okrug [The Society of Education of Warsaw], 1893.

Eyeck, Frank. *The Prince Consort.* Boston: Houghton Mifflin Co., 1959.

Footman, David. *Red Prelude.* London: Barrie & Rockliff, The Crescent Press, 1968.

Frichero, N. O. "The Frigate 'Svetlana' in America in 1871–72 from the Diary of N. O. Frichero 2nd." (in Russian). A. Tarsaidze (ed.). *Morskie Zapiski [The Naval Records]* XI (1953), 20–33.

Fulford, Roger (ed.). *Dearest Child.* New York: Holt, Rinehart & Winston, Inc., 1964.

Fülöp-Miller, René. *Rasputin, The Holy Devil.* Garden City, N.Y.: Garden City Publishing Co., Inc., 1928.

Furman, P. *Dolgorukova, Natalia Borisovna. Povest dlya Devits [Natalia Borisovna Dolgorukova. Story for Young Girls].* St. Petersburg: Ya. A. Isakov, 1872.

Gabriel, Grand Duke of Russia. *V Mramornom Dvortse [In the Marble Palace].* New York: Izdatelstvo Imeni Chekhova [Chekhov Publishing House], 1955.

Geiroth, A. *Opisanie Peterhofa [Description of Peterhof].* St. Petersburg: Imperatoskaya Akademia Nauk [Imperial Academy of Sciences], 1868.

Genealogisches Hand Buch des Adels. Freiherrliche Hauser B. Band I. Glucksburg Band I. 1954.

Gernet, N. N. *Istoria Tsarskoi Tyurmi [History of Czar's Prisons].*

Vol. III. Moscow: Gosudarstvenoe Izdatelstvo Yuridicheskoi Literaturi [government publication for jurisprudence], 1952.

Gernsheim, Helmut and Alison. *Victoria R. A Biography.* New York: G. P. Putnam's Sons, 1959.

Gertsen, A. I. *Biloe i Dumi [The Past and Thoughts].* Leningrad: Gosudarstvenoe Izdatelstvo [government publication], 1946.

Gladki, S. V. "Dvorzhitskie" (in Russian). *Novik* IV, 24 (1939), 29–32.

Gofman, M. L., and Lifar, Sergei. *Pisma Pushkina k N. N. Goncharovoi [Letters of Pushkin to N. N. Goncharova].* Paris: Cooperative Etoile, 1936.

Goncharova, A. and Khamtsob. *Steni i Bashni Kremlia [Walls and Towers of the Kremlin].* U.S.S.R.: Moscow Worker, 1957.

Gotie, Yu. V. "Borba Pravitelstvennikh Grupirovok i Manifest 29 Aprelia 1881 g" ["A Fight among Members of Government Groupings on the Manifest of April 29, 1881"]. *Istoricheskie Zapiski [Historical Notes].* Vol. II U.S.S.R.: Akademiya Nauk SSSR (Academy of Sciences), 1938. Pp. 200–299.

Graham, Stephen. *Tsar of Freedom.* New Haven: Yale University Press, 1935.

Greenberg, Louis. *The Jews in Russia.* Vol. I. New Haven: Yale University Press, 1944.

Greene, F. V. *Army Life in Russia.* New York: Charles Scribner's Sons, 1880.

Grenfell, Captain Russell, R.N. *Unconditional Hatred.* New York: Devin-Adair Co., 1958.

Grey, Viscount K. G. of Fallodon. *Twenty-five Years, 1892–1916.* Vol. II. New York: Frederick A. Stokes Co., 1925.

Hamilton, Lord Frederic. *The Vanished Pomps of Yesterday.* New York: Doubleday, Doran & Co., Inc., 1934.

Harcave, Sidney. *Years of the Golden Cockerel.* New York: Macmillan Co., 1968.

Hingley, Ronald. *The Tsars 1533–1917.* New York: Macmillan Co., 1968.

Hoyt, Edwin P. *Kreuzerkrieg.* New York: World Publishing Co., 1968.

Hyde, H. Montgomery. *Princess Lieven.* Boston: Little, Brown & Co., 1938.

Istoricheski, Vestnik [Historical Herald]. Vol. 80, 1900 and Vol. 1, 1913. St. Petersburg.

Kallistov, N. D. "Flot v Czarstvovanie Imperatora Pavla I" ["The Navy during the Reign of Emperor Paul I"] in *History of the Russian Army and Navy.* Vol. IX. Moscow, 1913.

Kane, Harnett T., with Victor Leclerc [Alexandre Tarsaidze]. *The Scandalous Mrs. Blackford*. New York: Julian Messner, Inc., 1951.

Kelen, Betty. *The Mistresses*. New York: Random House, Inc., 1966.

Kocherov, Samuel. *Courts, Lawyers and Trials under the Last Three Czars*. New York: Frederick A. Praeger, 1953.

Kondakov, A. I. *Direktor Narodnikh Uchilishch, I. N. Ulyanov [The Director of Public Schools, I. N. Ulyanov]*. U.S.S.R.: Akademiya Pedagogicheskikh Nauk RSFSR [Academy of Pedagogical Sciences], 1948.

Konovalov, S. "The Emperor Alexander II and Princess Ekaterina Dolgorukaya (Yurievskaya): Nine Letters" in *Oxford Slavonic Papers*. Vol. XI. Oxford: Clarendon Press, 1964.

Korevo, N. *Nasledovanie prestola [Succession to the Throne]*. Paris: Society of United Russians in Nice, 1922.

Krasny Arkhiv [Red Archive]. Vol. V. Moscow, 1924.

Kschessinska, Mathilde. *Dancing in Petersburg*. New York: Doubleday & Co., Inc., 1961.

Laserson, Max M. *The American Impact on Russia 1784–1917*. New York: Macmillan Co., 1950.

Lee, Sir Sidney. *King Edward VII*. Vol. I. New York: Macmillan Co., 1925.

Life of Alexander II. London: W. H. Allen & Co., 1883. (anon.)

Longford, Elizabeth. *Queen Victoria*. New York: Harper & Row, Inc., 1964.

Loubat, J. F. *Mission to Russia, in 1866*. New York: D. Appleton & Co., 1873.

Lyons, Eugene. *Workers' Paradise Lost*. New York: Funk & Wagnalls, Inc., 1967.

Malia, Martin. *Alexander Herzen and the Birth of Russian Socialism*. New York: Grosset & Dunlap, 1965.

Massie, Robert K. *Nicholas and Alexandra*. New York: Atheneum, 1967.

Mazour, Anatole G. *Rise and Fall of the Romanovs*. Princeton, N.J.: D. Van Nostrand Co., Inc., 1960.

McClellan, Elizabeth. *Historical Dress in America 1800–1870*. Philadelphia: George W. Jacobs & Co., 1910.

Miliutin, D. A. *Dnevnik D. A. Miliutina [The Diary of D. A. Miliutin]*. Vols. I–IV. Moscow: Gosudarstvenaya Ordena Lenina Biblioteka USSR [Government Lenin Library USSR], 1947.

Mirsky, Prince D. S. *Contemporary Russian Literature 1881–1925.* New York: Alfred A. Knopf, 1926.

Moorehead, Alan. *The Russian Revolution.* New York: Harper & Bros., 1958.

Mordovtsev, D. *Russkaya Zhenshchini Novovo Vremeni [Modern Russian Women].* St. Petersburg: A. Cherkesov, 1874.

Morison, Samuel Eliot. "Historical Notes on the Gilbert and Marshall Islands." *The American Neptune,* IV, 2 (1944), 87–118.

Morosov, N. A. *Povesti Moei Zhizni [Tales of My Life].* Moscow, 1961.

Mosse, W. E. *Alexander II and the Modernization of Russia.* New York: Macmillan Co., 1958.

Munster, A. Ataman Platov. *Voenno-Istoricheski Vestnik [War Historical Journal]* No. 10 (1952), 7–10. Paris.

Nagengast, William E. "Moscow, The Stalingrad of 1812: American Reaction Toward Napoleon's Retreat from Russia." *The Russian Review* VIII, 4 (1949), 302–15.

Narishkin-Kurakin, Elizabeth. *Under Three Tsars.* New York: E. P. Dutton & Co., Inc., 1931.

Nicholas II. *Dnevnik Imperatora Nikolaya II [Diary of Nicholas II].* Berlin: Slovo, 1923.

Nicolson, Harold. *The Congress of Vienna.* New York: Viking Press, 1962.

———. *King George the Fifth—His Life and Reign.* London: Constable & Co., Ltd., 1952.

Nikitin, V. D. "Iz Vospominanii" ["From Memories"]. *Vakhteni Zhurnal [The Log Book]* No. 4–5 (1935), 25–28.

Noviy Zhurnal [The New Review] No. 63 (1961). New York.

Novoye Russkoye Slovo (a Russian newspaper published in New York City).

Obolensky, Dmitri. "Iz Vospominanii Knyazya Dmitria Dmitrievicha Obolenskavo" ["From the Memoirs of Prince Dmitri Dmitrevich Obolensky"]. *Novik* (1950), pp. 1–18.

Obolensky, Serge. *One Man in His Time.* New York: McDowell, Obolensky, 1958.

Olga, Grand Duchess, Queen of Württemberg. *Son Unosti. Zapiski docheri Imperatora Nikolaya I, Velikoy Kniazhni Olgi Nikolaevni, Korolevi Vurtembergskoi [The Dream of Youth. Memoirs of the Daughter of Emperor Nicholas I].* Paris, 1963.

Padenie Czarskogo Rezhima [The Fall of Czarist Regime]. Moscow, Leningrad, 1926.

Paleologue, Maurice. *Le Roman Tragique de l'Empereur, Alexandre II.* Paris, 1923.

Parsons, Julia Stoddard. *Royalty in the Nineteenth Century*. Boston: Bruce Humphries, Inc., 1943.

Payne, Robert. *The Fortress*. New York: Simon & Schuster, Inc., 1967.

Perets, E. A. *Dnevnik E. A. Peretsa [Diary of E. A. Perets]*. Moscow & Leningrad: Gosudarstvenoe Izdatelstvo [Government Publication], 1927.

Pflaum, Rosalynd. *The Emperor's Talisman*. New York: Meredith Press, 1968.

Pilyavski, V. *Arkhitekturnie Ansambli Leningrada [Architectural Ensembles of Leningrad]*. Moscow: Architectural Academy of the U.S.S.R., 1946.

Polovstsov, A. A. *Dnevnik Gosudarstvenovo Sekretarya A. A. Polovtsova [The Diary of the Government Secretary A. A. Polovtsov]*. Vols. I, II. Moscow: Nauka (Science), 1966.

———. "Vospominaniya" ["Remembrances"]. *Vozrojdenie [Renaissance]* No. 2 (1949), 128–41.

Polyakov, A. S. *O Smerti Pushkina [About the Death of Pushkin]*. St. Petersburg: Gosudarstvenoe Izdatelstvo [Government Publication], 1922.

Pope-Hennessy, James. *Queen Mary 1867–1953*. New York: Alfred A. Knopf, 1960.

Pope-Hennessy, Una. *A Czarina's Story*. London & Brussels: Nicholson & Watson, 1948.

Potemkin, V. P. (ed.). *Istorya Diplomatii [History of Diplomacy]*. Moscow: Gosudarstvenoe Sotsialno-Ekonomicheskoe Izdatelstvo [Government Socio-Economical Publishing House], 1941.

Pridvorny Kalendar [Court Calendar of 1877]. St. Petersburg.

Reeves, Francis B. *Russia Then and Now 1892–1917*. New York: G. P. Putnam's Sons, 1917.

Richardson, Joanna. *Princess Mathilde*. New York: Charles Scribner's Sons, 1969.

Roberts, Brian. *Cecil Rhodes and The Princess*. Philadelphia: J. B. Lippincott Co., 1969.

Russian Encyclopedia. St. Petersburg: Brockhouse & Efron, 1894.

Russian Nobility. New York: Russian Nobility Association in U.S.A., Inc., 1953.

Russkaya Starina [Russia's Past]. Vol. I. St. Petersburg, 1898.

Salisbury, Harrison E. *Moscow Journal—The Land of Stalin*. Chicago: University of Chicago Press, 1961.

Savin, A. N. *Svatovstvo Cesarevicha Alexandra Nikolaevitcha [The Betrothal of the Heir to the Throne Alexander Nikolaevitch]*. Vol. I, Moscow: Institute of History, 1926. Pp. 57–116.

334 / BIBLIOGRAPHY

Schapiro, Leonard. *The Origin of the Communist Autocracy*. New York: Frederick A. Praeger, 1965.

Schub, David. *Lenin*. Baltimore: Pelican Books, Inc., 1966.

Schwezoff, Igor. *Borzoi*. London: Hodder & Stoughton, Ltd., 1935.

Sedykh, A. "Pisma i dnevnik Kniaghini Yurevskoi" ["Letters and Diary of Princess Yurevskoy"]. *Novosselye*, No. 6 (Aug., 1942), 51–56. Paris.

Seton-Watson, Hugh. *The Decline of Imperial Russia 1855–1914.* New York: Frederick A. Praeger, 1952.

Shebeko, N. *Souvenirs*. Paris: Bibliotheque Diplomatique, 1936.

———. "Za Zhivimi Dushami" ["In Quest of Living Souls"]. *Vozrojdenie [Renaissance]*, No. 196 (1968), 7–25.

Shurigin, Ya. I. *Petrodvorets [Peter's Palace]*. Moscow: Gosudarstvenoe Izdatelstvo *Isskustvo* [government publication *Art*], 1952.

Skinner, Cornelia Otis. *Madame Sarah*. New York: Dell Publishing Co., Inc., 1966.

Skipwith, Sofka, née Princess Sophy Dolgorouky. *Sofka. The Autobiography of a Princess*. London: Rupert Hart-Davis, 1968.

Sliozberg, G. B. *Baron G. O. Gintsburg* (in Russian). Paris, 1933.

Smirnova, A. O. *Zapiski, Dnevnik, Vospominanya, Pisma [Notes, Diary, Memoirs, Letters]*. Moscow, 1929.

Soljhenisyn, Alexander I. *The First Circle*. New York: Harper & Row, 1968.

Soloveytchik, George. *Potemkin*. New York: W. W. Norton & Co., Inc., 1947.

Spiridovich, General A. E. *Velikaya Voina i Fevralskaya Revolutsia 1914–1917 [World War I and the February Revolution 1914–1917]*. Vols. I-III. New York: All-Slavic Publishing House, Inc., 1960.

"Spiski Titulavanim Rodam i Litsam" ["The List of Titled Families and Persons in Russia"]. St. Petersburg: Pravitelstvuyushchi Senat [Governing Senate], 1892.

Stacton, David. *The Bonapartes*. New York: Simon & Schuster, Inc., 1966.

Strachey, Lytton. *Queen Victoria*. New York: Harcourt, Brace & Co., 1921.

Struve, Gleb. *Russki Evropeetz [A Russian European]*. San Francisco, 1950.

Talberg, N. D. "Muzh Vernosti i Razuma" ["Man of Loyalty and Reason"]. Jordanville, N.Y.: Holy Trinity Monastery, 1957.

Tarsaïdzé, A. G. "Dva svatovstva" ("Two Marriage Matches"). *Novik* (1952), pp. 30–40.

Tarsaidze, Alexandre. "American Pioneers in Russian Railroad Building." *The Russian Review* IX, No. y (1950), 292.

———. *Czars and Presidents—The Story of a Forgotten Friendship.* New York: McDowell, Obolensky, Inc., 1958.

Tatishchev S. S. *Imperator Alexander II.* Vols. I, II. St. Petersburg, 1903.

Thompson, J. M. *Napoleon Bonaparte.* New York: Oxford University Press, 1952.

Trotsky, Leon. *Stalin—an Appraisal of the Man and His Influence.* New York: Harper & Bros., 1941.

Troyat, Henri. *Pushkin.* New York: Pantheon, 1950.

———. *Tolstoy.* New York: Doubleday & Co., Inc., 1967.

The Tsar and His People. New York: Harper & Bros., 1891.

Tsarskie, Amuri. *Loves of the Tsars.* Nice: Kleidman, n.d. (anon.)

Tuchman, Barbara W. *The Proud Tower.* New York: Macmillan Co., 1966.

Tupper, Harmon. *To the Great Ocean.* Boston: Little, Brown & Co., 1965.

Twain, Mark. *The Innocents Abroad.* Hartford, Conn.: American Publishing Co., 1870.

Tyutchev, A. F. *Pri dvore dvukh Imperatorov [At the Court of Two Emperors].* Moscow: M. & S. Sabashnikov, 1928.

Vassili, Count Paul. *Behind the Veil at the Russian Court.* New York: John Lane Co., 1914.

Volkonsky, Sergei. *Moi Vospominanya [My Memoirs].* Munich: P. Oldenburg, 1923.

Von Laue, Theodore H. *Sergei Witte and the Industrialization of Russia.* New York: Columbia University Press, 1963.

Vonlyarlyarski, V. *Moi Vospominanya [My Memoirs].* Berlin: Ruskoe Natsionalnoe Izdatelstvo [Russian National Publication], n.d.

Von Richter, V. G. "Angliski Fayans 1812–1813 s Ruskim Izpbrazheniem" ["English Porcelain 1812–1813 with Russian Motives"], *Voenno-Istoricheski Vestnik (War Historical Journal),* VI (1955), 31–34.

———. "Kazak A. Zemlenukhin v Londone v 1813 godu" ["Cossack A. Zemlenukhin in London in 1813"]. *Voenno-Istoricheski Vestnik [War Historical Journal]* IV (1954), 33–41.

———. "Yeshche ob Angliskoi Keramicki s Ruskimi Syuzhetami" ["More about English Earthenware with Russian Subjects"]. *Voenno-Istoricheski Vestnik [War Historical Journal]* VII (1956), 25–27.

Vpered [Forward]. III, pt. 2 (1874). London.

Vsemirnaya Illustratzia [World Illustrated]. St. Petersburg, 1881.

Weeks, Albert L. *The First Bolshevik. A Political Biography of Peter Tkachev.* New York: New York University Press, 1968.

Westwood, J. N. *A History of Russian Railways.* London: Allen & Unwin, Ltd., 1964.

Williamson, David Geoffrey (compiler). *The Counts Bobrinskoy,* with a foreword by The Count Bobrinskoy. Edgeware, Middlesex: James V. Poate, 1962.

Windsor, Duchess of. *The Heart Has Its Reasons.* New York: David McKay, Inc., 1956.

Witte, Count S. Yu. *Vospominanya Detstvo. Czarstvovanie Aleksandra II i Aleksandra III (1849–1894) [Memoirs of Childhood. The Reign of Alexander II & Alexander III (1849–1894)].* Berlin: Slovo, 1923.

————. *Vospominanya [Memoirs].* Vols. I and II. Berlin: Slovo, 1922.

Woldman, Albert A. *Lincoln and the Russians.* Cleveland: World Publishing Co., 1952.

Yarmolinsky, Avrahm. *Road to Revolution.* New York: Macmillan Co., 1959.

Yourievich, Colonel Simon. His private diary.

Yourievsky, H.S.H. Princess Catherine. *My Book.* London: Eveleigh Nash & Grayson, Ltd., 1924.

Zaionchkovski, P. A. *Krizis Samoderzhavia na Rubezhe 1870–1880 godov [Crisis of the Autocracy on the Eve of 1870–1880].* Moscow: Moscow University Press, 1964.

Zaitzev, Boris. *Zhukovsky.* Paris, 1951.

Zenkovsky, Serge A. "The Emancipation of the Serfs in Retrospect." *The Russian Review* XX, 4 (1961), 280–93.

Zhukovsky, V. A. *Sochineniya V. A. Zhukovskavo [Works of V. A. Zhukovsky].* Vol. I. Moscow: I. D. Sitin, 1902.

INDEX